The

Multimedia Production Handbook

for the

PC, Macintosh, and Amiga

The Multimedia Production Handbook *for the* PC, Macintosh, and Amiga

Tom Yager

Academic Press Professional
Harcourt Brace & Company, Publishers
Boston San Diego New York
London Sydney Tokyo Toronto

This book is printed on acid-free paper. ∞

ACADEMIC PRESS PROFESSIONAL
955 Massachusetts Avenue, Cambridge, MA 02139

An Imprint of ACADEMIC PRESS, INC.
A Division of HARCOURT BRACE & COMPANY

United Kingdom Edition published by
ACADEMIC PRESS LIMITED
24–28 Oval Road, London NW17DX

Library of Congress Cataloging-in-Publication Data

Yager, Thomas.
Multimedia production handbook for the PC, Macintosh, and Amiga / Tom Yager.
p. cm.
Includes bibliographical references and index.
ISBN 0-12-768030-6
1. Multimedia systems. I. Title.
II. Title: Hypertext and hypermedia.
QA76.575.Y34 1993
006.6—dc20 93-19435
CIP

Printed in the United States of America
93 94 95 96 97 98 EB 9 8 7 6 5 4 3 2 1

Contents

Preface

If you're wondering whether this book is right for you, you've come to the right place. In this preface, I'll attempt to answer the most obvious questions that might be running through your mind. It's less an effort to sell you a book than to put you in the right frame of mind to receive the messages it sends. If you do buy this book, or if you've bought it already, this section will help you get more from the pages to come. In any case, please take the time to read at least a part of this section. If you don't, the rest of the book may seem so odd and disorganized that you'll have trouble getting through it.

Who Needs This Book?

This is an unusual book. To get the maximum benefit from it, or to decide whether to buy it, you'd be wise to spend a few minutes reading this preface.

A "multimedia producer," in the context of this book, is simply someone who has a role in producing multimedia material. I use the word "presentation" as shorthand for multimedia material. Apply the word in the broader sense, simply, "that which is presented to others." That presentation can be anything from 35mm slides of business graphics to a full-blown video production. The range between these two extremes is large, and so is the range of the audience for this book.

There is something here for people at most levels of skill with computers. Throughout this book, you'll find relatively few assumptions are made about your computer literacy. It is assumed you have a computer, and you've used it at least to run commercial applications. Except for the chapters involving advanced topics (like programming), there's nothing here most people can't get through.

What makes this book unusual, aside from its broad spectrum of coverage, is the manner I've chosen to provide that coverage. While I've written for books before, I am mainly a magazine writer, and I have decided to apply a magazine-like style to the writing of this book. The multimedia market moves and changes quickly, and it is defined by the innovative products that populate it. So this book focuses not on *technology*, but on the *products* that define it. That way, instead of subjecting you to a thick volume on theoretical issues, I can acquaint you with specific products that provide you a more practical, useful point of view. The theory, then, is mostly packed into Chapter 1, which you can skip if you're not interested in my views on the usefulness of multimedia. Beyond that, you'll find the book almost entirely devoted to the various classes of multimedia presentations, and the tools and techniques you can use to create them.

The Practical Perspective

While this book is product-oriented, it isn't a catalog of every multimedia product ever created. In fact, even though there are *lots* of products discussed in this book (see the resource guide in the back), the number of them discussed here doesn't even scratch the surface of the very crowded multimedia market. Instead, I've decided to select representative products for each of the categories I seek to cover in this book. My work as director of BYTE's Multimedia Lab has allowed me to see hundreds of different products over the years, and I have used that experience to narrow the field of products discussed in this book. A product's inclusion here doesn't equate to an endorsement. In some cases, the products selected were those I could acquire most rapidly. But in every case, I set standards that products vying for coverage here had to meet to be included. I'm confident that the specific products discussed in this book will, if you choose them, perform well for you.

An unusual book calls for unusual methods to create it, and the way this book was assembled certainly fits that adjective. I conducted all the research and writing myself, using a lab I created in my home. You can get a closer look at this facility on the instructional videotapes that were created to accompany this book. I'll discuss those tapes in more detail later in this preface.

The Research Lab

The lab constructed for this book was built with the cooperation of the vendors whose products are discussed in these pages. Their cooperation was limited to the provision of products, documentation and technical support. Everything that appears in these pages, and on the available videotapes was tried in the lab. None of what you read here was created by vendors, or even seen by them prior to the publication of this book. In fact, most of the sections of this book were written while the procedures being described were being carried out. I think you'll find this book has a very "hands-on" feel to it, and the research lab's organization is the reason for that.

Because multimedia is not married to any specific type of hardware, the research lab includes the three most popular computer platforms: PC, Apple Macintosh and Commodore Amiga. All three systems were equipped with similar base-level hardware, with the objective being the ability to create professional-quality results. There is no place in this book where you will find solutions that involve low-grade equipment or software. The material you create using the techniques described here will play equally well in Peoria or Los Angeles, in the backroom of a shoe store or the board room of a huge conglomerate. Throughout this book, I presume that you're more interested in getting your message out effectively than in finding the cheapest possible way to do it. Were the latter the case, this book would be of no interest to you; you don't need a book to teach you to use Magic Markers on easel paper. Neither, however, am I inclined to recommend you spend your money capriciously. The products used to research this book were neither the least nor most expensive available. I choose to draw the "professional quality" line a bit lower than some deep-pocketed folks. Some in the video industry, for example, would have you believe that to achieve usable results, you must invest at least $100,000 in video equipment. In this book, I'll show you how to knock an audience flat with video for less than a third of that. That frugal, yet professional, approach is evident in every chapter. It's my goal to show you how to create the hottest-looking material possible on a realistic budget. And in several sections of this book, I'll provide alternatives. I'll show you the *best* way to do something, but then sometimes back off a little and show you how to do it a little more affordably.

The lab makes this book special because it means all the material here is fresh.

Everything was gathered expressly for the book; nothing was recycled from other sources. Given the number of pages here and the number of products used, you might begin to see the size of the undertaking. It was a huge project, and to get it to you before the information went stale meant cutting a corner or two. I handled the layout myself, entering my text directly into a very capable publishing system (specifically, FrameMaker for Windows—see the acknowledgments and the resource guide) running constantly in my research lab. This allowed me a quick turnaround time, handing sections of the book off to the publisher the moment they were finished. As a result, the book's layout style may not be state of the art, and it's even possible that a typographical error or two has escaped my notice. I hope you'll be forgiving, though, because the number one goal of this project was to place as much useful information in your hands as possible, as quickly as possible. Thanks to an understanding and innovative publisher, a bevy of patient and cooperative vendors, and selected special people who helped out, I think we've managed it.

The lab is central to this book because as you read, you'll feel a part of the experience of using the products described herein. I tried to make you feel like you were in the lab alongside me, watching the products work, listening to my running commentary, and getting your own hands into the operation as it went along. I want to draw you in, because as I worked in BYTE's lab, and the new one constructed for this book, I became more and more convinced that multimedia holds the key to the future of communication. Chapter 1 has more to say about that. The videos use multimedia to make that point. Rather than distance you from the material by casting you as an outsider, I invite you into the lab as a part of it. As you read and, if you avail yourself of the tapes, watch, I think you'll appreciate this approach. It allows me to pipe information to you at a much higher rate. With you as part of my lab team, I can dispense with the some of the typical formality of technical writing and simply share what I've learned with you.

If you decide to jump into multimedia yourself, this book's resource guide might be your best place to start. I have tried to provide contact information for every company whose products contributed, incidentally or directly, to the creation of this book. I'm not selling anything but ideas. It's up to you to decide whether the vendors in the resource guide, or any of the other sources available to you, can give you what you need. My reason for including them is not to endorse them, but merely to offer a "here's what worked for me," condensed into a few pages. It would have been impossible for me to complete this book on schedule if the products I selected had not worked as advertised, out of the box, with few or no surprises. I expect you would enjoy a similar experience.

There are places in this book, however, where I found certain products to be worth special mention. While I must stop short of endorsements, I don't mind at all shining a spotlight on those products I've found that do what they do uniquely well. This market exists because of the innovation of daring vendors who turned ideas into products. Even though the multimedia market is now crowded, there are still many outstanding products in it that deserve recognition.

To close this section, I'll offer a few words about impropriety and ethics. Working for BYTE, I've often been caught in the flame of a vendor's wrath for my failure to include them in some piece of editorial. I've endured all kinds of accusations, and lest anyone leap to conclusions about this work, I'll tell you up front: no vendor paid for inclusion in this book, and no one was given preferential treatment. I selected the products included here based mostly on the evaluation skills I learned in my years as an analyst. The only exceptions are those few where, in the interest of keeping deadlines, products were selected on the basis of quick availability. It wouldn't be in my or my publisher's best interest to sell space in this book for money or other consideration. I want you to derive real value from what you read here, and my baser motive is to move you to interest in other works with my name. I wouldn't sacrifice your trust by aligning myself with any vendor, tilting this book's coverage toward any platform, or espousing anyone else's point of view. Quite the contrary: a fair bit of what appears in this book goes against so-called prevailing wisdom. I'll tell you what I mean by that in the next section.

What You'll Learn

What and how much you learn from this book depends on how you read it. If you go through it cover-to-cover, you certainly won't retain it all. What will stick to you are those things you find most applicable to your present condition. If, however, you skip around based on research you've already done, or based on assumptions you're making about where your interests lie, you'll retain more useful information.

Either way, effective use of the material in this book depends on narrowing down your breadth of interest. I'd like to think every chapter has something in it for everyone, but I know that's not so. The people who read the chapters on desktop video production very well might not give a hoot about computer-telephone interfacing. So in a way, this is a different book for every reader. Your interests will guide you to read or skip chapters accordingly.

To help you in this, I have organized each chapter to include a brief section describing what the chapter contains, what the benefits of the technology being discussed are, and how it ties into other chapters in the book. Given what you have paid (or may pay) for this book, it would be unwise to leave portions of it unread without at least seeing my justification for each chapter.

I won't try to make you a multimedia expert. Instead, I'd like to make you comfortable with the available technology and to offer enough practical examples of its use to help you decide whether or not *you* can use it. The safest promise I can make is that if you duplicate the configuration of some part of my lab and follow the steps I lay out, you can produce the same results I did. You can then adapt my work, a few steps at a time, to something that more accurately reflects your unique needs. But perhaps the more reasonable promise is the broader one: after reading this book, multimedia won't be as confusing as it was, and, if you use what you learn, you'll reap more benefits than you would if you had started from scratch. To understand what I mean by that, read the first chapter.

I've gone to great lengths to ensure that the procedures described in this book, and reinforced by the videotapes, actually work and can be implemented by anyone. That's not to say that nothing in this book requires study. In those sections where the technology can be a bit imposing, I tend to back off, giving you enough high-level information to get the job done, but avoiding a nose-dive into technical depths that will only cloud the objective. I want you to be able to do what I describe, and knowing the speed of the memory in the systems I use or precisely how information is encoded on videotape won't help you. If these low-level topics interest you, I encourage you to look up any of the many books targeted at software, hardware and video engineers.

About the Videos

If you flip to the back of this book, you'll find an information form for videotapes. These tapes were produced in the lab, while the book was being written, and offer greater technical depth than was possible in this book. I chose to offer tapes in addition to this book because using dark ages technology (a printed book) to make a case for something so dependent on color, motion and sound seemed arcane. For sections on topics like 3-D animation and desktop video production, videotapes seem an obvious choice. But other sections like presentation graphics benefit as well. It's impossible for me to show you, within the confines of the methods used to print this book, precisely how the tools I used work. Videotape gave me the freedom to show you not only the finished results, but also to let you look over my shoulder as I built the finished work. You can not only see and hear key elements of this book, but also view added material that appears nowhere on these pages. That's no come-on; there is some footage on tape that simply couldn't be translated to print. Also, because the turnaround time for video is far less than that of printed works, I used the tapes as an opportunity to provide even more timely information than that which appears here. Finally, the videos serve as figures for this book. If you leaf through it, you'll find relatively few graphics and figures. That's because, once again, multimedia is difficult to represent with a silent, motionless, colorless piece of paper. So the videos make reference to the book, and the book tends to use the videos as "living illustrations" of what's being described.

The videos are arranged in a manner not unlike this book. With a remote control, you can scan past the sections that don't interest you, skipping directly to portions that relate to solving problems you have. Except for special material (like introductions and late additions), the tapes are matched to the book text so that you can use the two together.

I'll warn you in advance: while the tapes were produced in the lab using leading-edge technology (the very technology described in this book), they don't represent the best you can do with a video production setup. I didn't, for example, trouble to turn my lab into a broadcast video studio. I also didn't have the luxury of dedicating a large block of time exclusively to the tapes. So the lighting won't be perfect throughout, and you won't find any rented models acting as talking heads. Instead, you'll find I did my own talking, not because I think I look great on camera, but because it was the expedient thing to do. You will find a lot of useful material crammed into a very small space (just like this book!), with less emphasis on glitz than on practical content. But there's just enough glitz to keep you interested—how can I not practice what I preach?

Here We Go

That about covers the disclaimers, sales pitches and other more-or-less useless information. The chapter which follows offers you an introduction to multimedia from a philosophical, but still practical, point of view. After that, it's straight to work. Thanks for joining me; I'm glad to have you along.

Acknowledgments

While my name is the only one that appears on this book's cover, I cannot take all the credit for the results. I have many people to thank, but there are some whose contributions stand out:

Jenifer Niles Swetland, my editor at Academic Press, whose patience and cooperation made my life much easier.

All of the vendors whose products were used in this book, but especially the "founding members" of my original BYTE Multimedia Lab: Truevision, Newtek, Diaquest, Panasonic, Sony, Apple, Commodore/Amiga, Ensoniq, Roland and AT&T Graphics Software Labs. That lab, the private lab it spawned, and this book would not have been possible without the cooperation of these daring early participants. These vendors, as well as those who joined later, distinguished themselves through their willingness to participate in a project for which the only payback was a more educated public.

The staff at BYTE magazine, but most especially Howard Eglowstein, Bob Ryan, Jon Udell, Tom Thompson, Stan Diehl, Selinda Chiquoine and Steve Apiki. Howard took over the final corrections for this book (remaining grammatical errors are, therefore, his fault), managing the process for me while I moved to Texas. Selinda helped solicit some of the equipment and software, and generally pitched in whenever the details were too much for me to manage. The others are co-workers and friends for whom I have boundless respect, and I hope their talents will bring them the satisfaction and rewards they deserve.

Greg Loveria, my long-time friend, who worked himself to a frazzle at the same time I did so that I'd think my lot wasn't so bad. Greg is one of those rare souls whose intellect and skill are matched only by his integrity, and I'm proud to be counted among his many friends.

And finally, my wife Teresa, who settled for the tiniest fraction of my time while I worked on this book. Her faith and encouragement kept me moving, and it is to her that I owe the greatest debt of all.

1

Introduction to Multimedia

Multimedia is about getting your message out more efficiently and more clearly; but what is it, and why does it work?

Technology marches on. Not long ago, the "thinking machine" was as improbable as putting men on the moon, but now computers are an inescapable part of our lives. Even those who eschew computer technology cannot survive without it. It's in their cars, their microwave ovens, and their television sets. Every time you pick up a telephone you connect your lips and ears to a vast worldwide network with millions of nodes, all controlled by a network of computers nearly as vast. Virtually every television program and movie you see wouldn't have been possible without computers, and even the old standbys—radio and newspapers—have grown quite dependent on complex computer systems.

These large-scale applications of computer technology made the small-scale applications possible. In the late 1970s, among the first application of then-new microcomputers was word processing. Printers, and the computers that drove them, were expensive, but the notion of using computers to communicate with one another was a compelling one. So legions of typewriters were banished from desktops, replaced by computers and printers. That's when the trouble began.

The written word is a medium *made* for a computer. Every keystroke of English turns into a neatly formed number between 0 and 255. To us, it looks like Ps and Qs, but to the computer, it's an orderly set of 8-bit bytes, each representing a single character, each fitting comfortably in a same-sized slot in memory or on disk. The written word slides nicely into a computer's world, but how well does it work for people?

You needn't search very far for the answer to that: not terribly well. Whoever said "a picture is worth a thousand words" wasn't whistling Dixie. Your brain knows what to use when it wants to tell you something. When you think, how often do you see letters flashing before your eyes? We never talk of "the little typesetter" or "the little desktop publisher" that guides us—it's "the little voice." Our thoughts come to us as speech. For some, thoughts are seen by the mind's eye as well. But the brain doesn't waste time with text except as the occasional visual cue. Instead, what we read is recorded and played back as speech, pictures, or both. The mind, then, does a sort of "format conversion" on reading text to turn it into something it can more readily store and recall: sounds and pictures.

The Brain's Filing System

When we were taught to speak and read, our lessons were composed of pictures and sounds, with the matching words presented for association. Right from the beginning, our minds eagerly stored and filed the brightly colored objects that caught our attention. Long before adults told us what to call them, our minds held well-formed images of virtually everything we had seen and many of the sounds we had heard. Though we were unable to control our immature minds and bodies to draw those images or speak those sounds, they were there, and the second time we saw something, our brains told us we had seen it before. Our ability to communicate this recall was limited to pointing and grunting (a trip to a local pub will let you see this endearing behavior in adults), but *we* knew what we meant.

We take our brains so much for granted that we don't give a second thought (bad pun, sorry) to how its filing system works. You needn't be a psychologist to realize that the brain's files are not arranged alphabetically by topic. Words have little place up there—they're too inefficient, and four out of five brains, given a choice in the matter, will pick the filing system that works best. It's such a universal phenomenon that it's become part of our vernacular. "I'm lousy with names, but I never forget a face." "I hate directions, but if I drive there once, I can find my way there again." "I don't know that song by name, but if you hum a few bars..." Only rarely can a written phrase open a file in the brain. When we say that something can "take you back" to a time gone by, we generally speak of a song, a smell, or a picture. The words "high school graduation" might bring back a memory or two, but the song you listened to on your car radio that day heard later can bring back the entire experience even decades after it occurred.

When the brain files information, it prefers to file it associated with some direct sensory input, some unique pattern it can easily match later. To use a computer database as an analogy, the brain files its records—memories—using one or more keys. Each key in this context is some sensory input that grabbed your mind's attention at the time. To be recalled most rapidly, one of the keys must be unique, or some combination of keys must work out to a unique sequence. Some events affected you more than others, and if your brain sorts its information, it seemingly places the most important first.

Consider the smell that precedes a summer rain. When that smell hits your nose, your brain instantly accesses its database, bringing up a selection of memory records that match that sensory key. If you fell in love for the first time on a day that smelled like rain, chances are the smell will evoke a fond recollection of that person (unless he or she dumped you). Less-important memories get lumped together, and generally, if the brain can't narrow the list of matches down far enough, it doesn't bother reporting its data to you.

The brain also employs what's come to be known as "fuzzy logic" in forming its memory keys. Even though there are dozens of species of duck, you probably know a duck when you see one as long as it "looks like a duck." To say that something "looks like" or "sounds like" or "smells like" something is indicative of a near-match in the brain's database. The sensory key came close enough, without matching exactly, to cause the brain to play back a recollection. It's this ability that allows us to recognize types of things: musicians are taught to recognize types of chords by the unique combination of sounds. Do they need to memorize every possible augmented chord before the brain files "augmented chord" as a key? No, but at first, the key is only good enough for a fuzzy match, and the musician will incorrectly identify other types of chords as augmented. As they hear more, the key becomes more and more specific, until the mind identifies the precise pattern of sounds. In that way, the mind is able to refine its memory keys: it can drop a loosely defined placeholder, updating it later when more specific data is available.

The main problem with words on a page is that the mind's fuzzy logic has to go through several layers of pattern recognition to connect the word or phrase with the thing it describes. The word "duck" does not resemble the object it describes. To work it out, the mind must identify the shape of each letter, then put the letters together, and then—this is the interesting part—*say* the word to itself to form a key it can use. A picture of a duck, or the sound a duck makes, is a key in itself, bypassing the layers of translation the word must follow to be understood.

So sounds and pictures are worth more than the equivalent weight of letters and punctuation; the former are essential to the workings of our own brains. Getting closer to the brain's own native means of storing information has long been an objective for those who have a volume of information to impart in a very short time. When a fire engine goes roaring down the street, is it a silent white truck with "fire engine" written on it in black letters? If it were, few cars would move aside, and the truck would constantly be mowing down pedestrians as they stopped to read the words on the side of the truck. Instead, the truck is painted in a bright color, festooned with brilliantly flashing lights, and given a howling siren. The words "fire truck" don't make your heart beat faster, but the sound of the siren, the decor of the truck, and the blinking beacons make you know there's trouble somewhere. A fire truck is a very basic, very effective example of the value of multimedia: with sound and visuals, it delivers a message that even the simplest mind can fathom in the merest fraction of a second, far faster than the nine-character written phrase can be read and understood.

Information Overload

A speeding fire truck has one message: "get out of the way." A screaming siren and a glittering array of lights are enough to make that clear. As the volume of information increases, conveying it becomes more complex. In an airplane's cockpit, the pilot and crew are literally surrounded by hundreds of buttons, switches and indicators. During a flight, there are countless things that can go wrong and a wide range of severities attached to these various failures. In the days before computers, pilots were expected to constantly watch all their gauges; the pilot had to know what the safe ranges for all of the indicators were and what to do to correct any problems he or she saw. At first, when the equipment was simple and there were only a handful of instruments, this wasn't difficult. But with more engines, multiple hydraulic systems, more moving parts and new ways to measure the craft's condition and environment, the cockpit became awash with controls and gauges, all needing to be tickled and watched. The two-way radio added to the list of things a pilot had to tend to, all while keeping the plane in the air.

An airplane's cockpit is a good example of information overload. Our brains are capable of doing several things at once—*multitasking*—but only to a point. You can't listen to two conversations at once and understand all the words of both, or listen to two songs simultaneously and hum both of them later. Similarly, you can't hold two newspapers—one for each eye—and read two articles at once. Where our senses are concerned, we're mostly limited to processing one thing at a time. In the days before computers, a pilot had no choice but to constantly scan the gauges. If the oil pressure dropped to zero while she was studying the gauges on the other side of the panel, she might not notice it until her practiced scan brought her back to the oil pressure gauge. That could take several seconds, long enough for a critical situation to develop into a catastrophic one.

The solution was to install lights. The oil pressure gauge knew what its safe range was, and a light came on when the pressure fell below or rose above that range. The plane knew when it was in a stall, when the landing gear was down, when the cargo door was open, when a hydraulic system had failed...and all these conditions got their own lights. Sometimes the lights go on when something's wrong, sometimes when something's right. Some lights blink when there's a serious problem. Others might change color. Some lights are just always on, and some only come on when you tap on them. An airplane's cockpit looks like a pinball machine's playfield. Once again, information overload.

The lights were a good idea, but there were too many of them and nothing to differentiate them from one another. So many of the lights have legends, decals with written phrases describing the condition indicated by the light. But remember what I said about the written word: it's a poor substitute for a visual or aural cue, especially when you're in a hurry. A blinking red light labeled "hydraulic failure" attracts no more attention than a blinking red "coffee ready" light. Somehow, a *priority* must be established. The hydraulic failure light can be made bigger than the coffee light, but how far can that go on? If indicators were all sized differently according to their importance, the cockpit panel could occupy the side of a building. Even with indicators of different sizes, the brain would lose its ability to discern between size A and size A+1. Its fuzzy logic would kick in and make them look very much alike. Once again, overload.

Priority is a problem that isn't easy to solve, but you must try to solve it when you have lots of data to present. The cockpit example is an extreme one, but some of the principles apply well to all kinds of information presentation. So let's presume the cockpit problem is one we will solve with multimedia. The solution may be some part science fiction, but for the purpose of illustration, we'll assume technology makes all things possible. Our project might proceed something like this: First, information is condensed. If you create a replacement for an aircraft instrument panel, but it still presents as many different pieces of data as before, it's no improvement. Several separate gauges are removed, and instruments' output are fed into a computer. The computer watches the instruments, in effect, and sifts through the data to report to the pilot only those things she needs to know. The reports come through a panel-mounted CRT, giving the pilot only one place to look to get a summary status of the aircraft. Let's take a single action: lowering the landing gear. The feedback the pilot requires associated with that action might be: acknowledgment of the request ("the button works/the computer knows you pushed it"), indication of progress ("landing gear on the way down"), and final status ("landing gear down and locked/landing gear *not* down and locked").

After condensing the information, priority must be assigned. The first message ("the computer knows you pushed the button") is pretty important because it lets the pilot turn his attention to other matters. Giving him instant acknowledgment of his request keeps him from mashing on the button again. The second message ("landing gear on the way down") is the lowest priority; it lets the pilot know the aircraft is working on his request, but it's not something that needs to grab the pilot's attention. It's there in case the pilot pushes the button, gets distracted, and needs to be reminded that he already pushed the button. The final message ("gear down and locked/gear *not* down and locked") is the most important. Until the gear are completely down and locked, the plane cannot be landed safely. If there is an equipment failure, it needs to be identified and the pilot notified immediately so he can abort his landing and look into the problem. In our cockpit, our CRT is a color one, and we also have a computer-controlled noisemaker that feeds into the pilot's headset. We might also outfit the seat base for electric shock, but for now, let's stick with visual and aural feedback.

Our color CRT gives us several ways to define the priority of information. Even though I've preached about the inefficiency of words, they're necessarily the building blocks for this book, so our cockpit display will put up most of its messages in text. An ordinary message—let's call it "priority 3"—shows in green characters on a black background. This high-contrast, constant display attracts no attention on its own, so like the traditional cockpit instrument, the pilot must decide to read it before the data it contains can be delivered. A more urgent message, "priority 2," will be set in text of a different color. If the rest of the screen is green on black, with the exception of one line of red text, the pilot's eye will be instantly, automatically drawn to the red. That's part of how the brain processes patterns. It looks for things that are sufficiently different from their surroundings. Remember the brain's tendency to fuzz things, though. You would have trouble setting up priorities 2.1, 2.2, and so on with differing shades of red characters. After the first couple of shades, the brain loses its ability to quickly discern one shade from another close to it in intensity. So color is useful for setting up priority of information, but only to a point.

Presumably, when the pilot is confronted with a priority 2 message on his display, we'll want to make sure his attention isn't elsewhere. We could install blinking lights throughout the cockpit to ensure that wherever the pilot looks, he'll know from the lights that he should look at the display. That's impractical, especially since the pilot could be admiring the fluffy clouds at the time, and there's no way to hang blinking lights on them. Instead, since we know all good pilots always wear their headsets, we'll use the noisemaker to make a unique sound that says "look at the CRT." If our noisemaker is sophisticated enough, perhaps it can really *say* that, in as many words, but a short bell-like tone, repeated every few seconds, takes less time and is just as effective for a pilot trained to its meaning. When the pilot has read the message, perhaps he can touch the screen over the message to make it go away and to make the bell sound stop.

For priority 1, we presume some grave condition exists that needs immediate attention, some condition that is *always* more important than anything else going on. For this, a change of color and a gentle sound cue aren't enough. The highest visual priority is established through the most compelling visual cue: motion. Making the characters blink is a simple example of motion. If the pilot is looking at the display at the time, no matter how many red text lines there are, if one of them starts blinking, his eyes will shoot there in an instant. Keeping the characters constant and blinking the background color is a way to eliminate the confusion of having the characters appear and disappear. However you manage the visual cue, you still have to cover the possibility that the pilot is looking away at the time. Priority 2's gentle bell isn't enough. Your pilot, after becoming a veteran of many flights, might become complacent and tune this sound out, figuring he has several more seconds to contemplate the clouds since priority 2 is never that serious. The sound for a priority 1 message needs to be unique and stirring, unmistakable in its urgency. This might be a good place for the electric seat shocker, but well-chosen sounds can easily make the pilot feel like he's been shocked, and once he turns his head, the blinking text on the display will give him an instant grasp of the problem.

The Real World

Our cockpit display example may seem completely removed from whatever business you're in, but it isn't. The basic problem—too much information—is one all of us must face. Another issue raised in the example—priority of information—is also common. The pair of them can gang up on you to make the information you're trying to present, regardless of its quality or the effort that went into it, invisible.

The process of running a business, a classroom, a government or any institution requires communication. To sell, teach or get re-elected requires the same skill: you must reach your audience. Despite the apparent simplicity of that phrase, "to reach" is a complex notion, and one that must take human nature into account. Reaching an audience is best viewed as a series of steps.

When a newspaper or magazine writer pens a story, she must create an opening paragraph, called a "lead." There are several ways to interpret that word, but I tend to think of it as a hook. The first paragraph should sink a hook deep into the reader, making him *want* to read the rest of the story. There's a notion worth repeating, with a broader scope: to reach an audience, you must make them *want* the information you're presenting. That's a foreign idea to some, because the old school philosophy holds that a captive audience is as good as a willing audience. Students who are in a scheduled class should automatically want to learn. Employees paid to attend a meeting should automatically pay attention. These precepts would hold true if people were predictable, but we're not. Even if you assume your audience is composed exclusively of "A" students or company boys and girls, it isn't fair for you to assume that a desk and blackboard, or a paycheck, is enough to ensure your message will get through. If you don't have a captive audience, the problem is even greater. As an architect selling a concept to a potential client, or a middle manager giving a proposal to upper management, your idea will be compared against untold others, likely in an environment over which you have no control. Captive or not, if your objective is to reach your audience, *never* assume they'll give you rapt attention. The concept of the lead applies to more than newspapers and magazines. Regardless of the form your information takes, you can construct a lead that intrigues your audience. With a strong lead, the sleepy student will sit up and pay attention. The executive, busy running his stock portfolio through his head, will shift his focus to your message instead. And the potential customer will take notice that your approach is different from the others, so perhaps what you have to show her deserves her attention.

Another concept of modern communication that frequently gets set aside is that most forms of human interaction are, at a basic level, sales pitches. You might be selling a car, an idea, your company's image, or even yourself, but it works out the same. If you think of business presentations in the light of salespersonship (did I say that?), some of the uses for multimedia become more apparent. I counsel those engaged in business presentations to forget about the bad reputation sales pitches have earned through their common misuse and to focus instead on the elements that make a good pitch and the objectives associated with those elements.

The objective of a pitch is a simple one to understand: you want your audience to buy whatever it is you're selling. If you're selling vacuum cleaners door-to-door, the meaning of the word "buy" is obvious. If you're the captain of the debating team, the meaning is only slightly different. While no money changes hands, a successful pitch means the audience leaves with something they didn't have when they came in—in this case, your views on some subject.

Getting your audience to buy what you're selling is only the most obvious objective. The best pitch is one that leaves the audience feeling like they made out well, and thinking better of you for their having been pitched. If you do your job right, they have greater trust and respect for you, and that trust and respect get extended to the idea, product or company you represent. So a sales pitch sells an *image* in addition to the primary sell. Building trust and respect isn't easy, and there's no magic formula. There are several places in this book where some technique's ability to impress your audience is called out, and impressing the audience is a large part of gaining their respect and trust. There's a tendency to assume that a slick (and there's nothing wrong with that word) presentation is a vehicle employed by reputable businesses. When people are asked their impression of a multimedia presentation, assuming it's well done, the word "professional" often comes up. In the business world, that's a description of one's activities that's not hard to live with. The basic link between the perception of the quality of information and the quality of its presentation is one that runs very deep. I can take a set of dry statistics, wave the wand of multimedia over them, and turn them into something that will make people say "wow." Some old-schoolers insist that sizzle might impress or entertain, but it doesn't serve any useful purpose. What they don't get is that nothing can be taught or sold to an audience that won't pay attention. I realize that there are plenty of people who see multimedia as a cheap trick, giving those who use it an unfair advantage. I say they're *right*, and as long as there are people who still believe that data is better dry than dressed-up, there will be plenty of opportunities for those who are willing to invest a little time and creativity in impressing their audiences.

If multimedia works so well, *when* should it be applied? Given three environments--new product launch, board of directors' meeting, department meeting--can you figure out which are candidates for the use of multimedia?

My job would be easier if there were a simple right answer to that question. Fact is, the criteria that determine whether multimedia is appropriate or not vary according to the situation. Perhaps it's a bit easier to say that multimedia, if done right, never *hurts*, but it takes time to create. Unless you can imagine a tangible benefit from the use of multimedia, it may not be worth the time to use. But when you ask yourself the question, "is it worth it?", make sure you cover the right bases. Instead of asking yourself deep, probing questions about multimedia's value to you, ask simpler ones:

- ***Will I, the interests I represent, or this information benefit from being seen and heard as well as discussed?***

There may well be some types of information that can't be significantly enhanced by multimedia. One such case that comes to mind is the political speech: while multimedia might play a very effective role in supporting the speaker's argument that the opponent is full of hot air, it is the politician's ability to deliver a stirring speech that becomes part of the measure of his or her worth. I hasten to point out, however, that no election since the proliferation of television has taken place without the help of TV advertising. There is no more accessible example of multimedia than television.

- ***Is there sufficient time to both research the subject and put a presentation together?***

Those who don't share my beliefs about the value of multimedia often tell me they fear that the "medium will become the message." I interpret this to mean that the way the information is presented becomes more important than the information itself. From my view, this happens most often when the producer spends more time building the presentation than collecting the data that went into it. Only rarely is this appropriate; video production, for example, often requires a very high ratio of production to research time. But for most other things, you must make sure your data gets the most attention. Despite my obvious affection for multimedia, I always counsel those who use it to use it judiciously. Gather the data *first*, then assemble it into an attractive form. It often takes willpower to avoid going overboard with powerful multimedia tools. They can do so much that sometimes users can get a little giddy and try to use every feature. I don't need to say much more about this beyond calling up the analogy of the newsletter done with 35 fonts because "that's how many the printer had." That first leap—from boring data to a very basic multimedia presentation—is a huge one in terms of benefits. Spending more time on a presentation pays off on a decreasing curve, so there's generally nothing to be gained from going nuts and trying *too* hard to impress.

- ***Do I have the right tools for the job?***

An amateurish multimedia presentation is far worse than one that doesn't use multimedia at all. The range of tools available for producing multimedia material is broad, and not all of them are intended for use in professional situations. All of the tools in this book are distinguished by their appropriateness for business, educational and other serious uses. Some multimedia tools are more toys for the curious than useful products, but you can't always tell from the packaging or the pitch. If you plan to use multimedia, don't be cheap. It's possible to stay within a reasonable budget and still get the results you want. Dabbling in low-end toy software is a good way to have your audience spend more time chuckling at your poor presentation than paying attention to its content.

- ***What will it take to show what I've created?***

Because there are so many different kinds of tools, their requirements vary. As you create your presentation, be aware that the more different media types you apply, the more demanding the presentation environment will be. The exception is video, which is one reason I think it's so effective: there are no requirements that can't be met almost anywhere. For other types of presentations, you must consider what equipment you'll need when showtime comes. If it's to be a computer-based presentation, you'll probably have to plan on bringing the computer with you—you can't count on your audience's computer having the right combination of hardware and software. For many, finding the right way to pack a desktop computer for travel is among the more trying elements of using multimedia. Remember, too, special requirements at your audience's site, those things that are not the same as where your presentation was built. If your computer-based presentation is to be given before a large crowd, will you have a data projector waiting for you? If there is audio involved, can the facility handle it? If you're traveling overseas, are you prepared to deal with the possible electrical differences? So much of the planning for a multimedia presentation has little to do with multimedia.

- ***Will I need help?***

Most multimedia works are done alone, or in very small teams. With more complex projects, you should plan far enough in advance to know whether the amount of work, or the kind of work to be done, will require the aid of others. You might need an artist to do a drawing, a musician to create a bit of music, or a professional speaker to lend his or her voice to your presentation. Tools have come a long way, and many of the things that once required outside assistance can now be done by you or bought "canned." Artwork is one example: many commercial artists sell their work to brokers that gather the art into electronic collections. So-called "clip art" is commonly used in desktop publishing, but with presentations, the concept has been extended to include color clip graphics, animation and video clips, and even music clips. This material is very convenient to use, generally requiring only a one-time license fee that covers unlimited use. Copyrighted material, such as a videotape of a TV show or a popular musician's CD, cannot be used in presentations without consent and fees (which are often quite high). Save yourself the hassle; if you need material you can't generate, buy it outright or pay someone to create it for you.

- ***Can this material be re-used?***

Re-use is an often-overlooked benefit of multimedia. The presentation exists in electronic form, making it easy to update or carve up for use in other presentations. If you're likely to give the same kind of presentation over and over again, you should develop your presentation the way good programmers develop their code: with modularity in mind. An animated company logo with underlying music, for example, can last for years. A pitch for one client can be quickly adapted for another, and neither client will realize the work wasn't done especially for them. As you create, if you're smart about it, you'll be building a library of material that will save you hours of work later.

Instinct vs. MTV

No matter what your material, and no matter what your audience, the need to grab and hold their attention is constant. Even if you're the only one in the room that's speaking, you have competition. The traffic, the whoosh of the air conditioning system, ringing telephones, daydreams and countless other distractions all conspire to obscure your message. Gathering professionals together for a meeting is expensive, and it only pays off if the majority of the attendees, or at least the key people among them, fully grasp the material they came to ingest.

Some of humanity's instinctive, centuries-old defense systems remain with us today, and they work both for and against us. While, as I said before, it may seem reasonable to expect a paid staff to sit still and absorb facts regardless of how they are presented, the fact is that it's not in our natures to behave that way. Unfortunately, our desire to expand our intellect doesn't stand on its own. The brain has lots of sensory collection devices at its disposal, and it tires quickly when those inputs are not stimulated. Some are fortunate enough to be able to sit and listen for hours without requiring other stimuli. But most people require a little more. Don't be too quick to judge those who have trouble focusing on a dryly delivered message. They may have fine minds, but ones that require more stimulation than a speaker and a stack of overheads can provide.

In a way, multimedia is cheating. It taps into the brain's natural tendency to key on color, motion and sound, a tendency that dates back to our ancestor's roots when this mechanism kept them from being devoured. Contrasts between colors draw our attention, perhaps because we're keyed to spotting predators sneaking up on us. If something moves, the eyes and mind are instantly drawn to it. These defense systems feed the mind and "wake it up," giving an audience a fresh interest in whatever material is being presented.

Aside from taking advantage of our natural tendency to be attracted to contrast and motion, we must also consider what pleases us. If roses were gray instead of red and yellow, would we appreciate them as much? If tropical fish were drab colors and stuck themselves, motionless, to the sides of the tank, would we be so captivated by them? The notion that anything enjoyable can't be worth doing is nonsense. The best presentations are those the audience enjoys; why not give your audience a little entertainment? I'm not talking about MTV or stand-up comedy, but simple things. Our eyes can remain focused longer on a colorful image than a bland one. We're fascinated by motion. These are traits we associate with children, but we still have them as adults. It's not pandering to build color and motion, and music for that matter, into presentations *purely to entertain*. Done with taste and moderation, it doesn't harm the seriousness of your message. If you do it right, it will help you drive the message deeper into the minds of those you're trying to reach. One of the great values of entertainment is that it can be the sugar that makes the medicine—the message—go down. You often hear filmmakers in interviews talking about a movie's "real message." You probably wouldn't pony up the price of a ticket to see the filmmaker's message. You pay to see the entertaining wrapper *around* the message. You don't have to be a film school graduate to take advantage of the same idea.

It's been suggested to me that perhaps I should be ashamed of my affection for technological tricks and so-called glitz in serious business applications. In fact, I don't feel guilty at all. Multimedia, if used properly, is a tool that helps you condense and prioritize information, using shortcuts to penetration and comprehension that have been known for ages. It's not deceitful, and it's far from unprofessional. Quite the contrary: a well-produced multimedia presentation sheds far more positive light on the entity presenting it than any stack of overheads, slides or flip charts could confer. The audience is often impressed that the presenter went to so much trouble just for them, and so they feel almost obligated to pay attention. But more than that, the tools make the information make more sense. From a purely practical point of view, those elements that are seen by multimedia non-believers as glitz are often easily defensible as valid means of packaging information for more efficient delivery.

The trick is not to go too far. My belief, which this book details, is that the medium must never be an end unto itself; it must never become its own message. Extravagant use of color is worse than none at all, and excessive, senseless motion is far less defensible than still imagery. I'd rather sit through a carousel of 35mm slides than watch some overzealous presenter's attempt at artistry. Perhaps that view surprises you, since in the preceding paragraphs I seemed to espouse doing whatever is required to snap your audience out of its presumed coma. There must be boundaries. Somewhere between the castor oil and MTV lies a dignified, professional middle ground that leaves room for creativity while tempering our natural rambunctiousness.

Much of the technology that falls under the species "multimedia" is exciting and fun to use, and some of it is almost thrilling. One of the most thrilling aspects is that you can now do, for yourself, a kind and quality of work that previously required several hours of attention from professionals dedicated to creating presentations (or whatever you're planning to create). You may be sick of hearing this analogy, but it's appropriate: the rise of multimedia is very similar to that of desktop publishing (DTP). When PCs first hit the market, newsletters, brochures and other small jobs were handled by print shops and typesetters. Their services were expensive, and if you didn't get what you wanted the first time, you had to pay for changes and then wait for those changes to be implemented. Today, it's taken for granted that companies are able to do their own small-scale typesetting and publishing, and even large-scale projects (like this book) are easily handled by the growing number of high-quality tools.

Desktop publishing, as a concept, was always a good idea. What kept it on the back burner for so long was technology. First it was storage: PCs didn't have enough disk or memory to run complex programs and store their results. Then displays became the bottleneck, because the first reasonable PC graphics followed the initial PC by several years. And finally, the hurdle that took the most time to leap, the printer. Daisy wheel and dot-matrix took budding publishers only so far; documents still had to be brought to typesetters to get multiple fonts, high-quality graphics and the clean, "jaggy-free" look of a professionally produced document. Laser printers arrived, and the rest is history. Now desktop publishing is an accepted part of the modern business milieu, taking its place alongside spreadsheets and databases as standard business applications. That place wasn't always assured.

Early on, it was surmised (mostly by those with a financial stake in the matter) that the consumers of typesetting services farmed the work out not because they couldn't do it themselves, but because they didn't want to. The arrival of the laser printer, fast-paced improvements in system performance and display capability, and the proliferation of scalable document processing systems provided evidence that people *did* want to do their own publishing. Bringing the project in-house means having control over it, and control over access to the material, from beginning to end. Costly surprises are reduced—staff time, supplies and equipment can all be documented—and the overall cost, even if dedicated staffers are hired, is much lower than farming documents out if a business does a sufficient volume in them. Now desktop publishing drives the sales and technological development of laser printers, scanners, displays and software. It makes sense for businesses to do for themselves whenever they can. Desktop publishing proved that once a sufficient demand exists, vendors will move to fill it.

Multimedia is following much the same track, with almost identical opposition. There are those who stand to lose a bundle if businesses begin creating their own "productions" (see the preface for my definition of that word). Video, computer-based business presentations, audio and telephone applications, interactive multimedia systems...these are among the things that companies have traditionally gone outside to have created for them. We're fortunate that technology is advancing so rapidly that now, unlike only a few years ago, these and other multimedia production tools are becoming increasingly affordable and accessible.

Where will it all end? I expect multimedia will eventually no longer be seen as a technology category of its own. The components that currently make up what we call multimedia will develop individually, and others will spring up that we haven't thought of yet. At some point, we'll begin to take for granted that audio, video and other multimedia data types are part of our interaction with computers. It won't be novel any more to see a real estate database with a moving video tour of the property as a data element. Attaching spoken notes to electronic mail messages, or using voice as a replacement for traditional textual messages (after all, voice is more natural), will become commonplace. And the usual choice between presentation overheads and slides will become a choice between computer-assisted presentation formats. Right now, the technology makes many of us a little giddy, and that fondness for the technology itself makes the technology's potential harder to pinpoint objectively. There are plenty of outspoken players on both sides of the issue; some have even said "multimedia is dead." I partly agree with that phrase, but only with my twist on it: multimedia, as an identifiable, cohesive technology class, never existed, so I suppose it could be called "dead." I use the word because it keeps titles down to a manageable length; can you imagine how well "The video, audio, business presentation, telephone interface, CD-ROM and interactive multimedia producer's handbook" would sell? As long as we both understand what the word means in the context I've chosen, "multimedia" is as good a word as any.

2

Media Types

The process of multimedia cannot be set apart from the media itself. Here's a brief introduction to the major media types discussed in this book.

Multimedia isn't a thing. It's a word that describes vehicles for the carriage of information. Those vehicles you can use today, and those that wait on the horizon, necessarily color the way you package your information for presentation to others. It's impossible to be more creative than technology allows, but fortunately, there's enough room to maneuver with what you have to work with today that you needn't worry much about hitting some ceiling in your expression of your ideas.

This is also an appropriate place to discuss platforms—the types of computer systems that house the devices that carry your data (it's beginning to sound like "the house that Jack built"). Every system, if you're willing to invest the effort, can handle all the useful media types. But some are better suited than others, and that's where this book's content begins to cross over into opinion.

Because every system can be coaxed into doing anything that's technologically possible (sometimes you have to develop your own custom chips, but that's the way life is), judgment about the suitability of a particular kind of system to a particular need becomes subjective. I've worked extensively with all three of the system types used to produce this book, and in that work, I managed to draw some conclusions about the effectiveness with which each platform addressed the exploitation of a particular media type. I offer those conclusions here, with this caveat: this book was written at least several months ago. In that time, it's possible that the platform that was behind in a particular technology is now surging into the lead. So what I offer is not advice, but information; a snapshot of the state of technology at the time this book was written. Luckily, much of what's described here is fairly evergreen and will track changes in technology.

Before you can set your imagination loose cooking up ideas for ways to package and deliver your data, you must understand the limitations and freedoms offered you by today's technology. We are fortunate to exist in an age where the honored buzzword "multimedia" has spawned an entire industry; at no other time has the development of communicative technologies been as rapid as now. We now have more ways to exchange information than ever before. In the first part of this chapter, I'll acquaint you with the most widely used media types.

The media types described below are discussed in much greater detail in the coming chapters. The intent here is to give you the foundation of knowledge the future chapters take for granted. It's an overview, so don't be frustrated if it raises more questions than it answers. The answers will come soon enough.

Audio

The addition of sound to existing personal computers made for the birth of popular multimedia. Some computers, including the Amiga and the Macintosh, had sound practically from the get-go. On those systems, and particularly on the Mac, sound became an integral part of the way the systems worked. It's gotten to the point where even Mac systems running office productivity software scream whenever they put up dialog boxes and belch when they eject floppies from the disk drive. That seems silly on the face of it, but this arbitrary use of sound is actually a good thing; everyday users have grown so accustomed to having their computers use sound to communicate that they actually prefer it. It makes computers seem a bit more friendly, maybe even more humanlike, and the choices of sounds give each person's computer a different personality.

Getting sound in and out of a computer isn't as straightforward as using a tape recorder, although recent advances in software help make it *seem* that easy. Amigas and all but the newest Macs can't record their own sounds; both systems require external sound recorder modules that plug into one of the computer's external ports (the parallel port on the Amiga, the modem or printer port on the Mac). This strategy limits the quality of the sound, for reasons I'll explain shortly. Another tack is that taken by the PC, which is traditionally deaf and mute except for the near-useless "beep" speaker. Fortunately, a thriving video game market for PCs resulted in the creation of what is now a mature, affordable add-in audio board technology. The market was created by manufacturers like Creative Labs (Sound Blaster) and Adlib, and with that market came de facto standards for the handling of sound on PCs. Those standards have been tweaked a bit to make room for higher-quality sound, and the current overall state of audio on the PC is, in many ways, more advanced than the standard audio on either the Amiga or Mac. Soon, audio capability will be built into most desktop PCs; major manufacturers including IBM and Compaq have already produced systems with integrated audio. As they sell more, the cost of implementing audio will get cheaper, and audio will soon be a check-off, a required item on buyers' shopping lists.

Whether internal or external, included or optional, most audio systems in modern computers have many implementation details in common. It's not necessary to understand the low-level science of sound to gain the needed grasp on how to put it to best use for your applications. It does help, however, to bone up on a few buzzwords and concepts that may not be familiar to you yet.

Current implementations of computer-based audio systems use some mix of three kinds of audio: passed-through, digitized and MIDI. The most useful products or systems are those that offer all three, because in using multimedia to deliver a message, it's always best to have as many vehicles at your disposal as possible.

Passed-Through Audio

Passed-through audio comes into the computer from some external source: a microphone, tape player, CD player, radio or television—any device that emits an electrical audio signal. Thc audio from the external source is passed through the computer's audio hardware. Sometimes the sound is passed unmodified and the pass-through is provided only as a convenience so all your audio connections can be made at the back of the computer. More often, though, the computer has at least some control over the shaping of the sound as it passes through. Volume control, accessible through software, is common, and on audio devices that support multiple pass-through audio inputs, making a volume control available for each of those inputs gives you the ability to deal with multiple audio sources under computer control. Some devices also let you adjust the bass and treble to give you some control over the sound's color, controls you can also use to "clean up" a badly made recording. And lastly, a few devices provide functions like stereo expansion, which widens the apparent distance between stereo speakers by injecting a brief delay, and low and high-pass filters, which filter out the lowest and highest-frequency sounds (which are often unwanted noise) to help minimize audio problems like booming bass sounds and tape hiss.

Passed-through audio is rarely seen on its own; it's almost always combined with some other media type, either another flavor of audio or some video technology (video overlay boards, described later, often include audio pass-through as a convenience). PC audio boards use audio pass-through so that you can mix external audio sources with those created by the board itself.

Digitized Audio

The most commonly seen (or, should I say, commonly *heard*) type of computer audio support is digitized audio. Here, sounds are electronically converted to digital information (through a process called *sampling*) and stored in the computer's memory or on its hard disk. Once stored, a reverse process turns the digital data back into sound and pumps it through speakers or headphones. In practice, digitized audio can be roughly analogous to using a tape recorder. You can use it to take spoken notes to yourself or to others, to record the minutes of a conference, or even to record music. But since these are all things you can do now with a $30 Radio Shack tape recorder, why go to the trouble and expense of recording them digitally?

The benefit, and one that lies at the heart of multimedia's reason for existing, is *control*. With a tape deck, you have a little control over the process. You can set recording levels to determine how loud the sound on the tape will be, and you can choose from a number of grades of tape and qualities of equipment that affect the quality of your recording. But once the information is laid down, you have to settle for what's there. What if you recorded an hour-long meeting, but only wanted to extract the fifteen minutes or so while your boss, whom you regard as a godlike creature, was speaking? On tape, you'd either have to resort to making a copy, shuttling around with rewind and fast-forward to find the sections you want, or you'd have to get a razor and a splicing block and paste your new tape together. In both cases, the time to prepare your boiled-down tape will be much greater than the tape's playing time. Wouldn't it be nice if you could skip instantly to the "good parts," mark them somehow, and have a new recording generated for you automatically?

That scenario is one that digitized audio makes possible. Once your sound is recorded and stored in the computer, it can be manipulated as digital data, in much the same way as a database or word processor file. Parts can be added, deleted and moved around, portions can be cut and pasted between multiple audio files, and just as you can set italics or boldface in a word processor document, you can use the computer to enhance portions of a digitized audio file. I'll save the details for the upcoming chapter on audio.

Voice Mail

Some digital audio solutions not only record and play sounds on the desktop, but can connect directly to a telephone line for so-called voice mail. If you take a typical digital audio board and add the ability to detect a ring on the phone line and to "pick up" that line that board can turn a computer into the equivalent of an answering machine (albeit an expensive one).

The most capable telephone audio interfaces are commonly referred to as "voice mail" boards. These add touch-tone decoding circuitry so that a program can not only answer the phone, play a digital audio message and record a digital audio response, but also guide the caller through a set of functions selected by touch-tone button presses. These systems, when built to be versatile and customizable, can be very powerful and can frequently do most of the work that previously required a human attendant. Whenever the main function of the system is to collect or provide recorded information (without having to analyze it), the so-called voice mail systems work fit the bill very nicely.

Less-expensive voice mail boards generally provide a fixed level of functionality; the application bundled with the board might give you a digital answering machine with the ability to collect your messages remotely by touch-tone. Better voice mail systems are programmable, either through an interface that doesn't require traditional programming or one that expects you to have a C programmer handy. A programmable system might be put to use as a dial-up information service or a multi-user corporate voice mail system. The better systems will service multiple phone lines from within a single computer, and almost all "serious" voice mail systems expect to be housed in a dedicated computer.

MIDI

The third common audio media type is MIDI, short for musical instrument digital interface. This is a standard for the digital representation and transmission of music that is now adhered to worldwide by virtually all makers of electronic music equipment. For as little as $200, you can buy portable musical keyboards that have MIDI jacks. The hardware side of MIDI is a mid-speed (about 3000 bytes per second for those with a passion for stats) serial network that can interconnect multiple musical instruments. You can, for example, connect two MIDI-equipped keyboards together, play a note on one keyboard, and have the second keyboard play that same note but with a different instrument sound. Connect enough equipment and you've got the rough equivalent of an electronic orchestra.

The computer's part in all this is usually as a data and communication manager. PCs usually do MIDI through internal interface cards, while the serial ports on Macs and Amigas require only an inexpensive external MIDI connector box. The connection between the computer and the electronic musical instrument is through a cable with five-pin round (DIN) connectors on both ends. Devices can then be daisy-chained together, and the MIDI standard provides a scheme for simultaneous computer control of multiple instruments, all connected to the same chain.

MIDI data isn't digitized audio. In fact, it's a lot closer to sheet music. Musical notes have numeric equivalents, and other controls (like the sustain pedal and the volume control) are reduced to numerics as well. These numbers become a stream of data that is processed by the instrument and turned into sounds. But because it isn't digitized audio, MIDI music is much more compact and modifiable than a digital recording. You could fit the entire MIDI representation of a lush orchestral work on a floppy disk; the same floppy couldn't hold more than a few seconds of high-quality digitized audio.

MIDI doesn't require a computer, but once one gets involved, it expands the number of ways you can change the data that represents your music. MIDI music can be recorded into a computer using a software package called a *sequencer*, which captures and stores the MIDI data stream. Once it's stored, the sequencer can be used to edit the music, change its tempo, or alter instrument assignments. More advanced sequencers can display the MIDI data in notation, like sheet music, and some can even add harmony and counterpoint melodies.

You can't turn a piece of recorded music into MIDI data. The most common way to turn music into MIDI is to have someone play it on a keyboard connected to a computer running a sequencer. The sequencer can be used like a recording studio, allowing the keyboardist to layer more sounds on top of existing ones, stacking chords, melodies, drums and other elements to create a finished musical score. Another way to create MIDI music is to enter it from the sheet music. Software exists that allows you to "draw" musical notation, either invented by you or copied from some other source, and then convert that notation to MIDI data. Music collected in this way often suffers from a stiff feel—computers always do everything right on time, unlike human musicians—but some sequencers can apply "humanizing" filters that add random delays to the notes to simulate the rhythmic imperfections of a human player.

The easiest way to get MIDI data is to buy it. Several companies are now in the business of selling canned MIDI music. Aimed at business presentation, video production and other serious multimedia uses, canned MIDI music is a simple and cost-effective way to add music to a multimedia production. The seller takes care of licensing and copyright issues (you *must* be careful about using music—even sheet music—from other sources), and usually packages the music orchestrated and ready to play on popular MIDI instruments.

A trend on the PC is to package a combination of a MIDI interface and a MIDI instrument on a single plug-in board. Without connecting any external instruments, you can play any MIDI score; just connect headphones or speakers to the back of the board, and you've got music. The Amiga also has some limited ability to play MIDI music through an internal four-voice audio music circuit.

In addition to electronic keyboards and PC music synthesis boards, there are a number of compact, stand-alone electronic instruments called *sound modules*. These have no keyboards, so they cannot be used to create music, but they produce music from a stream of MIDI data much the same way an electronic keyboard would. Sound modules usually cost less than keyboard synthesizers, and their small size makes them easily portable for presentation use.

The most versatile computer-based audio systems combine passed-through, digitized and MIDI audio. Thanks to the development of the MPC (Multimedia PC) standard, there are now a large number of add-in PC boards that do at least some of these things, and most of them handle all three types of audio in one relatively inexpensive package. Macs and Amigas can also be made to handle all three types as well, but they lack the variety of "do it all" boards available for the PC. Generally, for non-PC systems, you have to shop around more carefully to find the components you need, and you might not find them at all: I didn't bother equipping either the Mac or the Amiga in my lab to handle audio pass-through, but both systems do have digital audio and MIDI.

Audio Quality

If you choose to make use of digitized and/or MIDI audio, you'll need to find the proper balance between quality and cost. In both cases, you very clearly get what you pay for, although the greater cost associated with greater quality may not be immediately evident.

In the case of MIDI, the quality choice is a simple one: which instrument sounds best? Whether you choose an electronic keyboard, a sound module or an internal music synthesis card, there are enough different kinds of music synthesis to make the choice truly confusing. Determining the quality of a particular MIDI product means relying on your own ears to some extent (there are samples of several MIDI synthesis methods on the videotape), but there are some key things to look for when you start shopping for MIDI gear. The first aspect that deserves your attention is the synthesis method itself. Electronic keyboards, sound modules and internal PC music cards are all actually specialized computers, designed to produce music by creating patterns of digital data that are transformed to sound.

The synthesis method seeing the most widespread use (thanks mostly to PC game sound cards) is FM (frequency modulation). FM has the advantage of being very inexpensive to implement, making it the choice not only for sound cards, but also for home and arcade video games and most pinball machines. The instrument sounds produced by an FM synthesizer are created by tiny programs that chart the path the instrument's sound makes at various stages in its life. From the time the sound first appears (*attack*) to its decline to silence (*decay*), FM instrument programs combine basic building-block sound elements to create a finished sound that can change shape as it progresses. The program gets stored in the synthesizer's memory and can be called up later using a numeric instrument ID (*patch*).

The least-expensive, and most common, FM method is 2-operator. The Yamaha 2-operator FM chip is the one used in most low-end PC sound boards, home video games and arcade games. The phrase "2-operator" has a complex meaning, but it can be described as supporting a maximum of two sound variations in a single instrument patch. The 2-operator FM chip is monophonic, capable of producing 11 simultaneous voices. That means that 11 musical notes can be playing at one time. The number of voices that can play at once is referred to as *polyphony*, and 2-operator FM synthesizers are said to have 11-note polyphony. Eleven voices may seem like a remarkable number; after all, even the best pianist only hasten fingers, so 11 voices are probably more than you need, right? Regrettably, that's not so. When you hit a key on a real piano, the sound it produces doesn't start and stop sharply. It has sharp beginning and a gradual end—attack and decay—with the decay altered depending on whether you're pressing down the sustain pedal. With the sustain pedal down, you could run up all the keys on the keyboard, and set every string in the piano to vibrating at once. So even though you have only ten fingers, you can easily make the piano do 88-note polyphony. An electronic instrument must simulate the effect of a piano's natural decay by sustaining the note and decreasing its volume over time until it's silent. While the note decays, it occupies one of the 11 available voices. Three four-note chords played one after another, each one given a natural-sounding decay, would be enough to go beyond the 11-voice polyphony of 2-operator FM.

Internal PC music cards traditionally use two 2-operator chips to simulate stereo, placing 11 voices on the left and 11 on the right. More recently, 4-operator chips have found their way into mid-range PC audio boards, capable of supporting more complex patches, real stereo and more polyphony. The 4-operator chips typically get used one at a time because each one effectively replaces a pair of 2-operator chips, and the 4-operator chips produce better sound.

How good is FM? I've taken no small amount of flack for this point of view, but I stick with it: while FM is valuable because it's inexpensive and widely implemented, the quality of even the 4-operator FM sound is not equal to the demands of professional use. In the 1980s, FM synthesizers (like the popular DX7) were all the rage among professional musicians, but their use died out as more advanced synthesis technology became more affordable. Now you can find FM only in music stores that specialize in used gear, and there's a reason for that: compared to other synthesis methods, FM sounds cheap and thin. There are exceptions to that—one need only step into an arcade to hear masterful use of FM, but that's because the game manufacturers have talented people on staff who do nothing but program the FM chip to produce good sound. An FM-based PC game sound card, out of the box, produces music that sounds like a $69 toy keyboard. The instrument voices lack the depth that you'd associate with an acoustic instrument. And after all, it's *real* instruments like pianos, violins and horns that form our base of reference. It's perfectly acceptable for a synthesizer not to precisely imitate an acoustic instrument—one need only listen to a Vangelis or David Arkenstone recording to know that fully electronic sounds can be mesmerizing in their own right—but our expectations have been formed such that we demand an electronic instrument have depth and richness. The people you're trying to impress with your music expect that, too, and it's wise not to disappoint them. More often than not, I find FM music, unless you can get someone from Atari or Williams (arcade game manufacturers) to program it for you, is very disappointing. Its sole benefit is its cost to implement—it's so cheap to build an FM synthesizer onto a PC board, they're virtually everywhere and irresistibly affordable. As a way of previewing your music before your big presentation, FM works as well as any other method. But if an audience is involved at all, I advise you to find something better.

The "something better" I have in mind is the synthesis method that's quickly taking over: PCM. PCM, for pulse-code modulation, is actually the simplest thing in the world. If you accept that the best you can hope for in an electronic instrument is to make it sound like an acoustic one, then why not make a digital recording of the real thing and create a computer that plays those sounds back under MIDI control? The technology has been available for years, in expensive dedicated systems used by deep-pocketed musicians. With a PCM synthesizer, when you press middle C on the keyboard, the computer inside will play a recording of some instrument playing middle C. Done properly, it's crisp, rich and stunningly realistic, and we're fortunate that there are plenty of companies doing it properly and doing it for computers. PCM synthesizers are made by so many different companies that it's impossible to summarize their polyphony, but most of them handle at least 24 voices.

Most modern synthesis methods are relatives of PCM; at some point, they involve the playback of a digital recording of another instrument. You might also hear of "digital wavesampling" or "sampler," "wavetable," and other variations, but they all have the digital recording in common. Because the device is playing back digital data, it doesn't care how it was created, so some PCM instrument sounds are created from scratch without borrowing them from elsewhere, creating original synthetic sounds. But the depth and quality of the sound remains, and PCM instruments can deliver obviously synthetic sounds as well as they do sampled acoustic instruments.

A while ago, an item worth considering was a synthesizer's ability to be *multi-timbral*, meaning that it could play several different kinds of instrument sounds at once. The MIDI standard supports up to 16 simultaneous channels, each one distinct, and each channel can either be its own MIDI device or one of many patches inside a single MIDI device. In that way, one MIDI device can serve up an orchestra's worth of different instrument sounds. There was a time when MIDI devices were rarely multi-timbral, but no more: it's become expected, so virtually all the devices in common use for MIDI music are fully multi-timbral.

With digital audio, the quality issue takes quite a different turn. All other things being equal, with the quality of the circuits that process the incoming and outgoing audio being of the highest caliber (which is not always the case), the issues that define the quality of digital audio are *rate* and *resolution.*

When sound is digitized, the computer stores an approximation of the sound wave created by the thing making the sound. Sound waves are infinitely complex, but the computer must simplify them because it can only represent them as numeric values within a certain fixed range. Many of today's digital audio solutions let you choose the range within which the device will operate, so you can choose where you strike the balance between quality and cost. That range determines the accuracy of the digital approximation of the sound, and the ranges apply to rate and resolution alike.

Rate refers to the sampling rate, or the number of times per second the computer takes a snapshot of the sound wave coming into it, converts it to a number, and stores it. Each sample becomes like a point on a graph. When you join the points, you can see the computer's approximation of the sound wave. The closer together the points are, the more accurately the graph will depict the original wave. The sampling rate also determines the maximum frequency that can be represented. The rule is that the sampling rate must be double the highest frequency you wish to capture. A sampling rate of 11 KHz (KHz for kilohertz, or thousands of cycles [samples, in this case] per second) is sufficient, for example, to capture most human speaking voices, which fall easily in the range below 5.5 KHz. Music and natural sounds like waterfalls and bird songs, on the other hand, can reach up to 16 KHz or a bit higher. The top end of the human audible range is arguable, but experts believe that the top of the human-audible range falls somewhere between 16 and 22 KHz. Using the double-rate rule, to capture sounds at frequencies of up to 22 KHz, you must sample at 44 KHz. Not coincidentally, this rate is the one used by common audio CDs. By doing a little better than the range of the average human, sound sampled at CD rates comes as close to perfect as we can discern.

If the sampling rate determines the accuracy of a sound wave's digital representation, it only affects the accuracy of the X (horizontal) axis of the wave. The Y axis represents a wave's amplitude, or volume, and the range used to express that also profoundly affects a sound's quality. Once again, the closer together the points are on the Y axis, the better the sound will be. A sound card with an 8-bit resolution, for example, must boil each sample of a sound wave down to one of 256 possible amplitude values. Any sound can be heard clearly in 8 bits, but it cannot reasonably be compared with the original. The highest fidelity sound available to most computer users today is done in 16-bit resolution, expanding the range of numeric values available to represent each sample's amplitude to 65,536 (quite a leap from 256). The difference is more difficult to describe than it is to hear. A demonstration appears on the videotape. Lower resolutions generally make a sound thinner, less lifelike. With sufficient rate and resolution, a digitized sound can be as good as the original, and remarkably, a digital recording made with a desktop computer can be better than any you could make on even the most expensive analog (tape) recording equipment.

Rate and resolution have a direct relationship to the cost of digital audio. Standard audio on most Macs and the Amiga, and the low-end audio products available for the PC, max out at 22 KHz and 8 bits. This handles the human voice very well, but it falls apart if asked to represent music or other sounds that make use of the full spectrum. All three types of machines can be enhanced with audio boards that take the digital audio quality all the way up to the currently accepted useful maximum: 44 KHz at 16 bits. This matches CD audio (and that's why it's frequently referred to as "CD quality") and is generally thought to be capable of reproducing any human-audible sound with no perceptible loss in quality. Boards that produce results this good cost more than those that do less, and they certainly cost more than the built-in capabilities of the Amiga and Mac. But the real cost is not the price of the board, which may be significant in itself, but in storage. The numeric data that represents the sound wave must be stored somewhere, and for now, that's your computer's hard disk. If you're like me, you generally have precious little hard disk room to spare, and that's where the trade-off comes in: as the quality of digital audio increases, so does the room required to store it. The equation is simple: the sampling rate times the resolution, divided by 8 (the number of bits in a byte), tells you how many bytes of hard disk space will be consumed in a second by a particular combination of settings. A sampling rate of 44 KHz (actually, 44.1 KHz is the norm), for example, with 16-bit resolution, consumes 88,200 bytes of disk space per second. A mere twelve seconds of CD-quality digital audio eats up a megabyte of disk, and a minute takes up over five megabytes; *double* that for stereo. Compromise is obviously necessary, and most products that can deliver the highest-quality results also give you a healthy number of choices that are less storage-costly. Using our example above, backing off to 8 bits at the same sampling rate, for instance, cuts the amount of disk required in half. Cutting the sampling rate from 44.1 to 22 KHz cuts it in half again.

Do these compromises also cut the *quality* in half each time? That depends. First, it's a matter of individual taste. I'm no audiophile (one look at my cobbled-together home entertainment system will tell you that), but I have standards I consider reasonable. I have heard remarkable things done at 22 KHz and 8 bits; Amiga enthusiasts are particularly proud of the impressive sounds their pet system can be made to produce, even with its limitations. On the other hand, I have been in the audience of presentations in which music was used that was obviously captured at 22 KHz or worse. Looking around, I could see that I wasn't the only one grimacing. There are times when lesser rates will do, and that brings me to the second consideration: if you're running tight on disk space, the rule of thumb is to use the combination of rate and resolution that delivers the minimum acceptable results. You can sample several test clips of the audio you intend to use, stepping up the rate and resolution each time. Start from the absolute minimum and work your way up. At some point up the ladder, you'll hear something that strikes you as “good enough”; stop there and use that combination for the rest of your project. If, however, you have a lot riding on the production you're creating, buy yourself a bigger hard drive and use the best combination available to you. Even in the worst case, you'll spend a few hundred dollars for a bigger hard drive, but relieve yourself of the worry over the quality of your audio.

Audio's role in multimedia productions can't be overlooked. It provides guidance, it grabs attention, and it adds a touch of personality you can't get from any other source. By using audio in your work, be it a business presentation or a piece of electronic mail, you'll get one thing from your audience that you can't count on any other way: silence. If you can get them to be quiet, you can get them to pay attention. The last thing you want is to get the notice of your audience, only to have them start talking amongst themselves about how poorly done the digital audio or MIDI music in your presentation is. This is not a good place to cut corners.

The coming chapters on audio will provide you with more detail on the issues raised here, and they will also offer specific examples, illustrating audio's usefulness and details of its use in practical production applications.

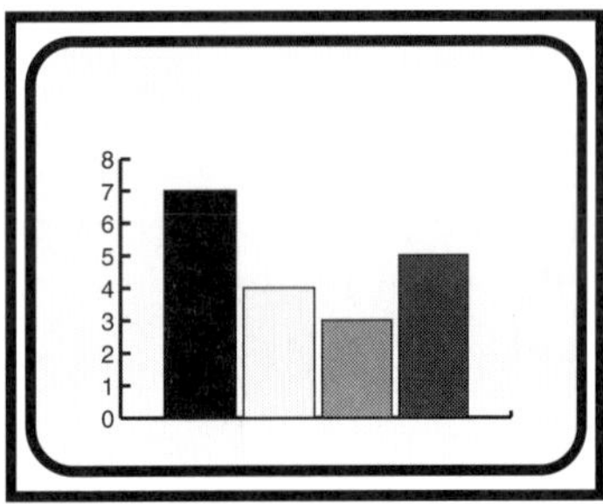

Graphics

When the Color Graphics Adapter first became available for the original IBM PC, pundits scoffed, insisting that no serious computer user needed color or graphics. Color graphics languished for some years as the domain of scientists and game players, but with the introduction of the EGA and VGA on the PC, the Amiga 1000 (in which color graphics were standard), and the first color Macs, color began to earn a well-deserved reputation as a useful tool for serious users. Now many programs take for granted that they're running on color displays and even text-mode programs make liberal use of color to present data more clearly.

As I mentioned in Chapter 1, sighted people absorb most of their information through their eyes. Graphics play a key role in bringing computers closer to human-style communication. Where humans rely on facial expression and body language, computers can employ graphics to communicate an unspoken message. Stationary graphics, 2-D animation and 3-D graphics and animation each strengthen the link between us and our data.

Stationary Graphics

Today, we're spoiled by the massive number of color graphics boards, monitors and other graphics products on the market. Not only do we expect color on our desks, but it is increasingly the case that we expect our color graphics to be faster and more realistic than ever. Stationary graphics, in which category I include programs' user interfaces, play a huge role in shaping our perception of information. If this concept seems foreign to you, consider ads in a magazine. The only tools available to the designers of those ads are color and shapes. They can't make it move or make noise (there have been exceptions to the latter, but not notable ones). Each purchaser of a full-page ad gets something like an 8x10-inch space in which to make their point, and they must make that point better than the competitor who likely has an ad in the same magazine.

As in advertising, graphics are one of the most powerful tools multimedia producers have. Interestingly, many graphics are actually made of words. Words, presented graphically, form a large part of most productions. To make those words presentable, they are set in a size, shape and style that enhances the message. The text is shown in a pleasing font, perhaps casting a shadow to one side, and with a graphical background that adds to the audience's enjoyment of the image without detracting from its content. The old notion that with the right information, all you need to do is present it in the most expedient way, doesn't cut it any more. So the art of typography has graduated from the printed page to the CRT. Popular illustration programs like Adobe Illustrator include the ability to manipulate text, and companies (Adobe in particular) are thriving with collections of exciting font libraries. For most of us, good-looking type set against an appealing background is most of a presentation.

Illustrations, whether drawn with a computer or not, become graphical images as well, as do photographs and statistical charts and graphs. The availability of inexpensive color scanners, which convert photographs and printed artwork to computer images, changed the shape of computer graphics. But just as much was gained by the arrival of easy-to-use paint and illustration packages. Paint packages, including products like Deluxe Paint and Tempra, create graphics through the simulation of real paint. Most packages don't bother to provide a very accurate simulation. They settle, instead, for providing a basic set of tools for drawing freehand graphics. You can draw lines with a certain color and thickness. You can use an airbrush to create graphics that simulate the fine-mist spatter of a real airbrush.

Geometric shapes become perfectly formed colored stamps that you can impress on your electronic canvas. As with real canvas, it's usually difficult to erase something once it hits the screen; paint programs require you to invest some thought in advance, and they call for more artistic talent than the alternative. Graphics created by paint programs and the like are referred to as bitmapped graphics.

The alternative, one more suited to the use of those of us with limited artistic skills, is the 2-D illustration package. These programs use shapes—circles, squares, curved shapes and user-formed polygons—to create graphical images in building-block fashion. In the hands of artists, these tools produce absolutely amazing results. But even for us grunts, the degree of control illustration software offers makes it easy to create first-class graphics. Each shape you create becomes an object, and when you stick it down on the canvas, it retains its individuality. You can move it, redefine its visual attributes (like the color, the color and width of the line that defines its edges, and the shadow it casts), and attach it to other objects so they can be moved together. Two-dimensional illustration software (like Adobe Illustrator and AT&T GSL's RIO) is probably the single most valuable graphics tool in a multimedia producer's collection, because the work produced with it can include graphics as well as text, and what you create can be reshaped and used for another purpose later.

Another advantage to illustration software is the ability to scale graphics cleanly. Paint software lays dots on the screen you're painting on. If you later wish to "blow up" some part of your drawing to show its detail, the best the computer can do is turn each pixel of the drawing into a bigger blob of color. The cost of scaling graphics this way is evident to everyone—images, particularly those including text and shapes with diagonal and curved lines, come out looking rough and choppy. Curved lines become approximations of curves that only look good from a distance, and what were smooth diagonal lines become as flights of stairs, with each step clearly and annoyingly defined by the expanded graphical blob that was once a tiny pixel. With illustration software, the drawing exists not as pixels, but as shapes. Each shape, because it retains its identity, not only knows how to change color and rotation, but can also change its size. So zooming in on a portion of a drawing created with an illustration program causes that program to redraw at your display's full resolution. This also works well for printed graphics, because printers, particularly those that employ the PostScript language, also deal best with shapes that can be resized. It is for these reasons that I will dwell on 2-D illustration packages in this book when it comes to the creation of original graphics.

Two-dimensional illustration packages also work better in most cases because they know how to do layering, in which each object in the scene understands its relative closeness to the foreground. If you laid one suit's set of playing cards one atop another on a table in order, the ace would be the only card fully visible. The 2 card would only be visible if you moved the ace aside enough to allow the 2 to be seen. Similarly, the 3 would only be as visible as the two cards atop it permitted, and so on. In computer-generated graphics, layering (sometimes called depth) simulates limited three-dimensionality by allowing you to hide objects behind one another in a manner similar to a stack of playing cards or pieces of cut paper. Almost all 2-D software lets you move an object to the front or the back of the "stack," making it appear as either the topmost or bottommost object in the view.

There is one time when the use of pixel-oriented graphics packages is the best choice: when you import images from another source, and that source is a pixel-oriented image. Such is the case with scanned photographs and graphics: scanners digitize printed images one line at a time, so they can't create independent shapes from the images they scan. In this case, paint packages, and the new class of image-editing software (like Photoshop and PhotoStyler), are the best choices for retouching and altering the characteristics of scanned images. If, for example, the image you've scanned comes into the computer too dark, an image editor can apply an algorithm called gamma correction to alter the brightness of the image. If your photograph is miscolored from bad handling at the processing lab, an image editor can color-correct the scanned version of the image. Blemishes and other imperfections can be retouched as well in the manner of paint packages.

Graphics Quality

With so much riding on graphics, it helps to know what the defining issues are. As with audio, there are two key elements that, taken together, describe most of what you need to know about a graphics system's quality: *resolution* and *depth*. The resolution of computer graphics displays is measured in pixels (picture elements), the smallest graphical quantity that can be represented. If you lighted one pixel on your screen, it would appear as a tiny dot. The number of pixels you can get on your screen at once is the resolution, usually expressed as a pair of numbers, with the horizontal (X) resolution followed by the vertical (Y). The most common resolution in use today is 640 × 480: all three of the systems used in my lab have this as their standard resolution. And all three systems have in common that they can produce a variety of resolutions with optional display hardware. If your system's display hardware (which is sometimes on the motherboard and sometimes on a separate card) supports multiple resolutions, which of them you can use is a function of the monitor you select. Every monitor is capable of supporting a certain maximum resolution; be sure you choose a monitor that can give you the resolution you expect to use. Some additional guidelines for monitor selection can be found in the final section of this chapter.

Most computer monitors take their input from the computer in RGB form, in which the red, green and blue components of each pixel's color is delivered on a separate wire. This provides the best-quality image, allowing for the precise representation of complex graphics. Some graphics cards can produce composite output, which you can watch on a television set or record to videotape. These cards are useful for video production and other kinds of work where videotape or a standard TV set is the final destination. The quality is not as high as RGB since all the components of the video signal are rolled together and sent over a single wire. A compromise, S-video or Y/C, splits the brightness and color information out onto two separate wires, providing a better-quality image through that separation. The idea is easy to understand: electrical signals sent over the same piece of wire can't help but interfere with each other. The more you can separate the electrical signals that paint your graphical image onto your display, the higher the quality of that graphic will be. RGB (three, four or five wires, with the extra wires carrying the signals needed to synchronize the monitor with the computer's graphical signal) is the greatest separation available to most of us. S-Video (two wires) is a good compromise, and composite (one wire) is what most of us settle for when we watch broadcast television or a videotape.

The depth of a graphics system affects the number of colors it can represent at once. It is entirely up to the computer's graphics board or on-board graphics controller to determine this. Depth is measured by the number of bits used to represent each pixel on the screen. A common baseline among modern graphics systems is 8 bits, meaning that a maximum of 256 different colors can be displayed at once. Although 256 colors may seem like an infinite number—imagine having that many crayons—those colors get used up quickly in multimedia work. A photograph, converted into a computer graphic by scanning, contains hundreds, if not thousands, of subtle variants of every color that appears. And in business graphics, a popular aesthetic device is the gradated background, in which two colors appear at extremes, and the space between them is filled with all of the shades that fall between those extremes. An 8-bit graphical representation of a photograph or gradated background often shows that colors were dropped to squeeze the image into 256 colors. Skin tones become mottled, gradated backgrounds lose their smoothness, and shadows become less well defined. Still, most people experiencing high-quality computer graphics for the first time are impressed by 8-bit images, and the fact that each pixel on the screen occupies only 8 bits (one byte) of memory keeps the size of 8-bit files down.

Because computers deal best with data in multiples of 8 bits, the next step up in color depth is typically 16 bits. That makes room for many more simultaneous colors—65,536—and this is enough to offer a more accurate representation. Sixteen-bit graphics are a comfortable middle ground, vastly improving the quality of the image without requiring a huge additional investment in storage space (double that required by 8-bit images). Each pixel takes up two bytes, though, and one unpleasant side effect of this is that the device that runs your display now has twice as much data to move around. On Mac and PC systems, the difference in display performance between 8- and 16-bit color modes is quite noticeable. In a graphical user interface, dragging a window to a new position—which causes the system to erase and redraw the window—is a good way to check the basic performance of your graphics hardware. In general, that test done with the display hardware in 8-bit mode will show much better performance than the same test done in 16-bit mode. For that reason, the Macintosh lets you choose your color depth on the fly: 8 bits for general-purpose work, 16 bits for more demanding graphics work.

With any graphical image, the set of colors that appear in one graphic might be entirely different from those that appear in another. How, then, does the computer pick which 256 or 65,536 colors to use to represent the image? Most graphics hardware operating in an 8- or 16-bit mode uses something called a color palette. The colors a painter lays out will vary depending on the kind of painting she intends to do, and they may change as the painting progresses. In the same manner, a computer graphics system's color palette lets the computer choose which colors will be used for a particular image. In an 8-bit system, for example, instead of each 8-bit value representing some absolute color, each value is a pointer into a table of colors. That table—the color palette—can be changed to suit the graphic. Each entry in the color palette specifies a certain color, built by combining percentages of red, green and blue, that will be displayed every time a certain color value (0–255) is drawn on the screen. This scheme lets the computer choose a different color palette for each image. So if you're showing a series of graphical images in slide-show style on an 8- or 16-bit system, the color palette hardware can ensure that each image is shown with a set of colors that are the best match for that image. So-called palettized images are a little easier to modify, since every color in the image is represented by an entry in the color palette. Image-editing tools can change the palette of a graphic so that every occurrence of yellow, for example, is changed to white.

The highest-quality computer graphics are produced by display hardware in the "true color" class. Instead of being governed by a color palette, true-color graphics use 24 bits per pixel of graphical data. Each 24 bits directly represents the true color—using 8 bits each of red, green and blue—of each pixel. With 16.7 million color variations, 24-bit images push the limits of humans' ability to discern one shade from another. Like CD-quality audio, by being just a little better than we are, true-color graphics come as close to perfect as computers can get. They also carry with them a cost similar to that attached to CD-quality audio; compared to 8-bit graphics, true-color images can take three times as much space to store. And if 16-bit color graphics take a lot of time to move around, 24-bit graphics take even longer. Except for high-end workstations, the performance of most display systems in 24-bit mode is unacceptably poor except for those times when you really need true color graphics. But the trade-off is worth it: a 24-bit graphical representation of a digitized photograph, shown in sufficient resolution, can easily be indistinguishable from the original.

Not wishing to stop there, some graphics hardware goes even further. Since modern computers prefer to store things not only in multiples of 8 bits, but in multiples of 16 or 32 bits, many boards store a remarkable 32 bits per pixel, a full four bytes for every colored dot on the screen. Since it's supposed that we can't possibly see more than the 16.7 million colors offered by 24-bit graphics, 32-bit graphics systems use those extra 8 bits for something else. Most often, those bits go to either the *alpha channel* or the *overlay* bits. The alpha channel uses the extra 8 bits to assign up to 256 degrees of transparency to each pixel on the screen. That way, when one graphic is pasted over another, the alpha channel can determine in which areas the upper graphic shows through, and in which areas the lower graphic will appear. The effects produced in the alpha channel, which sometimes get referred to as matting or compositing, allow you to combine two or more images by drawing a separate alpha channel mask that determines where an underlying image will show through and to what extent. That decision gets made for each pixel of an image with an alpha channel. An alpha channel value of 0 (which might be shown in a mask creation program as black), for example, would use the value of the foreground image's pixel to determine the displayed pixel's color. A value of 128 would blend the colors of the foreground and background pixels, creating a semi-transparent effect. And a value of 255 would use the background graphic's pixel color exclusively.

Boards that use the extra bits for overlay create, in effect, two separately manipulable graphics planes. Images loaded into the overlay plane appear on top of the primary image. An overlay plane can be used to put text over a graphic, to display transient user interface elements like push-buttons and cursors, and generally to serve whenever it's useful to have two distinct, independent images on screen at once.

2-D Animation

When you place the elements that make up a graphical image under a computer's control, it doesn't take much imagination to figure that the same computer that draws your image can make it move. Motion brings graphics one step closer to being alive, and motion attracts our attention because it *seems* alive. 2-D animation is the process of moving “flat” images, graphics created with 2-D paint or illustration programs, across the screen and possibly changing their shapes as they go. An animation program records the movement and shape changes, and builds an animation that you can play back later.

Most animation involves *tweening*, in which each step of a graphical object's movement is represented by a redrawing of the object itself. Animation software can simulate *cel animation*, like using old-fashioned paint on transparent celluloid. Better cel animation software can take over most of the redrawing for you, keeping track of those portions of the image that change and keeping you from having to redraw the rest, but in the worst case, you'll have to do what traditional animators do: redraw each image in sequence to simulate movement. The sequence of images is then played back rapidly, imitating motion by throwing distinct images at the eyes too quickly for the brain to discern between them. Cel animation, like paint programs, is a method most suited to those with a talent for art. You must have enough of a grasp of the subject you're animating to not only imitate its form, but to mimic its movement as well. That's a tall order for most people who haven't made studies of the subject.

For the rest of us, 2-D animation software involves the automatic tweening of objects from one location to another. To use this form of animation, called *key-frame* animation, you place the objects in your scene at one position and take a snapshot—a keyframe—that records the positions and attributes of all the objects in the scene. Then you move the objects to where you want them to end up, and take another keyframe. By defining the time distance between the two keyframes, you give the animation program everything it needs to create the animation. Every animatable attribute—position, rotation, color, and so on—is interpolated in software to simulate the smooth transition from one position, one rotational angle, or one color to another. You can create an animation by dragging out a square in the upper left corner of your screen and setting a keyframe there. Then you could drag that square to the lower right of the screen and set another keyframe, say, one second later. The software would then compute the intermediate positions the square would have to occupy in order to smoothly glide from the upper left to the lower right. So unlike cel animation, which might have required you to redraw the square in each of its intermediate positions, keyframe animation reduces the move to two operations. Some animation software lets you change the shape of objects over time as well. If you take that same square I mentioned above, making it a full square at both ends of the animation but a flat line in the middle, you create the appearance of a vertically tumbling square.

Text is a common target for animation. Even simple business presentations usually employ some type of animation to spice up the show. The ordinary build, in which the bullet items in a text slide become visible one at a time, is a form of animation. An imaginative presenter can reveal each item by sliding it in from the right or the bottom of the screen, creating a more appealing effect. Some programs, particularly those that combine 2-D illustration and animation (like RIO Animator), let you change the shape of objects as they move. Having an object grow in size as it moves, for example, simulates the movement of that object closer to the viewer. "Squashing" (compressing) it to reduce its height simulates the tilting of the object on its horizontal axis; compressing its length as it moves, simulates spinning around a vertical axis. 2-D effects often simulate 3-D movement.

3-D Graphics

Software that does three-dimensional graphics understands the concepts of perspective and shading as well as the most talented artist. A computer display cannot actually present anything in three dimensions; height and width can be shown, but depth must be simulated. This is done through perspective and shading. In perspective, parallel lines leading away from the viewer eventually intersect at the horizon, so that portion of an object that is farther away from the viewer appears to be narrower than the portion that is closer. The basic rule of shading is that colors get darker as the distance from the light source grows. The angle at which light falls on a surface determines how quickly the brightness fades, and the type of surface (stone, metal, plastic, and so on) further changes the effect of reflected light.

Three-dimensional graphics programs use mathematical formulas to simulate the effects of perspective and shading, concepts artists can study years to master. The light-reflecting characteristics of various types of surfaces have been measured and entered into shading algorithms, so the stone-shading algorithm reflects light like real stone, metal like metal, and plastic like plastic.

The first step in building a 3-D graphic is to start with a shape that has three dimensions. A 3-D object is very similar to an object created with a 2-D illustration package. Where the latter creates 2-dimensional images by drawing lines from one 2-D point to another, a 3-D program gives each line's defining point a third qualifier: depth. In the nomenclature of graphics, the horizontal points lie along the X axis, the vertical points along the Y axis, and the points along the depth line lie on the Z axis. Building (*modeling*) a 3-D object is necessarily more difficult than building 2-D objects; if a computer's display and its input devices are inherently 2-dimensional, how can you create 3-dimensional things with them?

Three-dimensional shapes most often start their existence as 2-D shapes. To create that third dimension, you apply processes including *extrusion*, *lathing* and *complex surface modeling* (all explained in the chapter on 3-D graphics) to single or multiple 2-D shapes. The most commonly used of these, extrusion, can take any shape, including text, and give it depth the way you would create a 3-D shape with a Play-Doh set: the 2-D shape becomes a cutout, and material is pushed through it until it is extruded to the desired depth. Of course, 3-D programs aren't *exactly* like Play-Doh (they don't get all crusty if you leave them out). Thanks to extrusion, all you need to understand about 3-D is how deep you want your extruded object to be.

Most 3-D objects are drawn in *wireframe*, showing only the lines that define an object's surfaces. Wireframe views draw quickly, since no shading calculations need to be performed. The next step up is *depth cuing*, in which lines get dimmer as they recede into the distance. Ordinary wireframes make you guess at depth;

depth-cued views of wireframe images make depth easier to see. From there, your next option is *hidden surface removal*. Here, those lines that couldn't be seen from your view of the object (assuming all the surfaces are opaque) are removed, showing your object as a 3-D wireframe in which all the surfaces are the same color.

The process of giving different colors to surfaces is called *rendering*, a step that typically waits until you've finished most of the modeling work. After your 3-D models are placed, you must set up simulated lights. Each light can have a different color and other characteristics that affect the appearance of the scene, and each can be placed in a different point in 3-D space. Lights can be omnidirectional (shining in all directions like a lightbulb), distant (casting light from a distance like the sun) or spotlights (casting light in an expanding, dimming cone from the source). Light affects an object's surface depending both on the object's surface characteristics and the shading model being used. Flat shading is the next step up from hidden surface removal. Each face of the object, defined by sets of connected lines, reflects a color depending on the surface's angle and distance from the light source. More realistic shading methods proceed from there, but they mostly involve creating a smooth gradation in brightness from the point at which light strikes an object's surface to the point at which the surface ends. Various shading methods handle this gradation with varying degrees of accuracy, letting you strike that all-important balance between quality and time. There are no shortcuts; the more realistic you want a 3-D scene to be, the more time it will take to render.

The absolute maximum in realism is achieved through a process called *ray tracing*. In normal 3-D work, shading is simulated by analyzing the distance of the light from the surface, the angle of the surface to the light, and the characteristics of the surface itself. With ray tracing, the computer draws a beam emanating from the light source and follows it as it reflects off and refracts through objects in your scene. Objects can reflect other objects, and light can be bent as if through glass or water. Ray tracing produces stunningly realistic 3-D scenes, but at a tremendous cost: ray tracing takes many times longer than traditional shading to calculate, sometimes incurring calculation delays of hours (or, in the most extreme cases, days) per scene. The results are often worth it, and most of the computer-generated graphics you see on television and in movies have been created using ray-traced graphics.

A 3-D object, once built, must then have its surfaces defined. While a block hewn from real granite knows what it is and understands how to reflect light, the same cube simulated in a 3-D graphics program doesn't understand a thing. It's your job to assign properties to the cube's surfaces. If you're fortunate, the 3-D package you choose has a built-in property for granite—simply select the cube, select "granite" from the surface attribute menu, and the next time you render your scene you'll see a convincing simulation of a granite block. Otherwise, you might have to load in a scanned image of a pattern similar to that of a granite block, and *texture map* it to the surfaces of your cube. Texture maps are like projections or decals of patterns onto 3-D shapes. At the very least, they let you attach a graphical image to each surface or wrap the entire object with it. Better 3-D software can analyze a texture map and create other attributes, altering a surface's depth (bump mapping), shininess, or transparency. Bump mapping can create a topographical globe or a golf ball, shininess mapping can make some portions of an object appear glossy or dull, and transparency mapping can make parts of an object show through to the objects behind it. All of these add to an object's realism without adding significantly to the difficulty of creating them.

Like 2-D illustration programs, 3-D graphics programs let each object retain a separate identity and set of attributes. Layering means something a little different in 3-D. Instead of pushing 2-D shapes to the back or pulling them to the front, 3-D programs let you set an arbitrary Z-axis depth for every object in your scene. They also let you place the "camera," the point of view used for the final rendered image, wherever you like. The Z-axis depth of each object determines whether it will obscure, or be obscured by, other objects in the scene according to the placement of the camera. Because the simulation of three dimensions is so precise, you can preview a 3-D scene with real objects (salt shakers, presidential campaign buttons, or whatever you have handy) and be confident that what you see in real life is close to what you'll get from your 3-D software if you align your objects properly.

The algorithms that define simulated 3-D shading are among the most performance-intensive things you can do with a computer. In fact, desktop PCs have only recently become equal to the task of doing 3-D calculations. Not long ago, the only computers that could handle the immense load of 3-D were those specifically engineered for the purpose. Even today, most commercial 3-D work is done on UNIX workstations because of their computing power and specialized hardware dedicated to speeding up 3-D. But the best desktop machines, with high-speed processors like the 80486 and 68040, are now more powerful than the workstations of just a couple of years ago. Three-dimensional software has come a long way, too, and now packages like TOPAS and 3D Studio, Lightwave and Infini-D bring a full range of professional capabilities from modeling to ray tracing to your desk for a fraction of what it cost the makers of science fiction films.

The simulated shading of 3-D objects places a high demand not only on a computer's CPU, but also on its graphics system. Realism of shaded 3-D scenes is enhanced by greater bit depths, because most scenes, particularly those with multiple light sources and shadows, render to thousands of subtle color variations. Here, the difference between 16- and 24-bit graphics systems becomes evident; even a simple 3-D scene can use up 65,536 colors, creating a banding effect as colors are dropped. Some 3-D packages, including TOPAS, can apply a process called *dithering* to approximate colors. If you needed a shade of light blue, but didn't have any more room in your palette for it, your program could create the appearance of light blue by mixing dots of blue with dots of white in an airbrush-like pattern. Dithering looks best from a distance; when you don't have the bit depth to represent all the colors in your scene, dithering is always better than banding.

3-D Animation

What 2-D animation brings to flat graphics, 3-D animation brings to the world of simulated 3-D. Keyframe animation is available for 3-D as well as 2-D graphics, but 3-D animation adds the ability to simulate movement along the Z axis to the repertoire of object motion. Better 3-D packages, those in the class discussed in this book, also let you animate other object attributes, causing objects to change shape and appearance over time. A process called *morphing* is part of some 3-D animation packages. It lets you gradually change the shape of an object to match the shape of another over time. The most capable morphing software lets you change one arbitrary shape to another; lesser software lets you change an object to another object with the same number of shape-defining points. In either case, you can use morphing to transform apples to vases, spheres to bowling pins—wherever there is some rough similarity between objects, morphing can be used to create a mesmerizing animated shape-shift between the two.

Most 2-D animation software creates animation that you play back on your computer's display. Three-dimensional animation packages can do the same thing, but the best results are derived from recording 3-D animations directly to videotape. This requires additional hardware (which is introduced in this chapter's discussion of video and detailed in later chapters), but it is the best method available for producing the kind of smooth, well-defined animation you've grown accustomed to seeing in television advertising.

Among the most common uses for 3-D animation is the flying logo, which is now so frequently seen that it's almost cliche. With 3-D animation, it's especially important to recognize your artistic and technical limits and work within them. Some things are easy to do with any animation system; others are difficult except for those who have spent years in training. You can have your company's logo fly into the foreground from the distance, for example, and it can tumble as it approaches. That's an easy effect that any first-timer can manage, assuming you have some way to get your company logo into the computer. But in contrast, if you wanted your 3-D logo to appear as if being drawn by hand, with smooth, sweeping motions revealing each character, *that* could be hard to do. Successful use of 3-D animation depends on understanding what you're capable of and what the software you've chosen can do.

One element that plays a huge role in 3-D animation is time: animation is created by rendering a series of still 3-D scenes, one after another, then recording them to tape or a disk file in a sequence that, when played back, creates the illusion of motion. The time factor boils down to this simple (but true) philosophy: there is no free lunch. With 3-D, the more realistic your scene looks, the longer it will take to render. A single frame from an ultra-realistic rendering, one that might include ray tracing, can take hours and, rarely, even days to complete on a PC. It takes 30 such still frames (by U.S. television standards) to create one second of recorded animation. In the typical case, ten seconds of animation takes several hours to record. If you stretch the limits and shoot for the best quality you can get, the same ten seconds could take an entire weekend or longer. Three-dimensional animation is one of those things you must plan carefully and use with discretion to maximize your presentation's impact.

Video

Videotape replaced film as the favored medium for sharing moving pictures with others, and it's little wonder: it's cheap, consumer-quality equipment is easy to use, and the results can be viewed instantly. In business, video's usefulness is taking a long time to be seen. Large companies invest vast amounts of money in promotional, educational and informational videos, money which is typically handed to professional video production houses. But advances in technology have made it possible for anyone with the right equipment and software to create their own videos.

The most recent advances provide us with a choice we previously didn't have: analog or digital. Analog video is, simply, videotape. Your home VCR is an analog video device, capturing moving images by writing an analog signal onto moving magnetic tape. The highest-end digital video (of the caliber used by television networks) is recorded on tape as well, but as a digital signal. For most of us, however, the term "digital" when applied to video means that a moving video signal is digitized, stored on a computer's hard disk (or other medium) and played back later.

Analog Video

Most people have what it takes to record their own video. Just as modern 35mm cameras make the process of taking pictures almost automatic, so many modern camcorders (combination video cameras/videotape recorders) do practically everything for you: they focus, set exposures, set audio recording levels, and some of them even remove the usual jitter of handheld recording electronically. It's as close to point-and-shoot as you can get.

As with still pictures, however, the best results are not those gained by letting the recording device do all the work. The specialized computers built into cameras and camcorders are complex and fascinating, to be sure, but they're still no match for the brain. A few extra touches, like an external microphone and a tripod, can add significantly to the quality of a recording. The basics of shooting good video are detailed later in this book.

There are very few times when the video you wish to present pops out of the camcorder ready to show. Even if you got everything right on the first try, chances are you'll want to add titles, graphics, and possibly special effects like animation. That's video production, and it's one of the most exciting aspects of multimedia. Video production is the process of turning raw material into a finished work, and we're fortunate to live in an age where computers can handle a lot of the work. There was a time when a video producer had to be an engineer, schooled in the nuts and bolts of video. With a computer at the helm, video production is simplified: in the best case, it's reduced to you telling the computer what you want your finished video to look like. You start by marking the start and end of each video clip. You then string the clips together, inserting graphics and titles as you go. Some systems let you lay out the entire plan for the video in advance, with the computer recording the finished piece in one swipe, completely unattended.

One of the joys of having a computer manage the process of video production (the involvement of a computer earns the process the title "desktop video production," even though the equipment needed to do it rarely fits on a desk) is that once the scenes on the source tapes are marked off and identified in the computer, you can rearrange them at will and re-use them in future productions. So-called desktop video tools also greatly reduce the total cost of producing your own videos. An in-house video production suite, capable of producing professional-quality videos for business use, could easily have run into the hundreds of thousands of dollars only five years ago. The same capability, and even more, can now be managed by setups costing a total of $30,000 to $50,000. That still seems like a lot of money, until you consider that video production houses can charge that much for one video. Of course, for that price, you also get their expertise, so you have to figure out where you draw the line. You may not be able to do all your video production in-house, but you can do enough of it to pay for itself if video has the potential to enhance your company's bottom line.

Digital Video

The end product of an analog video production session is a videotape. That's both a blessing and a curse. It's a blessing because a VHS tape can be played almost anywhere; most businesses have A/V carts in their conference rooms that at least contain a large TV and a consumer-quality VCR. The problem is that those wanting to view the video must go to the conference room to see it; that's inconvenient at best, and unless the viewing is part of an already-scheduled meeting, the inconvenience can limit your audience (those most inconvenienced by it simply won't show). It might be better if people could view the video at their desks, at their convenience.

Digital video technology, at least as covered in this book, refers to the ability to digitize moving video and audio from another source (usually a videotape) and store it digitally as a file. That file, which must reside on a hard disk, CD-ROM drive or other high-speed device, can later be decoded and turned back into a viewable video signal. That video is generally viewed in a window on the computer's main screen. In order to save space, the video's resolution is reduced and other steps are taken that result in a reduction of the size of the digital video file.

To put things in perspective, consider this: if you digitized a *single frame* of video at full size, aiming for the best possible digitizing quality, you'd wind up with a file nearly a megabyte in size. Since U.S. standard video requires 30 frames per second, that would be nearly 30 megabytes per second of digitized video; even a one-gigabyte hard drive could only hold some 35 seconds of video. That's clearly unacceptable, because even if you could afford the storage space for all that data, no desktop computer can move data to and from its disks that quickly. By reducing the storage space required for each frame of video, you not only give yourself more total recording time, but also cut down on the traffic between the disk and the computer.

Reducing the size of digitized video has become something of an art. The most obvious reduction is to cut the resolution of the video. By scaling the video down to a smaller window, say, half or quarter the size of the whole screen (or smaller), you can directly halve or quarter the size of each frame's digital image on disk. Further reductions can be achieved by reducing the frame's color depth. While the best results are achieved by digitizing to 24 bits per pixel (true color), you can often obtain acceptable results by capturing only 8 bits per pixel. The benefits of these two approaches are immediately evident: cutting the resolution to a quarter-screen reduces our sample frame's file size to 250K; trimming it to 8 bits per pixel cuts the size again to just 83K. That's more manageable, but at 83K per frame, each second of video still occupies a heady 2.5 megabytes. One final cut can be gained by trimming the frame rate, or the number of still frames needed to fill a second of video. As I mentioned, the U.S. television standard calls for 30 frames per second. Some systems cut that rate to anywhere from 15 all the way down to 7 or 8. The resulting video is choppy; smooth motion is impossible at reduced frame rates, so it's the least pleasant of the available size reduction methods, but it's commonly employed.

Reducing the file size further requires some real magic called *image compression*. Each frame of the video is analyzed and run through some advanced mathematical transformations that reduce the complexity of the image. Most image compression operates on the assumption that the image will be viewed from a reasonable distance, and from that distance, reductions in the quality of the image will be much less evident. Some compression schemes also depend on the distraction of moving video; if the images are always in motion, the impact of the detail lost to compression in each frame is less evident. In a constantly moving scene, the eye rarely has a chance to focus on any one area of the scene where the lost detail might be evident. With the application of modern image compression methods, the size of a frame of video can be reduced to as little as 5K, and now that ten seconds of video is almost small enough to fit on a high-density floppy. The above-mentioned gigabyte hard drive could hold almost two hours of compressed digital video.

Both PCs running Microsoft Windows and Macintoshes can be equipped to record and play digital video through direct extension of their operating software. Both enhancements let you use a video capture board (costing, at the time of this writing, as little as $300) to grab moving video from an external source. These digital video systems both perform compression on the digitized video after it's captured, letting you set the balance between video quality and file size. Playing the video back doesn't usually require any special hardware. So-called "software-only playback" decompresses and displays the video. Standard computer display hardware usually results in playback frame rates of 15 frames per second or less, regardless of the rate at which the video was captured or to which it was compressed. Special hardware can accelerate the video performance or the image compression/decompression, increasing the playback frame rate and possibly reducing the file size beyond the reach of software-only methods.

As with digital audio, digital video offers distinct advantages over analog systems when it comes to editing. However, some image compression methods can make digital video less efficient to manage than analog. Usually, images are compressed one frame at a time, with each frame becoming a distinct graphical image in a sequence with others. But some methods go one step further, trimming the file's total size even more by doing *delta compression*. As its name implies, delta compression analyzes not only the contents of each frame, but the differences from one frame to the next. Instead of storing the complete image data for every frame, delta compression stores only those portions of the frame that differ from the one before it. The impact, particularly on video shot against a stationary background, can be dramatic; delta compression, combined with other methods, yields the smallest digital video files possible. The trouble is, since each frame depends on the data contained in the frame before it (and the one before that, and so on), you can't instantly jump to any individual frame. In fact, there are only two ways to jump to a specific frame in a delta-compressed video file: you can play the video from the beginning to the frame you want, or you can request that certain frames be written without delta compression. These check frames, generally created at intervals you set at compression time, give you fixed frame locations to which you can jump without incurring the delay of decoding all the frames leading up to it. There's a catch to this, however: you can get very close to random access by placing the check frames close together, but doing so can remove some of the benefits of delta compression. Without them, seeking to a specific frame can actually take as much time as playing the video up to that point at regular playback speed. The trick is finding the correct balance between random access and effective compression.

Once you get your digital video set up for random or near-random access, you can edit video very efficiently by cutting and pasting. Digital video editing systems often use *picons*, or picture icons, to represent key elements of the edit. The picons are created when you mark the starting and ending frames of each video scene. You then put them together by dragging the picons onto a timeline. It can't get any easier than that, and it takes no understanding of video technology or even video editing to create digital video. That's both good and bad: tools that easy not only make it a breeze to create impressive work, but also make it effortless to create really horrible video.

If you already know what you're doing, or you are patient enough to invest the time to learn, digital video editing systems can open up whole new vistas of creativity. Transitional special effects, animated titles and graphics, all of the things that professionals using analog gear pay dearly to do can be done by these digital systems, in software. The trick is that digital data lends itself not only to being cut and pasted, but also to being modified. Software can create dazzling special effects simply by moving pixels around, and it can take its time about it: tools for post-production of analog video are expected to operate in real time, but digital video software is under no such pressure. Each frame can be loaded, modified with effects and other elements, and written to another file. The process can take as long as necessary. Because it's all done digitally, you can see reduced-quality previews of your video before you commit to a regeneration that might take hours. The concepts embodied in relatively low-end digital video systems can be scaled up to serve the needs of professional video producers. These systems, often referred to as *nonlinear editing systems* (because the digital video data can be accessed randomly, rather than linearly as with analog), use advanced hardware technology to accelerate capture, playback and compression. They often use their own directly connected hard drives, and the benefit of these more expensive systems is that they can create full-screen, full-color video; the best of them inject no perceptible loss of video quality. In fact, with the fancy video hardware and software built into these systems, it's possible to create an end product that's better looking than the pieces that went into it. The difference between low-end desktop video editing and full nonlinear professional systems is that with the latter, the final destination is almost always videotape, where desktop digital video editing typically ends with video in digital form.

Since even relatively short digital video files can take up several megabytes on disk, they are difficult to move from one system to another. Even though today's average desktop computer has sufficient power to play these video files, you can't count on it having enough disk space to hold the digital video you want to play on it (assuming you find a way to get the file there in the first place). That's where digital video starts to lose a little of its polish; the huge files it creates are cumbersome to move around. One solution is to mix digital and analog technologies: use analog technology to supply the video, but use digital technology to put it up on your computer's screen. A special class of VCR, the computer-controllable deck, has sprung up to support this kind of arrangement. Connected to the computer's serial port, a computer-controllable VCR can be commanded to seek to a certain position on the tape, play, rewind, stop, pause—anything you can do with a normal VCR, except that most of these computer-controllable models have the ability to do very precise seeks, sometimes seeking right down to a single frame. This has all the drawbacks of an analog system—access time and tape wear being among them—but it has one huge advantage over digital video: you can use as much video material as you need without worrying about disk space. It's more expensive than low-end digital video setups, but it can deliver full-screen video of very high quality at a full 30 frames per second (U.S.). The video can share the screen with your presentation or other applications through the services of a *video overlay* board, which puts the analog video in a window on your computer's monitor. You can have the video play in front of all the other data, or you can overlay the video with computer-generated images, creating composited titles and graphics. The Amiga doesn't use a video overlay board, but instead is set up to accommodate a very inexpensive device called a *genlock* that merges an external video signal with the Amiga's own display video. Because of this, the Amiga can be used to build systems that include external analog video for much less money than Macs or PCs, but you lose the ability to shrink the video down to fit in a small window on the screen; the Amiga's genlock can only reproduce video that fills the screen.

The access time problem of analog video isn't a problem at all for some applications. In a business presentation, for instance, it's easy to record your videotape with the segments in order so that the only delay is the time between the segments, which can be cut to a few seconds. A computer-controllable VCR does its seeking asynchronously, so it can be fast-forwarding to the next video segment while your presentation continues, and the segment can be cued up and ready to play one or two slides later. The access time issue, which is of particular concern when you need quick access to a randomly selected video segment (as with educational and other viewer-driven applications), can be solved by recording your video to a laserdisc. This isn't cheap (although, fortunately, you can record your own now without having to send your video to a service bureau), but you can encode your laserdisc so that you can rapidly seek to any location on the disc. Under computer control, a laserdisc seek can be as quick as a fraction of a second. Even though you can now record your own laserdiscs, recorders are expensive, and the blank media is quite costly (especially compared to videotape).

One technology that makes it far easier to use and distribute digital video is CD-ROM. This technology has existed for years as a cheap, efficient way to store lots of data—a single disc holds over 600MB, enough for several minutes of compressed digital video. As of this writing, recordable CD-ROM drives are just starting to approach affordability, and the blank media are expensive compared to videotape but very cost-effective compared to other methods of computer data storage. CD-ROMs can be mass-produced very cheaply, with per-disc costs as low as $2, and CD-ROM drives (readers) can now be had for less than the cost of a cheap color monitor. CD-ROMs have uses beyond digital video, to be sure, but without CD-ROM, digital video would have had a very difficult time catching on.

Putting It All Together

The wonderful thing about the *multi* in multimedia is that it offers you an endless variety of options for packaging your information. You can take a simple business presentation up a couple of steps by using computer graphics, or fly it straight to the moon with digitized audio and video in a window; how far you take what you learn here and elsewhere is entirely up to you. There aren't any rules, but there are some things to keep in mind when you combine media types.

All media types aren't equal; there are positive and negative aspects of each. The most effective combinations of media come from a careful balancing of the benefits of the combined media against the problems they bring with them. While I'm all for the fearless use of available technology, there are times when the total burden of a combination of media types outweighs their use. That burden manifests itself in many different ways.

The table that begins on page 67 describes the relative burden of each of the media types described in this chapter along the lines of CPU performance, disk storage and transfer rate, memory usage, graphics quality and performance, relative cost of software and hardware, and the expertise required to use the medium effectively. I'll set the stage for the table by describing each of the issues covered there in greater detail. The table, like the discussion that precedes it, isn't meant to be anything more than a very rough guide. You might find it useful when shopping for a system, or when planning some project that combines media types. In the latter case, the table can help you avoid potential bottlenecks; it's a bad idea to combine multiple media that share a "high" burden rating in a particular area.

Most of the burdens are related to the stress a media type places on the computer you're using to manage the medium. Most media exact some toll on a system, measurable in terms of CPU burden.

CPU Burden

CPU burden might be defined as the amount of time your computer actually spends "thinking" while it deals with some media type. Most modern personal computers are so fast that when you're running mundane programs like spreadsheets and word processors, the brain in your computer—the CPU—spends the majority of its time idle. Most programs are driven by your actions, so the CPU waits for you to type another character at the keyboard, move the mouse or otherwise kick the program you're running into some brief action. Between these events, the computer rarely does anything but wait for you. At least, that's the way it works under the old model.

Advanced operating systems (the foundation software that loads and runs your programs) make it possible for you to run *several* programs at once. That's called *multitasking*, and it's a powerful thing. Multitasking on the PC is managed by operating systems like Microsoft Windows and IBM's OS/2; the Amiga's standard operating system (AmigaDOS) is inherently multitasking; and the Macintosh can multitask through its MultiFinder in operating system versions 6 & 7.

With multitasking, a computer is no longer limited to running one program at a time. That might seem of small benefit, since you only have two hands and the ability to concentrate on one thing at a time. There are times, however, when you can make better use of your time by starting some task, then sending the computer off to finish it on its own. This isn't always an option since most things people do with computers require regular interaction; the computer needs to be "fed" more information prior to each step of the task you've asked it to complete. Many of the most time-consuming operations in multimedia, however, can be set up in advance and run unattended. Under a single-tasking system, like DOS on the PC, unattended operation is still an advantage because you can feed the program the information it needs, say, just before leaving for the night or the weekend, and have it run while you're someplace else. But on a multitasking system, with software that's programmed to work that way, you can set the computer up to perform some time-consuming task and then proceed to work on something else *on the same computer*. On the Amiga and Macintosh, many 3-D packages will do their computations in the so-called "background," allowing you to run other software at the same time in what's referred to as the "foreground" (that application which is currently ready to receive input from you is said to be in the foreground).

A multitasking system will help you when your computer has more CPU power than the task you're asking of it demands. The *apparent* CPU burden is diminished because you're not required to completely relinquish the use of your computer while your 3-D render or some other job runs to completion. There's a catch to that, however: whenever you run several things at once on the same computer, everything runs slower. A CPU doesn't get any faster under a multitasking system, it just slices up what it's got. One program running on a multitasking system gets almost all the CPU's attention. Run another program, and suddenly both programs get as little as 50% of the available power. Add a third program, and each gets as little as 33%, and so on. It's a little more complicated than that since most multitasking systems try to divide up the CPU's power to give the most to the programs that need the most, but the fact remains that no matter how you divide you computer's performance with a multitasking system, the numbers will never add up to more than 100%.

A multitasking system won't help you at all for the most CPU-intensive tasks. These are the jobs that will always take some significant amount of time to run, even when you dedicate 100% of the computer to them. 3-D animation is one such application; it needs all the performance it can get. Depending on its complexity, a ten-second animation can take hours or days to complete, and the difference between hours and days can be made by your choice of computer system. A media type with a moderate to high CPU burden is one that can cause you grief if you use it on a less than capable system. In some cases, a high-burden media type will make you wait so long for your results that it's barely worth it. If, for example, your ten-second animation took an entire week to render, tying up an expensive computer and your best video deck in the process, would it be worth it? Probably not, and when you come across a dilemma like this one, you have some choices to make. One choice is to opt for a faster computer. All three of the platforms used in this book cover an extraordinary range of performance. The least-expensive PC, Macintosh or Amiga can generally do the things its more expensive counterpart can do, but it will do them more slowly. I won't launch into a discussion here of what makes a fast computer fast. Some CPU chips are faster than others, and the speed at which the chip is run (its *clock speed*) also contributes to overall performance. But there are so many ancillary issues affecting performance that it would be useless to lay out a couple of paragraphs' worth of guidelines here.

Disk Burden

Disk burden is a problem in two parts. The first part is the relative amount of disk space a particular media type consumes. Stationary graphics, for example, respond well to data compression and can generally be squeezed into a manageably small space. Digitized video and extremely high-quality digitized audio, on the other hand, are very space-inefficient and can easily occupy megabytes of storage for a mere few seconds of material.

The other part of the disk burden issue relates to *data transfer rate*, or the speed at which data moves from the disk to the computer's memory (and vice versa). Generally speaking, a medium that exacts a heavy disk space burden also carries a similarly high transfer rate requirement.

While it's easy to shop for a computer with a large amount of hard disk space, it's considerably more challenging to find a system with a high transfer rate; that's not a figure most computer store sales staff can quote offhand, and the numbers might not mean much to you in any case. Most system manufacturers, however, build better overall performance—including faster disk transfer—into their more serious systems. A $1200 home PC will almost certainly have poorer performance in all areas compared to a $5000 business system. In my work, I find that systems sold as "fileservers" (the hub of a computer network) often provide the best available mix of CPU performance, ample disk storage and fast disk transfer rates. Most of these systems are also packaged in roomier cases that give you more connectors for expansion cards and more space for adding disk drives in the future. There are vendors who specialize in making relatively weak computers look tougher by putting them in powerful-looking tower cases, but most reputable system vendors price and package their systems appropriately.

Memory Requirements and Virtual Memory

Another element that figures into a medium's overall burden is the amount of system memory its reasonable use requires. Generally speaking, systems are sold with enough memory to run typical off-the-shelf business applications. Some media types, however, are managed by applications that exceed the memory requirements of the average business program.

Memory usage generally doesn't remain fixed. Programs tend to allocate memory to themselves as needed, and under a multitasking system, that memory is taken from a pool that's shared by all currently running applications. Just as with

CPU performance, whatever memory one application uses decreases the total amount available to other applications.

Some multitasking systems, like Microsoft Windows (and, optionally, the Macintosh's MultiFinder), employ a mechanism called *virtual memory* to expand the total apparent amount of memory available to applications. The amount of real memory in your system is determined by the number of memory chips you have installed, and no operating system can make that number any larger. Virtual memory makes some programs *think* you have more memory by setting aside a portion of your hard disk that masquerades as memory. That sounds like a big win—after all, a system withfour megabytes of memory can be expanded to an astronomical number (like 24 megabytes) simply by setting aside some of your hard disk. But while hard disk space is cheaper per megabyte than real memory, it is far slower. Besides, programs can't really run in virtual memory. It works by "swapping out" information from memory to temporary storage on disk. This sometimes works very effectively, particularly in those cases when you start up lots of programs but only actively use one or two. The programs you don't use will get swapped out to disk, freeing up real memory for the active programs that need it.

The trouble with virtual memory is that it's easy to misuse. If you run lots of programs at once, and some number of them are active at the same time, your computer will spend so much time moving data between memory and virtual memory on disk that the benefit of virtual memory is eliminated. When your system is swapping virtual memory around, it can slow down or stall some or all of your applications. Under normal conditions, those swapping pauses are so brief that they're unnoticeable. But when you're using virtual memory the wrong way, your system's performance can be cut to a fraction of what it should be by excessive swapping.

The point here is that no matter what you may have heard, virtual memory is no replacement for real memory. It's handy, but only works well when used properly, which starts with setting aside only a reasonable amount of virtual memory space. How much is reasonable is determined by the system, but a general rule is to allocate twice as much virtual memory space on disk as you have real memory. That provides swapping space for all the programs that can fit in your memory, plus enough slack to allow you to run a few transient programs that go over your memory size. Effective use of memory also means exiting applications that you're not actively using. Except for the tiny inconvenience of waiting a few seconds for your application to launch, you conserve nothing by leaving a program running that isn't seeing active use. If you exit that application, you'll free memory (real *and* virtual) and improve the performance of the other programs running under your multitasking system.

But even under a single-tasking system (or under a multitasking system that's only being used to run one program at a time), memory usage fluctuates. In some cases, the program lets you tune its memory usage to suit your needs. The trade-off is generally between either features or performance and memory usage. A 3-D graphics package, for example, might only be able to deal with scenes of limited complexity when run in four megabytes. A digital audio-editing program might run much more slowly in a diminished amount of memory. Generally speaking, the software vendor's memory recommendations make sense, but I've found it wise to disregard the "minimum" memory figure; shoot instead for the memory the vendor lists as "suggested" or "recommended." The latter usually refers to the amount of memory needed to make the application run with all its features intact, and with the performance the vendor intended. I can't recall a single time I've run a program in the minimum possible memory without some limitation.

Graphics Burden

Computer-generated graphics play a role, directly or indirectly, in most of the media types covered in this book. If the medium isn't graphics-related, then chances are the applications used to manage the medium runs in a graphical environment. Fact is, virtually every application discussed in this book runs in a graphical environment: Microsoft Windows, IBM OS/2, the Macintosh OS, and the Amiga Workbench and Intuition (the graphical components of AmigaDOS) are all graphical environments. They have in common that applications can be run by pointing and clicking with a mouse or other pointing device (like a graphics tablet or a touchscreen).

Beyond the graphical environment that you use to create your multimedia material, graphics also play a pivotal role in the presentation of some kinds of material. For those media types that have a moderate to heavy graphics burden, the choice of graphics hardware can have a distinct impact on the quality of your presentation.

Nowhere is the range of choices wider than on the PC. Microsoft Windows, the environment under which much of the PC software discussed in this book operates, will work with any display hardware that includes a Windows driver.

Sometimes this means having two display boards in your system, because the lowest-level software in your computer, that part of it that runs from the time you turn on the power to the time your operating system takes over, requires a graphics card compatible with a well-established PC graphics standard.

The most widespread PC graphics standard in use today is VGA. This was born at IBM and first used in its PS/2 desktop systems. Now virtually all of the graphics hardware that connects to PCs is either compatible with or attaches to a VGA card. Like the Mac and Amiga before it, the PC is now moving toward the inclusion of graphics capability on the motherboard, meaning that the electronics that once resided on a card in the system's expansion bus have migrated to the board that houses the CPU and other vital components. This is convenient, freeing up a slot for other uses, and most on-board VGA controllers can be disabled in favor of a replacement display card.

Replacing a PC's standard graphics adapter is generally motivated by performance, features or compatibility. The typical VGA adapter is no great performer at the high resolutions and/or color depths demanded by multimedia. Some on-board VGAs, and the new class of local bus VGA controllers, perform better because they have a more direct, high-speed connection to the system's CPU. But generally, these cards are "dumb," meaning that they have no special hardware to speed up graphics operations. Cards that do are called *graphics accelerators*, but before I discuss those, I should give the Mac and Amiga equal time.

The Macintosh, being tightly controlled by Apple, is the easiest of all three platforms to expand, and that's true of graphics cards as well. The standard graphics on expandable (what I'd call "serious") Mac systems have graduated to color, but except for the high-end machines, higher color depths and resolutions require the use of an add-in card. Fortunately, the standardization of cards and monitors imposed by Apple makes the move relatively painless. There aren't nearly as many choices here as for the PC, but the choices that do exist still offer a wide array of prices and capabilities. A standard Mac system (like the Mac IIci used for this book) can have its graphics expanded in a minute or two, without tools and often without any special drivers or other software.

The Amiga generally has fewer options available for it than either of the other two platforms. Fortunately, since the Amiga started its life as the most capable graphics system of its day, the options available for it now are generally very impressive. The Amiga's standard video has come a long way, too, and is (finally) equal to the standard set by the PC's super VGA and the Mac's standard color video: 640 × 480 pixels with 256 colors (8-bit color depth). The latest Amigas have a completely new graphics chipset that offers the widest range of resolutions and color depths ever seen on an Amiga, but as with the Mac and PC, for serious graphics, you'll almost certainly have to resort to an expansion card.

What constitutes "serious" graphics depends on your application. Obviously, digitized audio and voice mail don't place high demands on your system's graphics capabilities. Any kind of graphics, and especially 3-D and professional 2-D graphics, benefit significantly from improvement in two areas: color depth and performance.

A graphics card's color depth is determined in part by the amount of memory it has. The memory on a graphics card isn't used to run programs (although some high-end cards that have their own CPUs can run programs), but is used to store the bit patterns that are translated to colored dots on your display. As explained earlier, each pixel takes up memory as determined by the bit depth you're using, and there must be enough memory on your display card to store the bit pattern for every pixel on the screen. A PC VGA card with the old standard 256K of memory, for example, can create a display at the normal 640 × 480 resolution, but only with a bit depth of 4 (16 colors). Supporting 256 colors require 512K of memory, and 16 bits per pixel (65,535 colors) raises the memory requirement to one megabyte.

Those requirements map across platforms, and they are easy to compute—simply multiply the vertical times the horizontal resolution to determine the memory needed for an 8-bit-deep image. Multiply that number by two for 16-bit color, and double that again for 24- or 32-bit color. Note that having enough display memory for a particular resolution and bit depth doesn't mean it's supported; check the specifications for your display card.

It is one of the unfortunate side effects of more capable graphics systems that they perform more slowly than their simpler counterparts. The reason is tied to the increased need for memory at higher resolutions and bit depths: these images simply occupy more memory and therefore take more time to move around. There is a solution, however, and one that is coming to be more affordable: graphics accelerators.

A graphics accelerator is a display card that has a specialized CPU of its own, dedicated to creating and moving graphics with greater speed. Ordinarily, when a graphic is drawn or moved, it is the system's main CPU that must do the work. Graphics data must often be moved from the display card's on-board memory to the system's main memory, passing through the system's data bus and tying up your CPU. A graphics accelerator uses its built-in processing power to avoid passing information through the system's data bus. Because the graphics card can "think for itself," it relieves some portion of the burden on your system's CPU.

Graphics accelerator boards are most plentiful for PCs, but there is a fair assortment for the Macintosh as well. In both cases, it's possible to avail yourself of the benefit of accelerated graphics performance by paying only a slight premium beyond the cost of an ordinary display card. That benefit can be great, well more than enough to balance the drawbacks imposed by higher resolutions and color depths.

Overall Cost

The expense of implementing a media type is a very complex issue. There is the hidden cost of time to be considered, but for this discussion I will limit myself to the value of equipment and software.

Costs generally stratify into levels according to quality of results. The question that must be answered before you even begin charting your course is, "what's the minimum level of quality I can accept?" In nearly every case, the higher the quality you seek, the more you'll have to pay for it. Highly capable graphics cards are more expensive than less-capable ones, faster systems cost more than slower ones, and software created for professional use carries a price tag more dear than that which was built for the dabbler. There are times when frugality must rule the day, and for those times, here are some suggestions about where and where not to cut costs.

When buying computer systems, the one great bargaining chip (no pun intended) is the CPU speed. A slower main processor generally means lower manufacturing costs, so even a relatively small decrease in system performance can net a substantial reduction in purchase price. If the media types you plan to employ most frequently are marked in the table with low to moderate CPU burden, you can probably get away with a system that's a less than stellar performer. For PCs, that means settling for a fast 386 (33MHz or better) or a slower 486 (25 or 33MHz). In both cases, the difference in speed can save you hundreds of dollars. If you opt for a 386, you should equip the system with a math co-processor. The 486's math chip is built in, but it's optional for the 486SX. You can also save money on a PC by choosing a slower I/O bus; a system that uses the 16-bit-wide ISA bus can cost far less than one with the 32-bit EISA, but the latter may be justified for those media that carry a high disk burden.

Both Apple and Commodore offer plenty of choices for Macintosh and Amiga systems. Saving money in these cases means sacrificing some combination of performance and expandability. Here, systems built around the 68030 processor provide the minimum acceptable performance for most kinds of multimedia work, while the 68040 boosts the performance with an accompanying increase in price. The least expensive Mac and Amiga systems can't be expanded at all except externally. That's rarely acceptable unless you're certain that the kind of work you plan to do with the machine is not hardware-intensive and isn't likely to change over time. You don't want to get caught having to replace your system because you want to expand it. In the case of the Amiga, some clever third parties have created expansion cabinets that make non-expandable Amigas expandable. I can't vouch for the workability of this scheme, but it doesn't matter much; the 68030 appears mostly in Amigas with expansion slots.

A large part of the investment in any system is the monitor. Color is an essential component for most kinds of multimedia work, and that work is made easier by a good monitor. The PC and Mac both make monitor choices fairly straightforward, with standard connectors and *scanning frequencies*, or the speed at which the electrons zip across your screen painting pixels. Higher-resolution display cards require higher scanning frequencies, and the higher the resolution, the more you'll have to pay for the monitor. The best available monitors are able to synchronize to several scanning frequencies, making the match between card and monitor easier but exacting a high price. Some monitors "fake" support for high-resolution display cards by *interlacing*. Here, the screen's image is drawn in alternating passes: even rows of pixels, then odd, then even, and so on. Your home TV set works this way. It lets low-resolution monitors display high-resolution images, but it's not a perfect solution. Because it effectively cuts the scanning frequency in half, the picture is only updated half as often, sometimes showing an annoying flicker. Interlaced monitors, even ones that don't flicker, always suffer from jitter. When a thin line or a sharp-edged graphic is displayed with interlace, the line or edge will only be drawn every other pass. It appears and disappears several times a second, and it looks on screen like it's jumping up and down. Whether interlace works for you or not is a personal decision; for those not bothered by it, it can save a pile of money, but those who *are* bothered by it can suffer anything from minor annoyance to headaches and eye strain.

That brings me to an important point. However you buy your system, make sure you get to see the very monitor you plan to buy. Then you'll get to see the effects of interlace first hand, check the monitor's sharpness, see if you like the way the controls are laid out, and so on. Even if you buy the rest of your computer sight unseen, be sure you don't go that route with your monitor. Try to see the monitor running at the resolution you plan to use. One common mistake is to buy a smaller or larger monitor than you need. There is a relationship between resolution and screen size, and while it's partly a matter of personal preference, there are some common-sense ways to approach it. If you plan to use a high-resolution display card (1024 × 768 or greater), you should probably shop for a monitor with a diagonal screen size of 16 inches or greater. Not *too* much greater; bigger monitors take up a lot of desk space, pump out considerable heat and cost a lot more than their more compact cousins. I've found that a 16-inch monitor is sufficient for all but the highest resolutions for most applications. A 13- or 14-inch monitor will often serve nicely when you only plan to use your system at the standard 640 × 480 resolution. I will warn you, however, that monitors included with many systems, particularly those private-labeled by mail order and retail computer stores, are very poor. Many computer magazines perform regular roundups of monitors, and that's generally a good place to look for a bargain.

Larger monitors—those 19 inches and up—not only serve the highest resolutions, but also double as presentation monitors. Their drawback is that they are often unsuitable as desktop monitors, either taking up too much desk space or being too heavy to perch atop a system case. Their weight also makes them a challenge to move around, so consider placing your really big monitors on rolling carts if portability is an issue.

Other media-related costs have to do with equipping your system to handle media you want, plus the burdens that media places on your system. The basic task of equipping a system for multimedia these days amounts to adding a CD-ROM drive and possibly an audio board. The CD-ROM has become an essential component of multimedia, because the file sizes associated with digital media (particularly audio and video) are so great that there's no other way a vendor can get "clips" into your hands. A growing number of companies are shipping their software on CD-ROM, and some of them have moved to the *exclusive* use of that medium. It's cheaper for them than floppies, and far easier for you to deal with.

On the PC, equipping for multimedia can be as simple as purchasing a so-called *multimedia upgrade kit.* These kits, costing less than $1000 and available from a number of sources, include a CD-ROM drive and controller, a digital audio board (which records and plays audio at a variety of rates and resolutions), and an assortment of software. Some kits also include speakers or a microphone. A multimedia upgrade kit is often the cheapest way to get a PC ready for multimedia, but you can also buy the components separately. There are already so many PC sound boards that I've lost count, so you'll have little trouble finding one that meets your requirements for quality and cost-effectiveness.

A multimedia PC needs to be able to run Microsoft Windows or IBM OS/2. Versions of Windows after 3.1 have multimedia support built-in, and most upgrade kits include Windows 3.1 on CD-ROM. Both Windows and OS/2 expect a lot of memory and disk space (compared to DOS). While they claim to run on systems with 2–4 MB of memory, I recommend running them in 8MB. How much disk you need is determined by the kind of media you intend to use, but a 200MB drive is a good place to start.

Digital video on the PC calls for the addition of a video capture board that costs $300 and up, with more expensive boards including features like hardware-assisted compression and high frame rates. The boards often include Video for Windows, the software from Microsoft for capturing, playing and editing digital video, but you can also buy that separately.

Finally, 16- and 24-bit graphics cards can be had on the PC for well less than $1000. Boards with recordable output (composite or S-Video) cost a little more, and the best graphics boards from companies like Truevision can run into the thousands of dollars. There are bargains to be had, but it pays to stick with name brands. While Windows insulates you from some worries about hardware compatibility, you'll probably wind up running *something* under DOS. DOS software generally supports only a small number of very popular graphics cards.

The most expensive thing to equip a PC to do, by far, is video production. A 24-bit graphics card with video input and output and a VCR controller (internal or external) are the minimum requirements, but then you have to add the video decks themselves, monitors, some way of dealing with audio...it adds up. I'm not trying to discourage you, and you'll find the chapter on video production makes a compelling case for doing this yourself. But I want to make sure you don't get sucked in by video's benefits before you've considered the costs. True, it's cheaper than ever thanks to advances in technology, but look before you leap.

The Macintosh has its own audio, and generally, the newer the Mac, the better the built-in audio. Quadras, for example, include playback *and* recording circuitry. For other Macs, you have two choices: a relatively inexpensive, low-quality digitizer costing about $300, or a high-quality internal audio card for $1200 or more. Apple is addressing the limitations of its standard audio (22 KHz at 8 bits) in its newer systems, and with the cost of adding serious audio to a Mac, you'd do well to shop for a system that has its own high-quality audio circuit.

CD-ROM is an external device for most Macs, made easy to attach thanks to the standard SCSI interface. A drive will run you $500–$1000, the price inflated (compared to PCs) because you can't install the drive internally (the extra cost is for the external case and power supply). If CD-ROM is a helpful accessory for the PC, it is absolutely *essential* for the Mac. Don't bother trying to do Mac multimedia without one.

Mac digital video is well established, thanks to the early lead of Apple's QuickTime operating system extensions. Video capture boards are plentiful and cheap (some less than $500), and every Mac running System 7 can display QuickTime movies without special hardware. As with the PC, there are special boards that incorporate hardware compression that cost as much as $5000. At the time of this writing (only a couple of weeks after Microsoft announced digital video enhancements for Windows), the Mac is the best choice of the three systems discussed here for digital video. Because QuickTime was first, there are more digital video products (hardware and software) addressing a wider spectrum of capabilities than on any other platform.

It's easy to manage 16- and 24-bit graphics on the Mac. Some high-end systems have enhanced graphics built-in, and the others can be expanded to 24-bit graphics for well under $1000. Apple has its own graphics cards, but other companies offer extras like graphics acceleration and video input and output.

Because so much excitement was generated by QuickTime, it's easy to forget that the Mac is also a popular system for analog video production. While it still isn't cheap to equip a Mac for video, it is a little less expensive to built a minimal system around a Mac than a PC. Once you shoot for pro-quality results, however, the costs balloon until you've spent as much as with a PC, if not more. That may change, however, since the kind of self-contained video production system hardware that is available now for the PC (see the discussion of Matrox Studio in the chapter on video) is also being developed for the Mac and may be on the streets as you read this.

When it comes to multimedia, no system got more of a head start than the Amiga. The very first machine was equipped with 4,096-color graphics, four-channel digital audio, and hardware-accelerated animation capabilities that apply just as well to digital video. Now the Amiga has positioned itself as a recognized leader in multimedia systems, and with good reason: the Amiga is the most cost-effective platform for building a multimedia system around. The reason for this is mostly Commodore's good hardware and operating software design, but also the almost fanatical devotion of a number of small vendors who dedicate themselves to providing leading-edge solutions for the Amiga market.

Digital audio is a standard part of the Amiga, but no Amiga includes recording capability. But because the system is equipped with a fast, bi-directional parallel port, a low-quality external audio digitizer costs as little as $40; a $100 digitizer in the same package can sample at up to 56KHz. Want more? How about eight independent tracks of CD-quality digital audio for $1200? Commodore used to use the phrase "only on the Amiga," and there are so many good things happening there that it's easy to be impressed.

Most expandable Amigas include built-in SCSI, so internal or external CD-ROM is fairly easy to add. Drives cost between $500 and $700. One great benefit available to CD-ROM–equipped Amiga users is access to the mountains of public-domain software for which the Amiga is famous. The Fred Fish collection alone, spanning two CD-ROM discs, is worth the price of the drive, but there are also an increasing number of applications shipping on CD-ROM. That includes programs built for Commodore's CD-ROM–based stand-alone multimedia player, CDTV.

Digital video has existed longer on the Amiga than anywhere else, but capturing it can be something of a challenge since Commodore (unlike Microsoft and Apple) hasn't stepped in to define digital video standards. There are plenty of video digitizers, ranging from $140 to around $800. Many of the less-expensive digitizers can take a second or more to grab a single frame of video, so unlike Mac and PC digital video capture boards, Amiga video capture rarely takes place in real-time. The captured frames can then be assembled into ANIM animation files by software. Once those files have been assembled, the Amiga's on-board graphics accelerator can display digital video at a higher resolution and frame rate than standard PC and Mac systems.

High-quality graphics cards for the Amiga cost between $500 and $4000, and because the Amiga has traditionally been used for video work, many of these boards include video input and output. One unique product, the Video Toaster, combines video enhancement (24-bit video capture and display) with broadcast-quality video production capabilities for around $2500; you can learn lots more about the Toaster in the coming chapters on video production and 3-D animation.

Thanks to the Video Toaster and products that have sprung up to support it, there is no system that handles analog video production better than the Amiga. But even without a Toaster, the Amiga's unique expandability (the ability to support video overlay for less than $300, for instance) mates it remarkably well to multimedia setups that include analog video. That includes not only video production, but also other applications like interactive multimedia.

Expertise

The one necessity that's most difficult to quantify and predict is knowledge. Every media type requires that you know *something* to put it to use, even if that knowledge extends simply to understanding how to connect the output from a CD player to the input of a digital audio board. Much of what has traditionally been difficult to understand is now easier than ever thanks to better documentation and a new emphasis on ease of use in software. Technology has made many things easier as well by consolidating capabilities into small, easily managed devices. Digital audio systems once filled rooms; now they fit on a single user-installable circuit board. Computer-controllable video decks were once bulky, slow and cumbersome to interface and operate; now they are no larger than ordinary VCRs and run on commands anyone can understand.

Competence in multimedia production, for the most part, isn't something you can be taught. Like most artistic expression, it must be learned through experience. I'd be a fool to discount the value of the kind of guidance this book offers, but it's only guidance. Even those media types that are listed in the table as requiring a high level of expertise can be managed by most people. It just takes time and patience. The coming chapters of this book, and the accompanying video, can bring you a few steps closer to a worthwhile level of expertise more quickly than just diving in cold. But the rest is inevitably up to you.

One problem I faced when I undertook to learn what I've poured into this book is the considerable number of people who tried to convince me I couldn't learn it on my own, and that even if I learned, the results I produced with that knowledge would be unacceptably poor. I *still* hear that, even though I've written dozens of articles and produced many multimedia works. The wisdom of the naysayers holds that only professionals, those who make their sole living creating multimedia works, can create professional-quality work. In their defense, what they say has a point: most multimedia professionals have educations and backgrounds that give them a technical and creative headstart. You or I, starting from scratch, might never achieve the kind of dressed-up, uncompromisingly good work the most-talented professionals take for granted. While I don't want to take bread out of the mouths of those who depend on multimedia for their livings, I can't agree with the premise that "civilians" are incapable of producing good results. Will we always manage polished works of art, worthy of Madison Avenue? Hardly. Does every person have the ability to grasp and make reasonable use of media and the tools that manage them? Certainly not; I know of some individuals who, for no lack of brainpower or creativity, find it impossible to create a worthwhile multimedia production. That shouldn't stop you from trying, but neither should you be too hard on yourself if your efforts don't pay off as you'd like.

About the Table

The table that closes this chapter is a glancing summary of one of the key issues raised in the preceding pages: the relative burdens each media type places on your computer system and on you. The representations of the level of burden are intentionally vague because many of the media types cover a range of quality. Audio digitized at a sampling rate of 8KHz, sufficient for voice, has a low disk and CPU burden. Audio digitized at 44.1KHz in stereo, so-called "CD quality," carries a high level of burden. Rather than launch into a lot of explanatory detail here or in the table, I've chosen instead to represent what I consider to be the average burden, based on common usage and what I consider to be minimally acceptable results. I still hold that the minimum acceptable quality is the low range of professional quality: 256-color graphics rather than 16 or 16.7 million, 22 KHz audio instead of 11 or 44.1, and so on.

The table's purpose is mostly to set the stage for your multimedia education, but also to set your expectations. All of these media types can be combined in any way you choose; truly, anything is possible. What's *practical* is something else: you must consider what you can afford, what you have time to learn, the kind of results you seek, and so on. The table can help you get a loose handle on those combinations of media that make sense for you.

Table 1: Burdens of Media Types

	Media	CPU Burden	Disk Burden	Memory Burden
Audio	Passed-through	None	None	None
	Digitized	Low–Moderate	Moderate–High	Moderate
	Voice Mail	Low	Moderate	Low
	MIDI	Low	Very Low	Low
Graphics	Stationary	Low	Low–Moderate	Low–Moderate
	2-D Animation (create)	Moderate	Moderate	Moderate
	2-D Animation (play)	Moderate–High	Moderate	Moderate–High
	3-D Graphics	High	Moderate	High
	3-D Animation (create)	High	Very High	Very High
	3-D Animation (play)	Moderate–High	Moderate	Moderate

Table 1: Burdens of Media Types

	Media	CPU Burden	Disk Burden	Memory Burden
Video	Analog	None	None	None
	Digital (create)	High	High–Very High	Moderate–High
	Digital (play)	Moderate–High	High	Moderate

Table 2: Burdens of Media Types (continued)

	Media	Graphics Burden	Cost Burden	Expertise Burden
Audio	Passed-through	None	Low	Low
	Digitized	None	Low–Moderate	Low
	Voice Mail	None	Moderate	Low–Moderate
	MIDI	None or Moderate	Low	Moderate

Table 2: Burdens of Media Types (continued)

	Media	Graphics Burden	Cost Burden	Expertise Burden
Graphics	Stationary	Moderate-High	Low–Moderate	Low–Moderate
	2-D Animation (create)	Moderate–High	Moderate	Low-–Moderate
	2-D Animation (play)	Moderate–High	Low	Low
	3-D Graphics	High	High	Moderate–High
	3-D Animation (create)	High	Very High	High–Very High
	3-D Animation (play)	Moderate–High	Low	Low
Video	Analog	None–Low	Moderate	Low–Moderate
	Digital (create)	Moderate–High	Moderate	Low–Moderate
	Digital (play)	Moderate–High	Low	Low

3

Presentation Graphics

The first step toward using multimedia is to turn your data—text, statistics, specifications, what-have-you—into graphics. This chapter shows you how to bind these graphics together into a sequenced presentation, with all the aesthetic benefits various applications have to offer.

No multimedia work enters life "fully hatched"— they all start in some more primitive form, then evolve through your effort into a presentation. The most basic form of multimedia work is the business presentation, a phrase I use broadly with the understanding that the same techniques can be used to present stories to preschoolers or a patient's history to a group of specialists. The "business" in business presentation speaks more, for me, of the importance of the work. Generally, presentation graphics are not employed unless you're looking to impress your audience. If you want them impressed, and you're willing to take the time to create impressive materials, then presumably there's something worthwhile at stake.

This chapter, then, deals with that most basic transformation of raw information, even *ideas*, into presentation graphics. The evolution doesn't require you to be a graphics artist or even to know one. We're fortunate that this portion of the market has existed long enough to offer a wide variety of tools. Those tools have built into them the skill of artists, so at least as far as your artistic skill is concerned, what you don't know won't hurt you. Because this is a multimedia book, my objective is to get you interested in applying *multiple* media types to the presentation of information. Most of the tools discussed in this chapter can manage other kinds of media than graphics. We'll focus primarily on graphics, though, because it is fundamental to most of multimedia work. Whatever form your effort takes, it's likely that the kind of basics discussed in this chapter will be a part of your work.

What's a Graphic?

In considering how to use graphics to illustrate your own ideas, it helps to put the usefulness of graphics in perspective. There are some obvious examples, like television and print advertising, but there are examples even more basic than that. In life, nearly every form of visual communication we employ has graphical elements to it. The sign language of the deaf is graphical and beautifully expressive, painting pictures with colors that exist only in the viewer's mind. A book, even one without pictures, is a graphical work. Artists slaved over the shape of each font's characters, ensuring a balance between aesthetics and purpose. Combinations of letters on a page aren't merely words expressing an artful idea; their sweeping forms and interposed shapes *are* art.

If sign language and text are, as I suggest, graphics, then they exist mostly as practical, efficient expression. There is another kind of graphic that places aesthetics over substance or that uses creative expression to deliver a subtle message. Consider the logos of some large corporations. Most of them were designed by artists who were given long lists of abstract notions the companies wished the logos to express. Looking at AT&T's logo, for example, you might imagine that the company asked the designer to embody the company's global scope and its technological leadership into a graphic. The logos of 3M, IBM and General Motors show the companies' initials in large, bold letters, denoting strength and stability. Still other logos signify nothing except that they are readily recognizable: Panasonic and Microsoft both use simple type for their logos with no graphical treatment at all; Microsoft even uses different logo typefaces on its packaging and its literature because all that's important is that it be identifiable in some form. Each company had something a little different in mind when it designed its logo, but there's one thing they all want: recognition. In Chapter 1, I suggested that words are inefficient forms of communication because they have to be translated by the brain into pictures or thoughts before they can be processed. The exception to that, however, is the company logo. A graphic, even one built from text, can take on a meaning of its own. It can occupy its own unique space in your brain's filing system without requiring the normal conversion overhead of text. The reason is that logos are *designed* to cross that barrier quickly. Seen enough times, the text takes on a meaning of its own. You can see the IBM logo, or oddly, even the letters "IBM" on a page and have an immediate flash of recognition without having to parse the letters out to "International Business Machines." Some company advertising campaigns are built around increasing logo recognition: IBM was famous for taking out full-page ads in newspapers and magazines with nothing but the company's logo in the middle, swimming on an otherwise naked white page. As an exercise, imagine the messages that simple treatment could convey. When I was younger, I saw it as blatant arrogance. Now I realize its brilliance.

There is a point to all this (sorry if you just lost that bet): sign language, printed text and company logos each represent different kinds of effective use of graphics. Each reaches us at a different level, each follows a different path through the mind toward comprehension, but all three share a common element: simplicity. The sign for "love" is universally recognizable; even someone seeing it for the first time knows what it means. Someone could have constructed a complex sign that depicts the elements of love one after another—compassion, commitment, and so on—but the simple gesture of the hands over the heart says more than a flurry of charade signals could ever manage. Printed text, with its swirls and points and interlocking shapes is, at one level, a beautiful thing, but that beauty handily steps out of the way when there's work to be done. The aesthetics contained in a well-designed printed page please the eye quietly but don't interfere with the message. And the company logo, custom-built for swift delivery of any number of concepts, exerts a sort of subtle hypnosis on its viewer who gets caught up in the elegant shapes while the viewer's brain absorbs the message behind the picture. Without an underlying simplicity, the message is clouded. Text printed in too fancy a font slows the reader. A too-ambitious logo delivers no message at all, or worse, delivers a negative one.

My concern is that people sitting down to a presentation graphics package for the first time might feel compelled to stretch their artistic muscles. Granted, there are those who create art every time they toss shapes at a page, but most of us must rely on simplicity and a software package's innate style sense to keep us from going too far one way or the other. At one extreme lies banality: there is no prescription drug that induces sleep more effectively than a visually bland presentation. At the other extreme lie the hazards of "too much" and "too many": too much clutter, too many fonts, too many different colors, too many styles in a single presentation... There is just as much reason to fear one extreme as the other, for in both cases, the result is that the audience misses some or all of the message you came to deliver. That's a catastrophe, because presentations generally give you only one shot at making your point. And worse, even if only *part* of your presentation is bad, it casts a shadow over the rest of your work. So while the tools that exist make presentation graphics much easier to create than before, these tools carry with them the burden to use them wisely. Even the simplest of graphics packages dare not prevent you from shooting your own foot; it's up to you to keep yourself out of trouble.

Choose Your Tools

It's impossible for me to cover every tool and potential use of graphics in presentations. Recognizing this, I've selected a broad class of graphics programs to use as examples for this chapter. Programs discussed here are made specifically for the creation of graphics for presentations. I almost typed "*business* presentations" automatically, since that's the supposed target of many of the commercial applications I'm about to discuss. But the services these programs render are applicable to all kinds of presenters, all kinds of material, and all kinds of audiences. I've been in the audience of scientific and educational presentations built with tools like these, as well as the more typical sales, marketing, and business reporting gigs.

There are roughly three classes of presentation programs available for the systems I used to write this book. The lowest rung is occupied by programs that provide only the most basic features. Building the individual graphics screens, anachronistically referred to as "slides," is usually done through an interface similar to a paint package. What makes these packages (Curtain Call from Brown-Wagh, a Windows program, is one) suited for presentations is that they have some ability to sequence the slides you build with them (or elsewhere). But because the basic interface is that of a paint package, modifications can be hard to make since each drawn object is indelibly stamped onto the program's virtual canvas. Once it lands there, you can't reasonably change individual elements of your slide. The advantage of these low-end packages is that they are generally very inexpensive and quite easy to use. The disadvantage is the difficulty of modification and a lack of integration.

The next level up combines a 2-D illustration package with some presentation sequencing capability. This is a crowded domain, with titles like Macromedia Action! (Windows and Mac), Corel Draw (Windows), and Oxxi Presentation Master (Amiga). Software in this class generally has a capable 2-D illustration component (especially in the case of Corel Draw). The relative suitability of these packages can be measured by the combination of their ease of use and features set. Corel Draw, for example, is very powerful, but has a stiff learning curve if you only plan to use it for presentations. Macromedia Action! brings presentations together quickly but has a more primitive set of drawing tools. Action!'s sequencer is specifically geared toward simple animation. One of the best examples I've seen of software in this class is Oxxi Presentation Master for the Amiga. It combines an incredibly powerful 2-D illustration program, including some advanced features like text warping, with a solid sequencer. In fact, Presentation Master does so much that it crosses over into the top category, only lacking some of the self-contained qualities needed for full membership. I'll include it in my discussions, however, because it is an impressive piece of work.

What sets the most capable presentation programs apart from those below them is their integration. These do-it-all packages, including giants like Aldus Persuasion and Microsoft PowerPoint (Mac, Windows), and some less well-known but outstanding programs like Symantec More (Mac), try to give you everything you need to build winning presentations. Outlining, 2-D illustration, business charts, large template and clip art libraries, word processing, slide sequencing, limited interactivity, media integration and a host of other features are typical of these programs that do their best to fix it so you don't need to depend on external programs for anything. These are the packages I tend to use the most for my own presentation work, precisely because I prefer a high degree of integration as long as that integration doesn't adversely impact the worth of any of the individual elements. In the cases of Persuasion, PowerPoint, and More, I rarely find myself reaching for another piece of software to get something done. If I do want to produce portions of my work somewhere else, software in this class generally has a healthy selection of import filters. Word processor documents, bitmapped and vector graphics, and sometimes even spreadsheets can be made part of your presentation. Oxxi's Presentation Master even includes software to read MS-DOS format disks on your Amiga so you can import material from PC systems. The value of a strong import capability is that you can re-use material you produced for some other purpose, and you can also stick with those tools for which you have developed a preference. But the greater value by far is the work these most powerful presentation tools save you. If you're in a hurry, you can pour your text into templates and let the program guide you toward a finished presentation in just a few minutes. With PowerPoint and More, all you have to know how to do is type. As you learn more about the software, you can depart from the program's defaults and be as creative as you like. Even though these programs make it easy for first-timers to create presentations, they don't get in the way of more experienced users who want no limits on their expression. Aldus Persuasion is loaded with features aimed at more experienced users; graphics artists would feel right at home. But even an artist has to start somewhere, so let's get busy.

A Good Start

The best presentations are those that are built methodically, with the concentration on the message first and the visuals later. Since most works present ideas sequentially, a most effective start for your plan is that organizational device you learned in school: the outline. Back then, outlines were horrid things. Changes were unpleasant because one inserted or moved item could send you through a whole bottle of correction fluid. That was then. Now software turns what was an ordeal into a breeze. Outlining tools not only make changes easier, but they make the entire process of organizing your thoughts flow much more smoothly from the start.

Everyone who has ever done an outline probably has some strong feelings about the best way to do them. I don't, because I always hated doing outlines as a kid, and frankly, computers don't make outlines fun, they just make them easier to create and change. So my method, which is arguably not the best, doesn't kick in every cool feature an outliner has to offer. Perhaps it's my short attention span showing, but I prefer to get all my thoughts down rather than get caught up in advanced outline theory and practice.

How you do your outline and how that outline gets turned into a presentation depend largely on your choice of tools. Of course, you can't have a computer-managed outline without the software that creates it. Fortunately for those of us who do a lot of presentations, good outlining tools are built into many popular presentation packages. The PC and Mac have the best selection of all-in-one tools, including two that frequently top the charts: Microsoft PowerPoint and Aldus Persuasion. Both packages run on PCs (running Windows) and Macs, and both include outliners. They are so similar in basic functionality that I'll focus on PowerPoint for expediency; the screen shots were taken from the Windows version.

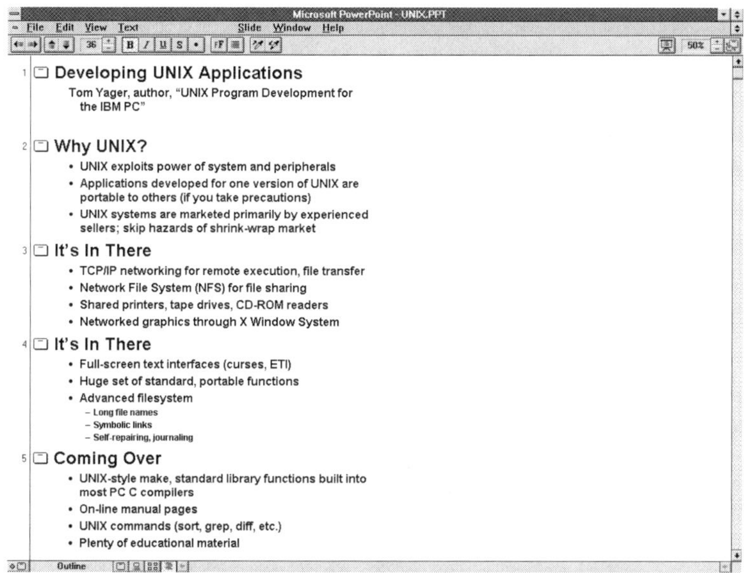

Figure 3-1: PowerPoint's outline view

PowerPoint's interface is typical of modern presentation graphics packages in this class. There are a couple of ways you can proceed. By default, PowerPoint drops you right into your first blank slide. From there, you're expected to draw your presentation exactly as it will be seen. I think that's a bad place to start, since you're inclined to worry about style rather than content. PowerPoint's outliner is a mouse-click away, and it's there that you can best address your presentation's organization.

PowerPoint's outliner, shown in Figure 3-1, isn't traditional in that it doesn't number items the way you might in a handwritten outline. The reason is simple: the outline you create in PowerPoint *becomes* your presentation. While numbers make perfect sense in an outline view, you can't reasonably carve up a numbered outline into a presentation; removed from their context, the numbers are useless. Each major heading becomes the title of a slide (you can see a little slide icon, along with the slide number, next to each title in Figurc 3-1). Lesser items appear on the slide under the title, prefixed with bullets. Still lesser items are indented further and prefixed with a symbol unique to that level. The appearance of the outline in PowerPoint is governed by a *master page*, a mockup of an outline that defines indentation width, prefix symbols, and other elements. The master page sets the style for the entire outline. If you decide you want to change your outline's basic appearance—to use a different character for the bullet, perhaps—the outline master page lets you make the change in one place and apply it to the entire outline.

Lacking numeric identification, a PowerPoint outline signifies levels by indentation: the wider the distance from the left margin to the first character, the deeper the level. You can "demote" a particular item in your outline to a deeper level by clicking on it and then clicking the button (near the top of the window) showing the right-pointing arrow. That might turn what is now a slide title, for example, into a bullet item under the title preceding it. Similarly, you can "promote" an item to a higher level (back one indent) by clicking the left-pointing arrow. Promote it enough times, and you'll have dedicated an entire slide to what used to be a lowly bullet item.

You're not limited to promoting and demoting a single portion of your outline. PowerPoint lets you drag-select (click the mouse button in the upper left and drag it to the lower right of the region you wish to select) as much of your outline as you like, and promote or demote it with the arrow buttons. With a little imagination, there are few limits to the shape of your outline (or presentation) when you take advantage of PowerPoint's features. Selection is a key element in the management of presentation data. When it comes time to change fonts and other visual attributes, you'll select the data you want to change and then tell the program how you want to change it. You should study the documentation for the software you've chosen to determine how to select data within it. In the case of the three platforms covered in this book, their standard software defines methods for selection that are common across applications on that type of system: text selection, along with other common operations, is handled the same way in almost all Windows programs as it is in PowerPoint.

Using the Clipboard

All the systems in this book support the notion of the *clipboard*, a metaphor for a storage space that holds some indeterminate piece of data. If you're like me, your thoughts don't always flow the way you want them to on the first try. The clipboard

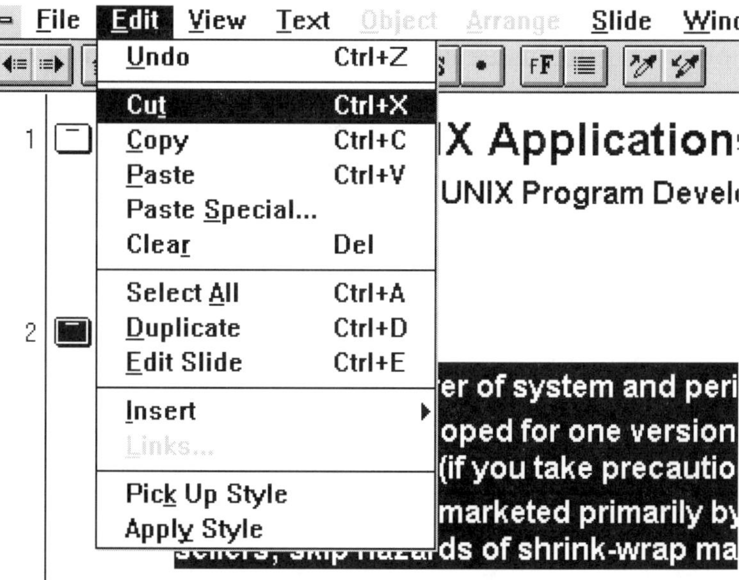

Figure 3-2: PowerPoint's Edit menu

lets you get your thoughts down in one place and move them easily to another. Most software that supports the clipboard for text (as with PowerPoint's outliner) also supports it for graphics and other types of data as well. Generally, if you can select it, you can put it on the clipboard. If you've used a word processor, then you may already be familiar with the clipboard model. Generally, you'll see an "Edit" menu (see Figure 3-2) on your application's menu bar when a clipboard is available. "Edit/Copy" (meaning the "Copy" option under the "Edit" menu) makes no changes to the project you're working on, but makes a duplicate of the selected text (or graphics, or whatever you've selected) on the clipboard. "Edit/Cut" deletes the selected item, be it text, graphics or whatever, and moves it to the clipboard. If you'd then like to copy the contents of the clipboard to some other location in your document (in this case, your presentation), then you need only select the "Edit/Paste" option. This will place one copy of the clipboard's contents at the current text insertion point, which is generally wherever the blinking cursor appears. Additional selections of "Edit/Paste" will place one more copy of the clipboard's contents at the cursor's position, and it will continue to do so until you replace the clipboard with another cut or copy operation.

The clipboard can only hold one item at a time. Each time you cut or copy something to it, the clipboard is cleared, and the item you just copied or cut is moved to it. That might seem limiting at first glance, but it avoids confusion. You'll get the hang of the idea that clipboard operations (cut or copy, then paste) must be done in pairs. Whatever can be moved in one operation can be moved directly through the clipboard. If you must split the operation up, you can use some portion of your document as a temporary staging area, pasting data there until it's all together, and then doing one huge cut and paste to move it to its final destination. Once you consider that no move you make is necessarily permanent, you realize you have all kinds of freedom to move data around in your outline. Whatever you change between saves to disk is effectively temporary; you can always revert back to your last saved version of the outline. You also have an option, under "Edit/Undo," that lets you undo the last change you made. What constitutes a single change varies from one package to another, but generally, whatever it makes sense to group into a single change is so grouped. Any number of characters added to an outline, for instance, without a mouse click or other separating action, is probably considered a single change. If you select a block of text and delete them with the "Del" key, that's one operation that can be undone with "Undo." Similarly, that which is undone by "Undo" can be un-undone: a change you make that you undo can be restored by selecting "Undo" a second time (some software changes the "Undo" menu item to "Redo" to reflect the change in behavior). Learning to make effective use of the clipboard is vital to getting the most from at least the Mac and Windows environments and many Amiga applications as well.

The clipboard can also create a link between applications. What you cut or copy from one program can be pasted into another. If, for example, you had a Lotus 1-2-3 spreadsheet displayed, and you selected and copied a range from that spreadsheet to the clipboard, you could then paste that selected region into a document managed by another program. If the receiving program is equipped to handle that specific kind of data, the format of the original data will be preserved. The degree to which data is interchangeable through the clipboard depends on the applications you choose.

Using Multiple Views

PowerPoint, like most other presentation software, offers you multiple views into your presentation. Each view gives you a particular advantage not offered by the others, a chance to speed your access to some part of the process of building a presentation. No matter which views you use in building your presentation, the other views are always available to you. Changes made to the content in one view immediately affect all the other views; the views are simply different vantage points on a single set of data. You can, for example, build your slides directly in the slide view, typing directly into the program's template and seeing your slides take shape exactly as they will be displayed. But you can always switch to the outline view to see the entire presentation in that format.

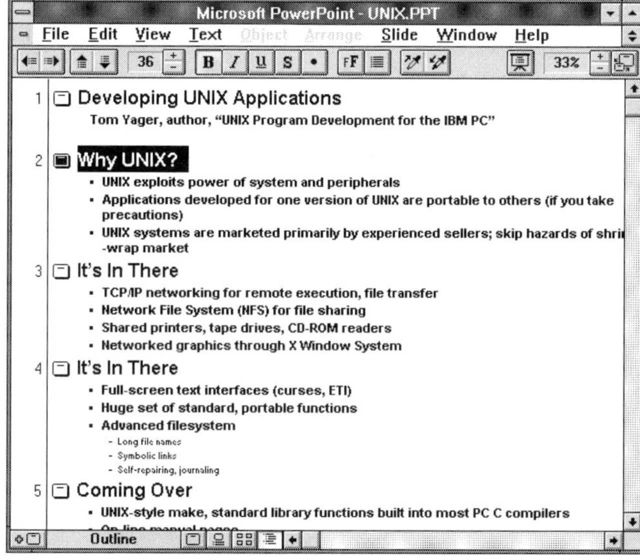

Figure 3-3a: The outline view

The *outline view* (Figure 3-3a) gives you quick access to your entire presentation. I recommended earlier that you build your presentation through this interface, but no matter how you build it, this is an efficient way to modify it. Only here can you see how your presentation flows as a sequence of ideas without the visual separation of slides. PowerPoint lets you move data around through the clipboard and by direct dragging and dropping: you can select the little slide icon next to each slide's title and drag that slide's contents anywhere in the outline. You can reorder body items in a slide by selecting an item's bullet and dragging it to a new location, even onto another slide. This interface is quick and intuitive. When you change the order of your outline, your spoken text must change, too, and the presentation program won't take care of that. Finally, a printout of your outline can serve as a concise guide to your presentation, particularly helpful if someone else is operating the equipment at your presentation site.

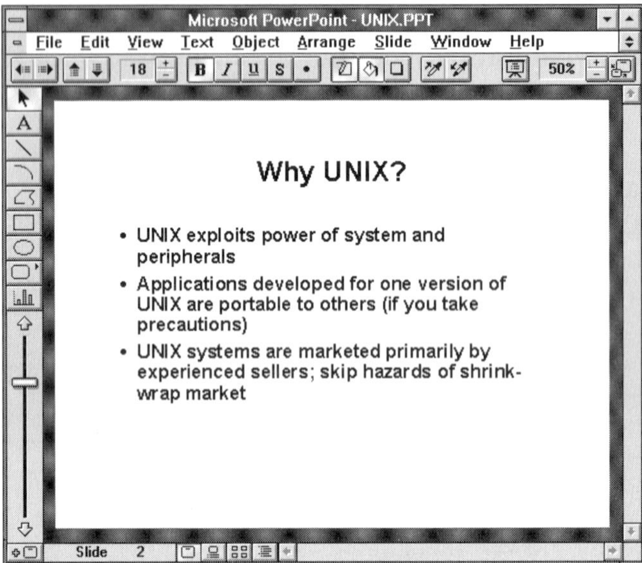

Figure 3-3b: The slide view

The *slide view* (Figure 3-3b) is the eye of the audience. It's here that you'll see what your slide will look like when it's displayed. The default for most presentation software is to make the slide look like a simple black-and-white overhead transparency. That's fine for now; you can change the look of your presentation without messing with the content. The slide view is useful prior to formatting because it gives you a quick look at how effectively you've managed to organize your ideas. You can step through the slides in this view in sequence, just as you will when you give your presentation. You can rehearse the fit of your spoken text to the slide here, too, with the added advantage that you can change the slide's content on the spot when you find a problem.

The slide view is generally only useful for changes limited to that slide; the outline and slide sorter views are much more appropriate for making more global changes.

The *slide sorter view* (Figure 3-3c) lets you see several of your slides at once.

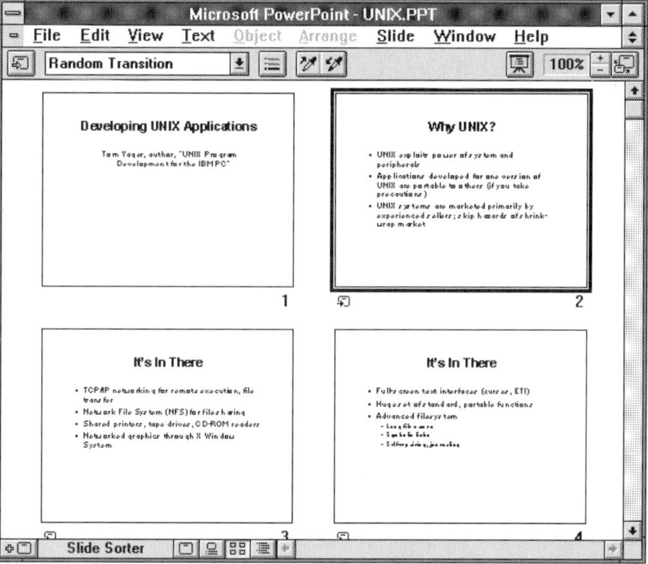

Figure 3-3c: The Slide Sorter View

The view is generally scalable to show you as many slides on screen at once as you need, with the obvious drawback that as you have more slides on screen, each slide is shown smaller. The sorter is a metaphor for the kind of backlit viewer you'd use to put 35mm slides in a certain order. A single slide or group of slides can be selected with a mouse click and moved around. Moving slides in this view changes the order of the presentation. Slides can also be deleted and duplicated here; all the functions of the clipboard's "Edit" menu apply to slides in this view. In the case of PowerPoint, slides cut or copied to the clipboard are pasted at the location of the last mouse click, a location marked with a tall, blinking vertical line.

You can also use the sorter to move slides easily between presentations. You can copy slides to the clipboard from one presentation, then open another presentation and paste those slides into it. In that way, you can build a library of reusable slides containing things like company logos, your name and title, and other material that needn't be recreated for every show.

Presentation packages differ most widely on the amount of help they offer in building the spoken portion of your presentation. Some include fairly capable word processors, while others leave the job of constructing the spoken text to other applications. What you can typically count on is a *notes view* (Figure 3-3d), in

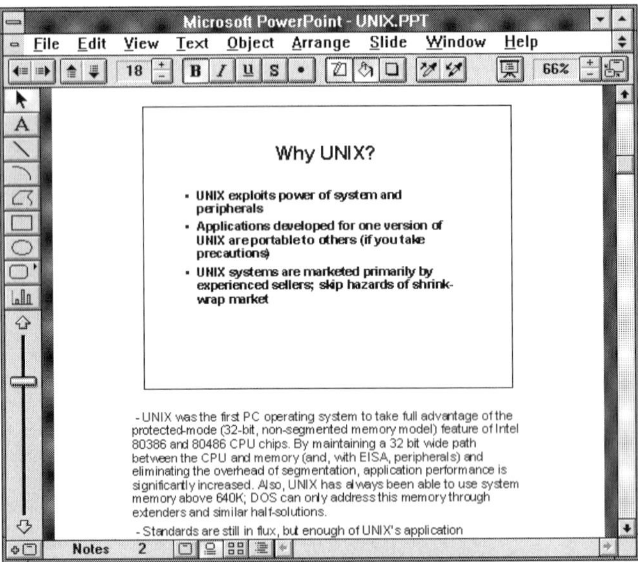

Figure 3-3d: The notes view

which each slide of your presentation is shown with a set of notes attached. If you don't have too much to say, you can use the notes view as a script. If it's your style to speak from a summary of your thoughts written on 3 × 5 cards, a printed version of the notes view is a perfect substitute. The graphic of the slide on the same page as your notes will help keep you on track.

Another popular use for notes is to turn them into audience handouts. If your presentation is part of a course you're teaching, for instance, you might print the notes out and provide them to your students in a binder. They can then refer to those notes to refresh themselves on the material you presented. Even when you're not teaching, audiences often appreciate having a set of notes to refer back to after your presentation is over. Unless you have some reason *not* to make hardcopy available, you should at least give those who ask a way to get the material from you after the speech is done (possibly charging a fee for duplication and for the information itself if you like).

What to Put In, What to Leave Out

While it's fine that outlining tools make it so easy for you to create and change your presentation, you need to focus on your content before you think too deeply about your tools. If you've never done a presentation before, you'd be well advised to consider a few simple guidelines before you dive in. Even if you have done this before, you might see something in this advice that makes the target a little easier to hit. This bit has nothing to do with formatting and visual style; that comes later. For now, let's think a bit about what makes good content.

If you use the outline style to build your presentation, there are two ways you can create that outline: before or after you create your spoken text. Either way is fine: some of us write much better if we just sit and type, while others require the structure of an outline. Another aspect that affects how your slides take shape is your preference for a detailed script. I tend to write down every word I plan to say, fearing that showtime may come and I'll be too tired or too something else to get my thoughts together. On a good day, I can improvise, following the basic structure of the script without reading from it. That's how I prefer to work, since it allows me to spend more time looking into the audience. But if some distraction leaves me unable to ad lib, the script is there like a security blanket. Braver souls, particularly those with lots of presentation experience, require only an outline, confident that they can call their material to mind under the most adverse conditions. Regardless of how you handle your speaking role, every computer-based presentation has one key element in common: the slides.

Brevity, it's said, is the soul of wit, but it's also the soul of presentation graphics. If you can't decide the right approach to a particular show, always err on the side of simplicity and brevity. You should consider each slide a precious commodity, one that must be used sparingly and with care. A good presentation is one that neither has too many slides nor too much information on any one slide. Let's take those issues one at a time, working backwards.

It's a popular misconception that presentation slides should convey the entire content of the presentation on their own. The idea is that someone looking only at your slides should be able to get the thrust of your message without any help from you. That might make sense with a few more media thrown in, but presentation graphics on their own should *never* be counted on to deliver your message. For the vast majority of presentations, that delivery should be handled in person.

Think of each slide as a paragraph, or, for particularly complex ideas, a chapter. The slide's title should summarize the slide's purpose succinctly. Keep the title to as few words as possible. Don't worry about complete sentences, and use only essential words and punctuation. If you finish your script or outline before your slides (as I prefer to do), the slide title can be taken from one of two places: the lead that introduces the idea of the moment or the idea's summary. It's okay to "telegraph" the conclusion in the slide's title; you can still set up suspense by choosing an interesting title and slowly revealing how you reached that conclusion with the rest of the slide.

How you word a slide title is a matter of personal style. Some prefer to make sure all the words in the title are spoken at some point while the slide is displayed; this gives the audience an obvious pointer as they try to match what they hear and see. Other presenters prefer to make their audiences think a bit by consciously avoiding duplicating the text of the slide in the spoken presentation. The audience must tune in a little more to follow you, but it also gives them a quiet sense of accomplishment: each time they tie something you say to an item on the screen, they'll get a little burst of "oh, now I get it" that may help hold their attention. The value of this little reward is debatable, but it's a device that I and others have used with some success. Of course, there's nothing that says you can't mix the two styles in a single presentation, except for the minor risk that you'll confuse someone who gets used to the one style (that might be part of my "no surprises" rule, discussed later).

It's a good idea to keep everything on your slide brief, but it's particularly important for the title since it will be set in a more prominent type size and style than the slide's body. Each letter takes up more room, and with presentation software, when you run out of room, the program wraps the text the way a word processor does. Every time a title spills over onto a new line, you lose someone in the audience; the eye scans headlines much more easily when they are contained on a single line. The visual style of the title has something to do with how long it can be, but don't count on reducing the type size to make room for long titles. Just make them short. As an example, the PowerPoint presentation shown in this chapter's figures uses very brief slide titles. They all fit on a single line. In fact, they are generally limited to two or three words. That's a reasonable limit for text you hope to have stick in someone's mind as a unit. The title, "Why UNIX?," for example, could also have been done as "What Are the Benefits of UNIX to Developers?" Certainly the latter paints a more complete picture of the slide's content, and on the face of it seems the superior title. But that longer message is more suited to your spoken text. "Why UNIX?" is something that will stick in the audience's mind, as will other well-chosen two- or three-word titles. I've proven this to be true in my own presentations: frequently, in the Q & A session following a presentation, audience members frame their questions by referring to specific slide titles. That wouldn't be possible if each slide were headlined by wordy titles.

The succinctness you apply to your titles should be carried through the body of your slides. Boiling a concept down to a few lean words is something that takes practice to perfect. Since you must never read your slides to the audience (let me say that again in case you missed it: *never* read your slides to the audience), it doesn't matter if the items on your slide sound good when you read them aloud. Once again, be parsimonious: forget complete sentences and throw out nonessential words. Maintain basic sentence structure and rules of grammar, but compress your material by leaving words out. You have a little more room to breathe in the body than in the title, but it's also not a bad idea here to avoid having the text wrap to subsequent lines. Succinctness in this context means expressing only the briefest summary of the idea behind the spoken text. There is no particular rule about how much spoken text should be attached to an item in the body of a slide. Remember that your slides are an outline, so leave the detail to your speech. Keep things moving, however, because you need to strike a balance that leaves each slide on the screen long enough to be read and understood but not so long that the audience looks away (and possibly misses your next slide).

There are lots of rules of thumb regarding how many items you are allowed per slide. I don't much go for hard and fast rules; there are always circumstances that confound the rules and those who try to follow them. In a slide like the ones in the sample presentation (shown in the figures), a reasonable goal is five major body items plus the title. In some cases, you can allow a breakout of lesser items under one of the five major items. Rather than find devious ways to squeeze more material onto a single slide, start a new slide with the same title as the current one and continue there. Whenever you find you have too much material for one slide, that's a reasonable approach, but only after you've been through the body of the slide to ensure that only what's essential is taking up space there.

One of those things that makes rules hard to follow is the fact that not all slides fit the cozy mold of the outline style. You might want a slide to contain a table of data or a quote from an expert, and we haven't even talked about graphics. In those cases, my guidelines fly out the window. You can't reasonably hack up a table or someone's quote to make it more terse. These exceptions make the design of presentation visuals more challenging, but even the ordinary slides require a little thought.

The Look of It

I've been downplaying the visual aspect of presentations because I wanted to make sure you realized the content is always more important. I'd rather see a well-thought-out presentation done with crayons and construction paper than a visually stunning presentation with second-rate material. Your audiences will likely be less accepting; they want *both* brains and good looks. Does that mean you have to enroll in night school for graphics design?

We're fortunate that the latest crop of presentation tools come with a valuable accessory: templates. In the simplest case, a presentation template gives you a set of forms into which you pour your text. The template takes care of setting off the title, formatting the slide's body text, and putting both on top of an appealing graphical backdrop. The templates also serve as an educational tool, since you can readily pick out the best aspects of the templates included with your software and combine them on your own. I'll discuss some of the techniques here, but I seriously recommend you take a look at some templates (this book's videotape includes a selection of sample slides as well).

Type and Format Considerations

The basic concepts behind good-looking presentation slides roughly match those of printed matter. The idea is to please the eye without confusing it, and those who have worked in print know how fine that line is. Presentations present more of a challenge: at least someone who is given a brochure can devote their entire attention to reading it. Audiences at a graphical presentation don't have that luxury. While their eyes are busy scanning the visuals, their brains will be doing double duty absorbing the words coming from you. Making your visuals too complex, too hard to read, or too distracting will force the audience to focus exclusively on what they see, shutting out what you're saying until they figure the slide out. Since I propose leaving the detail to the speech, having the audience's ears go numb for even a few seconds could cost you whatever it is you set out to accomplish.

I've already harped on brevity (failing to practice what I preach, perhaps), and brevity has a significant impact on the effectiveness of your visuals. A slide with less information can be set in larger type and generally offers more creative layout options than a slide loaded with text.

The size and shape of text in your slides is mostly determined by master pages, sometimes called "templates" or "style sheets." I referred to these earlier with regard to the outline view, where a master page determines the outline's appearance. There is also a master page that governs the appearance of slides (some applications support multiple master pages), setting, among other things, typefaces, sizes and styles. This "master slide," as I'll call it, makes it easy for you to give your presentation a consistent feel. Consistency may seem boring, but it's actually a wise thing to shoot for in a presentation.

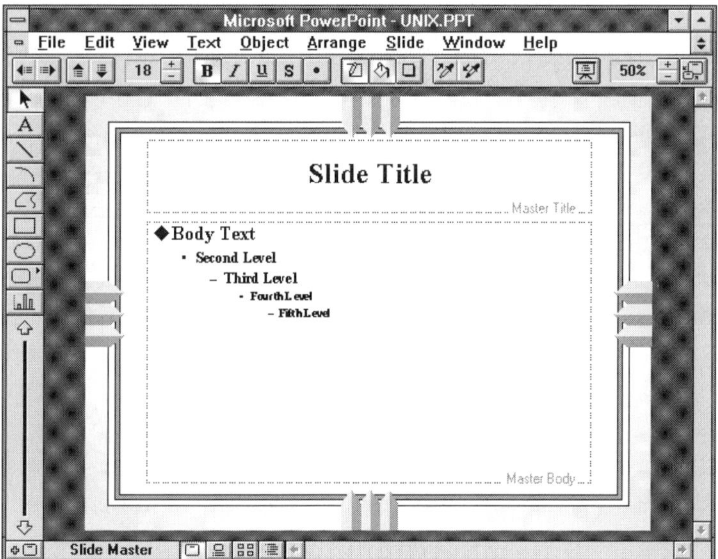

Figure 3-4: A master slide

The master slide (Figure 3-4) doesn't lock you into doing things a certain way. In PowerPoint, each slide can selectively inherit elements from the master slide. By default, however, every slide's appearance is completely governed by the master slide. In addition to typeface characteristics, colors and background graphics are determined by the master slide as well. You have the power to change anything you like about the appearance of an individual slide, but if things get out of hand, you need only select PowerPoint's "Reapply Master" menu option to return the slide to its consistent self.

Significant changes, particularly to a slide's background matter, that set a slide apart from the one before it catch your audience by surprise. If that's the effect you're looking for, then fine: changing the background of a slide is a good way to get it. But surprise is rarely a good thing in a presentation. I realize that sounds conservative, but every purely aesthetic thing you do has the potential risk of losing someone in the audience. If you transition from the buttoned-down look of the master slide in Figure 3-4 to a more spritely background with bright colors and lots of excitement, the audience will be so rattled by the abrupt change that you'll be lucky if they hear you at all. I don't mean that your audience is loaded with anal-retentives who only relate to shades of gray (if it is, then you're on your own). Even a roomful of teenagers can be so distracted by abrupt changes in graphical style that the message will be put on hold.

When you put your first slide on the screen, you're building a set of expectations in the audience's minds. The title appears in a certain place with certain colors behind it, the border looks just so, and the body text is set in this font and with that spacing between lines. This kind of analysis doesn't happen consciously—it's the mind trying to save itself some work. It analyzes the layout of the first slide and makes some notes to itself. You might say it memorizes the master page, and from that first slide, the mind expects to see something similar for the slides that follow. Once that pattern is established, any surprise shatters it. The trouble is, it takes time for the mind to adjust to the new look. It must first figure out that there has been a change. It tries to apply the rules of the pattern to the new layout. Only after it registers multiple "misses" does it decide the old pattern's a wash, and bring in a new one. But tearing it away from that old pattern is a tough job. It takes time, and it's hard work. Your audience has to work hard enough just understanding your material; you shouldn't burden them with surprises.

If You Must

Does that mean you can never change slide styles within a show? I'm not so staid that I think the answer is an absolute "yes," but I do think a single style, applied throughout an entire presentation, is the best approach for most work. Later in this chapter, I'll discuss a few ways you can make your slides more exciting without causing your audience's brains undue exertion.

If you're hell-bent on making changes to your slides' styles mid-show, there are some ways to bring it off while minimizing the negative impact. Some presentation packages let you select or create a *color scheme* that exists for an entire set of slides. It's possible to set up a scheme that includes all kinds of clashing, incompatible colors, but commercial presentation programs like PowerPoint include color schemes (often linked to the master slide) that take care of color for you. They don't make it impossible to stumble into clashing colors or inadequate contrast, but they help you stay within a limited set of colors (which includes various shades of those colors). That's the first step toward managing style changes.

If you change a slide's background, try to keep other elements in place; accommodate your audience's memorized patterns of previous slides as much as possible. The best way to manage background changes is to leave your text styles and positions completely untouched. If the title and body text looks just like the slide before it, your audience's minds may not register a miss on the memorized pattern. Similarly, if you change type styles and positions, you might consider altering your background to keep the pattern sound. If you move your title, for example, you could rework your background so that the title on the new slide has graphics behind it that are similar to those in the earlier slide. If your text changes size, resize background elements so that they have the same proportional relationship as in earlier slides.

There are some changes that simply don't make sense. If you're of a rebellious nature, some of the rules I've discussed here might lead you to go out and do the opposite of everything I've advised. Be my guest, but if you throw out everything else I've said, at least try to adhere to a few simple layout guidelines:

> ***Use headline or display fonts for titles.*** Companies that sell fonts, like Adobe and Bitstream, roughly classify the fonts they sell according to their best use. Adobe even sells packages of fonts by application class, with package names like "Letters, Memos & Faxes" and "Overheads & Slides." Generally, headline or display fonts either have no serifs (the decorative points and swirls that adorn the ends of the "pen strokes" that form letters), or gentle serifs. Serifs, which enhance readability at smaller type sizes (like the one used for this book), can be distracting or even gaudy when magni-

fied to the large type size of a title. Generally speaking, the larger the title, the less ornate the font should be, unless you're specifically after a decorative look for effect. There are some fonts that look fine in both titles and body text. You could do an entire presentation in nothing but boldfaced Times Roman and be pleased with the results; same for the ever-popular Helvetica. In fact, these two fonts are so widely used that they, or imitations of them, are available for practically every kind of system. These two fonts, in their bold, italic, and bold italic variations can serve you very well and save you from the agony of having to pick just the right font. Your friends won't make fun of you for using "old, reliable" fonts in your presentation, and if they do, well, I guess they weren't *really* your friends, were they?

Keep titles above your body text. I know that probably sounds obvious, but I've seen presentations where the presenter moved his titles to the bottom-right corner of the slide "because he could." Oh, the atrocities committed with presentation programs for that most irrational reason. Those schooled in reading English and most other languages have been taught to scan from top to bottom, left to right. Your audience should always come upon titles and subheadings before body text, so use what you know about your language's scanning order when laying out a slide. Generally speaking, that means placing titles and subheads above or to the left of body text. It *is* acceptable to place large text elsewhere on the slide, as long as it doesn't replace the title. You might have a block of large text after the slide's body text, for instance, if you wanted to drive a point home emphatically.

Use bullets appropriately. Presentation software lets you selectively precede a block of text with a bullet (•) or other graphical device that gives the audience a hint that a new body paragraph has started. Don't use bullets for titles, quotes, or any single block of text that isn't ordinary body text. It's okay, for instance, to have a slide that contains only a title and a single body item, with the latter preceded by a bullet. This maintains continuity with the slides before and after it, which presumably have more than one body item. But generally speaking, bullets should be reserved for those times when you have multiple text blocks that start at the same horizontal position. The text block should have a hanging indent so that text that wraps to the next line starts below the first character of the text above it and is not placed under the bullet. When you have a set of bulleted items, it's generally not a good idea to break them up with nonbulleted text. And finally, avoid the temptation to use cute bullets, like those included in some symbol and "Dingbat" fonts. If you decide to use cute bullets, use them consistently. You must realize, though, that using a cute bullet consistently means it's not cute anymore, so you might as well stick with boring old round bullets. If the font you've chosen doesn't have bullets, use a hyphen before resorting to "o" or "*." The hyphen, like a bullet, is roughly centered in the text row, making it flow better into the rest of the text.

Don't go too big or too small. Choosing the "just right" size for your type is an important job. Type that's too big shouts at the audience, while too-small type is either hard to read or whispers a message that needs more emphasis. It can be difficult to decide on type sizes while you're designing your presentation. Few of us create presentations on the large-screen monitors or projection TV systems that are used to display them. The watchword is *proportion*: if your text looks good and is readable on the screen you're using, chances are it will look good when it's displayed. That's another reason to stick with master slides, though, because if you get where you're going and discover that you used the wrong size font, all you have to do is jump into your presentation program and change the font sizes in the master slide to make them right throughout your show. Another difficulty unique to too-small text is that it can break up when projected or shown on a large screen. A presentation built at the typical display resolution of 640 × 480 looks great on a small screen, but a big monitor or data projector doesn't enhance your image's resolution; it just makes bigger pixels. So what were smooth diagonal lines and curves on your screen can become blocky and ugly at higher magnifications. Don't use type that looks small on your little display on the assumption that it will look fine when it's blown up. Stand a few feet away from your display—several feet for large displays—and use that view to decide whether the font sizes you've chosen are acceptable. There are formulas for that, telling you how far away to stand according to display size, but I don't place much stock in them since most presenters have precious little control over the environments in which they present. I prefer to counsel first-timers to assume the absolute *worst* conditions: a small, fuzzy monitor in a well-lit room. There's more to assuming the worst than choosing type sizes; colors and contrast play a role, too, and I'll get to them.

Centered text is attractive. I tend to center everything I can. Maybe I'm lazy, but centered text is pretty reliably good-looking. Some things shouldn't be centered. Individual lines of body text should never be centered; the entire block of text can be centered both horizontally and vertically, keeping the distances between the right and left margins equal according to the longest line of text. This is often more easily said than done; few presentation packages I've seen do this automatically. But if you're looking for a trick that adds a little polish to your presentation's appearance, centered text is a good one. Staggered justification works, too. You can, for example, set the slide's title at one inch from the left margin, and have the body text indented three inches. That makes the distinction between the title and the body text very clear and is a good style to use if the title and body are set in a similar font and size.

Don't embed outline-style sequence IDs or references to external material in your slide. Outline-style numbers and letters have little place in a presentation. As I mentioned earlier in this chapter, removed from the context that allows you to see a large portion of the outline at once, outline sequence numbers and letters lose their significance. Sometimes, when the presentation is accompanied by printed matter, some identification can help keep the two sets of materials in sync. In this case, place page numbers book-style in the bottom corner or bottom center of your slide, set in an unobtrusive size and style. Avoid embedding numbers in your titles, too. "409 U.S. 443: Authority to Make a Search" doesn't impart any more useful information than "Authority to Make a Search." Unless you give your presentation in the law library and you don't mind if your entire audience leaves to look up that reference, casting lines to material outside your presentation serves no purpose. If references to external material are necessary, place them in smaller type as footnotes on your slide, so audience members can note them if they wish. A better solution is to provide handouts that list the external references, so you can keep that clutter out of your slides.

Simplify all slide text. You can't make your material more important by using important-sounding words. I spoke earlier about compressing the number of words used in your text, and you can often trim words by stating your ideas more simply. "The Process of Making a Dial-Up Binary Data Transfer Connection to Another Party" becomes "Using Your Modem." Employ common, conversational speech tastefully to simplify your text. "Connecting Your Modem to the Wall Jack and Serial Port" can be "Hooking Up Your Modem." Your audience can get its mind around "hooking up" a lot more readily than the long-winded version. Save the detail for your spoken text. Wordiness and highbrow speech should be avoided in body text, too. "Maximum incidence is between the third and fifth decades" becomes "Mostly affects ages 30–50." I realize that you may see these examples as extreme cases and think yourself incapable of making such colossal blunders. But almost all presentations are built to impress someone, and we all have a tendency to want others to see how smart we are. Impress your audience with the quality and thoroughness of your material and with a confident delivery. You will *lose* points by relying on important-sounding text to impress.

Background Graphics

Most graphics (excluding text in this reference) are placed in the backgrounds of slides, set behind the text. Since graphics are done two-dimensionally, the whole business of what is background and what is foreground can get dicey. And once you figure out what a background is, what do you put there?

In the simplest case, a background is simply the color used for everything but the text. If you use solid-colored backgrounds, all you have to do is pick a color that contrasts but doesn't clash with the color of your text. But while the advice I've given to this point may make me seem boring, I'm *not* for solid-colored backgrounds. Tasteful use of color and shapes provide a little eye candy for the audience. Why carry the message to them in a paper bag when it travels just as well in a leather briefcase?

As with most things, there are rules about contrast and clashing. Color theorists can lay out the formulas that determine which colors go together best, and how many shades of contrast are required to provide optimal recognition. All that precision is a very good idea when you're publishing a magazine, but presenters needn't dig themselves in quite so deep. I mentioned earlier that many commercial presentation programs employ prepared color schemes. Within them, you'll often find colors that are obviously meant for background or foreground use. There are no rules, but you can be relatively safe sticking with dark backgrounds and lighter-colored text. Deep grays and browns are favorite background colors of mine, particularly since they support almost any color text.

These days, it's rarely necessary to construct your own background graphic; just use one included with your presentation software. If you can't find one you like, or if you just want to be a little creative, it's not difficult to invent good-looking backgrounds. Even if you don't use a prefabricated background, you should study the ones included with your software and note the design elements in them that you find most pleasing. Most often, your own backgrounds will combine the best features of those you've seen elsewhere.

There are a few issues to ponder when you select or create a background graphic. The relative conservativeness of your background graphics is determined by color scheme and shape selections. A conservative background relies on muted colors of the kind you might find in a business suit. Grays, browns, and deep blues make good background color palettes. Most backgrounds involve gradation of some kind, and sometimes several gradated shapes on one slide. Sticking with the conservative colors in your background also means limiting the range of your gradation: it's best to go from mid-tones to deep shades, rather than allowing gradation to or from high brightness levels. Doing a gradation from one conservative color to another (blue on top, to deep brown below creates a very attractive horizon appearance) can help you get a little more mileage out of a conservative scheme.

A conservative background most often uses a far background (a solid color or gradated pattern), sometimes with differently shaded rectangles or polygons behind the text but in front of the far background to stir visual interest and set key portions of your message apart from the rest. Some software lets you create a beveled edge, giving an intermediate background shape the 3-D appearance of a plaque. This also fits well within conservative guidelines. Other shapes, like circles, can be tastefully employed in areas of the slide that are not overlaid with text, provided they are set in colors that don't contrast significantly with the rest of the background.

A less-conservative background uses combinations of colors and shapes in more daring ways. Bright colors (solid and gradated) may be employed, and greens, purples, reds, oranges, and other colors you wouldn't see in a business suit make an appearance. The sky's the limit for shapes in the background, and there are no rules about how text overlaps them. In fact, one of the appealing things about free-form backgrounds is the freedom they give you to create backgrounds that break the old "rectangles behind everything" rules. In conservative backgrounds, a line or block of text is entirely backed with a rectangle or simply allowed to float above the far background with no intervening shapes. But in a nontraditional presentation background, those intervening shapes can cut across the neat, parallel lines created by text. Triangles, sharp-edged polygons and rotated rectangles seem to be popular choices for background shapes when you're after a more modern look.

Whether you go conservative or go nuts, there are things to avoid in backgrounds. A background should never be busy, having too many shapes or too many color variations. The definition of "too many" is a matter of personal taste, but I tend toward the conservative side and generally limit myself to one or two colors in the background (with gradation supplying shading variations of those colors). No background shape should so obviously contrast with the far background that it draws the viewer's focus from the text.

Foreground Graphics

Text isn't the only thing that floats above the background. Most presentation software lets you place graphics on your slide, either created with the presentation package itself or imported from another source.

Foreground graphics can serve lots of different purposes. Functional graphics are generally used either to represent statistical data or to illustrate some concept or process. Nonfunctional foreground graphics can be eye candy, appealing shapes with no more than aesthetic value, but more often, the graphics lend something to the message of the slide (although indirectly).

Company logos are probably the most popular form of foreground graphic. The most common usage is to feature a small logo on the bottom of the slide, in one of the corners, that is part of the master (and therefore appears on every slide in precisely the same place). Logos can be more prominently featured in slides that remain on the screen for long periods (presentation beginning, intermission, and end), soaking the audience in your company's name while you're not speaking. It's considered in bad taste to have your logo too prominently featured during speaking portions of your presentation, but if marketing is the obvious objective of your show, or you're presenting to people from within your own company, go for it.

Bringing your logo into a presentation program can either be a simple matter or a challenge. If you have a type-based logo (like the Panasonic or Microsoft logos I mentioned earlier in this chapter), it might be pretty easy: just find a matching typeface and type out your logo. If you can't find an exact match, or you can't get the spacing between letters just so, it may not matter as long as you don't feature your logo prominently. Even then, unless it's ugly or otherwise unprofessional-looking, even an approximation of your type logo will pass with the audience.

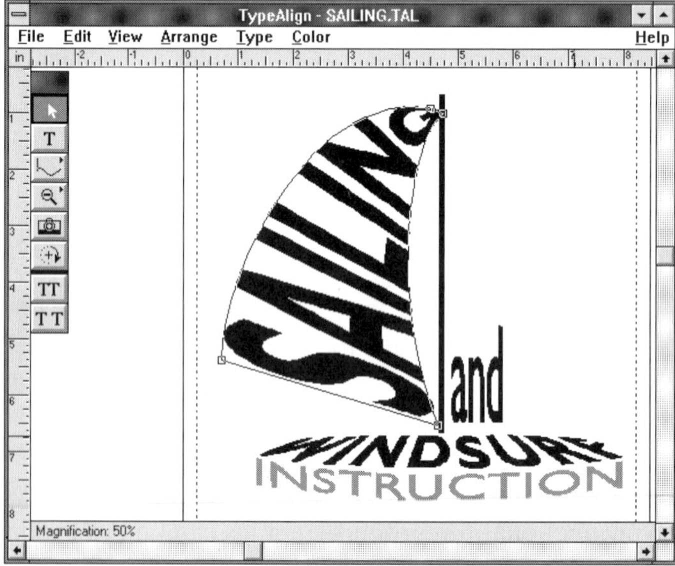

Figure 3-5: Adobe TypeAlign

If you want to go for realism, or if you haven't yet designed a logo for yourself, you might spend a few bucks on some type-effects software. Adobe, the type king, has its own effects package called TypeAlign. With it, you can change the shape of type by stretching, squashing, rotating, twisting—just about any 2-D effect you can imagine is possible with an effects package like TypeAlign. If your logo looks like the one in Figure 3-5, no one will wonder what your company does. There are other ways to get text effects. Some software, like Oxxi's Presentation Master for the Amiga, builds text effects capability into a 2-D drawing system. Presentation Master includes its own set of scalable fonts and TypeAlign-like tools for wrapping the text around line paths and altering its shape. Adobe Illustrator, too, can manage some impressive text effects if you first convert the text to shapes (a simple, automatic procedure).

Graphical logos can be a bit more difficult. A logo based on simple geometric shapes can be recreated by the drawing tools built into most presentation programs. If your logo is more complex, you have a couple of choices: you can scan the logo into your computer with a scanner or a video capture board, or you can have your logo converted into a vector graphic. The scan/capture option creates a bitmap. Most logos are line drawings, shaded or unshaded, and I find that bitmaps are not the best way to represent them. The primary disadvantage is that the logo is not readily scalable to different sizes. A bitmapped scaled down gets jumbled, with shapes bumping into each other and huge hunks of detail missing. An enlarged bitmap gets blocky as little pixels become big rectangular blobs. The only time to resort to a bitmapped logo is when the logo is a photograph, a complex freehand drawing with irregular strokes, or a painting or sketch. Then you almost have to use a bitmap, but I suggest scanning or capturing it at various sizes to avoid the unpleasant effects of scaling.

Vector graphics are far more effective and versatile carriers for logo art. They scale cleanly and have a professional, finished look. If you hired a design firm to do your logo, there's a chance they used an illustration program to create it. If you haven't already done so, you might arrange to obtain your logo from them in electronic form. You need to pay some attention to the file formats supported by your presentation software. If the artist did your logo on a computer, chances are the logo is most easily delivered in EPS, or Encapsulated PostScript format. EPS files are complex representations of vector art, and they're not always readable in presentation software. It's a common format on the Macintosh, so programs there are more likely to support the use of EPS files. Oxxi's Presentation Manager for the Amiga handles EPS graphics, too. Windows has its own vector graphic format, WMF (for Windows Metafile). Windows-based illustration software (like Adobe Illustrator or Corel Draw) can convert the EPS graphic to a WMF, but both of these are expensive if all you plan to do is translate your logo graphic. Again, a good graphics design shop should be able to help you with the conversion if it's to be a one-shot deal.

One unusual route for converting logo and other graphics from bitmap to vector form is to use an edge tracer. Adobe (who else?) offers a separate package, called Streamline, that converts a bitmap to a scalable vector drawing by finding the areas of highest contrast and drawing lines around them (edge tracing). If you put your hand on a scanner and ran it through Streamline, you'd end up with a black-and-white vector graphic, an accurate outline of your hand. It doesn't work miracles—you can't turn photographs into vectors and maintain their appearance—but you can usually convert a bitmapped scan of a line-art logo to a scalable vector graphic. Corel Draw has a tracer built into it as well.

Clip Art

Just as with prepackaged backgrounds, most presentation software includes a library of "clip art," so named for the huge books of stock art from which printers would clip drawings as they needed them. Clip art can free you from having to pay to have specially drawn graphics created for your presentation. Most libraries include common objects—people, computers, buildings, signs, business equipment—and decorative or functional visuals like bullets, arrows, and decorative borders (Figure 3-6 has a few examples). The art is most often used to illustrate a concept, to draw the viewer's eye toward a key point made in nearby text, or to provide a harmless distraction to keep the audience interested.

The clip art libraries bundled with presentation software are usually samples provided by companies in the clip art business. A catalog or mail-in card is tossed in so you can contact the vendor for more artwork. Making this art part of your presentation slides is a trivial task. The interface differs slightly from onc package to another, but you usually only need to select the name of the clip art file, drag out a rectangle in your slide where you'd like the artwork placed, and the figure appears there.

Some collections of clip art are organized (as with PowerPoint) as objects on presentation slides. You use the clipboard to transfer the graphics on those clip art slides to one of your presentation slides: click on the object you want to use, copy it to the clipboard, bring up the presentation slide on which you want the art to appear, and paste the clipboard's contents onto your slide.

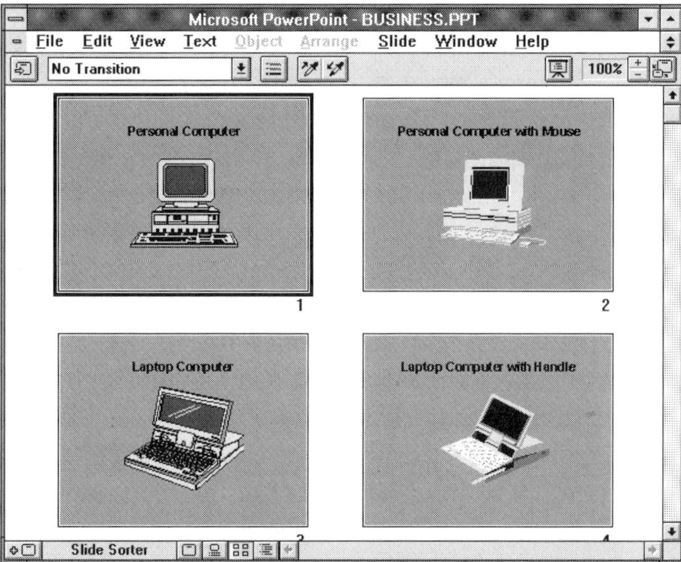

Figure 3-6: Clip art

As with most artful elements of presentations, it's far too easy to go overboard with clip art. You should use it sparingly, if at all. Unless you're presenting to an audience you know to be informal, avoid cute clip art; most libraries include caricatures, comic-style balloons for holding text, and other graphics that are meant to lighten things up. Something that strikes you as funny or harmless might lead someone in the audience to believe you don't take your material, or worse, your audience, seriously. When in doubt, play it safe: stay serious, but keep your slides visually interesting.

Custom Graphics

Some presentations call for graphics that must be created specially for the presentation. Product and technical drawings, maps, schematic diagrams, and many other types of graphics find their way into presentations, and when drawn well, these graphics can do wonders for an audience's opinion of the material and of you.

While it's true that you don't have to be an artist to build an effective presentation, drawing your own graphics is something you should approach with some caution. If you're artistic, then pay no attention to the advice that follows.

If you decide to draw your own graphics, you shouldn't spend much time wondering whether to use a paint or a drawing package: there are very few circumstances where drawing software, which produces vector graphics, isn't the best choice. Creating presentations frequently requires the moving and resizing of the graphics you put into them, and as I've said, vector graphics scale much more cleanly than the bitmaps created by paint programs. For nonartists, the ability to select and modify parts of your slide graphics after you've drawn them saves a lot of time.

Not being an artist myself, I'm poorly equipped to offer a list of things to do to make your own graphics look good. I "cheat" when I create custom graphics by making models that are only the roughest approximations of what I wish to represent. That fits this medium, because minute graphical details are almost always lost between the drawing and the showing. Even if details are visible, you usually don't want the audience leaning forward and squinting intently at the screen. The only exception to this is when you're using graphics as technical illustration, and your speech directs eyes toward the screen and calls out specific points of interest on the slide. Resist relying on detailed graphics too heavily unless you have good control over the environment in which your presentation will be shown. If you carry your show from town to town, relying on rented A/V equipment to get your images in front of the audience, you might wind up with a dim or fuzzy data projector or a screen that's too small for the audience size. In cases like that (which are not at all uncommon), a presentation dependent on graphical detail might as well get flushed.

For those cases where graphical detail is not essential, take advantage of the audience's imagination. The brain will fill in details where they don't exist—all you have to do is present a basic shape that can be uniquely identified as something familiar to most of the audience. When you're using a drawing tool, it sometimes helps to imagine yourself using construction paper. When you were young, a brown rectangle topped with a green circle was a tree. Similarly suggestive shapes (see Figure 3-7) work very well in presentations, but unlike your school days, you don't have little blobs of glue oozing out from the sides of your creation. The benefits of simplicity are obvious, but probably the best of these benefits is that simple graphics come together very quickly. The clock in the figure, while not exactly a masterpiece, probably took 20 seconds to create with the drawing tools built into PowerPoint. If the concept I wished to illustrate was "time," then what would have been served if I had spent several minutes more placing and rotating digits around

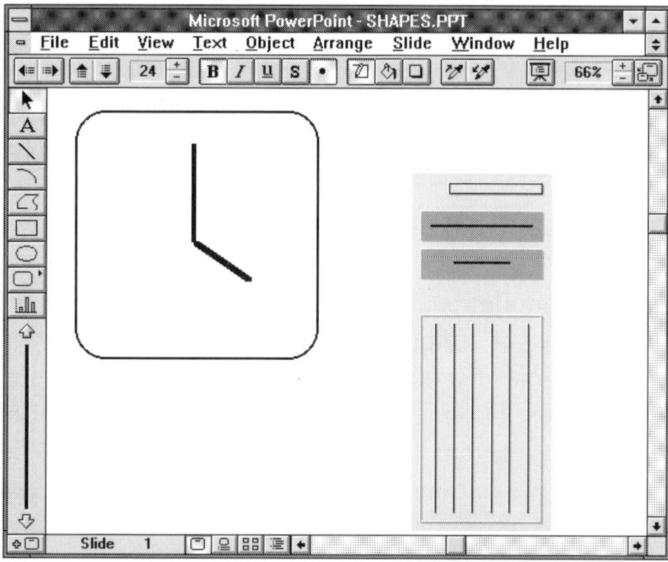

Figure 3-7: Simple custom graphics

the clock's face? When you design graphics like these, you can stop as soon as whatever you're drawing becomes recognizable. Little embellishments, like the vents in the drawing of the computer in the figure, can add a little fun to the process. The more complicated the drawing gets, however, the greater the risk that something will go wrong. If you want to fool around with your drawings, and you have the time, at least do frequent saves so you can always back up to the last version of the drawing if things get out of hand.

As with logo graphics, custom graphics can come from outside sources. Line drawings from CAD programs, scanned photographs, a frame of captured video, and all manner of graphics created elsewhere can usually be placed in presentations. It may call for conversion (as discussed at the top of this section), but if the graphic you want to include exists in some form someplace else, you rarely have to recreate it. In the hands of someone who knows how to wield a drawing tool, you can afford a greater degree of detail and the odd flourish. Skill at creating computer-generated art needn't always be learned; I've met many who seem to take to it within minutes of their first exposure to drawing tools. Whether acquired or automatic, if you have the skill, throw my cautious attitude to the wind (or wherever else you'd like to throw it). While I firmly believe that passable graphics can be created by anyone, the ability of a presentation to earn its audience's respect is enhanced by attractive graphics. If you have the means to create or purchase graphics that go beyond simple clip art to a more precise and artistic representation of your idea, consider taking advantage of that resource. The more you've got riding on your presentation, the more mileage you'll get out of attractive graphics.

Charts and Graphs

Probably the most familiar use of a graphic in a presentation is the chart or graph, which turns columns of numbers into something viewers can understand at a glance. Trends become instantly evident, the relative magnitude of climbs and drops is made obvious. Drop a few spreadsheet cells onto a slide, and most people in the audience won't bother to swim through the numbers there. The graphical representation has always been more effective, and some support for charts and graphs is part of most presentation packages.

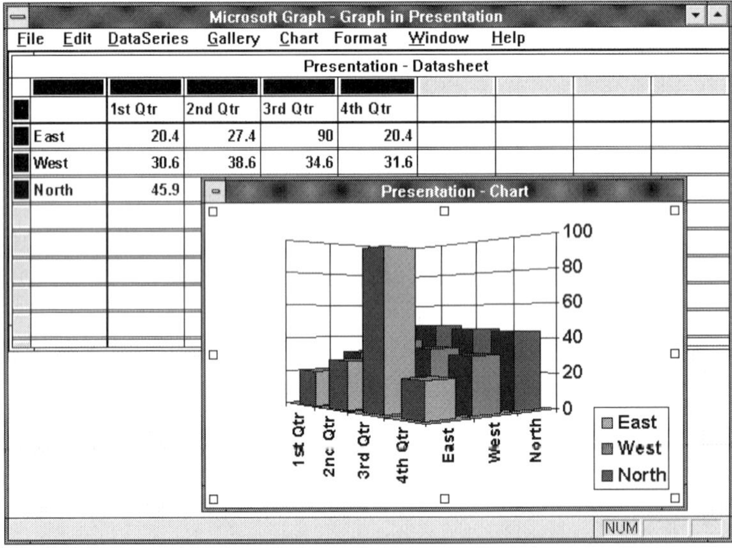

Figure 3-8: Statistical charts

Chart data usually starts as a spreadsheet. If the data doesn't already exist as a spreadsheet file when you're ready to create your chart, the presentation program probably has some facility for keying the numbers directly into the charting module (see Figure 3-8). One of the advances of modern presentation graphics programs is the incredible range of data representations they offer you. We're all familiar with (and soundly bored by) the reliable old pie, bar, and line graphs. Presentation software adds color and scalable fonts to the mix, along with something relatively new: 3-D. The chart shown in Figure 3-8 adds the appeal of simulated 3-D to the bland domain of business charting. It's true that virtually *everybody* uses 3-D charts now, but if they're done well, they're not yet so overused that they're out of style.

A good presentation program, like PowerPoint, defaults to an acceptable chart style. If you find you want to explore a little bit, just keep the running theme of this chapter—simplicity—in mind. In this context, that means a few things:

> ***Don't cram too much data into one chart, or at least cram it carefully.*** The chart in Figure 3-8 is readable because it presents a manageable amount of information in a 4 × 3 matrix of bars. The height relationships between bars are evident (even though perspective limits the visibility of some of the bars), and the text labels all line up well with the rows and columns they tag. When you increase the number of data elements, you force yourself to move to smaller label text, and you make it hard for the audience to keep the data separate. Some chart formats, like pie and line, are suited to representing lots of bits of data, but only if the majority of the data can go unlabeled. If you present a line chart that has three years' worth of data, for example, improve the chart's readability by leaving out some axes and labels. There aren't many ways to stuff 36 vertical axes into one chart without making it impossible to read. If you cut back on the frequency of the labels (see Figure 3-9), you can reasonably raise the information density in the graph.
>
> When a chart includes a lot of data (like the one in the figure), it limits the number of chart formats that will work with the data. I tested most of PowerPoint's chart styles before I settled on the 3-D line graph shown. Presentation software is built with this exploration in mind, making it easy for you to switch styles without affecting your data. Try other things, too, like the format of your labels (I shortened the ones shown in the figure from full-length names), the size of your type, and choices of colors to make dense charts easier to understand.

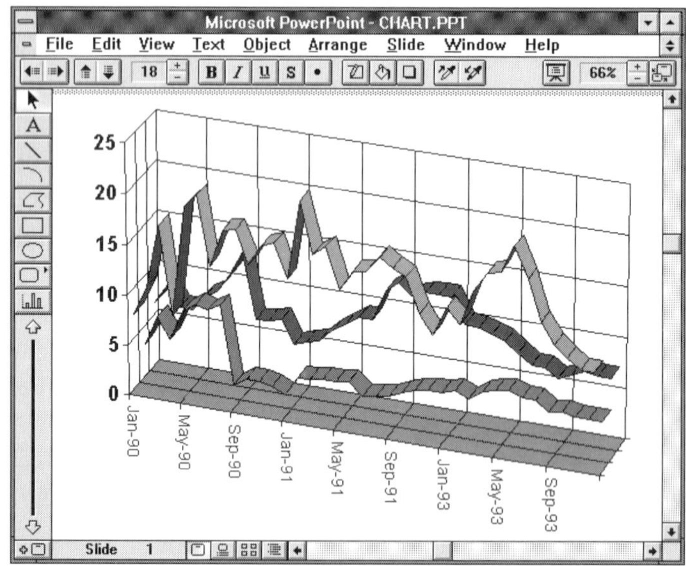

Figure 3-9: Packing data into a chart

Make sure 3-D works. Graphs look wonderful in 3-D, but they have a flaw that can prove to be fatal. I can't think how many presentations I've sat in on where the presenter had to say something like, "...and if you could see the East's January data—um, it's sort of hidden in the back there—you'd notice that there was a sharp drop that month." The flaw is that 3-D styles, particularly the popular 3-D bar chart, can conceal data. Make sure that the data not visible from the 3-D viewing angle you've selected isn't vital. Certainly, any data to which you refer in your speech must be visible. But data which is part of any trend you describe shouldn't disappear behind some less-important series that obscures it.

There are some ways to work around the problems 3-D creates. If you're lucky enough to have all your data represented by one row of bars, and the other rows are there for incidental comparison, you can move that more important row of bars to the front (by making it the top or bottom-most row in the mini-spreadsheet that holds your chart data). If more than one row is important, simply use multiple charts, each on a separate slide. In each slide, move the row you're talking about in your speech to the front, subjugating the others.

Sometimes a change in viewing angle is all that's needed to bring an obscured data item into view. Presentation packages that include 3-D charts usually let you spin the entire chart. You can look up at it from below, down from above, or peer in on it from the left or right. It's as though the chart were a tangible three-dimensional collection of colored towers or flowing ribbons, pinned in place inside a three-walled box. The viewing angle interface lets you hold that box in front of you as though it were on a tripod. Grabbing one handle rotates the box left-to-right, and another tilts it vertically. It's okay to use unusual viewing angles in your presentation, as long as the point you're trying to make is clear.

Avoid distractions inside the chart. Generally, the chart shouldn't have anything in it but the chart graphics, the title, and the labels. If you load up the chart with arrows and text boxes, you disrupt the flow of the chart. There are ways to do it tastefully, but there's another reason not to circle peaks and low points and call them out with arrowed text: some audiences will feel condescended to by that treatment. It's better to call out points of interest in your speech, or use a pointer (like one of the laser models that projects a bright dot onto the presentation screen). If you want to know why this is better, watch your audience: when you use your speech to highlight some key feature of a chart, audience members will scan the chart for the item to which you refer. When they find it, they'll shake their heads "yes," and by finding it themselves, they'll feel a small (but worthwhile) sense of accomplishment. If that notion seems silly to you, consider that keeping your audience involved is the best way to keep them interested (and awake).

If your slide contains only the chart, you can break with the presentation's style for that slide. Specifically, it's not necessary to have both a slide title like all the others, and the title that the charting module places above the chart itself. Fill the screen with the chart. If a chart is a part of a slide that includes other elements, it's best to use as many elements of your presentation's master slide format as possible.

Use axis labels instead of legends whenever possible. A legend, the little box that cross-references bar or line colors with names that make sense, draws the viewer's eye from the graph itself. The same purpose is sometimes served better by axis labels. A legend box with more than three or four items in it is worse than useless. A 3-D bar chart, for example, can accomodate both row and column labels. That's better than forcing the audience to shift their focus to the graph, to the legend, to the graph again, and so on. Line charts in which the lines overlap sometimes don't give you much choice but to use legends. Pie charts accomodate data labels well.

Regardless of the chart type you use, when using axis or data labels, eliminate those labels that aren't essential. If, for example, you've got a pie with 17 slices, but only four of them are referenced in your speech, consolidate some slices by adding their values together and reducing the size of your data spreadsheet. The data label "other" is a wonderful thing. Of course, make sure you only use it once in any chart—you don't want to get stuck pointing to that "*other* other" slice in your pie chart.

Making a Show of It

So far, I've devoted this chapter to the elements that make up a presentation. Coming chapters in this book will talk about some other elements, like digitized audio, animation, and video, that some presentation software can accomodate. But let's stick to our knitting and wrap up this chapter by talking about how a bunch of slides become a presentation.

One thing all presentation software, even the cheapest, simplest ones, have in common is the presentation sequencer. Some programs use timelines with icons, others use outlines and slide sorters, but whatever the interface, the idea is to put your slides in order and set them up for a live presentation.

Just getting the slides in order is trivial. If that's all it took, *everybody* would use computer-based presentations. Fact is, getting a finished presentation to an audience is enough of a challenge to scare off some of those most in need.

Making the Transition

A presentation given with a slide projector is punctuated by the telltale push-out/ black or white screen/pull in sequence. It's the same thing between every slide. No matter how pretty the slides are, slide projectors make them ugly with the abrupt transition from one slide to the next.

Some enterprising individual came up with a way to minimize the visual rattle of slide shows. By using two slide projectors instead of one, and alternating your slides between them, there could always be an image on the screen. A special device called a dissolver makes the slides cross-fade into one another, a very appealing effect. It's a cheap trick, but it gives a slide show a more polished look.

Considering that slides in a computer-based presentation are digital data, you gain the freedom to paint that data onto the screen just about any way you like. Images can just pop onto the screen, but you can make your show more interesting by using *transitional effects.* A transition defines how the contents of each new slide are painted over the old one. The range of effects available to you are determined by the software you're using and the capabilities of the computer and video system you're using. On the least-capable Mac or PC, your choices of effects are extremely limited because the computer can push information out to the screen fast enough for only the simplest effects. Even the cheapest Amiga can manage an impressive array of effects, because accelerated display hardware is standard on every machine. If you want something you can't get on your system, you can transfer your presentation to another system that gives you what you're missing (I'll present some options shortly).

The simplest transitional effect, and one that all systems are capable of producing, is the *wipe*. The graphics from the new slide are painted over the new one in a sweeping motion. The direction of that motion provides some interesting variations. Top-to-bottom and bottom-to-top wipes are common, but you can also wipe the new slide in from a corner, or from the center of the screen to the outer edges.

A wipe is a safe transition because it can generally be carried out smoothly, even on a slow machine with an unacclerated display controller. There are variants of the wipe, like checkerboard (the new slide replaces the old in a storm of little boxes), slats (like checkerboard, but with horizontal or vertical bars), concentric circular and rectangular wipes, and a host of other effects. They have in common that they don't move any of the graphics around on the screen. They just reveal the new slide in place of the old one.

More capable systems can manage effects that involve moving the graphics around. The *push* is one effect that's best left to systems that can handle it: the old slide is shoved from one edge (or diagonally) by the new slide until it's completely off the screen. Presentation software sometimes lets you do things that don't make sense for the system you're using, and this effect is a good example of that. On a system that's not equipped to handle it, a push looks horrible. The movement is far from smooth, and doesn't even maintain a constant speed. I'm sorry if it sounds snooty, but I tend to want to avoid using anything in a presentation that calls out the limitations of the system I'm using. A bad-looking effect is far worse than not using one at all. A $500 Amiga can do perfectly smooth pushes and other complex effects. I won't harp on that; it's just the best machine for delivering presentations of the three I used for this book. Macs and PCs need a little more work. Either system, equipped with a Truevision graphics card (like the NuVista+ for the Mac, or the Targa+ or ATVista for the PC) becomes able to do a lot of effects a standard Macintosh display controller or PC VGA board can't (or shouldn't) touch.

The high-end PC or Mac systems, upgraded with Truevision boards, and Amigas can sometimes get at some really impressive effects. *Page turns* peel the old slide away as though it were paper (you can see the "back," usually a solid color or a reverse-image of the slide) to reveal the new slide. *Page rolls* roll the old slide off in a curling motion. A *pour* makes it appear that the graphics are being poured in from the top of the frame. These are just a few of the effects better software and better systems allow you.

How important are transitional effects? That depends on how you use them. Using an effect is usually better than just popping a new slide up on the screen all at once. It's eye candy, and the really nifty effects give the audience something to "ooh" at. Good, smooth, well-chosen effects add to your presentation's professionalism. The audience gets the feeling that you went the extra mile just for them. If you can convince the audience that the material is important to you, it's easier for them to see it as important.

Like all other visual attributes placed at your disposal, it's easy to do too much with transitional effects. I tend to err toward consistency here, too, opting for simple wipes and dissolves for most slides, and reserving flashier effects for emphasis. There's another reason to keep your transitions refined. I've spoken with several people who experience an uneasiness, something like vertigo, when a presentation employs too much motion. Whatever the reason, it's best to choose a small group of effects that you think look good and use them throughout your show.

The most popular presentation packages let you apply effects in two ways: specifically and randomly. Specific effects tag each slide with the effect you want to use to bring it onto the screen. Using random effects simply chooses an effect at random each time you move to the next slide. If a presentation package has a limited set of effects, and you've previewed them all to make sure they don't look ridiculous, go ahead and use the random setting. I prefer to exert more control over my own work, and there are times when a particular transition is best, as with builds (hey, what a segue...).

Builds

A *build* is the incremental revealing of some part of a slide that was either not visible or was graphically de-emphasized (by setting it in a dimmer color, for instance). Outline-style presentations are enhanced by builds that reveal the body items one at a time as your speech progresses. You can also set the body item you're discussing in a brighter color or a bolder typeface, but leaving them all visible. PowerPoint, and most other commercial presentation packages that include outliners, will create builds automatically. A build can also be used to reveal graphics, or to rearrange the slide to change its focal point.

One way to do a build is to create multiple slides that share much of their content. Each slide is an element in a sequence, and you can employ transitional effects to add visual impact to the revealing of the material that changes from slide to slide. When you play the sequence back, it will appear to the audience that they are viewing one slide, the contents of which change as you speak.

Some software lets you do animated builds. On the Amiga, which, once again, is specially equipped to handle animation, you can get away with it. A simple animated build would have a bullet item "slide" in from one side of the screen. A Mac or PC can rarely do even that simple motion smoothly, and I think jerky animation is terribly unprofessional. If you really want to use animation in your presentation, you might use software like that described in the chapters on 2-D and 3-D animation. The animation capabilities of off-the-shelf presentation software is generally limited and best left alone. Unless you know your system can handle smooth animation, stick with transitional effects for builds.

Moving It Along

The presentations I've been describing here are all given live, with a mix of computer-generated graphics and live speaking. You need to synchronize your slides with your speech. If you pay half-attention to everything else, pay particular attention to this part of the operation. If the aural and visual halves of your presentation fall out of phase even temporarily, you lose *serious* points with the audience.

If you've never given a computer-based presentation before, you might think that syncing is no big deal: after all, you can see the screen, and you'll *just know* when it's time to move to the next slide or kick off the next build. The fact is, many presentations, particularly ones given to large groups in banquet rooms or auditoriums, force the presenter to do the entire show without seeing the screen at all. Your podium might be set so you can't see the screen from where you're standing, or it may be that you have to crane your neck to grab a look at it.

Even if you *can* see the screen, you shouldn't spend much time looking at it unless you're using a laser pointer or interacting with the screen in some other way. You've seen the show, and if you need something to do with your eyes, look into the audience. Anyone who's done any public speaking will tell you that eye contact with the audience is vital to being taken seriously. Twisting your head halfway around like an owl to see which slide's on the screen is going to have you taken much less seriously.

As I said earlier, I tend to script my presentations explicitly: every word I intend to speak is on paper. Synchronizing a presentation done this way is easy: I just litter my script with marker text that tells me when to move to the next slide. I use "***[* click *]***" as my marker, since I construct my presentations to be moved forward with a mouse-button click. Some software also allows you to define a timed interval between slides. Even though it might be tempting to teach the computer to run the slides without your help, using intervals for the entire show is a bad idea. If an audience member interrupts you with a question, or if you embellish or forget some portion of your speech, the computer will keep flipping away, oblivious to the fact that you've changed the tempo. PCs, Macs, and Amigas will all accommodate longer-than-normal mouse cables or extensions, so even if the podium isn't that close to the system you're using, you should be able to snake a cable up to the podium for the mouse. Unless the facility is specially equipped for computer-based presentations, you won't have room for the monitor or a keyboard. Besides, if you're on a stage, you can walk with the mouse in your hand, and if you're podium-bound, a mouse takes up very little room.

If you use an outline and ad lib, you need only work from an outline that matches your slides. Whether you script your speech or not, here are a few pointers:

Practice, practice, practice. And then practice again. You should rehearse your speech out loud in front of the computer several times before you appear. Don't trust that all will go well: I promise you that you'll find material that doesn't sound good, slides that don't match the message, or synchronization problems. Wouldn't you rather find them when you're alone rather than when standing in front of a roomful of people whose opinions matter to you?

Don't pause between slides. Your speech will be very choppy if, every time you move to the next slide, you stop speaking until the new slide is on the screen. It's hard not to do this, but teaching yourself to maintain a flowing stream of speech while controlling the presentation is a key to professional presenting. To make it easier for myself, I place those "click" markers in the middle of sentences. After rehearsing a couple of times, the markers become invisible to me. I talk right through them, but I train myself reflexively to hit the mouse button when they appear.

Consider display delays. When you're laying out your script, or when you're giving your presentation, you should consider the time it takes your system to load the next slide. The length of the delay depends on the software, and sometimes on the complexity of the graphics on the slide. If you follow my advice about letting your speech flow and you don't consider slide loading time, you'll wind up referring to slides that aren't on the screen yet. This is one issue that you can resolve in a rehearsal. I don't place the "click" markers in my speech text until I've done a dry run on my show. Consider, too, that some transitional effects take longer to complete than others. Just make sure you're not talking about a slide (or a part of a slide) that's not visible yet.

Keep going, no matter what. If you mess up, don't get flustered. The most common mistake is accidentally to advance two slides or builds forward instead of one. Like typing, you'll probably instinctively know you've done it. Few presentation packages let you back up one slide with the mouse. Even if the keyboard is handy, don't use it unless you've skipped a positively essential slide. If you do need to move backward, say nothing about it (the "I planned that" air effectively covers all kinds of gaffs), or, if you have to leave the podium to back up a slide, simply say "excuse me for a moment" and do your thing.

Clicking forward two slides is trivial compared to some of the things that can go wrong during a presentation. I've seen plenty of system crashes, power outages, and software bugs. I've even seen, if you can imagine it, *hecklers* at business presentations. Yes, it is embarrassing when your show is disrupted. It throws you off your rhythm, and there's no way to rehearse for the countless crises that can befall you on that stage. It's at times like these that the strength of your script is paramount. If something goes wrong with the equipment (if you can't see the screen, watch the audience: they'll start looking at the screen, then looking at you to see if you notice), how you deal with it depends on whether you're doing a solo gig or not. If you can, bring a colleague who knows how to operate the system and is at least familiar enough with the software you're using (and your script) to catch up to you. If the system crashes or your software fails, give your helper a high sign. Turn the data projector or monitor off, or unplug it from the back of your system (make sure when you're setting up that unplugging the input results in a black or solid-colored screen—it usually does). He or she can then reboot the computer without having the audience see the exercise on the screen, plugging the output back in when they have located your current slide.

If you're alone, leave the podium for a moment and turn the system off. If your presentation was scheduled for a break, and the normal time for that break is within reach, dismiss the audience for that break and get the system running again. If you can't break, or you can't bring the system back up again, go on without it. Audience handouts are helpful in this case: bring up the house lights and ask them to follow along with their printed copies of your slides. Failing that, just push ahead with your speech. You might give a little extra detail.

Whatever goes wrong, resist the reflex to laugh nervously or to joke about it. Equipment and software failures, even if they're not your fault, reflect poor planning in the minds of the audience. If you joke about it or show you're flustered, you call attention to the problem, and show the audience that you're too rattled to continue. Try to keep your cool, or at least *pretend* not to be bothered, and do whatever you must to disrupt the flow of the presentation as little as possible.

Look into the audience. I said it once already: eye contact with the audience is important. For me, that means rehearsing my script so many times that I have parts of it memorized, or I can at least paraphrase effectively enough to lift my eyes from the podium or table frequently. Each time I look up, I scan the audience, shifting my focus to make sure I hit every section of seating (or, in the case of a small room, each person) every minute or so.

Should you look directly into the eyes of audience members? If you can do that without stumbling, go ahead. Locking eyes with someone is a fairly intimate gesture that can make both the presenter and the audience member uncomfortable, and except for small meetings, I tend not to make direct eye contact. Instead, I use a trick I learned as a stage actor: I look at the spaces between people in the audience, or just over the heads of a row of them. It appears to individuals in the audience that I'm always looking at the person next to them, but they still get the feeling that I'm interacting with the audience (and, by association, the individual).

For those cases when you're in close quarters, real eye contact is unavoidable and necessary. Don't spend more than a few seconds looking at one person unless you're responding to a question or purposely directing your presentation. Even then, look at others in the room (to make sure they know they're still included), and break it up by glancing briefly at your script or at the screen if it's right in front of you. When you're looking someone in the eye, something that you'll have to do even in large rooms when an audience member poses a question, speak while looking into his or her *eye*. You see, even though both of you have two eyes (if you're like most people), you can't look at both of someone else's eyes at once. Normally, we shift our gaze from one eye to another. During an ordinary conversation, this doesn't seem at all odd, but in a business discussion (for instance), you don't want to look shifty-eyed. So pick an eye and look directly into it. If you haven't practiced this widely used method before, be prepared that it will feel strange to you. Another trick you can use for emphasis is to go longer without blinking. When you're speaking to and looking at someone, the longer you go without blinking, the more attention you'll get.

Either do something about hecklers or ignore them. If some member of your audience is disrupting your presentation somehow, either do something decisive about it or do nothing at all. If they're being really obnoxious about it, such as a pair who are talking loudly while you're trying to speak, you can sometimes quiet them by spending a little more time looking into that part of the audience than others. Don't let it be heard in your tone of voice or seen in your expression that you're perturbed. If the disturbance continues, pardon yourself from the podium and ask someone else to speak with the inconsiderate people; avoid handling it yourself. There's a certain aloofness that speakers should practice. In smaller audiences, such as classrooms, and when you don't have any assistants, walk over to the problem-causers and whisper a very brief, very direct plea for order. "If you must talk, please step outside so you don't disturb the others" is a nice way to say, "shut up or get out."

A persistent problem audience member sometimes must be asked to leave or escorted out. This doesn't have to be traumatic; chances are, the rest of the audience wants the troublemaker gone as much as you do. If you're presenting in a hotel or conference facility with security, excuse yourself from the podium and fetch a guard or other assistant. Return with them, but point out the problem to them from the back of the room. While they take care of business, return to the podium and busy yourself with your papers or the water pitcher. Don't look up again until the problem is gone, and then when you do, say nothing about the matter and pick up where you left off. Don't try to start your presentation again until the offender is gone; you can't possibly be as entertaining to the audience as watching someone get booted out of the room.

Make time for the audience. The best way to ingratiate yourself with your audience is to spend time with them after the presentation. If you're speaking at a trade show or other event where time is strictly allocated, try to allow at least five minutes at the end to take a question or two. This makes you more accessible and likable to the audience, but it also gives you a chance to prove you know your business. If you get shooed out of the room and you still have time, spend a few minutes willingly with those audience members who wish to engage you in civil, productive conversation. Even a couple of torturous minutes followed by an "excuse me, but I'm already late for my next meeting" will leave a better impression than if you walk directly from the podium into a waiting car.

Don't be stiff. It's normal to be nervous when you're presenting, but even the best graphics can't rescue a badly delivered speech. The worst and most common mistake is to give a lifeless, inflectionless reading of your speech. When you rehearse, practice inflections that give your delivery a more conversational tone. You don't have to sound like a pal, but even that's better than sounding like a robot. Gestures and facial expressions are welcomed by the audience, and walking on the stage or at the front of the room is fine, too, as long as you don't pace—make sure you stand still for most of your delivery, but it's good to move around. It helps you dissipate some of your nervous energy and gives the audience more of a performance.

Try to be prepared to sacrifice or add material. If you're speaking as part of a panel, or if you are speaking in a timeslot, you might be the one called on to cut your material to put everyone else back on schedule. Don't whine about it. Think in advance about which portions of your material you can trim to save time, and mark them somehow. If you have to advance through several slides to skip something, simply explain that you're short on time, so you're passing over some material. You can often do the multiple slide advances while you're offering a brief summary of the material you were forced to skip. Don't use phrases like "I was going to say" or "I had wanted to discuss..." This shows that you're not happy about having to cut material. Once again, that's unprofessional. Roll with it.

While you're building your presentation, if you find you need to cut good material to bring the time down (which often happens when you rehearse), instead of cutting it completely, move the spoken portion of the material to a separate page and mark your script or outline with a reference to the cut material. If it turns out you have more time than you thought you would, you can put the material back in. Don't worry about the slides. Let the last one stay on screen, and introduce your added material with a sequitur like "I'd like to digress for a moment..." Present your added material in its entirety, and then offer a verbal segue back into the main show script.

Get there early, start on time. This is the last of my presentation tips, and it's an important one. Make sure you show up well in advance of the audience to check your equipment and set up your software. Test everything you can, and then leave your opening slide on the screen while audience members file in. Unless you're to be introduced and make an entrance, the audience should see you when they enter. This is their cue that the show will start on time. Be or look busy before the show starts. Try not to get involved in discussions with audience members prior to the show. When the scheduled time to begin strikes, get underway immediately. I use a series of special timed slides that count down the minutes to the start of the presentation so everyone can make their trips to the soda machine and elsewhere and still get back in time. Start precisely on time, but don't acknowledge or be bothered by stragglers, no matter how late they arrive.

Getting It There in Style

There are times when the material and that which you have riding on it need the best packaging you can give them. It may be that the system you use to build your presentation doesn't let you present it the way you want to. If you have to travel, that system may be too bulky or too precious to carry with you. Before you start building your show, you should consider how it will be shown. If you have a Mac or PC-based presentation, you may be able to load it into a notebook, laptop, or luggable system. Even desktop Macs, being so little and cute, are perfect for toting around, and there are padded, reinforced cases built specifically for the job. You can carry a slimline pretty easily, too, except that a small PC sometimes also means an underpowered PC. I noted earlier that even the least-expensive Amiga outperforms both Macs and PCs as a presentation system, and while there's no Amiga laptop (yet?), models like the 4000 are fast, relatively lightweight, and compact.

Of course, there's more to putting on a world-class show than just picking the right system. Only rarely do you find that any system, out of the box, is capable of giving the best presentations it can give. Building the perfect presentation-giving machine usually means investing in some nonstandard hardware. Even though the Amiga has at least a bit of an edge, there are ways to give its presentation power a little extra juice; more on that shortly. Making the most of a Mac or PC usually means installing a more capable video board. The best video board for a computer-based presentation, given live, is one that combines high color and some kind of acceleration. You can save a considerable amount of money by deciding that you can settle for one or the other (color or speed); which you sacrifice is up to you. The toll exacted by color without speed varies depending on the device. Many of the least-expensive high-color display cards are slow enough that your audience can see your graphics being drawn onto the presentation screen. I have seen presentations that use this gradual drawing of a slide to an advantage, but it takes an extra measure of planning and rehearsal that might not otherwise be necessary. Without that advance planning, the slow drawing of a slide can at least throw your timing off, and at worst, it can create a negative impact on the audience's impression of you and your material.

Speed without high-color is probably the safer choice. Presentation software is generally geared toward only moderately capable display systems, typified by the Mac and PC standard of 256 colors at a resolution of 640 × 480 pixels. This resolution and color depth is easy to accelerate, and a great many display cards do that. A fast display means your graphics hit the screen more quickly; it's not uncommon for even the least-expensive display accelerator to cut the time needed to draw a display down to a fraction of a second. On the PC, most low-end display accelerators act like an ordinary VGA card until some software, like Microsoft Windows, activates the board's accelerated graphics subsystem. Because of this, you can simply replace your PC's primary display with a 256-color accelerator. At the time of this writing, prices were falling on high-color (16- and 24-bit) accelerated graphics cards as well, but support for them in PC software is still relatively poor. On the Macintosh, which is built to easily support multiple display cards (and multiple displays) and has had cheap high-color cards for long enough to enjoy almost universal support in applications software, upgrading your display card is probably easier than on any of the other systems: only rarely need you do more than plug in your new card and turn the machine on. I have alluded to the Amiga's rather impressive graphics capabilities, with the only drawback being that Commodore (the Amiga's maker) implements improved display hardware by introducing new systems; all Amiga systems have their display controllers built in, and there aren't any cards I know of that replace the Amiga's internal display controller and duplicate its functionality (as add-on PC and Mac adapters do). With the newer Amigas, you can generally "get by" with what's built into the system, because that system's standard graphics support is better than that on comparably-priced PCs and Macs. Upgrading an Amiga's display card usually means getting more color, and often means adding a second monitor.

A two-monitor system can be a little inconvenient when you're giving your show on the road. After all, the monitor is usually much heavier than the system itself. It has its advantages, however. Some Mac presentation tools, for example, can take advantage of the system's innate ability to support multiple display cards and monitors. They can use the display connected to one display card exclusively for graphics, while the program's interface or even your speaker's notes are displayed on another monitor (which you can place within your exclusive view on a table or podium). It's not so direct with the PC; Microsoft Windows, which is the base of much of the graphics software on that platform, doesn't handle multiple displays. You can, however, derive a similar benefit from using a DOS presentation sequencing program (like Panorama from Graphics Software Labs) combined with a dedicated presentation display card such as the Targa+ or ATVista from Truevision. On the Amiga, there is a handful of specialized graphics cards you can use to build a two-monitor system, but no prevailing standard. You should consult a knowledgeable dealer who can help you match presentation software with a supported high-color display card.

The absolute pinnacle of presentation quality is achieved by building a system that's meant for video production. The upcoming chapter on that topic will introduce you to some components and configurations you can use when the quality of the graphics is so important that you can swing the fatter budget.

There is a device, a specialized high-speed computer system, that incorporates several of the advantages I've discussed above. It's small (as small as or smaller than most notebook computers), rugged, fitted with international power and video connections, and built for the traveling presenter. It's called the VideoShow HQ, and it's made by General Parametrics. You pay extra for the system's travel savvy and tuned performance, but it's worth it to those who have grown accustomed to lugging heavy, bulky desktop systems around because they want the speed. The VideoShow weighs 6 to 8 pounds, and fits in a briefcase. When you get to where you're going, you can control the VideoShow from the podium with either an infrared remote or a remarkable wired remote that includes a color LCD display that lets you see your current slide or preview upcoming slides. You'll read more about the VideoShow HQ in this book because I found it an important, vitally useful product, but it can only get proper treatment in the video.

Presentation Sequencers

So let's say you create your presentation on a PC, but you wish you could show it on a Mac for its portability, an Amiga for its video capabilities, or a VideoShow HQ for its unique mix of features. Or perhaps you created your presentation elsewhere and you want to move it to a PC to take advantage of some peripheral that's best used in a PC. Or, perhaps you'd like to create and show a presentation that's a few quality steps above what you get out of an off-the-shelf presentation package.

These scenarios often involve using tools that are more specialized than the do-it-all presentation packages discussed throughout this chapter. They require splitting the process between the creation and the showing of your presentation, and you use different tools for each side.

I've talked somewhat about dedicated 2-D illustration software before, so I won't run that whole scene again. Software like GSL's RIO, Corel Draw and Adobe Illustrator weren't necessarily built for presentation graphics. Because they were built to do *more* than that (all the way up to camera-ready commercial art), they can be counted on to pull the load required by even the most exacting presenter.

With few exceptions (Corel Draw being among them), the tools that create the best graphics offer you no help with getting them to the screen in sequence. Therefore, a class of software called *presentation sequencers* has sprung up which specializes in taking graphics created elsewhere and building presentations out of them. Panorama from Graphics Software Labs (PC), MediaMaker from Macromedia (Mac), and Showmaker from Gold Disk (Amiga) are all programs whose primary purpose is presentation sequencing. They generally have in common the inability to *create* anything: the graphics, animation, video clips and digital audio most of these packages can bring together must come from elsewhere. Some packages give you limited video titling capabilities.

To the extent your system supports it, presentation sequencers can incorporate transitional effects, external videotape and digital audio and music into your presentation. The advantage of these specialized tools is that being specialized means they generally offer you more creative options than the sequencers built into commercial presentation software. Panorama, for example, will use the special features of a Truevision Targa+ or ATVista card to combine high-color graphics with smooth transitional effects. Mediamaker lets you pull together your presentation the way you might edit film, and it has powerful options for tying in external devices. And Showmaker can hook into a Video Toaster, probably the most powerful graphics card ever created (among other things—see the chapter on video production), to turn your presentation into crisp, slick-looking video suitable for recording and distribution (or even broadcast).

One of the less-known advantages of a presentation sequencer is that it allows you to create your presentation on one type of system and move it to another. The best portable presentations are those which were planned from the start to be moved to another type of system. Some things can't be moved. If, for example, you use Aldus Persuasion on the Mac and plan to move your presentation to GSL's Panorama on the PC, you need to avoid using Panorama's built-in builds and effects. In general, when you're going to move graphics somewhere else, and you don't have a matching program on the other system (Mac Persuasion or PowerPoint files are readable by the PC version of those programs), create slides that depend on none of the special features of the software you're using to create them. Do a build by duplicating a slide's contents, adding one line per slide. If you're not sure where you're going with your graphics, create standalone slides that incorporate inset graphics and charts, rather than counting on the sequencer to pop that inset up in a window on your slide.

Very often, when you make the move from one system to another, you'll need to employ some kind of conversion. Some presentation software does that for you, allowing you to save your slides in some widely implemented graphics format. GIF, a format created for the Compuserve on-line service, is probably the most portable format for 8-bit color graphics. GIF files are efficiently compressed, so they're much easier to send around. A well-recognized format for high-color (16- or 24-bit) images is TGA, named for Truevision's high-color Targa board. Unfortunately, there are many variations of this file format, and not every application that reads TGA files understands all those variations. While compression is available with some software, I've had trouble reading compressed TGA files across systems.

If your presentation creation and sequencing software simply can't meet in the middle with a common graphics file format, you will probably have to resort to a conversion program. The PC has several, with Image Alchemy, ImagePrep and PhotoStyler among them. The Mac has Adobe Photoshop, and the Amiga has Art Department Professional. At the very least, these programs will read in a graphics file in one format and churn it out in another. Most of them will also do color depth conversions, useful if you want to show your 24-bit files on a system that can only display 8-bit color. The color depth conversion built into the better graphics utilities generally produces more impressive results than the convertors built into presentation software. You can also use most tools in this class to effect other commonly needed changes as well, including gamma (brightness) and color correction.

How Will You Show It?

Even after you get your presentation together, there's still plenty to worry about. The coming chapters will cover the aspects of audio, animation and video that might be part of your presentation, but let's assume for now that you have just a basic batch of slides that you plan to show with a computer. Some computers are more suited to travel than others, and before you leave, you need to think about how you're going to show what you've created at your destination. Here's a checklist of things you might consider before heading out for a presentation road trip:

> ***Use a system that travels well.*** The best choice for a presentation that primarily uses graphics is a portable computer. If you purchase a system especially for the purpose, don't get too attached to the idea of running the thing on batteries. A battery-operated laptop or notebook computer gives you the ability to modify your presentation on the plane or at a rest stop, but other than that, you'll generally have power available wherever you're going to be. The advantage of PC systems that plug into the wall is that they often have at least one expansion slot. The best PC systems I've found for presentations are so-called "lunchboxes," compact, fully functional PCs that fold up to be roughly the size of their namesake. The newest of these systems employ color LCD displays, and in a small room, one of these with a sound board installed in it is all you need to show your stuff. Macintosh Powerbook systems are just about perfect for the job, save that (at this writing) there are none with color displays. If you add an external monitor, you're all set, but a monitor is often the heaviest, most damage-prone part of a system to transport. There are no specially portable Amigas, but newer ones do have built-in composite color video output and RF modulators. The latter ensures that no matter what kind of TV you find, even if it's an inexpensive consumer model with no A/V inputs, you can hook your computer into it. Desktop Amigas are lightweight enough to be easily portable.

Of all systems, the VideoShow HQ is probably the most reliably portable. It's tiny, lightweight, and rugged enough to survive baggage handlers without flinching or failing.

Consider the display at the destination. If you can, call ahead to find out what kind of display you'll be using to show your presentation. If it's a trade show, the video display hardware will probably be supplied by an A/V contractor. The quality of these contractors ranges from great to incompetent, so it's a good idea to arm your system with both RGB and composite video outputs. For the Mac, I recommend travelling with a video output convertor box (like the WTI VideoMax) or a video card with composite video output. The Truevision NuVista+ is a particularly good choice because this one gives you high-color graphics with RGB, composite and S-Video output; *that's* what I mean by covering all your bases. On the PC, you might do well to use a Truevision ATVista or Targa+, both of which offer you the same range of output types as the NuVista+. A less-expensive option is to use a regular or high-color VGA card with an external scan convertor (like the Hyperconvertor from PC Video Conversion). There are also several VGA cards with integrated video output, but you should be concerned with output quality. Too many inexpensive VGAs with composite outputs put out a very poor-quality signal. Colors bleed, text is fuzzy, and the image on the screen doesn't help your image any. I prefer external scan convertors, but if you choose a composite output-capable VGA, make sure you have a chance to see it in action before you buy it. Newer Amigas, as I mentioned above, have built-in composite output. All Amiga systems can be fitted with a composite video output using an inexpensive cable available through Amiga dealers and mail-order houses. Inexpensive Amigas like the 1200 are particularly attractive for traveling presentations; they are small, lightweight, fast enough for advanced presentations, and cheap enough to be replaceable if something goes wrong. The VideoShow HQ, with an optional expansion board, will also connect to just about any kind of monitor.

If you create your presentation on a 640 × 480 monitor, keep in mind that unless you're showing it on the same monitor, your graphics could run off the sides of the screen. This condition is extremely common when a PC or Mac presentation is shown through a television set or a projection TV with a composite or S-Video input. When you create your slides, it's a good idea to leave a margin (10% is usually adequate) around the edges. Some presentation software does this for you, keeping you within a *safe area* that includes these margins. It might look better to you if the slide completely fills your screen, but you can count on a composite/S-Video monitor having a completely different size. Moreover, even if you use a data projector (with RGB inputs that project a 640 × 480 image), leaving margins will allow for the maladjustment of image size that frequently plagues presenters. The margins need only be applied to your foreground material, so if you do show on a regular 640 × 480 monitor, the background can fill the screen. There's no problem with using a background that runs off the sides of the presentation screen.

If composite or S-video output of your presentation is likely, you should also worry a bit about colors. Again, the screen you sit in front of to create your presentation doesn't look a bit like what you'll get from an A/V monitor, TV set, or projector. When you use NTSC or PAL video output, the two extreme ends of the brightness spectrum must be avoided. Driving any color to its full brightness may cause the display to bend or otherwise behave erratically. If you choose a color that's too dark, you run the risk of having it vanish completely when you give your presentation. You have some control over brightness (the NuVista+ on the Mac, for example, has a Desk Accessory that lets you change brightness of the board's output) at the presentation site, but keeping brightness levels within a slightly narrower range than the hardware is capable of is wise. In a color system that lets you create colors by setting red, blue, and green values on a range of 0 to 255, you might limit yourself to using values between 50 and 220. That's worked for me, but of course, a blue value of 220 isn't a predictable standard that's the same shade on every system or graphics card. It's always best to test the limits of your system in advance: if you think you'll be showing your presentation on a composite or S-Video monitor, preview it there and watch for color problems. Some presentation and 2-D graphics software will adjust your colors automatically to "NTSC legal" values, meaning that the brightness levels are adjusted to fit an acceptable range for composite or S-Video output. The standard color palettes shipped with popular packages are usually made up of legal colors, but don't count on that. Preview it first.

One popular device for presenting to small groups is the LCD projection panel. These panels sit atop overhead projectors, and light shines through the same crystals used to build laptop/notebook computer displays. These are prone to all kinds of problems like overheating, but they're easy to carry and most destinations can be counted on to have an overhead projector. Be warned, though, that the trend toward *reflective* projectors is a bane for users of LCD panels. Reflective overhead projectors beam the light down onto a mirrored surface, and the reflected light is then sent through the lenses to the screen. This works fine for flat, high-contrast plastic overheads, but LCD panels can't deal with it. To use those, you still need the clunky old fan-cooled projectors that bring the light up from underneath the surface on which you place your material. If you know you're using an LCD panel, it's important to build higher contrast into your slides. Subtle effects like gradated backgrounds are often lost, and just about the only thing you can count on doing reliably are very dark characters on a very light background. Dark crystals, which appear when you use dark colors, absorb the light from the projector and speed overheating. If you use dark backgrounds through too much of your presentation, your panel may shut itself down, or the crystals will start to fade from the heat. Using light backgrounds also helps work around the frequent problem of insufficient brightness, caused when the projector used isn't strong enough, or when it's pulled back too far from the screen to accomodate a larger audience. I'm not a huge fan of projector panels except for the smallest of audiences, especially when data and video projectors serve the same purpose and are getting so cheap and lightweight.

Prepare the system for travel. Assuming that *something* will go wrong is still a wise stance, even though technology has become more reliable. Your system will get knocked around no matter how you travel. You can minimize the potential for damage by bringing essential components of the system with you as carry-on baggage. If the system is larger than airline's carry-on limit, you can give it a slightly improved chance of survival by removing expansion cards and the system's hard drive. The cards can easily be unseated from their sockets during the ride. While there's some potential for the cards to rattle around inside the case and do damage to themselves or the rest of the system, removing them is actually a trick to ensure that you'll open the system and reinsert the cards when you get it to its destination. If you leave the cards in, at least open the system's case and reseat the cards before you turn it on.

Even though hard drives have gotten tougher over the years, with auto-parking heads and mechanisms that dampen the effects of shock, they are far from impervious. Having seen packages fall off the conveyor and get purposely thrown from the plane to the ground, I know that there are plenty of dangers awaiting a hard drive in travel. Removing the drive not only protects a vital system component, but also makes you more independent: if you have the expansion cards and hard drive separate, and the system gets damaged beyond usability, you can borrow or rent a system of the same type and have it ready to run in minutes.

Hard drives aren't always easy to remove from systems, and it's not an exercise you should attempt if you're at all nervous about it. You can also solve the hard drive problem by storing your presentation on removable media, like a Bernoulli or Syquest cartridge, or a high-capacity "floptical" drive. Macs and SCSI-equipped Amigas readily support external drives, and some desktop PCs and laptops have their hard disks mounted into slide-out cartridges that are easily removed for travel and security. No matter what medium you choose, always have your presentation, and the program you plan to use to show it, on floppies or tape. Also carry all the operating system software you need to rebuild a system from scratch, including a disk diagnostic and repair tool. Such tools are standard with the Mac and Amiga. Something like the Norton Utilities is useful for PC systems.

If you must carry a monitor with you, be aware that it is probably more sensitive to damage than any other component. It only takes one good jolt to render a monitor useless, so pack it carefully. Use the original box, and, if you can, double-box it by placing the monitor, in its box, inside a larger box stuffed with spongy material (like packing peanuts or bubble-wrap). The double box will protect the monitor from the common condition of external perforation (from a kick or a collision with another package in the cargo hold). It will also give the monitor a better chance of surviving a fall or a sharp impact.

Travel guidelines for other kinds of equipment, including video decks, will follow in coming chapters.

4

Digital Audio and MIDI Music

Audio is a vital component of almost all types of multimedia work. This chapter focuses on the basics of integrating digital audio and electronic music into presentations of all kinds.

If multimedia makes computers more human, then audio is a vital part of the process of "humanizing" computers. If you can teach a computer to speak or make music, you are removing from it some of the impersonal quality that detracts from computers' usefulness as presenters of information. While I'd never suggest that a computer that can make sound is a viable replacement for a person in a business negotiation, classroom, or other setting, advances in technology have made it possible to expand the computer's role as a communicator.

Audio is a deep topic. Innumerable books have been written on the subject of audio production, with entire multi-hundred page tomes dedicated to specialized subjects like miking (the selection, placement, and usage of microphones) and cables. This book isn't the place for that kind of nuts-and-bolts detail, although I'll readily admit that there are times when I turn to books like these for my own projects. Instead, this chapter will give its attention to helping you understand the state of the accessible art in computer-based audio, with an eye toward its practical use in the kinds of multimedia works highlighted in this book.

If the phrase, "state of the *accessible* art" above struck you as odd, here's my explanation: Audio, like other highly evolved areas of multimedia technology, covers a broad spectrum of price, quality, ease of use, and intended application. A portable tape recorder costs as little as $25 and can be operated by anyone, while a fully decked-out digital recording studio can cost millions to construct and requires years of experience to use properly. Between those extremes lies a mind-numbing collection of thousands of different audio-related products. I could wallow around aimlessly in that sea, but fortunately, the systems I've used to pull this book together made it easier to decide which audio products and techniques to include here.

This chapter doesn't contain everything you need to know about audio, even if you only apply what's contained here to the coming chapters of this book. The audio production that's part of *video* production, for example, is a category unto itself and can't reasonably be discussed in detail until the upcoming chapter on video. So this chapter is about "presentation audio," which assumes the computer will be used not only to capture and shape the audio but to present it as well.

This chapter covers digital, passed-through and CD audio; an upcoming chapter is devoted to MIDI. A well-rounded multimedia work usually includes some combination of these. The coming chapters on interactive multimedia and video production discuss the combined use of these media.

Audio Hardware

With most machines, before you can record and play your first second of digital audio, you'll need to invest in some additional hardware. I described some of the requirements in Chapter 1, but I'll do a little recapping here along with some added detail.

The hardware you need to make your system deal with audio depends somewhat on the kind of work you plan to do. As I mentioned in Chapter 1, audio quality is determined partly by the combination of two factors: sampling rate and resolution. These two things are easy to shop for when you're buying hardware. Vendors of digital audio gear post at least the maximum rate and resolution of their hardware in their promotional literature and on package exteriors. Be aware that some hardware offers different capabilities on the record and playback side. Some PC audio boards, for example, will play back at 44.1 KHz in 16-bit stereo but can only record in mono.

There are other points to consider when shopping for computer audio hardware, and these are not always as easy to manage as rate and resolution. The PC in particular offers some unique challenges because it has more audio board choices than the Mac and Amiga combined. The packaging of audio differs from system to system, so I'll discuss each platform in turn below. As is true with the rest of this book, my comments below are based on products available at the time I wrote this book. I know, for instance, that Commodore has grand plans to upgrade the Amiga's audio capabilities, and for all I know, their new systems are available as you read this. I can only write about what I've seen, and that necessarily dates this material. Where I can, I have added a few words about what I see as the future of a platform's audio technology.

Macintosh

Of the three system types discussed in this book, only newer Macintosh systems are equipped to record audio. Systems so equipped have only microphone inputs. The systems also include low-grade microphones, showing Apple's intended use of the built-in audio as a "note taker," useful for such tasks as attaching a spoken comment to a piece of electronic mail. That's a use of audio that falls below the coverage floor of this book. The Mac's microphone input isn't limited to use with the included microphone. You can, of course, buy yourself a better microphone and plug it directly into the jack. More common, however, is the use of line-level input from devices like CD players, audio tape recorders, and VCRs. For this, you'll need a device that turns a line-level signal into a mike-level one. A line-level signal has a higher voltage and will overload a device that expects a mike-level input. There's little potential for damage (unless you plug an amplified audio source, such as headphone or speaker outputs, into a mike input), but a line-level device plugged into a mike-level input yields heavily distorted results. You might solve the problem with an *attenuator*. This is an unpowered (i.e., it requires no power supply of its own) device, usually an adaptor plug/socket combination or a cable, that trims a line output to a signal level acceptable to a microphone input.

Another approach to audio on a Macintosh is to use an external sound digitizer module. The only one I've used is the MacRecorder, currently sold by MacroMedia. This is a little plastic brick, slightly larger than a cigarette pack, with three inputs: a line jack, a microphone jack, and a built-in microphone. There is a thumbwheel on the side that controls input volume. It connects to your Mac through either its serial or printer port. The MacRecorder records in mono only, in 8 bits at a rate of 22 KHz. This is consistent with the audio playback capabilities of all Macintosh systems; most of the machines in service today can be counted on to play audio files recorded at this rate and resolution. If you need stereo, you can hook up a pair of MacRecorders and use them simultaneously, but the cost of the device makes this a poor solution. Besides, music is the material most likely to benefit from being heard in stereo, and at 22 KHz and 8 bits, music doesn't sound too hot. Stereo "not too hot" is no improvement and, in my view, not worth the investment in a pair of MacRecorders. As far as it goes, the MacRecorder is a useful device. The cable to the system is nice and long, so you can place the box where it's most convenient for you, or even hold it in your hand (if you're using the built-in microphone).

There is no gentle step up from the MacRecorder—you must leap directly from there to a high-end sound card like Digidesign's Audiomedia II. This is a NuBus board, so you'll only be able to use it if you have a Mac with NuBus slots. At over $1000 (the MacRecorder is a bit over $300 at this writing), the Audiomedia II is loaded with features aimed at the home music studio or demanding digital audio producer. It is serious overkill for the average business presentation, but is built for *multitracking* (see the section on this below). In that role, the board's price seems a little less unreasonable. The AudioMedia II offers four independent channels of 16-bit, 44.1 KHz digital audio and includes an audio digitizing/playback software package. To exploit the board more fully, you'll need the optional Deck software. As its name suggests, Deck simulates the behavior of a multi-track tape recorder. Again, there's more detail on multitracking below. While the Audiomedia II can create 8-bit, 22 KHz files playable on unenhanced Macs, most uses for the board will require you to have an Audiomedia II in your playback system as well.

Future Macs will certainly include at least the ability to play back 44.1 KHz audio. The question that remains unanswered as I write this is whether Apple will stratify its systems' audio capabilities, endowing high-end systems with good audio, while leaving lesser machines with the standard 22 KHz audio. Whatever the future, with the huge installed base of Macs that are limited to 22 KHz playback, you should stick with that quality if you plan to distribute your work to other Mac users. If that's not a concern for you, then I suggest you check the specifications on late-model Mac systems. Apple may well have gotten around to upgrading its audio by now.

Amiga

The Amiga's built-in audio capability is reasonably well-suited to multimedia production: four independent (multitrack) channels of audio playback with stereo output, at 8 bits and with rates of up to 56 KHz. At this time, there is no standard recording capability, but the Amiga's high-speed parallel port makes good-quality audio digitizers easy to come by. A stereo model, like the Perfect Sound from SunRize Industries, costs less than $100. A more advanced unit like the Aegis SoundMagic from Oxxi (which includes mike and line inputs and an overload indicator) is still very reasonable at under $200.

Audio files created with devices like the Perfect Sound or the SoundMagic can be played back on any Amiga; no additional hardware is required. If you want better than 8-bit sound quality, you'll have to spring for an internal audio card. As with the Mac, Amiga audio cards can only be installed in Amigas built with expansion slots; low-end models cannot accommodate cards directly, but there are vendors that offer odd little external chassis that let you use Amiga cards with non-expandable Amigas. That's rarely a good solution, since the expandable Amigas are also the ones with the best overall performance.

Of the enhanced-quality audio boards available for the Amiga, I've used SunRize Industries' AD1012 and AD516. These are both multitrack record/playback boards offering eight independent tracks of digital audio. The AD1012, at under $600, records and plays at up to 44.1 KHz at 12 bits, while the AD516 (under $1500) offers full 16-bit sound. Both of these boards come with Sunrize's Studio 16 software, which, by itself, is worth the price. You'll read more about the AD516 in the chapter on video production, and you can see and hear it and Studio 16 in action on the videotape. Both of these products will let you "mix down" high-quality, multitrack audio to Amiga-standard audio files that are playable on unenhanced Amigas. These cards don't replace the Amiga's built-in audio, and they can only be used with the included Studio 16 software or applications that include SunRize audio board control (like Blue Ribbon Soundworks' Bars & Pipes Professional, discussed in the chapters on MIDI and video production).

One difficulty unique to built-in Amiga audio is the high-pass filter. The Amiga's audio output has its high frequencies clamped by an electronic filter, presumably as a means of noise reduction. There are various solutions to this, including external hardware that amplifies the high frequencies to add them back and public-domain software that switches out the high-pass filter. Files played back with the filter in place can sound muddy. If you plan to use the Amiga's built-in audio playback, ask a dealer about that public-domain software switch.

Commodore has announced its intention to build a digital signal processor (DSP) into future Amiga systems. What that means depends on how Commodore implements the DSP. The SunRize AD516, for example, uses a DSP to deliver 8 channels of CD-quality audio, and Commodore could do the same thing. It's more likely, however, that the DSP will provide a more incremental improvement over current Amigas' standard audio. I expect it will offer an overall improvement in sound quality, perhaps accompanied by support for 12- or 16-bit standard audio playback. As with the Mac, I highly recommend you check with Commodore or an Amiga dealer to find out what the audio capabilities of the newest Amigas are.

PC

The PC was the last to get standardized digital audio capability, but there are now a huge number of audio boards for PC systems and an increasing contingent of systems with built-in audio. The standardization was imposed by the Multimedia PC (MPC) specification, a standard more or less created by Microsoft. To be an MPC-compatible system, a PC must include a CD-ROM drive and controller and a digital audio board capable of playing and recording at least 22 KHz, 8-bit audio. The standard extends to software, so unlike the Mac and Amiga, you can mix and match hardware and software with relative impunity.

The MPC standard does not require multitrack audio, so most PC audio cards will do stereo record and playback, but the left and right channels cannot be used independently. You can install two (or possibly more) digital audio boards in a PC to provide multiple audio channels, but to date, no digital audio software can use a pair of boards with full multitrack capability.

A feature unique to PC audio cards is that almost all of them have some type of passed-through audio support. The Pro Audio Spectrum 16 from MediaVision, for example, has mike and line inputs as well as an internal connection to a CD-ROM drive's audio outputs. When you're not recording, you can use a software audio mixer to pass any or all of the signals on these three inputs through to your speakers (or headphones). Each input's volume is independently controlled, and the mixer also lets you set the playback volume for the digital audio and on-board MIDI synthesizer. This makes the PC particularly well suited to interactive multimedia applications that use external audio sources (like laserdiscs and VCRs).

The best quality offered by mainstream MPC-compatible audio cards from vendors like MediaVision (Pro Audio Spectrum series) and Creative Labs (Sound Blaster Series) is 16 bits, in stereo, at 44.1 KHz. Microsoft has its own high-quality audio card, the Windows Sound System.

While Mac and Amiga audio hardware offers some clear "you get what you pay for" choices, those lines are not as well defined for PC cards. The broadest class of cards, the basic capabilities of which include 16-bit, 44.1 KHz, stereo audio, mike and line inputs, and some sort of on-board music synthesizer, includes several choices under $500. Some of these cards (like the Pro Audio Spectrum 16 and the Sound Blaster Pro 16 ASP) include CD-ROM controller circuitry on-board, making it possible to add CD-ROM to your system with a raw drive that costs a little more than a floppy drive. Virtually all of these boards also include the aforementioned passed-through audio capability.

There is no well-defined step up from the broad assortment of MPC-compatible audio cards. There are a few multitrack boards for the PC, with prices ranging from around $1300 to over $10,000. IBM has one of the few multitrack (two-track) audio cards in the mainstream, the M-Audio Capture and Playback Adapter.

A growing trend among PC vendors is to build audio capability into systems, giving them out-of-the-box MPC compatibility. Most vendors do this by buying in bulk the same "multimedia upgrade kits" offered by vendors like MediaVision and Creative Labs, kits that include the sound card, a CD-ROM drive, and a worthwhile assortment of standard software. You can buy these kits, too, not only for your existing systems, but also to save the hidden costs that some vendors impose for the convenience of preinstalling the kits in new systems. Prices of complete upgrade kits are falling so rapidly (prices nearly halved themselves in only two years) that I dare not be more specific about the cost of upgrade kits than "well under $1000."

With the advent of inexpensive DSPs, both audio board and system vendors are making plans to take advantage of DSPs to bring more audio power to their products. At this writing, Microsoft's Windows Sound System, Creative Labs' Sound Blaster Pro 16 ASP, and Turtle Beach's Multisound MPC-compatible audio cards all use a DSP as the central means of getting audio in and out of the computer. PC vendors, most notably IBM, have already announced intentions to place DSPs directly on the motherboards of future systems. In a few years, there won't be any market for any but the highest-end sound cards. I expect motherboard audio will be as commonplace as motherboard disk and display controllers have become.

Technology Snapshots

PC, Mac, and Amiga systems have in common a range of choices in the arena of digital audio. What you get is partly a function of how much you spend, and if you're building an audio system for your computer, it helps to consider just how much technology you need.

Rate and Resolution

For now, settling for reduced audio quality is a good way to save money. That won't always be true—once the switch to DSPs is complete, all audio hardware will probably support CD-quality or close to it. Until then, you can expect it to remain true that 8- and 12-bit and audio cards can be had for less than their 16-bit counterparts. What makes that the case is the cost of the electronics. It's far cheaper to build an 8-bit audio card, because 8-bit components have been around for a long time and they needn't be as fast as 16-bit components (which have twice as much data to move around). Similarly, the cheapest audio cards for the PC are those that top out at the 22 KHz sampling rate. Again, fast components cost more money than slow ones.

How much audio quality do you need? That depends. The higher the quality, the more the hardware will cost you. Also, the better the audio, the more disk space it will occupy. For these reasons, the best choice for audio hardware is the device that delivers the minimum acceptable quality at a competitive price. With that in mind, here are some common rate/resolution combinations and a few words about what they are and are not suited to. There is a companion section in the videotape that lets you audition each of these combinations for yourself.

8–11KHz, 8 bits: This is an acceptable range for a person's speaking (not singing) voice. This is a very space-efficient rate range, in which 60 seconds of audio occupies only 480–660 K bytes on disk, less if data compression is applied. The drawback of audio recorded in this range is that it sometimes does not play well through an amplified source. You might not, for example, want to use an 11 KHz audio narration with a business presentation shown before a sizeable audience. It might work well in concert with some other audio source, such as a "voice-over" above a piece of music or a video soundtrack from a tape or laserdisc. A last consideration is that some PC sound cards deliver sound in this range very poorly, with an unacceptable level of noise (often heard as a high-frequency "putt-putt" sound). Listen to your audio through headphones before you decide to use it.

22 KHz, 8 bits: This is, by far, the most widely used digital audio quality. It incurs moderate disk usage, with a 60-second file occupying 1320K (twice that for stereo). With most audio products, 22 KHz is more than enough to capture very clear human speaking voice. It is also the minimum acceptable rate for music. Because the 22 KHz sample rate excludes sounds above 11 KHz, high-frequency instruments like hi-hats and brushes will sound muffled. There are some kinds of music that work better at 22 KHz than others. Rock can sound pretty good; classical doesn't. But don't take my word for that—you'll always want to preview your audio through headphones before you decide it's good enough for public consumption. Because this is the "universal" rate and resolution, it's a good target if you plan to distribute your audio for multiple types of systems. One caveat: some PC audio cards play 22 KHz, 8-bit files more cleanly than others. A loud hiss is the most common complaint.

22 KHz, 16 bits: With 16-bit technology becoming more affordable, this combination is probably the best compromise between disk space and audio quality. Sixty seconds of audio at this quality will cost you 2640K of disk space. You might wonder why, if the 22 KHz, 8-bit quality is unacceptable for some kinds of music, the 16-bit setting would yield any improvement. The difference is the greater dynamic range offered by 16-bit sound. Remember Chapter 1's discussion of rate and resolution, and the difference between 8-bit (256 possible values per sample) and 16-bit (65,536 possible values) resolutions? You use *twice* the disk space, but making the move to 16 bits yields audio that has *256 times* the range of dynamic expression. Noise is reduced to a whisper, if not eliminated completely. There's probably more precise language I can use to describe the difference in sound quality, but I'll sum it up thus: I haven't yet found a piece of music that couldn't be reasonably represented at this rate and resolution. Again, the rate is a limiting factor, but if you boost your highs a little with an equalizer (some PC cards have bass/treble controls in software), the sound is very pleasing. I think this is a good choice for presentation work and is even passable for low-end video.

44.1 KHz, 8 or 16 bits: This is where most computer audio equipment tops out. The advantage of using 16 bits is, as I discussed in the preceding paragraph, the reduction or elimination of noise. A little quick math will tell you that it takes just as much disk space to record 22 KHz, 16-bit audio as it does to record 44.1 KHz, 8-bit audio. For my uses, I'd opt for the 22 KHz, 16-bit sound for the reasons I've described. But for videotape work or any application where the audio is to be re-recorded on some other medium, 44.1 KHz, 16-bit audio is the best way to go. This is so-called CD-quality, so named because it matches the sampling rate of CD audio devices. But there's more to matching the quality of a compact disc than matching its sampling rate. With a well-made audio card, this is the "no compromises" setting, but it will also call out the flaws in a poorly made device. If the board's output is inherently noisy, you'll be disappointed. When you're giving up five megabytes per minute of audio (*ten* for stereo), you have the right to expect exceptional quality. Quality problems are most evident on badly made PC cards; the Mac and Amiga audio cards I've used that support this rate and resolution have supported it well. On the PC, the closest to a sure thing I've used for CD-quality audio is the Turtle Beach Multisound. There are bound to be others; make sure you get a chance to audition your audio card before you buy it. Turtle Beach, at least at the time of this writing, offered inexpensive CD test drives which let you listen to the Multisound's quality on your home stereo. You might also browbeat a well-stocked dealer into setting up a couple of comparison systems for you—bring a pair of headphones you trust.

Multitracking

All professional audio recording for music CDs, film and television is done on multitrack equipment. What sets this gear apart from your home cassette recorder, aside from quality and cost, is that each track can be independently recorded or re-recorded, and each track can be independently controlled on playback. On your home stereo, and with almost all stereo digital audio hardware for PCs and Macs, you can record and play in stereo, but you can't separate the left and right channels and control them independently.

Take this example: Let's say you were putting together an interactive multimedia program, and you wanted it to have a constantly running musical background, provided by digitized audio. That's easy enough, but let's say that you also wanted to be able to play voice narration or sound effects in sync with the user's actions. You might want the computer to make a "click" sound when the user presses a button, for example. On an MPC-compatible PC sound card, the only way to do that is to install a *second* card and write some special software that directs the second card to play the sound effects and narration.

The easier solution is to use a system that supports multitracking directly. The best system for this is the Amiga, which has four independent channels of digital audio standard in every system, large and small. Its multitracking is done by *dynamic allocation*. The four audio channels are managed by the operating system and are allocated to programs as they are needed. For the example I used above, the program would ask the Amiga for two audio channels for the stereo music soundtrack. The operating system would hand out those two channels, leaving two free. When the program hit a point where it wanted to use narration, it would ask the Amiga for an audio channel, and it would instantly get the next free one. If music *and* narration were already playing, taking up three channels, you'd still have room for sound effects on top of that. Once an audio clip has finished playing, the audio channel or channels it used are freed and made available for requests.

Another unique aspect of the Amiga's audio hardware is that it can be shared by multiple applications. On the Mac or PC, the first program that asks for the audio device "owns" it until it exits or explicitly returns the device to the system's control. On the Amiga, any unused audio channel is available to any application that wants it. So you can have several programs running at once, all doing their own audio and sharing the same basic hardware. That may seem like an absurd idea, but there are times when it comes in quite handy, as with video production and interactive multimedia.

The unique advantages offered by the Amiga's audio architecture are amplified by the SunRize Industries AD516. This board offers eight dynamically allocated audio channels, each with 16-bit resolution and supporting sampling rates of up to 44.1 KHz. It is the Amiga's innate multitracking capability and its real-time operating system, that lead me to recommend it most highly for audio work.

If you're using a PC, chances are you'll have to settle for doing without multitracking. The only board I know of that does it is IBM's M/Audio Capture and Playback Adapter. This is a two-track board that works best with IBM's own OS/2 operating system and IBM's interactive multimedia development tools (like the Audio/Video Control, or AVC).

Digital Signal Processors

A DSP isn't just an audio chip. It is a computer-on-a-chip, a microprocessor, that specializes in the fast manipulation of digitized signal data. DSPs are used not only for audio, but also for digital video and imaging applications. One strength of a DSP is that it can perform complex operations on high-volume streams of digital data. The Microsoft Windows Sound System card uses its DSP for on-the-fly data compression and decompression. The compression ratio offered by the card is 4:1—well worth the effort—and the DSP lets you do the compression processing on data as it comes into the system, without incurring unreasonable system overhead. Microsoft also included limited speech recognition capability in the Windows Sound System card; a standard application lets you navigate through the Windows environment by speaking commands into a microphone.

Microsoft isn't the only company using DSPs, although they were one of the first to the general PC market with a product that made its DSP do something more than just pass audio back and forth. As previously mentioned, IBM and Commodore have both announced their intention to build some kind of DSP-based audio onto their system motherboards. Some board manufacturers are offering DSP-based expansion cards that combine fax, modem and telephone voice mail on a single low-cost card. The SunRize AD516 uses one DSP to provide eight channels of CD-quality audio. That all of these things can be done in software, with a single chip, is some indication of the incredible power of DSPs. But the real potential of DSPs won't be seen for a couple of years or so. Only after the market is crowded with installed DSP-equipped systems, and some standards are devised for taking advantage of their capabilities, will the most impressive software start to appear. DSPs are the future of digital audio.

CD Audio

When you connect a CD-ROM drive to your computer, you get more than a

600MB, read-only storage device. You also get a computer-controlled CD audio player. You can drop an ordinary compact disc into a caddy, insert it into your CD-ROM drive, and with the right software, you can use the computer to select and play parts of your audio CD. The ability to pop up a little software remote control in a window and play your discs is only a convenience: it's silly to turn a multi-thousand dollar computer into a $169 CD player. The real value of a computer-controllable CD player is that you can use it to provide exceptional quality background music for your multimedia work with no disk space or system performance overhead. With MPC-compatible audio cards, you can often run a cable between the card and the back of an internally installed CD-ROM drive. The audio mixer software that comes with the board has a slider dedicated to the volume of the CD audio port.

That you can use CD audio as part of your multimedia presentation doesn't mean you should. A great many articles have been written on the dangers of copyright infringement, and I see no need to launch into great detail on the subject here. Suffice it to say that in the U.S., and in many other countries as well, it is illegal to use a piece of pre-recorded music in a public performance without the permission of the copyright holder. That permission invariably costs money and takes time to secure. Because I sympathize with musicians and songwriters whose works are stolen this way, I'd like to say the jails are filled with presenters who snuck copyrighted material into their presentations. That's not true, but neither is it true that nobody gets caught. Record companies will pursue cases of copyright infringement, so why mess with it? There are companies, like Fresh Music and Killer Tracks, that sell audio compact discs especially for those of us who use background music in our presentations. The discs usually come with limited-use licenses, allowing you to use the music freely for as many computer-based presentations as you like. If you want to re-record the music, as with a video production, you'll probably have to pay extra, but a few companies offer so-called buy out discs. A buy-out disc can be used for anything, even commercial broadcast, without any additional fees beyond the purchase price of the disc.

This kind of canned music is enormously useful, especially for PC-based presentations where it's so easy to control the playback of a CD audio disc from inside a presentation program. These production music discs usually give you an hour or so of music, split into segments timed to last some multiple of 15 seconds long: 30, 60, and 120 second are common, and some discs will give you multiple lengths of the same piece of music. This is meant to be an aid to those who use the music for radio or television commercials (which must be precisely timed), but it's also a big help for presenters. In my live presentations, I use a canned music CD to fill the room with music as the screen displays a countdown to the start of the show. The tracks of the CD I use are arranged such that I can step up the tempo with each song change, with the lead-in cut being a "stinger," a cross between a musical fanfare and an electronic sound effect that does a good job of grabbing an audience's attention.

MIDI

The Amiga and Mac have both been popular choices for professional musicians because MIDI interfaces for these systems are very cheap (less than $50), system software provides a standard means of sending and receiving MIDI data, and software is plentiful. Amiga and Mac MIDI interfaces plug directly into the systems' serial ports (or, in the case of the Mac, MIDI interfaces can also plug into the printer port, which is also serial).

The benefit of MIDI to musicians is obvious: a computer with an inexpensive MIDI interface and a sequencing package gives a keyboard musician the equivalent of a multitrack recording system. Depending on its design, software can take care of everything from recording and playback to automatic transcription of sheet music.

For nonmusicians, MIDI still plays an important role. It provides an extremely efficient means for adding background music to a presentation. On systems like the PC and Mac that don't readily support multitrack digital audio, MIDI gives you the layer you need to present music and narration as separately controlled tracks. The same kind of canned production music that's available on compact disc can also be had in MIDI format. MIDI music can be reorchestrated, time-compressed or expanded, and otherwise modified by nonmusicians to make a better fit for its intended use.

Just buying a MIDI interface for your computer isn't enough to make music. A MIDI interface is just a dressed-up serial port; you have to connect it to something to get music out of it. An MPC-compatible PC and the Amiga have the ability to play MIDI files directly. The base-level MPC system supports 11 or 22 voices of polyphony using an FM synthesizer. The FM synth is built onto the sound board, and, as I mentioned earlier, is best suited to game sound effects and the like. It's also useful for previewing music that you'll eventually play through better-sounding equipment. There are a growing number of MPC sound cards with on-board professional synthesizers from notables like E-mu, Roland and Ensoniq. Any MPC-compatible sound card using non-FM synthesis is worth a listen. The E-mu Proteus chip is probably the most widely implemented alternative synthesizer, and it delivers clean, pure, professional-sounding music. The same can be said of the Roland chip, and there will certainly be others.

The Amiga's built-in synthesizer is actually a fairly sophisticated device, but it's limited to four-voice polyphony. The Amiga uses its multitrack digital audio capability to play digitally sampled instrument sounds. Four voices won't buy you much, although great things are possible if you choose the right instruments. Most often, the Amiga's internal synthesizer serves the same purpose as an MPC system's FM synth: to preview music that will be done better later.

Most of the time, using MIDI means connecting to an external device. A quick visit to any well-stocked music store will show you that your choices are endless. If you play, virtually all serious keyboard synthesizers, electronic pianos, and even organs have at least limited MIDI capability. You can get a workable MIDI keyboard for well under $500, but the cost of something that produces truly professional results is much higher. Fortunately, there is a very active market in used keyboards (musicians who can afford it are always trading up).

A more popular choice for an external MIDI synthesizer is the so-called sound module. These come in a variety of shapes and sizes and run along the same price range as keyboard synthesizers. The best ones, like the extraordinary Roland SC-55 Sound Canvas, offer hundreds of high-quality instrument sounds, 24- or 32-voice polyphony, and clean audio output. Some of them have limited controls, opting instead to place things like volume, left/right pan, and effects (like reverb) under the control of MIDI software. Being self-contained, sound modules make a better choice for MIDI playback in a kiosk or desktop application than a bulky keyboard. Sound modules are also great for trade show displays and other applications where being compact and rugged are virtues. Top-end sound modules are often keyboardless editions of professional keyboard synths, mounted in heavy-gauge, rack-mountable cases that are built to take a beating.

Passed-Through Audio

Sound doesn't always come from inside the computer, and it's not always under the computer's direct control. Some sources, like a speaker's microphone or a cassette player, have a role in a presentation but don't work exactly like more technical media. Often, the computer plays no role at all. In a live presentation, for example, the microphone is usually run directly to the room's PA system, separate from the connection made to computer-controlled audio devices.

When you're using an external audio device (which also includes the audio output from a video device), the computer is usually limited to acting as an audio switcher or mixer. PCs seem to have an upper hand in this, with most MPC audio cards able to manage multiple external inputs. The boards have the ability to adjust the volume of each audio source, and those with good software let you build control of the on-board electronic mixer into your applications. Control of an audio mixer isn't something you find in most commercial presentation or authoring software. To get to an MPC board's audio mixer, you generally have to make a call to Windows' Media Control Interface.

Using Digital Audio

How you use digital audio depends on several factors: your system, your operating system, your digital audio hardware, and your application. Because each of these covers such a broad range of possibilities, I'm forced to limit my discussion to the basics: playing, recording, and editing.

The playing of audio comes first in that list because there's a good chance that at least some of your audio will come from somewhere else. You can speak into a microphone, but you may not have the skill to create your own music or sound effects. So a key part of using digital audio is figuring out where to find canned production audio when you need it.

The PC and Mac have well-established canned audio markets, mostly because CD-ROMs—the favored means of distributing prerecorded audio—have been readable on large numbers of these systems longer than on the Amiga. Voyetra and Prosonus are among the companies selling CD-ROM compilations of digitized production music. As with the CD audio discs I described above, the digitized music on these discs is intended for use in computer-based presentations. Some of the compilations drop the clause restricting the music's use in video and other distributed media.

Prerecorded sound effects can be obtained from a variety of sources. On the serious side, MediaSource sells a series of CD-ROMs with topical sound effects. The discs also include digitized photographs and some production music, with all of the items on the disc cross-referenced in an interactive database. If you want to make the ambient noise of an arcade part of your presentation, just type in "arcade" as a search keyword, and the database will turn up the proper file. You can then copy the file to your hard disk for use in your presentation. On the silly side, Microsoft offers collections of sound effects taken from cartoons and old movies, and another company sells digitized snippets from the Star Trek television series (old and new).

Because you'll usually copy the files to your hard disk before you use them, many vendors offer each cut on the disc in a couple of rate/resolution combinations: one for quality and one for space efficiency. You can choose, based on your intended use, which sacrifice to make.

Playing Digital Audio

Each of the systems used for this book handles the playing of audio files a little differently. The Amiga, with its standard audio capability, has an astounding number of public-domain audio utilities that can be used to add audio playback to applications that don't manage it directly. Because the Amiga is inherently a multitasking system, many programs let you issue a command from inside the program. You can, from the AmigaDOS command line, load and play a digital audio file. More common, however, is direct control of Amiga audio from inside an application. Interactive multimedia programs like AmigaVision and Scala Multimedia have built-in support for the Amiga's multi-channel audio system. Because the Amiga is a real-time system, it's possible (with the right software) to achieve very precise synchronization of audio with other events.

If you have an unusual audio device like the Sunrize AD516 installed in your Amiga, you're a bit less likely to find integral support for it in applications. In that case, you may resort to using ARexx, the Amiga's scripting language and inter-program communication system. With ARexx, two applications running on the same Amiga can send commands and messages back and forth. Most commercial

Amiga software now supports ARexx, with some of the better software letting you insert an arbitrary ARexx command as an event. You could, for example, use ARexx from inside an Amiga presentation program to take remote control of a Sunrize AD516 to add CD-quality digital audio to your presentation.

Because the Mac has supported audio for so long, the Macintosh's standard audio playback facility is supported in some form by most applications that claim to be multimedia-capable. If it's not, there are public-domain programs that make it a little easier to use audio from within applications that don't support it directly. The standard Mac audio interface is fairly primitive, as I mentioned, but it is at least equal to reproducing voice for narration. Newer Macs have better audio.

As with the Amiga, if you install an audio board in your Mac, you may have a bit of trouble getting to it from within the application you choose. You'll find that some Mac hardware vendors worry about supporting only one Mac program: Hypercard. Hypercard is an interpretive programming environment for the Mac. Some other Mac programming environments let you use Hypercard-specific software drivers (called XCMDs for external commands, and XFCNs for external functions) without requiring you to use Hypercard.

An MPC-compatible PC probably offers the most options. The structure of the Windows multimedia extensions provides a layer of hardware independence none of the other systems match. No matter what sound card you use, as long is it comes with Windows drivers (and no PC sound card vendor would be caught dead without one), you can use it with any multimedia-capable Windows application. There are always exceptions, but in this case they're easy to spot: avoid audio boards that don't have MPC-compatible Windows drivers.

Playing a digital audio file from within a packaged Windows program or one you've written yourself can be handled one of two ways. First, the program can make a direct request of the multimedia extensions to play the file. Second, the program can use OLE (Object Linking and Embedding) to place an icon representing the sound file in your document or presentation screen. Double-clicking on the icon launches the playback application (usually the included Media Player), loads the sound file and plays it. Depending on the type of application, OLE can save you the work of integrating multimedia into your presentation or program.

Assuming that your choice of system is either equipped with or expanded to include digital audio playback, the functions available to you are mostly determined by your software. The minimum you can expect is that you'll be able to play an audio file from beginning to end. That's acceptable for the simplest uses of digital audio, as when you tag a spreadsheet cell with an audio comment. But if you have something more involved in mind, you might want to consider some of these shopping list items when you're looking for software:

Can you play a portion of an audio file? Normally, you'll play your audio files in their entirety, but there may be times when you want to play only a part of a clip. Programs that allow this generally let you specify "from" and "to" parameters (sometimes referred to as "in and out points") expressed in some time notation. Partial play lets you consolidate the files associated with a multimedia presentation by combining several audio clips into one and building the in and out points for each clip into your program.

With music, you can use this capability to use one piece of digitized music differently depending on the context. Using a single piece of music, carved up into segments, provides a sense of continuity while remaining fresh—the audience is introduced to a different piecc of the song throughout the presentation.

Partial play also lets you trim unwanted material from an audio clip without editing it. In a custom-written application, you can place the setting of the in and out points in the user's hands, providing some of the benefits of editing without the trouble of building waveform editing into your program.

Can you adjust the playback volume? Not all digital audio files are recorded at the same volume level. To compensate for this, and to accommodate listeners' comfort, most systems offer some kind of central volume control. On the Mac, for example, there is a Control Panel applet (shown in Figure 4-1) that lets you adjust the volume of all digital audio playback. It's often helpful to have a separate control in the software. For one, it saves the user the inconvenience of popping up some other program to adjust the volume. It also presents an opportunity to set per-application playback levels on systems that support it, with the volume returning to the overall system setting when the application exits.

Some multimedia development tools, like AmigaVision, let you associate a playback volume with each audio clip you use as part of your presentation (see Figure 4-1a). The volume setting for that clip doesn't affect any of the other audio you use, and the setting can be changed at any time (in

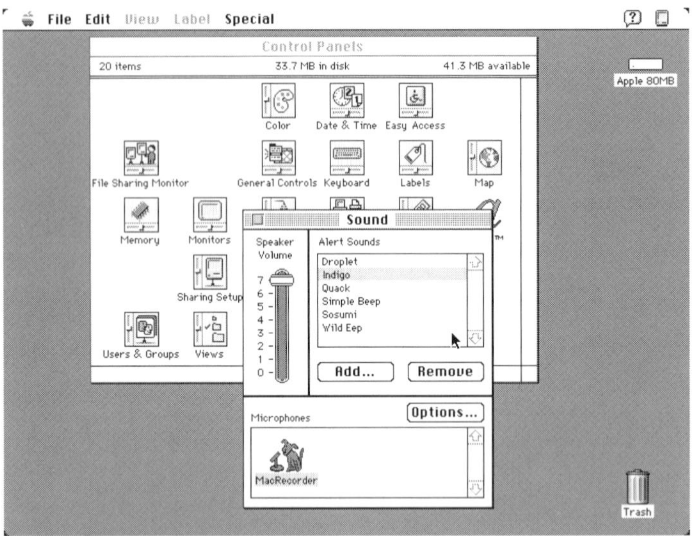

Figure 4-1: Macintosh sound Control Panel

Figure 4-1a: AmigaVision sound control

AmigaVision, all you have to do is double-click on the icon that represents the clip).

In building any interactive application that supports audio, it's wise to place a master volume control within easy reach. If you have the means, "remembering" that setting and applying it the next time your program is launched is a good step.

Adjusting volume settings under Windows from within your presentation or program requires using the Media Control Interface (MCI). At this writing, MCI control of an audio mixer is not part of the standard, but many MPC audio boards support it.

Can playback be paused or cancelled? There are plenty of situations when a user wants the computer to shut up. When the phone or some other distraction intervenes, it's nice to be able to put the audio playback on hold, and continue with it later. Similarly, you should allow the user to cancel the playback of a currently playing file and offer the option as well that the presentation should continue without sound. In a private setting or when headphones are being used, there's little call for a muting control. But whenever there are others around, there's always thc chance that the sound your show is making will cause someone grief.

Frequently, when audio is played through the service of some external application (like the Windows Media Player shown in Figure 4-2), you'll

Figure 4-2: Windows Media Player

have the option of playing it with a control panel attached. A volume control is rarely part of this panel (OS/2's media player, shown in Figure 4-3, is an exception), but tape recorder-like transport controls, including "pause" and "stop," are always present. It's not at all difficult to organize your graphics to make room for the panel, and you can generally place the panel where you want it. If you're building a custom application, you should consider giving users access to at least a limited set of audio transport controls.

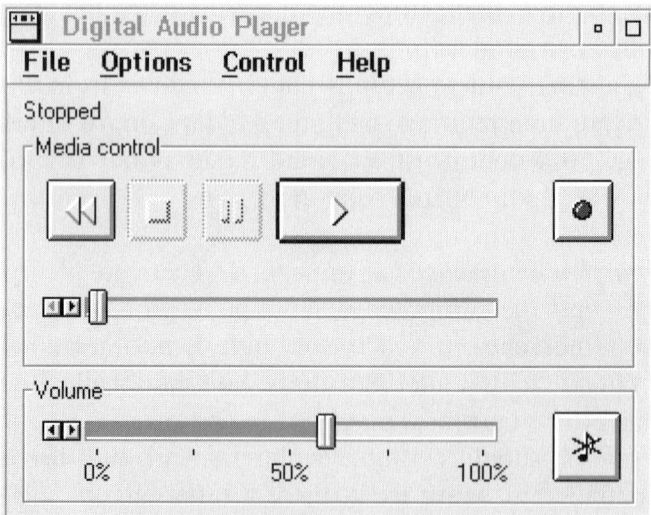

Figure 4-3: OS/2 Media Player (with volume control)

Will the software preload and cue audio clips? Most systems load as much of a digital audio file into an in-memory buffer as possible before playback begins. Depending on the system, this caching can inject a noticeable pause. Sometimes, the disk activity associated with the buffer loading can slow other things (like animation) down. At the very least, the delay between the request for playback and the actual hearing of the clip can be noticeable. If your use for audio depends on having the playback begin at a relatively precise time, or if quick response to user actions is important, you might want to preload and cue your audio clips. This process takes advantage of idle time (as when a stationary graphic is being viewed by the audience) by loading the memory buffer with the first portion of the clip and preparing everything for playback. That way, when you (or the user) request that the clip start playing, it plays instantly.

Some software, particularly presentation tools, are smart enough to look ahead to the next audio clip and do the preload and cue for you. Doing it yourself depends on the software you're using having built-in support for audio. It's sometimes impossible to split audio playback into two phases (preload/cue, followed by play) using external programs. In fact, when you use a mechanism like Windows' OLE to play audio, a playback request incurs a loading delay not only for the audio file but also for the application that plays the file. Delays of several seconds are not uncommon when you're forced to rely on external programs for audio playback. The exception is the Amiga, which lets you run the audio playback application simultaneously with the presentation software. The presentation software can manipulate (through ARexx, most likely) the audio player to eliminate loading delays.

In a custom-written application, two-phase audio playback is a tradeoff. With rare exceptions, it's the only way to ensure split-second accuracy of playback start. It's also extra programming, and depending on how your presentation script (or whatever you use) is organized, it may not be convenient to look ahead to the next audio file or to find an idle period during which preloading can take place unnoticed.

Can multiple audio files be played at once? If you've got a PC, managing the simultaneous playback of multiple audio files is a trick that usually requires multiple audio boards. The Amiga is best at it, with its set of four dynamically allocated audio channels. But the Mac, even with its single-channel playback, is increasingly being taught to manage playback of at least two overlapping audio files. There is clearly great value to this, particularly in those cases where you desire both music and narration but MIDI is inconvenient or unavailable.

Playing multiple clips at the same time makes it essential that the playback volume of each be controllable in some way. You can't have two full-volume clips playing at the same time; distorted playback is the most common result. Some software, particularly on the Mac, will automatically cut the volume of all the clips so they "add up to 100." In other words, if you play two clips at once, each will play at half of its recorded volume so that the two clips together will approach the same loudness as either one played alone. This scheme doesn't let you create foreground and background sounds. Having music and narration play at precisely the same volume obscures the speech and turns the music into a nuisance. The best software will give you independent control over the volume of each track of audio. If you can't get that control, you may have to use a sound editor to change the playback level of the clip. Such changes are permanent, however, and running long clips through an editor just to adjust their volume is tedious.

Recording Digital Audio

To record digital audio, you'll probably use a sound editor. There are some dedicated audio recorders (like the Pocket Recorder in Figure 4-4, included with MediaVision sound cards), but even these usually include at least minimal editing

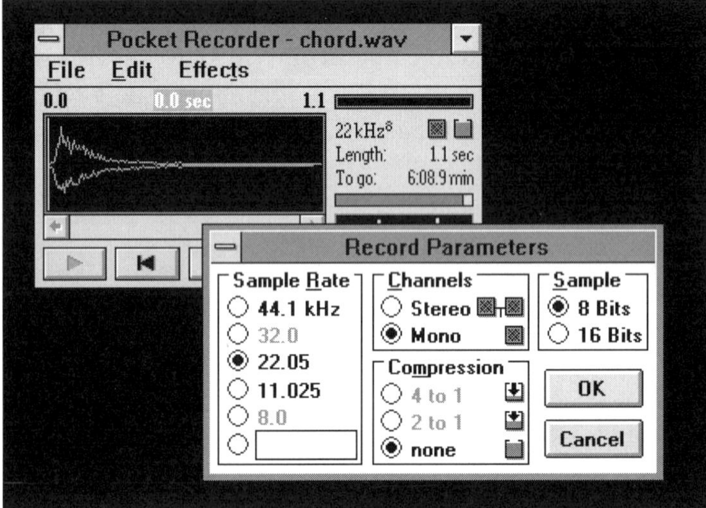

Figure 4-4: Mediavision's Pocket Recorder

capabilities.

There's nothing difficult about most digital audio recording. The sound recorder application will let you choose from among your system's available sampling rates and resolutions. The software I use defaults to what seems to be a reasonable setting: 22 KHz and 8 bits. If you have a range of settings available to you, you might consider doing some test samples at various rates and resolutions. The idea behind this is to find the minimum acceptable setting. Every step down from the maximum that you can afford to take will net you considerable savings in disk space. If time is tight and you can spare the storage, sample at the highest available rate and use a sound editor to *resample* the sound at a less demanding rate/resolution combination (more on that shortly).

The Impact of System Hardware on Audio Recording

Depending on your system and sound hardware, your sound recorder program may present options that you can't reasonably use. A slow system, a slow disk, or a disk that is heavily fragmented can keep you from using the top sampling rates available to you. The setting of 44.1 KHz and 16 bits in stereo requires the moving of some 175K bytes of data to disk per second. That's not unreasonable for most modern systems; today's disk controllers can often manage transfer rates of multiple megabytes per second. But to record digital audio at the best available rate requires that a steady stream of data be maintained. If the stream is broken, as when the disk is forced to seek to find empty space or when another program requests attention from your computer's CPU, you might not experience any problems. If your processor is fast enough and you have enough memory, the recorded audio will probably be buffered in memory to allow the disk controller time to catch up. If these things are not in your favor, however, you might lose data. When data is lost during a recording session, your application might stop, or it might not even know it dropped the data. In the latter case, you'll hear skips in the playback where the material is dropped; data loss always presents itself as a complete interruption of sound, never as a reduction in sound quality.

If your system drops data during audio capture, there are a few things you can try to make your system able to maintain a faster data rate to the hard disk. First, close all applications except for the sound recorder. This will free up memory, and it will also help ensure that another application won't step in and distract your CPU while you're recording. Another step is to adjust your system's disk cache. If you're not accustomed to tinkering with such things, it's probably best not to try. But if you feel comfortable reconfiguring your system, you should consider that disk caches, both hardware and software, can prevent you from getting the maximum audio capture rate. Understanding the problem requires understanding how a cache works: when a disk cache is running, data written to the disk by a program doesn't actually go straight to the disk. Instead, it gets held in a memory buffer. That buffer is "flushed" to the disk either when it fills or when a predetermined amount of time has passed. The benefit of caches is that they make most disk I/O asynchronous; that is, the program doesn't have to wait until the disk controller is finished writing the data to the disk. Data can be written to memory almost instantly, and the cache hardware or software takes care of writing that data to disk later. The problem arises when large amounts of data are streamed to the disk. The cache intercepts the data as usual, but because the data doesn't stop coming, the cache fills quickly and starts flushing to the disk. If the disk controller or the drive isn't fast enough, the audio data streaming into the cache will be coming faster than it can be flushed out. When the cache overflows, data is lost.

The surest way to deal with problems imposed by caching is to disable the cache. A software cache is generally a driver or program your system loads when it boots. On the Mac, a software cache resides under the System folder, usually in Extensions; on the Amiga, you'll probably find the command that starts the cache in `s:startup-sequence` or `user-startup`; and a software cache on a PC is almost certainly loaded in `config.sys` or `autoexec.bat`. Eliminating the cache completely will have a drastic impact on your disk performance. You can usually settle for adjusting the cache size and retention time. Reducing either (or both) will have the effect of making overruns less likely, because the cache will start emptying to disk sooner after the data stream starts coming. You'll also benefit from the memory saved when a software cache's size is reduced. I tend to be very conservative; my disk caches are set to 256K.

Solving problems with a hardware cache is similar, although some disk controllers that have on-board caching don't allow you to change their settings except to disable the cache completely. You may have to do that, and you'll find that most of the benefits of the hardware caching can be reinstated by installing a software cache of a reasonable size.

If your cache isn't a problem, you might have a fragmented disk. Fragments occur when you've stored and deleted a lot of files on a disk. Deletions leave holes that the operating system fills with new data, but sometimes the holes aren't large enough to store the entire file. When that happens, the file is split into fragments. The more holes you have in your filesystem, the more likely it is that large files (like digital audio) will have to be split up. When the drive has to seek to find empty space for a large file, the stream of data flowing to the drive is interrupted. If the controller and drive are fast enough, they can catch up. But even with really fast hardware, a badly fragmented disk (with *lots* of holes) will create a problem for demanding audio captures. Macs, PCs, and Amigas all have utilities available for them that fix a fragmented disk by filling the holes and moving all of your disk's free space to a contiguous (uninterrupted) block at the end. These utilities are sometimes called *optimizers* or *defraggers*. They're generally safe, but it's wise to make a backup of your disk before you run such a utility. If you can't find a good utility, making a complete backup of your hard disk, erasing all of the data on it (reformatting is a certain way to accomplish this), and then restoring the data from the backup will also close the gaps in your filesystem. None of this is either for the faint of heart or for someone in a hurry; all of these solutions can take hours to complete.

Selecting and Connecting Your Audio Source(s)

Recording audio on an MPC-compatible PC sometimes requires an additional step that can't be managed from within the sound recorder. MPC audio boards usually let you record from any connected sound source—external line and mic-level inputs, CD audio and internal synthesizer are typical selections—but you have to select the input you want to use before you begin recording. Some applications will let you do this, but because recording source selection isn't part of the MPC specification, you're sometimes forced to use the audio mixer software that came with your board to choose the record source. Figure 4-5 shows MediaVision's Pro

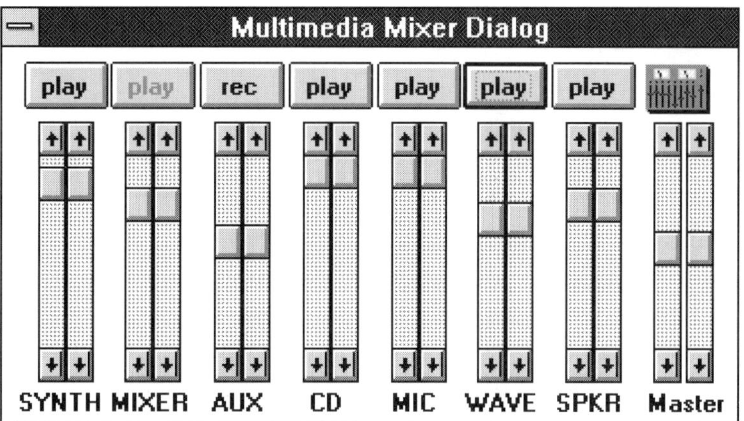

Figure 4-5: MediaVision's Pro Mixer

Mixer with the line (AUX) input selected for recording (note the button marked "REC" above the AUX volume slider). This particular mixer lets you select multiple record sources so you can do live source mixing. This rarely comes in handy, since you can't reasonably adjust source volume levels during a capture. You'd need that if you wanted to try to record narration with a microphone over music coming from a CD in one take. A good sound editor makes that kind of thing much easier to do after the fact and ensures better results.

If you want to use multiple sources, your best bet is to invest in an audio mixer. The best of these are found at music and video stores, and affordable mixers of somewhat lesser quality appear in Radio Shack catalogs. The difference between a good mixer and a bad one is noise. A really cheap mixer will let you combine audio sources all right, but probably at the expense of a loud hiss or some other distortion of the audio. You might also run into equipment that injects noise when you move the volume knobs or sliders during recording. Even a good mixer will add some noise, but the key is to find one that creates as little as possible. One technique that helps minimize mixer noise is to keep audio levels fairly "hot" (or high). That simply means that when you adjust your mixer, keep the mixer's master volume as low as possible, and use the volume controls for the individual audio inputs to set the overall volume. Most mixer noise is created by the mixer's amplifier, and the master volume determines how hard the amplifier works (and therefore how much noise it adds). Once you find mixer settings that deliver the best results for a particular combination of sources, write them down. Don't forget to record any applicable recording volume settings of your computer's mixer as well.

Making connections between your sound hardware and whatever's making the sound isn't always as easy as it seems. Just because you've got the right plug on the end of your audio cable doesn't mean you're ready to go. One gotcha is the signal level. You can make fine adjustments to the signal level with a mixer, but there are two distinct flavors of audio signals that must be recognized and dealt with accordingly: mic and line. Mic-level audio input comes from a microphone, which is an unamplified sound source. Microphones convert sound to electrical signals, but the voltages associated with those signals are extremely low. Line-level audio is amplified, so it uses higher voltages. The two signal levels are incompatible with each other. If you plug a microphone into a line-level input, you'll either get no sound at all or a very faint, scratchy sound. If you plug line-level audio into a mic input, you'll overpower the audio hardware and get loud, raspy, heavily distorted sound.

Your system's sound hardware might only offer you one type of audio input. Many Mac systems have only mic-level inputs, while some Amiga sound digitizers offer only line inputs. PC audio boards usually offer both, but even if you're stuck with one that doesn't, you're not out of luck. You can drop a line-level signal to mic level with an *attenuator*. Any Radio Shack or well-equipped audio or video store will have one. They usually take the shape of an adapter plug—you plug the adapter into your system's mic input, and then plug the cable to your line-level source into the adapter—or a patchcord that lets you make an attenuated connection directly. Bringing mic-level sources up to line level is more expensive. Mixers are probably the most accessible devices for this, but you can sometimes find small amplifiers that serve the same purpose.

Not all audio plugs are created equal. Most connections to sound hardware are made through either 1/8" diameter phone plugs (a thin, subtly pointed plug about 1/2" long) or RCA plugs (a hollow circle of metal surrounding a rounded cylindrical plug in the center). These plugs are depicted in Figure 4-6. Some systems, like

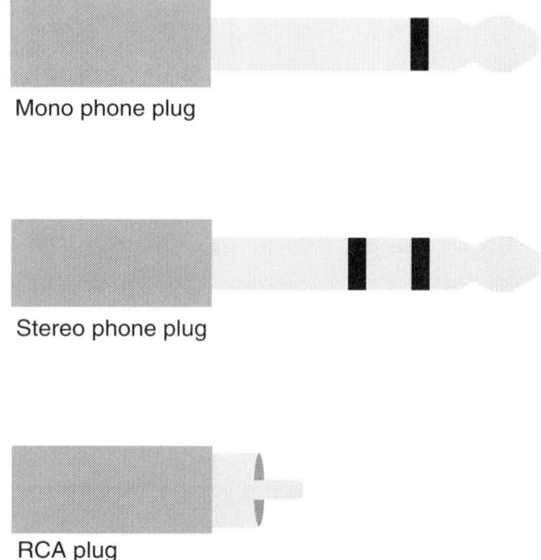

Figure 4-6: Common audio connectors

IBM's Ultimedia PS/2, have sockets for the older 1/4" phone plug. Phone plugs also come in two varieties: mono and stereo. Stereo phone plugs have two rings near the tip instead of mono's one. It's been my experience that you never have the right cable for the job. If you plan to do much audio work, you should invest in an assortment of adapters and cables of various types and lengths. You can find adapters to convert phono to phone plugs, plugs to sockets, stereo to mono, and so on. You can generally use any kind of adapter you like as long as you don't alter the signal level (unless you need that). Before you get caught out, make a list of all the things you'd like to hook together and purchase cables and adapters that cover all the combinations. Remember to include what you may need to translate between stereo and mono. A PC's line input is usually stereo, and you can save yourself some hassle when recording from a mono source if you buy an adapter that splits the mono signal into two mono signals. This doesn't create stereo, but it lets you work with the signal as though it were. Similarly, you'll want a cable that combines stereo signals into a single mono signal, particularly when working with the Mac, most models of which accept only monophonic mic-level input. When you make the trip to purchase these supplies, you may find different grades of cable and connectors. If you don't plan to do CD-quality recording, high-grade cables might be an unnecessary waste of money. If you plan to change your connections a lot, or if you will use your cables for field work (see the coming chapter's coverage of shooting video), high-grade cables are often sturdier and can be flexed many more times before the wire inside breaks. So-called professional cables often have gold connectors. Gold conducts electricity better than other metals, and gold connectors are usually combined with low-loss cable that helps keep the signal in and external noise out. Frankly, you may never notice the difference in sound quality between low- and high-grade cables and connectors, so I'll leave it to you to decide for yourself whether the inflated cost of the top-of-the-line stuff is justified. I have found that the *really* cheap cables and adapters have a tendency to short out or come apart after much less use, but that won't be a problem for you if you'll be hooking things up once and leaving them alone.

Levels and Microphones

If you've prepared your system for audio capture, you should just be able to hit the Record button on your audio recorder application and let it fly. Most programs are tuned to start recording almost instantly, but there's no harm in giving yourself a bit of dead space before you start the sound. You can always take that gap out later with a sound editor or by specifying a nonzero in point with playback software that permits it. Better sound editors let you see a graphical representation of audio levels before you start recording. As with analog (tape) recording, you should aim to make the loudest passage in your recording match the maximum undistorted loudness of your recording equipment. Sound recorders that show recording levels usually indicate maximum loudness by turning the graph red or blinking a "clipping" light when you've gone too far. Both mean the incoming sound is too loud to be recorded without distortion. Use the meter to adjust either your audio source's volume or your sound hardware's recording level. Find the loudest passage in your music and test against that, or speak in what you expect will be your most forceful voice if you're doing narration. Watch the graph and trim the volume until the red graph or the clipping light go away. Don't overadjust; stop trimming right after the clipping warning disappears, because you normally want the recording to be at the highest possible volume. You can sometimes watch the meters when you record, too, and if you get a clipping warning while you're rolling, notch the volume down and start a new take. Don't let any distorted audio, even if it's only a short piece, creep into your audio.

Recording with a microphone adds to the list of things you need to consider. I won't get into doing complex multiply miked recording sessions—I said this chapter was basic—but I'll stick instead to narration and the like. "The like" might include placing a microphone near an open window during a rain shower or a crickets' serenade to capture some ambience. Whatever kind of sound you're going after, if you have serious plans for it, use at least moderately serious gear. Narration recorded with a cheap microphone at 8 or 11 KHz won't be noticed, but even at 22 KHz, a bad microphone will have a very noticeable effect on the quality of your audio. A bad microphone often has a limited frequency range, failing to pass the lowest or highest frequencies and creating recordings that sound tinny or muted. There's no need to suffer, because low-end professional microphones are quite affordable.

Another absolute *don't* for serious audio recording is the handheld mike. It might be convenient, and it may blend well with your Elvis impersonation, but every time your fingers move even a millimeter along the shaft of that mike it will be recorded as a loud rumble or thump. You can train yourself (as newscasters do, for example) to hold a microphone quietly, but you also need to pay attention to *where* to hold the microphone. You should never hold a microphone directly in front of your mouth. Watch a little network television news to see how the pros do it. The microphone is held vertically, with the top sitting several inches below and slightly in front of the chin. Consonants (like *P*) will not pop, *S* will not hiss, and the quality of the tone will be more natural as sound flows over the microphone instead of straight into it.

If you take my advice and don't hold the microphone in your hands, you'll have to find something that can hold the mike for you. Some sound hardware now comes with microphones that stick to the front of your computer's monitor. They're handy there, but not very practical—microphones should be no more than four or five inches away so that room noise doesn't play too big a part in your project. I've grown fond of lapel mikes, which you can clip or pin onto your tie or jacket lapel. Lapel mikes, which sit more than my preferred distance from the mouth, call for either a very quiet room or good equipment. Professional lapel mikes have a limited coverage area that points straight up (at your face) and helps keep the noise around you out of the session. If you're using a more traditional stick microphone, drop into a music store and grab a mike stand. I prefer floor-standing models to desktop units because the desktop stands can absorb even small vibrations (as when you rest your hand on the table) anywhere on the table and transmit them to the microphone. If you have the space for it, a model with a counterweighted boom will give you plenty of options for positioning the microphone where you want it. Add a short gooseneck to the end (mike stands have standard threads for accessories) and you gain a few more options. You'll find a good stand is as important as the mike you put in it, and the only thing you have to remember about using the stand is not to adjust it while you're recording.

When professionals record audio to tape, they usually keep rolling through multiple takes because rewinding between takes wastes too much time and can throw a narrator off. When you're using digital audio, disk space is too valuable a commodity. Unless you have a bottomless hard disk, you should overwrite your botched record sessions.

The End Product

The result of a digital recording session is a sound file. The Mac and Amiga both have standard sound file formats that let you take files directly from recording to playback in any application that supports sound. The MPC specification settled what was a messy situation on the PC where several incompatible sound file formats existed. Now you can expect Mac and Amiga-style convenience as long as you stay in Windows and stick with tools that use the multimedia extensions. Sound files include headers that identify the rate and resolution used to record the sound, and indicate whether the data is compressed. You can mix files recorded with different settings with relative impunity as long as you keep a few points in mind.

Whether the sound file you create can be played is mostly determined by the hardware on the playback system. If the sound will never be played anywhere but on the system you used to record it, then you'll have no trouble. If you intend to distribute your sound files for use on systems whose configurations you cannot control, you might have to scale back the sound file quality to ensure the files can be played on the majority of target systems. You can't reasonably distribute Mac audio recorded at anything higher than 22 KHz and 8 bits, because there are a lot of older Mac systems out there. The MPC specification allows for audio hardware that's no better than the Mac (22 KHz/8 bits), so you're stuck with that on the PC as well. The Amiga is the only place where you can go to town, for as long as the audio player you supply can drive the internal sound generators at the rate you desire, you're in business. The audio hardware hasn't changed since the original Amiga 1000. The spaciousness of CD-ROM distribution of software allows for some flexibility: you can offer two versions of your audio files that cover both the minimum standard and higher quality. If your presentation relies on digitally recorded music, it's worth offering both so that users with better audio capability can hear the music in much closer to its original form.

If your system doesn't support audio file compression, you might derive a similar benefit from running the audio files through external compression programs. Such software is available as shareware or freeware, and you can buy data compression engines as libraries that you can plug into you custom software. Transparent audio file compression (like the Mac's ADPCM format) is best because neither you nor the user have to do anything special, but failing that, you can at least use data compression to shrink the audio files down and save diskettes (if that's your distribution medium).

Editing Digital Audio

Audio capture turns sound into digital data that can be manipulated by software in ways that tape recorders can only fantasize about. You can cut and paste portions of your audio clips, mix audio to create overdub effects, and apply complex transforms that modify pitch, time, and equalization, and you can add effects like reverb and echo. Some audio editors are extremely simple in their design and features. Of the systems used for this book, only Windows includes any kind of standard sound editor: Sound Recorder (shown in Figure 4-7) captures audio (at the default rate and resolution, in mono only) and can perform only the most rudimentary editing duties. It's workable in a pinch and serves as an unintimidating introduction to PC

Figure 4-7: Windows Sound Recorder/Editor

audio. You can't select portions of your audio file per se, but you can request that everything before or after the current position be deleted. You can insert the contents of another audio file at the current position (pushing the rest of the current file's audio to the point after the inserted file), and you may also mix the contents of another file with the one you're working on. The entire file may be brought up or down a fixed percentage of volume, speed can be increased or decreased by a fixed percentage, and an echo effect may be added.

Working with Sound Recorder or any other sound editor doesn't make adjustments to the hardware or to the method used to play the file back in order to accommodate your editing requests. The original sound file is modified by each action: add echo and it's there to stay. If you double the speed, Sound Recorder does it by throwing away half the sound data. Halving the speed after that in an attempt to return the file to its original state results in a 22 KHz clip that sounds like it was recorded at 11 KHz (or worse). What Sound Recorder's missing, among other items, is an Undo function that lets you audition your changes before you commit them. That's reason enough to invest in a real sound editor.

Sound Editing Basics

Microsoft provides a sound editor of its own for the PC called WaveEdit (see Figure 4-8). This is tossed in with Microsoft's Multimedia Development Kit (MDK) and is also included with the Video for Windows digital video software (discussed

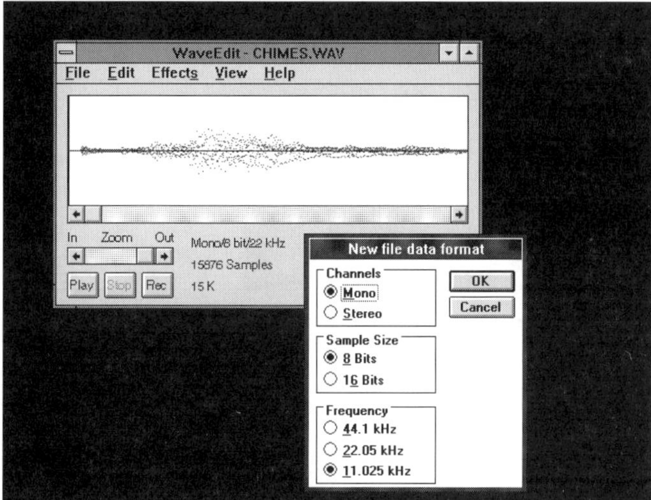

Figure 4-8: Microsoft WaveEdit

in an upcoming chapter). By your reading of this book, this utility or its like may be a part of the standard Windows release. It's a sturdy editor that forsakes cute features (like echo) in favor of some you can really use. WaveEdit's practical features set a reasonable minimum standard that you should expect any sound editor to meet. The features I discuss relate to most sound editors.

WaveEdit puts up a graphical view of sound file data using scattered dots. I spoke in Chapter 2 about the properties of amplitude and frequency and how they could be represented by a graph. Sound editors do just that. WaveEdit plots amplitude by the relative vertical distance between the center line and the farthest dot. Frequency can't reasonably be graphed when the data is viewed as above; there isn't enough graphics resolution to put up a meaningful display. If you're curious about what sound "looks like," WaveEdit will let you zoom in on the data. The selected portion of the wave shown in Figure 4-9, which is highlighted by a black rectangle, represents 100 samples from a file captured at 22 KHz. That amounts to roughly five thousandths of a second worth of audio. You could chop that selected portion out of the file and not notice it. This kind of zoomed-in view is useful only for satisfying scientific curiosity; you can't do any real editing at this level, but it does provide a fascinating glimpse of the shape of sound.

You'll do most of your sound editing from a zoomed-out view that either shows the entire file or at least shows a second or so's worth of data. From that

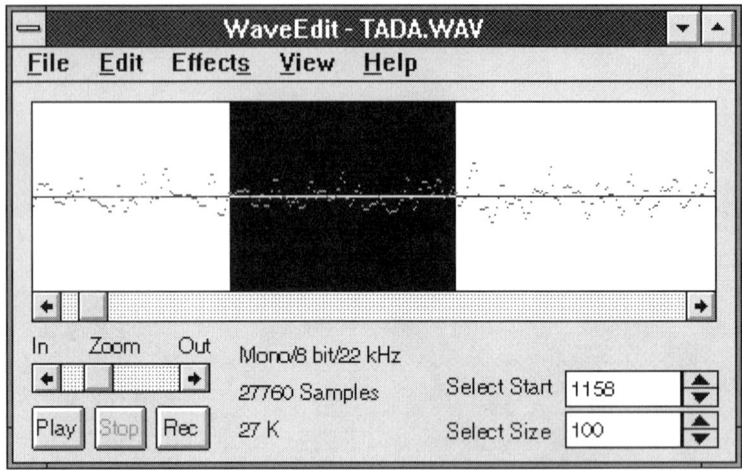

Figure 4-8: A zoomed-in view of audio data

view, one of the most common editing tasks is the cut. It's here that you'd remove the silence that marks the distance between your pressing of the Record button and the start of the sound. Silence is represented in a sound editor's graph as something close to a flat line. If you recorded from a noisy sound source or with cheap audio hardware, you'll have to accept that silence shows not as a flat line, but as a wave with lower amplitude than your sound. Sound recorded with a microphone is also rarely silent because of ambient room or outdoor noise, and silence is a distant goal for someone who holds a microphone in his or her hand while recording.

To select audio in a sound editor, you drag the mouse pointer (moving while holding the button down) across the portion of the graph that represents the sound you want to affect. You can play the selected portion to make sure you got the selection right, and you can usually "tune" your selection by moving the left or right edge of the selected area in or out. Selected audio can be cut or copied to the clipboard, or it can be deleted outright (without placing it in the clipboard first). Better editors have Undo options in their Edit menus that let you reverse your last action, even if you play the changed version of the file before trying to undo the change. You've got plenty of room to experiment as long as you practice some care.

Silent passages can be removed not only from the ends of recorded audio, but also from anywhere in the file. Removing silence is a good way to trim the size of a file, but use this method sparingly. Don't remove the brief pauses that give speech its natural rhythm. But if you consult your notes for several seconds, you can (and should) get rid of that gap with one cut. When you remove silence, make sure you're zoomed in close enough to see where the silent period really begins and ends. If you're zoomed out so far that you can see several seconds of audio data on the screen at once (which is usually the default view—see the Mac's SoundEdit Pro in Figure 4-9), the accuracy of your selections will be limited. You

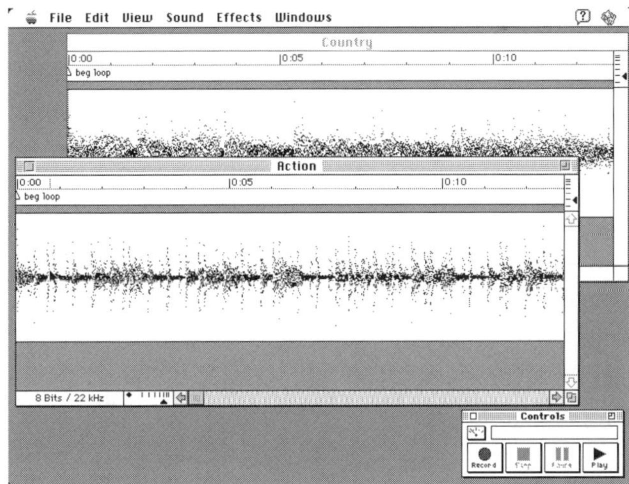

Figure 4-9: SoundEdit Pro (Mac)

can often make a coarse selection, then zoom in to tune it up in a view that lets you see the detail.

Silent passages aren't the only kind of material you cut from audio files. You can cut sentences from files containing narration, and with some practice, you can even edit digitized music down to a shorter playing time. The only way to learn either of these skills is to practice. Each sound editor has it own way of representing sound data. Becoming proficient at trimming sound files means teaching yourself to recognize the relationships between the sound you've recorded and its graphical representation on the screen.

Narration is easier to edit than music because the graphical waves create a pattern that maps to speech fairly directly. You can learn to spot the patterns by starting with short phrases. Figure 4-10 shows a SoundEdit Pro window with the phrase "this is a test" shown graphically. As an aid, the word "test" is highlighted.

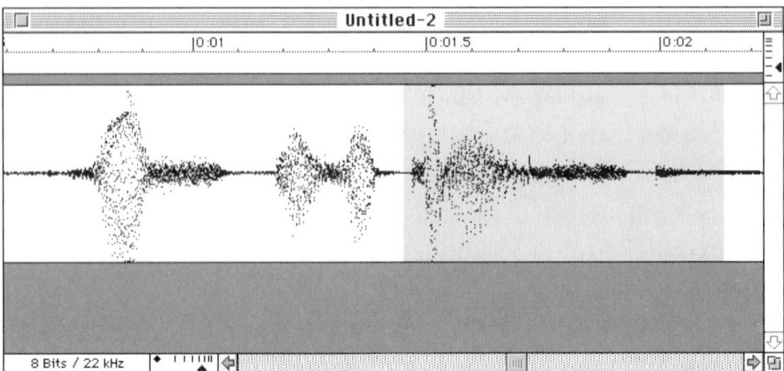

Figure 4-10: "This is a test"

You'll notice that there are four sizable "humps" in the graph that are clearly associated with the four words in the phrase. You should also note the relationship between the wave amplitude and the sound being made. The highest peaks in a speech wave are usually caused by open-mouthed vowels and percussive consonants (like the *T* in "test"). The difference is that percussive consonants show as very brief peaks, while vowels (like the *i* sound in "this") appear as more rounded humps of longer duration.

Given the appearance of that graph in the figure, would you know where to cut to remove the entire word "test?" Does the selection in the graph include the whole word, or is more or less of the sound selected? Actually, the selected portion of the graph in the figure *does* include the entire word "test," but the appearance of the end of the selected region might throw you off. The sound there looks so close to silence that you might be moved to place the end of the word more to the left. The drawn out *S* and softer *T* at the end of the word show as waves of very low amplitude. But looking closely, you can still see where the sounds occur. It's situations like this that make it imperative that you play selected regions before you cut them. Longer spoken clips leave you no choice. While the words of a single sentence can be picked out with a little practice, you can't expect to identify a phrase in the middle of a long passage by looking at the wave patterns.

The data that you cut won't always wind up in the trash heap. Sometimes you'll cut data to move it elsewhere in the same file, or to move a portion of a clip to another file. In these cases, the data will be pasted into the sound editor window at the *insertion point*, usually shown by a solid or blinking vertical line. You need to apply the same care in choosing an insertion point as you do in selecting data for cutting or copying. If you're working with speech, the insertion of new material should maintain natural speech patterns. There should be a brief silence between sentences; just select the silence that precedes the phrase you're moving along with the phrase before you cut it. That way, when you paste it you can set your insertion point close to the end of a phrase. If no such silence exists, you can graft silence from another part of the file, create a special sound file that contains a few seconds of silence and copy some data from it, or use your sound editor's "generate silence" option (if it has one).

Audio Effects

Better sound editors let you do far more than just cut and paste audio data. The term *effects* refers less to mostly useless gimmicks like echo, but rather to more practical calculated changes to audio data. As an example, consider the piece of music whose beginning strains are shown in Figure 4-11 (the application is Turtle Beach's Wave for Windows). This tune opens with percussion, and let's say that while you liked the tune and chose to use it, you didn't want such a jarring introduction. You could mitigate the tune's initial punch by having it fade up gradually from silence. This effect, the "fade-in," is a commonly used sound editor feature, and is very easy to apply. Simply drag over the first second or two (depending on how long you want the fade-in to last) to select it. Then apply the fade-in effect by either choosing it from the editor's menu of effects or, as is the case with Wave, choose a "gain-adjust" option or its like. An automatic fade-in will change the audio data so that the data at the beginning of the selected region is reduced to silence, and the volume is gradually increased until, at the end of the region, the playback volume is as it was in the original file. A gain-adjust effect brings up a dialog box that lets you determine the starting and ending volume. This is helpful if you don't want to completely eliminate the starting drumbeat, for example. You could use the gain-adjust effect to set the fade-in to start at something greater than zero volume. The result of a fade from silence is shown in Figure 4-12.

The list of available effects varies from one sound editor to another. It has very little to do with your hardware, since effects are created in software and are not run back through your sound hardware until you play the file after the effect is completed. So any computer that can run a particular sound editor can use all of its effects. The only problem is that some effects use more of your system's resources

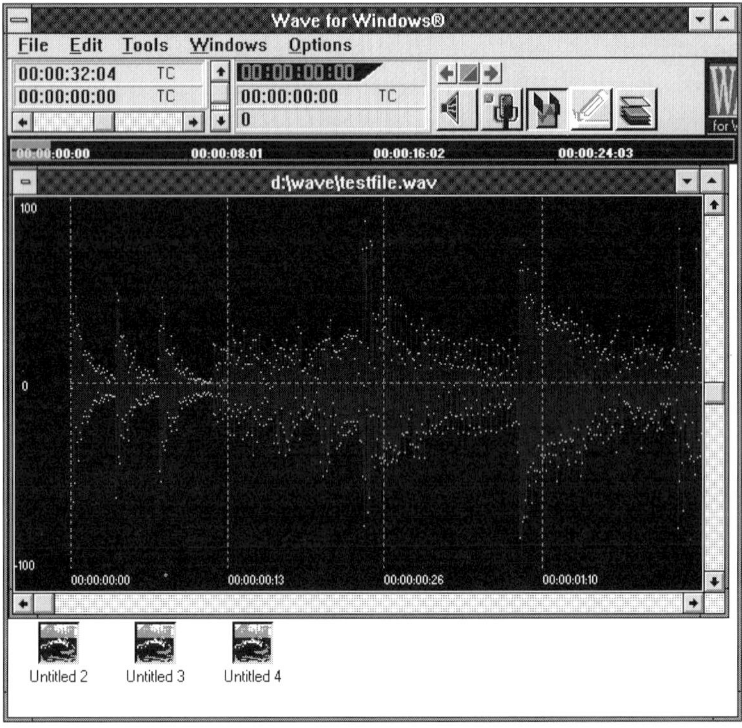

Figure 4-11: A few bars of music

than others. Effects like fade-in, fade-out and echo are easy for any computer to manage, but there are some that take a long time to complete on computers that aren't performance champs.

To give you an idea of the kinds of effects you can perform with a good sound editor, I've compiled a list of some of the effects offered by three software packages in my lab: Turtle Beach's Wave for Windows, Macromedia's SoundEdit Pro for the Macintosh, and Sunrize Industries' Studio 16 for the Amiga. This isn't a complete list, and not all effects are available in all of the packages. I selected the ones I thought were most useful in a professional setting.

Fade-in, fade-out: These should be familiar to you. While generally applied at the beginning and end of a file, respectively, they can be applied to any selected portion of your audio file. If you use cut and paste to add a music introduction to a piece of narration, for instance, you might do a fade-out on the tail end of the

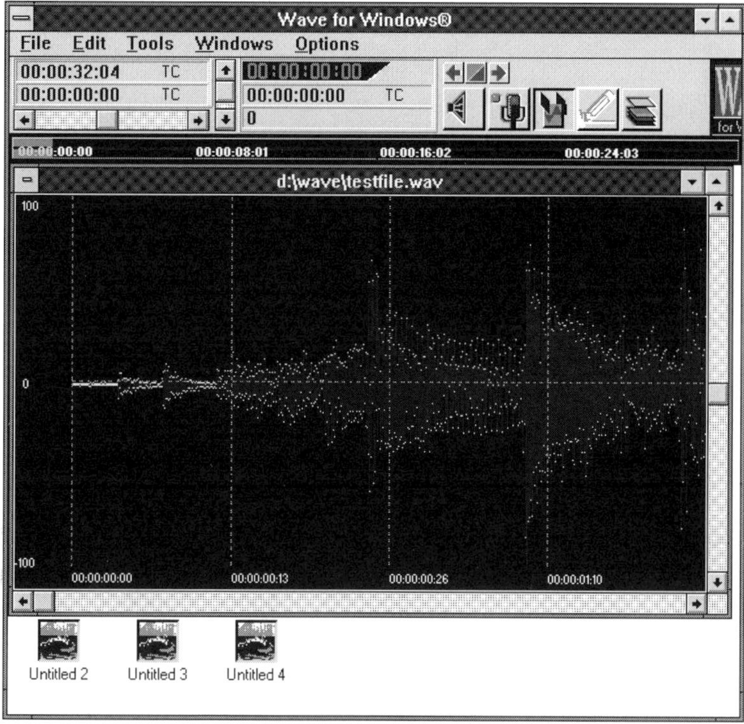

Figure 4-12: Fade-in

music to create a nice transition. In this case, you'd make the change to the new sound file (the one with both the music and the narration in a single file) to avoid inflicting a permanent effect on the music file. You might want to use that file later without fading the end out.

Gain-adjust: I've mentioned this one, too, since Wave for Windows uses this to create its fade effects. But the same mechanism can be used to apply an amplitude increase or decrease to a selected portion of a sound file. You can use a gain-adjust effect to create an "automated mix" that brings the volume level of a music soundtrack down to make room for live or recorded narration. Music should always get quieter when speech is to be heard above it. Figure 4-13 shows a music clip that's had a portion near its center adjusted to make way for narration. Such a trough should be made gently by fading down to the reduced volume, then fading back up to restore the full volume at the end of the trough. This required three

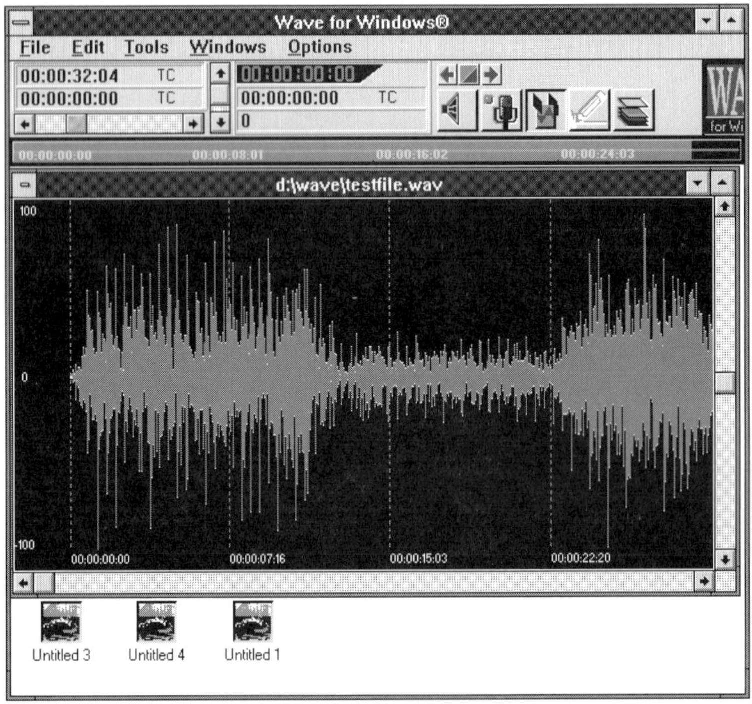

Figure 4-13: The gain-adjust effect

operations in Wave (fade-down, gain-adjust and fade-up); your sound editor might handle the whole operation in one shot.

A gain-adjust is also handy to apply to an entire file when you're using playback software that doesn't allow you to set the playback volume. You can use gain adjust to make sure all your audio clips play back at an acceptable volume. You can also use it to make the best of a bad audio capture. You can't really repair a file recorded from a too-loud audio source because the clipping distortion (shown when the wave goes off the top of the graph) remains even after you knock the volume down. Gain-adjust can rescue a file recorded with a too-weak signal, provided there's more real sound than noise; using gain-adjust to bring up the volume will make both the sound and the noise louder.

Equalize: An equalizer boosts or diminishes sound that occurs within a given range of frequencies. When seen as part of a home stereo setup, an equalizer usually has a set of six or more sliders, with each one assigned to a fixed range of frequencies, with low frequencies on the left, high frequencies on the right, and midtones in the center. Raising the sliders on the left boosts a sound's bass; raising high-frequency sliders makes cymbals, chimes, wind instruments and other high-frequency sound sources more prominent. Lift the sliders in the middle, and you'll boost the relative volume of the vocals. In the same way, pushing any of the sliders *down* will make quieter the sounds that are covered by that slider's frequency range.

Professional musicians and others who deal with audio for a living generally use a device called a *parametric equalizer* to alter the frequency curve of their sound. While a home-stereo equalizer can effect only broad changes (moving a slider affects *all* of the frequencies covered by it), a parametric equalizer can be more precise. To use one, you dial in the basic frequency you wish to affect, the range of frequencies around that basic frequency that you'd like included, and the degree of boost or diminishment to apply to the range you've created. This method lets you zero in on just the sounds you want to change. A fixed equalizer, for example, generally has one slider that covers all frequencies of 16 KHz and higher. Raising that slider heightens not only the high-frequency sounds you want, but also the amplifier and sound source hiss you don't want. With a parametric equalizer, you can create a custom-tuned frequency range that boosts only the music but doesn't extend high enough to let the noise through. In fact, with good equipment, you can use parametric equalization to quiet high frequency noise (hiss), hum, record scratches and other unwanted sounds. You might not be able to get rid of them completely because some noise exists in frequency ranges that also include sound you *do* want.

Equalization, in the context of digital audio, is a powerful ally. Music recorded at lower sampling rates can sound flat; equalizing up the highs and lows can help that. I sometimes use interviews conducted by telephone in my presentations, and I find that equalization can lend a more natural tone to what would otherwise be annoyingly scratchy speech.

Figure 4-14 shows the equalizer dialog (the effect is called "filter" in this program) of SoundEdit Pro for the Mac. You'll note that while it looks like a typical home equalizer, it's actually parametric. The vertical lines that mark the frequency ranges can be moved around (just grab the line with the mouse and move it to the new frequency). One slider can represent a span of frequencies as little as 500 Hz apart. I particularly like SoundEdit Pro's approach because it lets you choose—

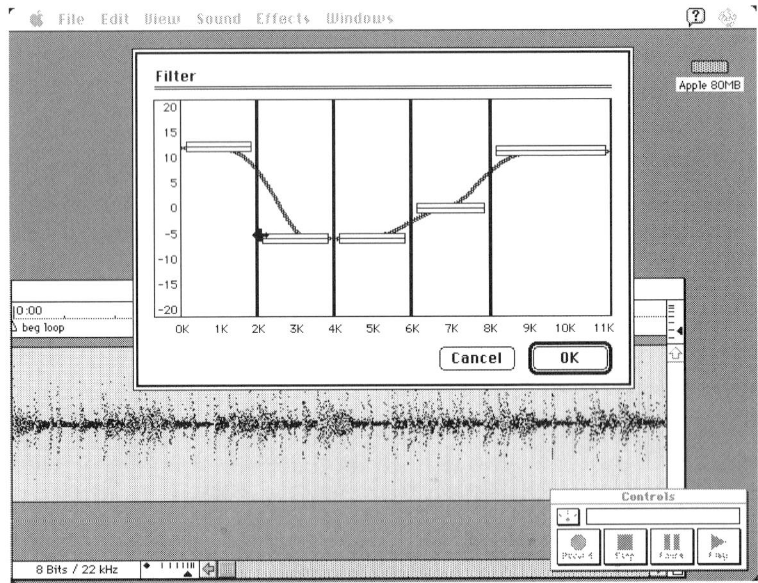

Figure 4-14: SoundEdit Pro's equalizer

fixed or parametric—what kind of equalizer you want to use.

Resample: An audio file is stored with a header that identifies the sampling rate, resolution, mono or stereo, and compression method (if any). As you pull together the audio files for a project, you may want to make them all the same type. You might wish to save yourself space by taking a file recorded at 44.1 KHz and knocking it down to 22 KHz, or you might do that to ensure more global compatibility with older systems. On systems that support it, you might want to apply compression to an audio file that wasn't recorded with it. Whatever your reasons, changing the characteristics of an audio file requires resampling. This effect's name is misleading—it almost sounds like the sound is re-recorded by your audio hardware at the new settings. Instead, like all effects, the audio file is operated on entirely in software. The only possible exception, which I haven't yet encountered but have been told to expect, is hardware-assisted compression. Your sound board might have a chip on it that can do audio data compression much faster than your computer can. If that's the case, and if you're using a sound editor that somehow knows about that chip, resampling to compress an audio file might use your sound board's compression chip.

Resampling can't improve a sound file, so there's rarely any reason to resample to a higher sampling rate. The file will take up more space, but it won't sound any better. Resampling to a lower rate, converting a stereo sample to mono or applying compression all make perfect sense as long as the quality of the sound file you're working with isn't significantly reduced. You should always be on the lookout for ways to reduce the size of your audio files, but take care: when you resample, unless you're sure of the results, make the destination of your resampling operation a new file instead of overwriting the old one. That way, if the resampling makes the file sound bad, you can revert to the original.

Time compress/expand: Life would be grand if every piece of audio fit perfectly into the slot made for it. In a precisely timed presentation, an audio clip that's too long or too short can throw off the rest of the show. You might also have a piece of music or narration that's simply not lively enough to fit the style of the rest of your presentation. Time compression and expansion takes a selected portion of an audio file and simply makes it play faster or slower *without altering the pitch.* That last bit is important. You could make a dull speaker talk faster by just playing his recorded voice back at a higher speed, but raising the playback speed also raises the frequency of his voice—the faster you play, the higher the pitch. Time compression and expansion alter only the time it takes to play a selected region of an audio file. It doesn't sound any different except that it takes up more or less time. With good software, minor adjustments to playback speed are absolutely imperceptible from the original. And if you haven't heard the original speech or music before, even more radical shifts in tempo can't be discerned.

Time compression or expansion is usually applied to an entire file to make it fit a certain length. In radio, for example, a commercial that runs three seconds over the magical 30-second mark can be time-compressed down to 30 seconds without a noticeable impact. The interface offered by the sound editor usually lets you adjust the playback rate either as a percentage of the normal rate or by specifying the amount of time you wish the selected region to occupy (see Figure 4-15). This can be a very time-consuming effect; the calculations required to make this work are extremely complex and require your computer's full attention. Time-compressing a 20-second audio clip down to 15 seconds using my Mac IIci took almost four minutes; at that rate, a three-minute song would have taken more than half an hour to process. A faster Mac would have cut that time down. Wave for Windows lets you select the accuracy of the transformation (see the figure). The

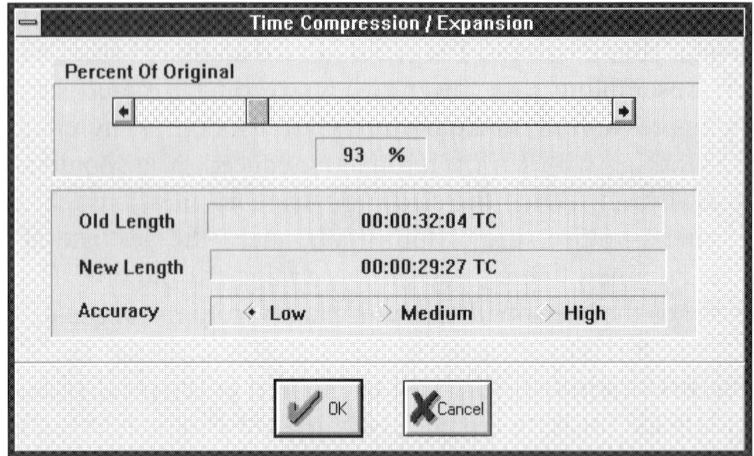

Figure 4-15: Time compression/expansion (Wave)

lower the accuracy, the faster the conversion.

Multitrack: True multiple-track audio is a rarity for personal computers. A minimal definition of multitracking is the ability to play two or more channels of audio simultaneously. Real multitracking, in the fashion of professional recording equipment, means being able to listen to already-recorded audio while you digitize a fresh track. You might do this to add a vocal to an instrumental layer you recorded earlier. This process is sometimes called "overdubbing," but it's not all you should expect from true multitracking. To be an acceptable replacement for an analog multitrack audio recorder, a digital system must also allow you to "mix down" several channels of audio onto one or two channels. This creates a master audio file that can then be played on non-multitrack hardware.

If you happen to have an Amiga or a PC (more likely, PS/2) system with an IBM M/Audio board, your hardware is already capable of supporting multitrack audio. The Amiga supports four tracks of medium-quality audio, while the M/Audio board supports two channels of moderate to high-quality audio. At the time of this writing, however, software for these two systems support the multitrack capabilities on playback only. To get real multitrack editing, you'll probably have to invest in an add-in multitrack audio board regardless of your system. One shining example of this is the Sunrize Industries AD516. This eight-channel audio board plugs into an Amiga and includes Studio 16, a very impressive multitrack recording and editing package. The coming chapter on video production will discuss the AD516 at length; for now, you can catch a glimpse of it in Figure 4-16.

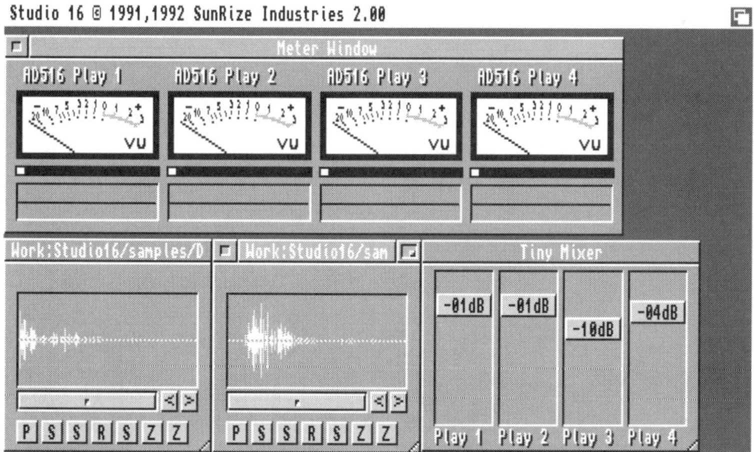

Figure 4-16: Studio 16 multitrack sound editor

The benefits of multitracking in multimedia production are many, but using it often requires an investment of time and money beyond what ordinary single-channel audio production calls for. As I said, most audio editors don't do multitracking, even on multitrack-capable systems, so you should decide how important multitrack audio is to you before you take the plunge. The only application for which it is vital is video production; too often, desktop-produced video suffers from poorly produced audio. Apart from video's obvious need, only the most audio-intensive applications call for multitrack hardware and software. If you'll be combining audio from several sources, you require the highest sound quality, and you have a complex plan in mind for editing those sources together, your project will probably benefit from a multitrack board and software. Keep in mind that this hardware is moderately to outrageously expensive (the AD516 offers the most "bang for the buck" at $1495 for eight channels, software included). If you fall in love with the notion of using an add-in card for multitrack audio playback at the user site, it'll raise the price of your playback system considerably.

Mix, Paste Mix: You can obtain some of the benefits of multitrack audio by using an editor that supports Mix or Paste Mix functions. Mix is implemented in some audio editors, including Wave for Windows, which let you keep multiple audio files open at once (see Figure 4-17). With Mix, you can create a new sound file that

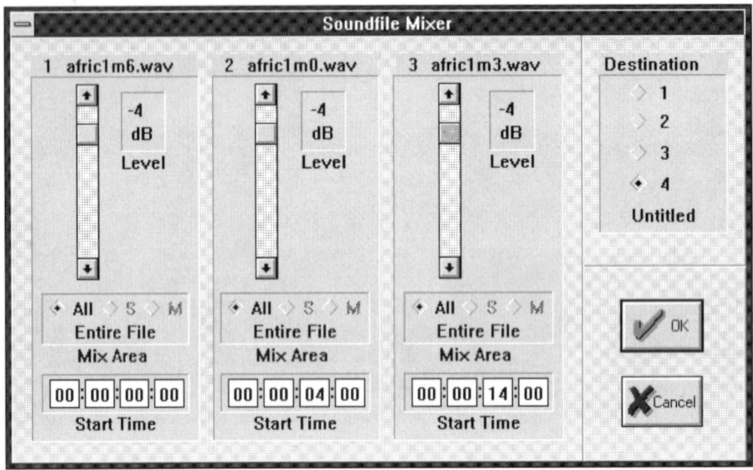

Figure 4-17: Mix dialog box (Wave for Windows)

is the combination of two or more existing and open files. You can generally control the relative volume of each of the mixed pseudo-tracks, and you may also specify an offset (delay) to stagger the playback start times for each of the component sound files. You could have your music track start with a delay of zero to place it at the beginning of the new file, for example, and mix in narration that starts five seconds after the music.

You may find that your software requires that all the component files for a Mix operation be of the same type. If you have files captured at differing rates and resolutions, you'll need to use resampling to coerce all the files to the same type. While resampling a low-quality file to a higher rate and resolution won't do much to improve the quality, it is reasonable to resample to a higher-quality setting when you're preparing for a Mix. You might resample narration originally recorded at 22 KHz, for example, to match a music track's 44 KHz. Then, when you Mix, you won't be dragging the quality of the music down to that of the narration.

A more common sound editor function is Paste Mix, which works with editors that only allow one open sound file at a time. With it, you can combine any two sound files in a manner similar to Mix, through the use of the clipboard. You start by selecting and copying a portion of the secondary sound file (let's say it contains your narration) to the clipboard. You then open the primary sound file (with the music, perhaps) and set the playback cursor or insertion point by clicking the mouse button at the spot where you want the secondary audio clip to land. Then select Paste Mix. More primitive editors will simply forge ahead, dropping the volume of both clips by half for the duration of the mix and blending the files together starting at the current insertion point. Better editors will let you set the blend levels; the default half and half mix might not produce the kind of foreground/background effect you seek. With some editors, you can also arrange to fade gently to the volume levels you specify for the mix, fading back to the primary sound file's standard volume at the end of the mix.

Cross-fade: One of the most common sound editing operations is the splicing of one audio file onto the end of another. If you place the splice during a period of silence (which you can arrange by using fade-out on the first clip and fade-in on the second), it will be unnoticeable, but there will be "dead air" where the clips come together. You might prefer the more gentle, professional-sounding cross-fade, where the tail of one clip actually overlaps the head of another. The two clips fade in opposite directions (tail down, head up) simultaneously, creating a pleasing dissolve effect that works particularly well when you change from one musical theme to another. Editors that allow this (including Wave for Windows) let you set the duration of the overlap; the fade will span the overlapped portion, with the volume of the tail hitting zero just as the end of the clip arrives. You should plan ahead for a cross-fade by trimming any silence or noise from the end of the tail clip. Otherwise, you'll hear the audio cut out abruptly before its volume is reduced to zero. Similarly, if the head clip has dead space in front, the cross-fade won't sound as smooth.

MIDI

Electronic music, represented in MIDI file format, is an efficient and easily managed way to add music to a presentation. There are several vendors (including

Voyetra and Prosonus) that offer MIDI files designed specifically for use in multimedia presentations. As a means of storing and delivering electronic music, properly applied MIDI is in all ways preferable over digitally recorded audio. MIDI isn't quite as effortless to use as digital audio, but you don't have to learn much to reap MIDI's benefits.

Like other media, the way you use MIDI music depends on your skill and creativity. If you're a keyboard musician, you can use MIDI to create your own presentation music. If you have at least a sense of rhythm and an understanding of the way music can shape a mood, you can use software like Blue Ribbon Soundworks' SuperJam to tie simple chords together into a computer-generated composition. And with little or no musical talent of your own, you can still take advantage of MIDI's unique versatility.

The first choice you need to make when putting together the music for any type of multimedia work is whether you plan to use custom or canned music. Custom music is that which you create yourself or commission to have created for you specifically for a certain job. It involves recording one or more tracks, played on a keyboard synthesizer, electronic piano, or other MIDI-equipped instrument, into a computer through a MIDI interface and sequencing software. In contrast, you buy canned music from a source, usually a clearing house for production music. A canned music diskette might contain several tunes that share a similar mood, or they might represent a mix of styles and playing lengths. Some canned music is available in all three multimedia audio formats: MIDI, digital audio file, and CD audio. Of these, only MIDI is changeable and adaptable. I can't stress enough that it is, by far, the smartest way to go when packaging music for a presentation.

In, Out and Through

Working with MIDI, as a musician or not, requires a basic understanding of how MIDI works. MIDI is actually a specialized local-area network, not all that different from the networks used to bind computers together. MIDI devices are bound together in daisy-chain style: each new device added to the network is cabled to the device that was previously on the end of the chain rather than directly into the computer. I should point out that musicians often use more expensive MIDI interfaces that do support multiple direct connections to the controlling computer. This is valuable only when you plan to use so many MIDI instruments that multiple networks must be used. Production music is seldom so demanding, but we'll get into that after we get some vocabulary down.

As I mentioned at the beginning of this chapter, MIDI starts with a MIDI interface, a device that gives your computer the ability to send and receive MIDI data. Macs and Amigas have serial ports that are able to support MIDI directly, and MIDI interfaces are, therefore, quite inexpensive. The trend in MPC-compatible PC sound cards is to include MIDI interfaces but to make the necessary MIDI connecting cable an extra-cost item (but a fairly inexpensive one). The justification for the latter, I expect, is that sound-card vendors don't expect many people to use external MIDI. I hope to change that, at least in your mind.

A MIDI interface has at least two connectors, labeled *in* and *out*. The names are descriptive enough, and they refer to the direction of data flow relative to that interface. The simplest MIDI connection involves hooking up a single MIDI playback instrument, sometimes called a *sound module*. If all you plan to do is play canned MIDI music, you only need one cable. Because played music data flows out from the MIDI interface, you plug one end of the cable into the interface's *out* port. The other end plugs into the *in* port on the sound module. That's often all you have to do. MIDI playback doesn't require a two-way connection to the playback device; normal operation doesn't expect any feedback from the sound module.

Chapter 1's discussion of MIDI covered some instrument considerations, including the number of simultaneous voices or *polyphony*. Multiple playback devices are most often needed to work around device-imposed limits on polyphony. A complex musical score, one that is comprised of many layers of different kinds of instrument sounds, can be more than one sound module can handle. That's when you'll want to connect another module to the chain, and use a sequencer to split the load between the two devices. You might also add a module that produces a type of sound that the other device can't create. Some sound modules create realistic reproductions of acoustic instruments, while others produce sounds that are clearly and intentionally synthetic. You can mix the two styles together or use multiple instruments of the same style to build a plusher, more thickly layered sound.

The set of connectors offered by a MIDI instrument sometimes differs from what you find on a MIDI interface. You will generally find *in* and *out*, but a MIDI instrument frequently also has a third connector labeled *through*. This is an extension of the *out* port on the computer's MIDI interface; connecting a new device to the *through* port of a preceding device is roughly the same as hooking it into the MIDI interface's *out* port. That is, when you're adding a new device to a MIDI chain that includes at least one module, you join the new device's *in* port to the preceding device's *through* port. That way, the data that flows from the computer is transmitted simultaneously to all the devices in the chain.

Each join, be it computer-to-module or module-to-module, is done with a MIDI cable. This is a flexible cable with large, round five-pin male connectors on the ends. Cables are readily available at any music store or mail-order house that sells electronic musical instruments. MIDI cables are always male at both ends, because all MIDI instruments have female sockets. The only time you'd use a male–female or female–female cable is when you're joining lengths of MIDI cable to create a longer cable.

The *out* connector of a MIDI instrument is often left open when you're using canned production music. Some MIDI sound modules are able to transmit data back to the computer, and depending on the sequencing software you're using, that feedback may be valuable (check your software documentation). It has no importance in the playing of music, but it is sometimes used by software that includes the ability to reshape a sound module's instrument sounds. More frequently, however, the *out* connector is used on a keyboard synthesizer, external sequencer, or other device that produces MIDI music of its own. By connecting an electronic keyboard's *out* port to a computer MIDI interface's *in* port, you can record the notes you play on the keyboard as musical sequences that can be recorded, manipulated, and played back later. Unless you make that connection to the keyboard's *out* port, the notes you play can't be heard by the computer. They may make sound through the speaker or headphones connected to the keyboard, but only a cable to the MIDI interface's *in* port enables it to record new music.

Some computer MIDI interfaces also have *through* ports, allowing that the computer may be placed somewhere other than at the head of the MIDI chain. You might have another computer at the chain's head, but more likely, you'd use a keyboard synthesizer with a built-in sequencer.

One of the toughest concepts for new MIDI users to grasp is the difference between the *out* and *through* ports. It's actually not that difficult to understand if take the words at their literal meaning. The *out* port on any device, be it computer MIDI interface, sound module or keyboard synthesizer, transmits data that originates in that device alone. If you could look at the data emanating from a keyboard's *out* port, you'd see that, no matter what other data was coursing through the rest of the MIDI chain, the *out* port would show only what you commanded the keyboard to send out. The *through* port, in contrast, only passes data whose origin is a device earlier in the chain (most often the computer's MIDI interface) to the next device in the chain. You could connect a keyboard synthesizer's *through* port to our imaginary MIDI data viewer and bang on the keys all you like; you'd never see so much as a blip. But every bit of data originating at the computer could be seen, regardless of what you were doing with the keyboard at the moment.

If all that still seems confusing, consider the block diagram in Figure 4-18. It

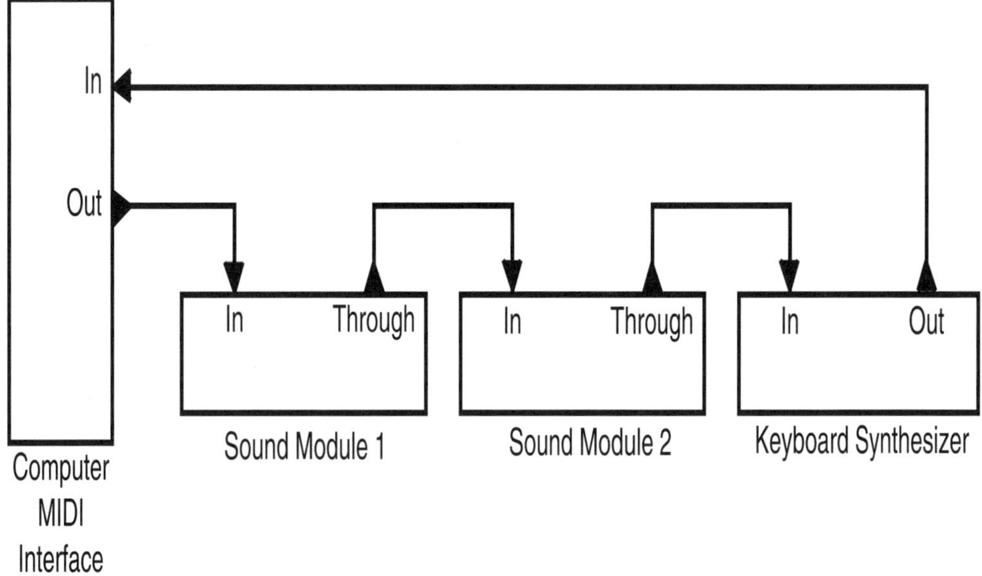

Figure 4-18: A typical MIDI network

shows what might be considered a typical MIDI setup for a musician: a computer MIDI interface (shown at the left) at the head of the MIDI network, two sound modules hooked together by *through-in* connections, and a MIDI keyboard at the end that can feed new music data back into the computer. This arrangement would allow you to use all three external MIDI devices—sound modules 1 and 2 and the keyboard synthesizer—to play music sequences. A keyboard synthesizer can be used as a playback device. In fact, it contains the same components you'd find in a sound module. The difference is that keyboard synthesizers, being larger and having more room to devote to controls, generally have more directly accessible features than sound modules.

Channels and Patches

Once you get your MIDI network hooked up, you have a few more buzzwords to contend with. The first is the concept of the *channel*. A computer's MIDI interface, by its nature, transmits every piece of MIDI data to every device in the chain. A simplistic view of this leaves one wondering how a particular device knows when to sound off and when to keep quiet. Consider a choral score, separated into four parts: bass, tenor, alto, and soprano. It would defeat the purpose of the score if all of the singers sang the same part. They, in effect, split themselves into channels, creating four distinct groups of singers that follow their own staff in the musical score. Each singer knows what part he or she sings. Any number of singers can sing a particular part, but each individual singer can only sing one part at a time.

MIDI channels follow that analogy in a rough fashion. Instead of four channels, MIDI has sixteen, and instead of named parts, MIDI simply uses channel numbers. How channels are used depends on the device and the software; I've seen some particularly creative applications of channels, so there aren't any hard and fast rules. What you're most likely to be faced with, however, is still complicated enough to require a bit of thought.

Most often, a MIDI channel is associated with an instrument sound. You might put a piano sound on channel one, strings on channel two, and horns on channel three. You would need to teach all of the devices in the chain (including your computer) to use this instrument/channel mapping. It's fairly easy with the computer. Most sequencing software lets you organize a piece of MIDI music into tracks that correspond with specific MIDI channels. The device down the stream from the computer that makes the string sound might be smart enough to take it from there, provided you embed the *patch number* into the sequencer track associated with MIDI channel two.

MIDI devices usually have built into them a variety of instrument sounds, called *patches* in homage to the old days when creating a new sound with a synthesizer meant changing cables on a patch panel. Each patch is identified by a patch number (usually from 0 to 127; some devices offer more than 128 instrument sounds). A sequencer can, based on data embedded in a MIDI sequence, send a command down the MIDI chain that says "tell the device listening to MIDI channel two to switch the instrument associated with that channel to patch number 17." The device will then make the switch, and from that point on, any music played on

MIDI channel two will sound like strings (provided strings are located at patch number 17 for that MIDI device).

How patch numbers relate to instrument sounds depends entirely on the device. Many sound modules and keyboards now adhere to the *general MIDI standard*, which defines a set of 128 instrument names that can be used predictably across devices adhering to the standard. With general MIDI devices, the "kalimba" and "pan flute" sounds are always in the same place. Thanks to this, you can create sequences that have embedded patch numbers and expect that they'll sound similar as long as they're played through general MIDI-compliant sound modules and keyboards. General MIDI doesn't mean that the songs will always sound the same. "Electric piano," for example, is a patch that sounds very different from one device to another. But general MIDI's purpose is not to enforce homogeny. It is, instead, meant to allow you (and others) to create music that can be reproduced anywhere else without requiring the use of the same equipment you used to create it. Even though a Roland electric piano patch sounds nothing like that coming from a Yamaha device, it's still recognizable as an electric piano. Prior to general MIDI, you'd have been just as likely to have a tuba play when you expected a piano.

The world's not perfect yet. There are still plenty of nonconforming MIDI devices, particularly among professional keyboards that can load new sounds from floppies and memory cards. The Ensoniq EPS 16 Plus I use, for example, can make no sound at all until I load an instrument disk. Because of this, the EPS 16 Plus can't reasonably be a general MIDI instrument. I can, however, use this keyboard to create music that will eventually be played through a general MIDI device. I must do that, because I'd hate to have to insist that everyone who plays my music do so on an EPS 16 Plus (even though it's a fine keyboard). So even when I'm not using a general MIDI-compliant device, I can create my music in a way that takes advantage of the standard and allows others easier access.

A single MIDI device rarely listens to only a single MIDI channel. More often, a single device can listen to multiple channels at once (usually all sixteen if it suits you). It can separate out the channel data internally, maintaining an internal map of channel/instrument relationships. Because of this, you can have the equivalent instrumental diversity of an orchestra coming from a single MIDI device. So you don't need a separate MIDI device for every different instrument you plan to use. One well-chosen sound module is very likely all you'll need to play MIDI sequences that use several instrument sounds.

You can have multiple MIDI devices listening to a single MIDI channel. You may also assign multiple instruments within a single device to a particular channel. This is a useful technique called *layering* that makes your music fuller by piling multiple instrument sounds onto a single note. Layering the percussive piano and soft strings on the same MIDI channel, for example, produces a combination that's commonly applied to romantic music. You might construct a completely new piano sound, mad scientist style, by layering different flavors of piano on top of one another or mixing multiple percussive sounds (piano, guitar, kalimba) together. You can layer instruments with impunity (there's is no arbitrary limit on the number of instruments you can stack on a MIDI channel), but remember that devices do have finite limits to their polyphony. Let's say you have a sound module that supports 16-voice polyphony. If you instruct it to listen to MIDI channel one, and place a piano patch on that channel, you'll be able to listen to up to 16 notes of piano at once. If you layer strings on the same channel, you limit yourself to eight notes. Layer again, and you'll have still fewer. Layers work best when you have multiple MIDI devices, for only by adding new devices can you add notes to your MIDI network's polyphonic range.

Most MIDI devices don't assign a strict number of notes of polyphony to a MIDI channel. Instead, they'll simply allocate the notes they need, regardless of the channel being used, until they run out. As soon as each note becomes silent, the polyphonic slot it occupied is freed for the next request. Some devices will let you assign a priority to certain channels and instruments to ensure that no matter what else happens, you'll always have a certain number of notes reserved for that channel. You might find this useful because when a MIDI device runs out of polyphony, it either doesn't play new notes or it "steals" notes that are currently being played. The result is either gaps in the music or notes that end before they're supposed to. Both sound awful, but the impact can be minimized if you reserve notes for the most audible portions of your score. If you have a piano and an organ that both play the same chords, you might reserve some notes for the piano channel so that it never drops a note. The organ can drop notes without doing serious damage as long as the piano sound is more prominent.

A basic part of the configuration of a MIDI network that includes multiple devices is the division of channel assignments among those devices. This is difficult or impossible to do with devices that don't include front panels with displays. How you split MIDI channels among devices is up to you. You won't necessarily want an even split (sixteen divided by the number of devices) unless you have multiple devices of the same exact model. Otherwise, allocate channels based on consideration of polyphonic limits, layering and the relative quality of the device's sound. You'd likely allocate more channels to a device with lots of polyphony and high-quality sound. If you can't come up with uses for all sixteen channels, don't fret. Make a wild guess about their assignments and let them be. If a sequencer doesn't send any data out for a particular MIDI channel, the instrument assigned to that channel makes no sound. Don't blindly layer seemingly unused MIDI channels because that will reduce your polyphony.

The command to change to a different patch can come at any time during the playing of a MIDI sequence, and you can change any channel's patch as often as you like. When you request a patch number change, it is acted upon by all MIDI devices listening to the channel on which that patch change was sent. If all of the devices are of the same type, or they're all general MIDI-compliant, then that's not a problem. Otherwise, you'll want to be careful about having two or more different nongeneral MIDI devices sharing a channel. A MIDI patch change command is just a patch number, not a clear identification like "piano." Two devices with different instrument mappings, both set to listen to the same MIDI channel, will almost certainly respond to a single patch change command by creating a layered sound you weren't expecting. Avoid the problem by giving dissimilar devices channels of their own.

If you find all this channel and patch jazz really confusing, don't worry. There are plenty of MIDI sound modules built for folks who just want to use canned music and don't want to fuss with understanding MIDI. They are intended for use in single-device networks in which one MIDI module is connected to the computer's MIDI interface. The module listens to all sixteen MIDI channels itself, so all you have to do is load the canned music and play it. For this kind of work, you don't even need a sequencer. Let's take a look at some of the choices available to you as you shop for electronic music hardware.

MIDI Devices

If you don't already have the hardware, creating a MIDI network to add music to whatever you're creating must start with the selection of gear. Computer MIDI interfaces are, with the exception of high-end units laden with features aimed at those who make a living in music, so similarly capable that there's no real need to comparison shop. But as far as the devices that create and play the electronic music are concerned, the choices are many.

The choices available to you start with MIDI sound modules. As I said earlier, these are compact boxes that listen to MIDI commands and produce sound; they have no other purpose. These units range in price from a few hundred to a few thousand dollars. You'll also find that sound modules differ as widely in price as in design. Some have computerized front panels with backlit LCD displays from which you can adjust the device's sound characteristics directly. Others have only more primitive labeled knobs on the front panel that let you set playback volume and, sometimes, the default instrument sound used to play music that doesn't specify a certain instrument. The extreme can be found in the expansive rack-mountable modules that feature dauntingly complex front panels and often include diskette drives or memory card slots.

The look and feel of a module has a lot to do with its origin. The larger rack-mounted units often descend from similarly capable keyboards. In fact, many of the most popular professional keyboards from companies like Ensoniq and Korg have identical rack-mount sound modules; all they lack is the keyboard itself. These occupy the top range in both price and learning curve, but also tend to deliver the best sound quality and choice of instrument sounds. They frequently also include features that make them as much computers as musical instruments. The Ensoniq EPS 16 Plus keyboard synthesizer (which is also available in a rack-mount module) I use in my lab sports a floppy drive, a SCSI port for a hard drive or a CD-ROM drive, and expandable memory, features you'd expect to find in a desktop computer. Indeed, when you have a keyboard like the EPS 16 Plus in your production facility, you can sometimes do without the computer. This keyboard, like many other professional instruments, has a very capable built-in sequencer that can handle up to eight independent channels of MIDI music.

MIDI devices that include front panels may allow you to change the shape of the sounds the device makes. In the case of the Ensoniq EPS 16 Plus, you have an astounding number of programmable parameters associated with each instrument sound. Once you reshape the sound the way you want it, you can save that sound as a new instrument on disk without obliterating the old one. Some other non-disk-based systems can store your instrument sound changes in "nonvolatile memory," memory that doesn't get wiped out when you turn the power off. You can make changes to instrument sounds, turn the device off, and have those changed instruments waiting for you when you turn the device on even days later.

Patch Programming

The ability to reshape an instrument sound may appeal to you if you have a keen ear and you're willing to invest the time to learn what the various sound-altering parameters mean. The end product of your exercise will be an instrument that differs in some tiny or substantial way from the standard instrument sound included with the device (or stored on a disk or memory card you purchased). Reshaping an instrument is a way to make it your own, to help ensure that the instruments in your music won't be duplicated elsewhere. You can see to it that no one wears the same dress to the party as you, so to speak. Changing the shape of a sound is also useful if you find a sound that's *almost* what you're looking for, but it lacks some quality you can easily add.

There are two ways to change an instrument sound in a synthesizer: through the synthesizer's own front panel and through a software tool called a *patch librarian*. The latter is a helpful program that runs on your computer and talks to your synthesizer through MIDI cables. The patch librarian stores and retrieves the parameters associated with instrument sounds. More capable librarians let you modify patch parameters as well.

The list of modifiable sound parameters varies from device to device. Making changes to an existing sound or creating a new instrument sound from scratch is called *programming*. That word may bring to mind a frightening vision of flowchart templates and pocket protectors, and in truth, some synthesizers present a very intimidating interface to those who wish to create custom sounds. Others are obviously designed to make changes as painless as possible. Because of the vast numbers of different synthesizers that exist, I can't afford to launch into detail about synthesizer programming here. It would be too difficult to give you information you could use regardless of your choice of equipment. I can, however, relate a couple of basics that apply pretty broadly to just about all programmable synthesizers.

Probably the easiest thing to change about a sound, given a module or keyboard that permits it, is its *amplitude envelope*. An envelope contains something, and in this case, the amplitude envelope contains the volume levels associated with an instrument sound. Typically, the envelope is represented as a graph or as at least four pairs of numeric parameters: *attack*, *decay*, *sustain*, and *release*. Each parameter pair determines the length and loudness of the instrument at a specific phase in its life. These four parameters were chosen to allow sound designers to make a synthesized instrument behave as much like a real instrument as possible. A piano makes a good example of amplitude envelope programming. When you strike a key, the string vibrates and reaches its full volume very quickly (it sounds immediate, but it's actually a tiny and measurable length of time). That's the attack. The attack time is the period an instrument takes to reach its attack (usually its loudest) level. The attack level is the loudness the instrument reaches at the end of its attack. The time and level are often represented by synthesizers as arbitrary numbers on a known scale; level is frequently seen as a percentage of the instrument's maximum possible volume. The combination of time and level make a good graph, with time occupying the *x* (horizontal) axis and level occupying the *y* (vertical) (see Figure 4-19). The steeper the slope, the faster the attack. Shorter attack times

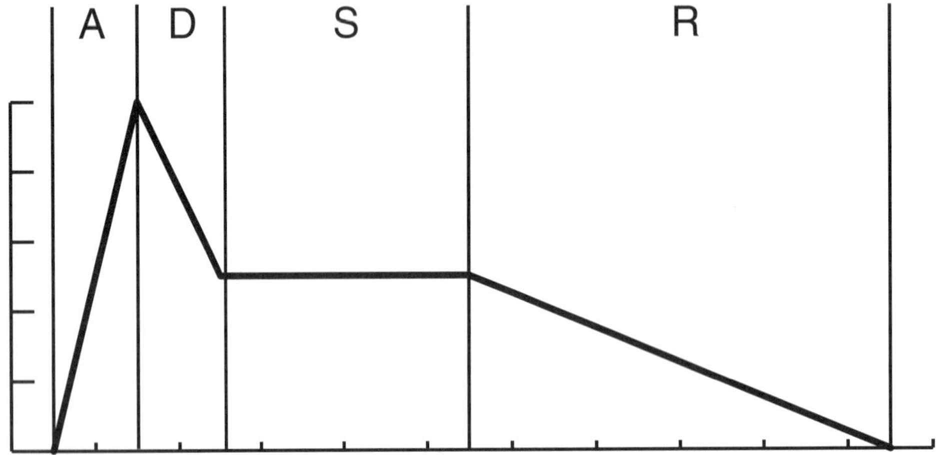

Figure 4-19: An amplitude envelope graph showing attack, decay, sustain and release

are associated with percussive instruments (like the piano). A medium attack lends softness and realism to wind instruments, while long attacks are often reserved for warm strings.

After the attack comes the decay. A piano note reaches its full volume quickly as the string is hit, then drops down to a slightly lower volume while the string vibrates. The decay time and level determine the path the amplitude envelope takes to bring the sound from its maximum attack level to the decay level. Wind instruments and strings have no decay (the decay level is set to be the same as the attack level), unless you're looking to create a unique effect. A rock sax, for example, might start with a loud punch and decay to a softer volume.

The sustain follows the decay. The sustain level is the volume the instrument eventually reaches if the key or sustain pedal is held down. The sustain time determines the maximum duration of the fade from the end of the decay to the end of the sustain. A piano with its sustain pedal held down will eventually reach zero volume; so will a guitar. A wind instrument has indefinite full-volume sustain; the holding of a synthesizer key or a sustain pedal provides an infinite supply of "wind."

The release wraps it all up. This is the path the envelope takes to bring the sound from its sustain level to silence. The piano, like most acoustic instruments, has a quick release. The guitar, whose strings aren't normally damped, is an exception. Orchestra triangles and chimes are another, and a timpani produces a sound with a moderate to long release as well.

While you might modify an amplitude envelope to make a sound more realistic, you'll usually do it to create a different kind of instrument sound from one of your synthesizer's patches. A synthesizer string sound often has a slow attack, no decay, full-volume sustain, and a long release. By applying a piano envelope (short attack, reduced-volume decay, long sustain to silence, fast release) to the string patch, you can create a surreal-sounding "string piano" that you can layer with another percussive sound to give it additional depth. Modifying the amplitude envelopes of drum sounds can create some stirring effects as well. A popular gimmick for some rock music is the "reverse envelope cymbal," which uses a slow attack and an instant release—the opposite of the natural cymbal's envelope.

This type of synthesizer programming is also often applicable to another envelope, the *filter envelope*. The filter affects the "brightness" of a sound. It's not a complete match, but you might think of the difference between muted and unmuted trombones and trumpets. You might also think of a filter as hands cupped around a harmonica. When the mute or the hands are opened, the sound gets brighter. The filter envelope determines, in effect, how muted or bright the sound is at various points in its life. These points are rarely tied to the amplitude envelope.

Performance Parameters

The amplitude and filter envelopes affect the shape of the sound, but you can effect some changes to the instrument sound as you play. Again, different synthesizers and sound modules offer different performance parameters, but I'll focus on a few of the common ones.

All of the parameters below have in common that they can be captured by a sequencer, along with your music, while you play. Changes to these parameters, as effected by the controls described, are recorded in real time and can be heard in playback exactly as they're heard during a live session. Keyboards differ in their range of performance features and the ability to generate MIDI data for these features. This list isn't complete—there are some truly unusual parameters and controls—but it represents the ones you're most likely to encounter.

Volume is a pretty basic control, but many keyboards don't send volume control changes out as MIDI data. The ones that do send it out as a sort of master control, changing the volume of all the music being played at the time (even if that music involves multiple instruments). Even this is helpful, however, allowing you to apply a greater dynamic range to your music and even to manage fade-in and fade-out effects.

Patch change is sent out as MIDI data by most keyboards. If you're playing on a keyboard that allows quick instrument assignment changes while you play, you can create very rich compositions that include transitions from one instrument to another. There's no real limit on how many patch changes you can have in one piece of music, but keep in mind that your synthesizer may need a little time to effect the change. Don't do an instrument change while notes are being played; the results will be unpredictable and almost certainly unpleasant.

Key velocity is a feature of most professional keyboards, but it is now finding its way into inexpensive instruments as well. The basic version of the concept is simple: the harder you strike the key, the louder the instrument will play. This lets you play a synthesizer like you'd play a piano, applying volume dynamics to the music by hitting the keys with varying degrees of force. Some keyboards can do more with key velocity than make the sound louder. Some, like the Ensoniq EPS-16 Plus, can also change attack and other characteristics based on velocity. The EPS-16 Plus also supports what Ensoniq calls *poly-key pressure*. Most velocity-sensitive keyboards sense a single velocity which is applied equally to all the keys. If you play softly with your left hand and bang on the keys with your right, most keyboards will play a loud sound based on the greater pressure of your right hand. Poly-key pressure senses velocity for each key individually, so the sounds played with your left hand would play softly, while those played on the right would be louder.

Aftertouch uses a keyboard's velocity sensing mechanism to change the shape of an already-playing note. If you're playing a saxophone sound from your keyboard, you can add expressiveness to it by placing a rasp, a volume increase, or a pitch bend on the keyboard's aftertouch. Applying greater pressure to the key after you've sounded the initial note will cause whatever effect you've tied to the aftertouch to modify the instrument sound. The harder you press on the key, the more the effect. *Polyphonic aftertouch* appears in the features lists of some keyboards, and refers to the ability to apply aftertouch effects on individual notes. Most keyboards with aftertouch can only apply it to all notes being played at once.

Keyboard synthesizers are frequently endowed with devices specifically designed to change the shape of an instrument sound while you play. Three such common devices are the *sustain pedal*, the *pitch wheel*, and the *modulation wheel* (frequently abbreviated as "mod wheel"). The sustain pedal's purpose should be self-explanatory: it serves the same purpose as the same-named pedal on a piano. Some keyboard synthesizers let you reprogram the purpose served by the sustain pedal. You might, for example, use the pedal to jump to the next patch number without interrupting play. Professional keyboards sometimes provide connections for two pedals so that one can be devoted to a special purpose such as this, while still leaving a dedicated sustain pedal.

The pitch wheel (which may be a slider or other device on some keyboards) bends the notes you're playing up or down depending on the direction in which you push the wheel. When done as a wheel, pitch bending involves pushing a large-diameter, thin wheel of plastic with ribbed edges up to bend the pitch up, and down to bend the pitch down. The wheel is spring-loaded to return to center (normal pitch) when you release it. Synthesizers with pitch wheels let you program the interval used for the top and bottom of the bend. The wheel bends the pitch over a continuous range between normal pitch and the extremes you set. Changing the interval does not change the feel of the wheel; it still rolls up and down the same amount regardless of your settings.

The modulation wheel applies some change, programmed by you, to the sound as the wheel is moved. This wheel is not spring-loaded; if you move it, it stays put when you let go. The more you push the wheel toward the top of its range, the more modulation is applied to the music you're playing. Modulation can take several forms. Popular uses include vibrato and tremolo, filter (with that word applied as in the description of filter envelopes, above), and A/B mixing. The latter case doesn't occur on all synthesizers. A/B mixing is used when two patches, or a single patch with two component sounds, are layered. At the bottom of the mod wheel's range, the A sound is heard. At the top, B. In the middle, equal parts of A and B mixed together. You might have a layer that places a piano on A and strings on B. Through the mod wheel, you might be able to switch instrument sounds and even gradually fade layered strings into your piano part as you play.

The EPS-16 Plus has a couple more special performance parameter devices. They are *patch select* buttons. This pair of small rectangular buttons sits just above the pitch and mod wheels. Pressing them alone or in combination offers instant access to up to three variations on the current patch. An organ sound, for example, might have a snappy percussive organ on one variation, a chorus effect (see "effects," below) on another, and the same patch done an octave lower or higher on the third. Most Ensoniq patches, delivered on diskette, include patch variations.

The videotape offers a look at (and a listen to) these and other performance characteristics.

Effects

A MIDI instrument, be it a keyboard or a sound module, may offer one or more built-in effects. It wasn't that long ago that if you wanted to change the way your instrument sounded, you had to use an external effects box. *Reverb*, which simulates the reverberation of a sound in a large room or concert hall, is probably the most-used external effect. It is still applied to at least the vocals of virtually every song recorded. Far from the boxes full of springs of old, modern technology has turned reverb into a small number of inexpensive components. These components are so small that they fit comfortably inside keyboard synthesizers and sound modules. Other effects have been scaled down as well. Not every synth offers every effect; indeed, some synthesizers, even good ones, don't have any built-in effects. All of the built-in effects I've seen have in common that they can only process the sounds made by the keyboard; you can't plug a microphone into a synthesizer and sing through its effects module.

Because of its popularity, reverb is easy to find as a built-in effect. Synthesizers that have it let you tune reverb parameters, at least including *depth* and *blend.*

Reverb depth roughly adjusts the "size of the room," with deeper reverb settings making for longer-lasting reverberations. The blend adjusts the mix between the original sound and the reverb effect. Unless you're after a strange sound, you'll never use a mix of 100% reverb. If your synth allows, play a passage and nudge the blend and depth slowly until the sound is "wet" enough to suit you.

By far the most widely implemented effect is *chorus*. Here, one instrument is made to sound like several. The synth makes a copy of the sound, detunes it a tiny bit (which you can sometimes set), and mixes the original and detuned sounds together. With the advent of massive polyphony and multi-device MIDI, if you want to thicken your sound with layers, you can use real instruments that are all tuned to the same note. Some instruments don't work well with chorus; the detuning can make your music sound cheap.

Echo (also referred to as *delay*) is finding its way into more and more synthesizers. As when you shout into a canyon, electronic echo records a sound and plays it back after a fixed delay, repeating that cycle a fixed number of times, reducing the volume of the echoed sound each time. Done well, echo can work wonders with all parts of a piece of music: lead vocals, lead instrumentals, drums and background chords. The trick is not to use it for more than one or two of these. Reverb and echo are often used in combination, with echo sometimes reserved for lead riffs and other foreground sounds.

Distortion doesn't sound like something you'd want in your music, but it's handy to have around for hard-edged rock. A synthesizer can simulate a rock guitar passably well, but it doesn't really take off until a little distortion (also called *fuzz* or *overdrive*) is added. This gives an instrument a raspy tone, as when it's played through an amplifier that's had its volume turned up a little higher than it can handle. It's not just for guitars—distortion, in moderation, can also enhance sax, piano, and other patches that you want to paint with a few spikes.

Flanging and *phasing* are throwbacks to psychedelic days, and appropriately so: at full intensity, they sound like a drug experience (not that I'd know what one sounds like, mind you). If you've ever heard the Beatles' "Lucy in the Sky With Diamonds," then you may recall this continuously sweeping modulation that cycles a sound from tinny-high to rumbly-low, raising and lowering a filter in a sine-wave pattern. It is often accompanied by a panning of the sound between the left and right stereo channels that is timed to match or complement the flange. Very weird. Flanging and phasing have their applications, though, if you use them sparingly and in a very mild mix that leaves them only barely perceptible. It blends in an unpredictable quality that can keep a listener occupied. Of course, you can use them more aggressively if you're after an eclectic sound.

Compression doesn't mean the same here as it does when it's used in relation to computer data. Instead, this effect squeezes the dynamic range of the music you play. The flavor of the sound is difficult to describe, except that it sounds a little like an instrument being played through a stage amplifier. Lead instruments are often compressed to give them a little extra "crunch."

These effects are important even if you're not invoking them as you play. If you don't play your own music, you can instruct MIDI sequencing software to make these effects happen (assuming your equipment supports it).

Sequencing

The process of capturing and manipulating MIDI data is called *sequencing*. This is a good term because it strikes a difference between the way MIDI data is captured, stored, edited and played back, and the way you'd use a tape recorder. MIDI data is a sequence of instructions for playing notes, triggering effects, setting configuration parameters, changing the volume...in short, MIDI can capture nearly everything you do as you play.

MIDI is a far-reaching standard, covering everything from cables and serial data rates to the representation of the data itself. The MIDI code for a particular note on the scale is precisely the same on every MIDI device ever made, and it will always be so. Few standards are as well defined and adhered to as this. That's not to say that vendors haven't occasionally gone their own way. The standard leaves room for "system exclusive" MIDI messages that provide some function not covered by the standard. You usually don't have to worry about system exclusive or, for that matter, any kind of MIDI data. You'll most likely use a sequencer to manage your sequences of MIDI music.

Even if you're not recording your own MIDI files, you'll want at least a basic sequencer around if you plan to use electronic music in your presentations. You'll often need to change a song's patches to match the instruments you're using or to alter the mood of the piece. You may also use a sequencer to alter the tempo, key, number of repeats, and other musical attributes without understanding music yourself. Of course, a musician will get more out of a sequencer, but they still offer much to those who have at least some sense of musical aesthetics and are willing to experiment.

I won't take the time here to offer you a course in MIDI sequencing. Instead, I'll give you a look at a couple of popular sequencers, and I'll talk about a few of the most common sequencing operations. I highly recommend you follow this up with some study of your own. All of the systems used for this book have very inexpensive sequencers available for them; you may even find something in the public domain or as shareware.

As an aside, I'll remind you that some keyboard synthesizers, and some high-end sound modules (usually those based on keyboard synths) have built-in sequencers. Some of these, like the one built into the Ensoniq EPS-16 Plus, are very capable. However, synthesizers' built-in sequencers don't solve the problem of getting the MIDI data into your computer for use with other media. While I find built-in sequencers a tremendous convenience as I compose and arrange my own music, computer-based sequencing software is much more powerful and easy to use.

If you don't yet have a sequencer, you'll have to start by selecting your software. There are several factors that contribute to such a decision. Fortunately, most of the tougher questions only need to be asked by "serious musicians." That's not to suggest that your use of music isn't going to be serious, but by and large, multimedia producers call on far fewer of a sequencer's features than do professional musicians.

Representation

Perhaps the largest issue is that of musical representation. If you're planning to do any editing of individual notes or groups of notes, you'll want to think about how you'd like to view them. If you've had some musical training, you may like to see *notation*, notes drawn in traditional style on a five-line staff. Some software does better notation than others. At the top are packages like Passport Designs' Encore (Mac/Windows), which are built mostly for those who transcribe notation for publication. But Encore can "go both ways," converting the MIDI data you play into its minimal sequencer into notation, and converting notation to MIDI music that you can play directly. Encore and its like are tremendously useful when you have sheet music (be careful of copyrights—make sure the sheet music is either your own creation or is clearly in the public domain) that you'd like to turn into presentation music. Entering music as notation is excruciatingly painful, but like any task you manage with a computer, it gets easier as you do more of it. Some music stores that cater to schools and instructors will have sheet music of orchestral and symphonic classical and traditional pieces. I can't stress enough that you must be cautious of copyright. If the music or the arrangement is copyrighted, you place yourself at some risk by using it. The risk of using more modern music is greater; record companies and music publishers actively pursue copyright violators.

In the middle tier of notation-based sequencers, you'll find Electronic Arts' Deluxe Music Construction Set (Amiga). This is a simple but very respectable sequencer/notation editor that has less of an emphasis on visual aesthetics and publishability than Encore. I've found Deluxe Music to be the quickest way to get sheet music into the computer. I also use it to compose music from scratch. Being from Electronic Arts, there are parts of it that feel a little unpolished, but I recommend it very highly to anyone using an Amiga for notation-based editing.

The lowest tier of notation-based sequencing is found in software like Bars & Pipes Professional (Amiga) and Cakewalk Professional (Windows) that offer limited notation as an alternate view on a piece of MIDI music. The notation is *extremely* limited and is only useful for checking your timing and doing cut and paste operations; it's a little easier to locate musical phrases in notation than in the traditional sequencer "bars" view.

Most popular sequencers use a graphical shorthand for representing musical notes. Passport's Trax and Master Trax Pro (Mac/Windows) use bars, as does Blue Ribbon Soundworks' Bars & Pipes Professional (Amiga). They offer an unintimidating view of music for nonmusicians. The bars represent the music very directly: the vertical location of the bar signifies the note value, the horizontal placement signifies the starting time of the note, and the bar's length corresponds to the note's length. Bars let you see more of the music at once than notation, and you needn't understand the theory of note values, rests, and so on.

Figure 4-20 shows a view of a pretty typical MIDI sequencer, Passport's Trax. Take a look at the bars in this figure. You'll note that the left side of the view is taken up by a graphical keyboard. The bars are aligned with this keyboard so that the vertical placement of the bar matches the note on the keyboard at that level. You can also move the mouse around the screen in this view and get a constantly updated readout of the note value the mouse is pointing to.

The bars view is, for the most part, the best place to make minute note changes

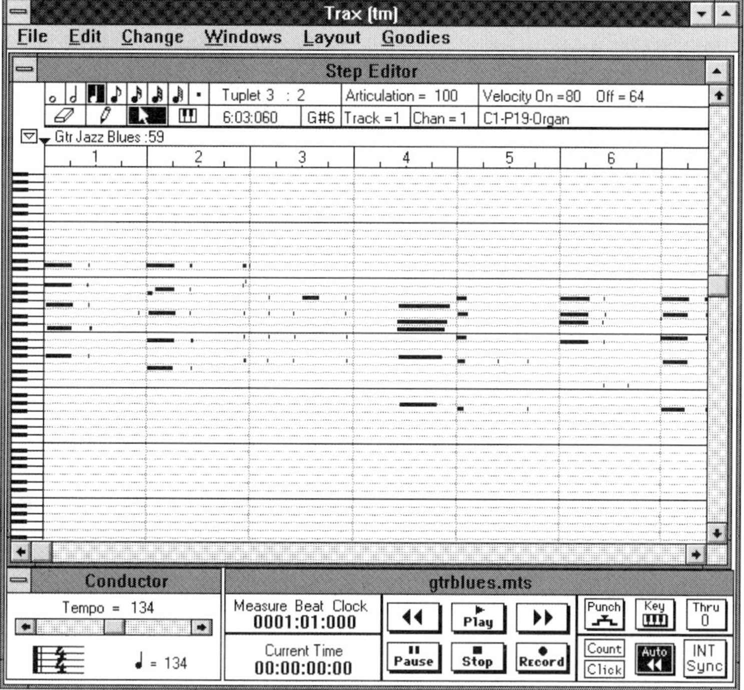

Figure 4-20: A "bars" representation of music

to a piece of music. Notes, or bars, can be selected, cut, copied and pasted, moved up or down to change their pitch, shortened or elongated to change their duration, and moved horizontally to have the music they represent start playing at a different time. Editing music in this view can take some getting used to, especially for musicians. The best way to learn to edit this way is to practice. Take a piece of music that you're very familiar with and create exercises for yourself that cover all the basic operations the editor makes available to you.

The bar view in Trax shows one track's (usually one MIDI channel's) worth of data. You can jump from channel to channel with relative ease. Bars & Pipes Professional (shown in Figure 4-21) offers a bars view similar to Trax, but takes the business of bars one step further. The view shown in the figure is Bars & Pipes' main interface, and as you can see, the program offers miniature bars views of, in this case, eleven tracks at once. The MIDI data is not editable in this view, but a pointer scrolls through the bars as you play your sequence so you can see your

Figure 4-20: Bars & Pipes Professional

music. You can also get a very clear picture of where the busy and silent passages are in your music.

Changing Instrument Assignments

It's very likely that the thing you'll spend much of your time doing in a sequencer is changing instrument or patch assignments. I'm forced to introduce yet another synonym for "patch": *program.* I avoided using this term before to prevent confusion, but I can't use correct MIDI terminology without it now. The stream of data captured by a MIDI sequencer can include *program changes*, commands embedded in the MIDI stream that cause the synthesizer to change the instrument sound associated with a particular MIDI channel. You might recall that MIDI programs are referred to by number. One of the advantages offered by good sequencers is that they have built into them the program number/instrument name mappings for several popular MIDI synthesizers and sound modules. I use the Roland SC-55 Sound Canvas sound module, and fortunately, that unit conforms to the General MIDI specification. That makes changing instrument assignments very simple.

A piece of canned MIDI music will have its own instrument assignments. Program change messages are usually embedded into the beginning of each track of

MIDI data. Even if you change the instrument assignments using the front panel of the synthesizer, they'll be changed back to the defaults provided by the canned music as soon as you start the sequence playing again. Changing the instrument assignment for a particular track or channel sometimes involves bringing up a dialog box similar to the one in Figure 4-21. As you effect changes to a song's instru-

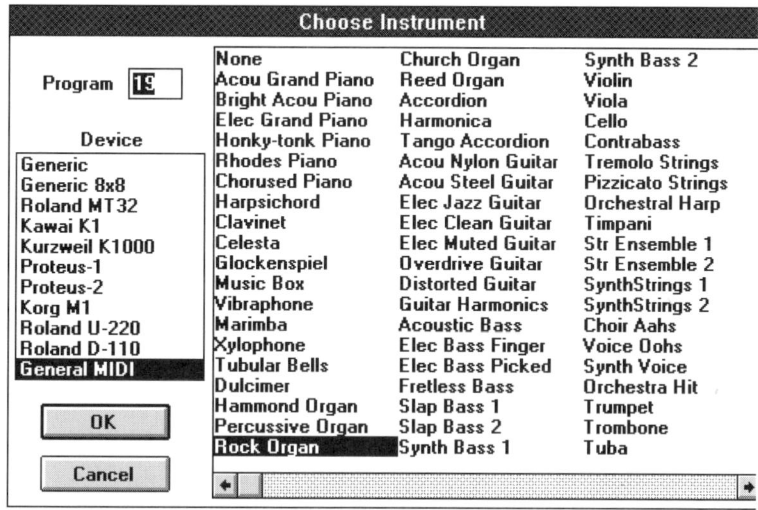

Figure 4-21: Changing a channel's instrument

ment assignments, keep in mind that changing the instrument for a channel makes that change for all sequencer tracks that play on that channel. Most sequencers let you create multiple tracks of music that will be played through a single MIDI channel. In fact, if you have a piece of music with multiple tracks but with only one instrument (as when the left and right hand of a classical piano piece have been transcribed into separate tracks), it's common practice to point all of those tracks at the same MIDI channel. If you later decide that you'd like to change the instrument assignment of only *one* of those tracks, you have to do something else first. Before you can change the instrument assignment for a track that shares a MIDI channel with other tracks, you must change that track's channel assignment. So, in the example of the two-track piano piece, let's say we started with two tracks, both assigned to play through MIDI channel one. If you wanted to change the bass, held in track two, to another instrument, you'd first have to reassign it to MIDI channel two. Actually, you could reassign it to any other unused MIDI channel, but it sometimes helps simplify things to set a MIDI score up with a direct tracks-to-channels mapping.

Your sequencer might not know the instrument names associated with your synthesizer's program numbers. In that case, your changes to the instrument assignments will have to be entered numerically. You'll find a list of program numbers and associated instrument names in your synthesizer's documentation. One caveat: some documentation differs in the representation of the program numbers. All MIDI instruments have room for 128 basic programs. Some synthesizer documentation lists program numbers as being in the range of 0–127, while other manuals show it as 1–128. This can create some frustrating "off by one" problems when you're hunting around for a particular instrument. If you plug in a program number that doesn't sound like the instrument it's supposed to represent, simply try the next one up and the next one down. Then make that same adjustment every time you change an instrument assignment for that synthesizer.

Altering Performance Parameters

I spent some time earlier talking about those things that modify the shape of sound as you play. A sequencer can capture and store your manipulation of performance-altering controls, and it can also add the data that control normally generates to an existing MIDI score. Volume changes are the most common alteration, and sequencers add the ability to change the playback volume for an individual MIDI channel, a feat that's difficult to manage from most synthesizers. The Trax interface seen in Figure 4-22 shows the track view common to many sequencers. Trax, like many others, gives you a volume control for each track. In this case, you can slide the controls back and forth while the sequence is playing to create a mix. Those individual volume levels are stored with the sequence and are reflected in the playback.

Other performance parameters aren't as easy to modify. Most of them require entering your sequencer's event view, in which the individual numeric messages that make up a MIDI sequence can be seen. Not all sequencers have event editors; you have to move up from Passport's basic Trax to its more capable Master Trax Pro (Mac/Windows) to gain the event editor shown in Figure 4-23. Just a quick look at its interface reveals how complex MIDI data is once you zoom in on it. If this looks a little daunting, keep in mind that I've seen much more frightening event editors. The one in Master Trax Pro is quite friendly as editors go.

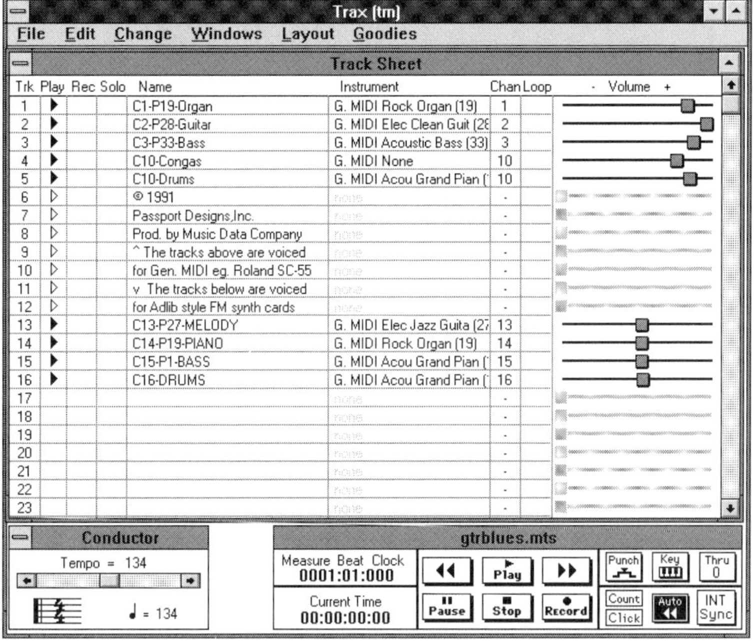

Figure 4-22: The track view (with volume sliders)

Using an event editor to add performance parameters to a piece of music or change existing parameters requires that you learn your sequencer's representation of event types and their corresponding data. Master Trax Pro uses little icons to identify the MIDI event type on each line, and the data associated with that event is grouped onto the same line for clarity and ease of editing. This sequencer can represent note, program change, pitch bend, aftertouch, poly-key pressure and arbitrary controller events. The icons represent the MIDI event types that are covered by the MIDI standard; others are lumped into the "arbitrary controller" category and are represented by a controller number and a corresponding data value. This accommodates odd controllers such as the breath controller (you blow into it), but also allows MIDI instruments to embed special data into sequences without resorting to the more confusing system exclusive event type. Roland's SC-55 Sound Canvas sound module, for example, uses a special controller event to provide more than the 128 standard instrument sounds.

Before you enter the event editor and start making low-level changes, you should capture a short sequence of known events from your keyboard (if you have

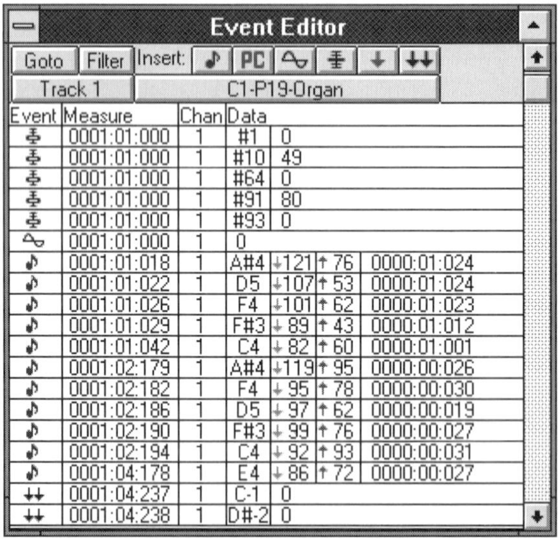

Event Editor

Goto | Filter | Insert: | PC

Track 1 | C1-P19-Organ

Event	Measure	Chan	Data			
	0001:01:000	1	#1	0		
	0001:01:000	1	#10	49		
	0001:01:000	1	#64	0		
	0001:01:000	1	#91	80		
	0001:01:000	1	#93	0		
	0001:01:000	1	0			
	0001:01:018	1	A#4	↓121	↑ 76	0000:01:024
	0001:01:022	1	D5	↓107	↑ 53	0000:01:024
	0001:01:026	1	F4	↓101	↑ 62	0000:01:023
	0001:01:029	1	F#3	↓ 89	↑ 43	0000:01:012
	0001:01:042	1	C4	↓ 82	↑ 60	0000:01:001
	0001:02:179	1	A#4	↓119	↑ 95	0000:00:026
	0001:02:182	1	F4	↓ 95	↑ 78	0000:00:030
	0001:02:186	1	D5	↓ 97	↑ 62	0000:00:019
	0001:02:190	1	F#3	↓ 99	↑ 76	0000:00:027
	0001:02:194	1	C4	↓ 92	↑ 93	0000:00:031
	0001:04:178	1	E4	↓ 86	↑ 72	0000:00:027
↓↓	0001:04:237	1	C-1	0		
↓↓	0001:04:238	1	D#-2	0		

Figure 4-23: A MIDI event editor

one) so you can learn how your actions translate to events. Synthesizer manuals provide lists of controller numbers, patch numbers and such, but your sequencer's representation of these events can't be predicted by your MIDI device's manufacturer.

If you become proficient at it, the MIDI event editor can also help you make minute timing and pitch changes to your music. If you hit a bad note, you may have an easier time locating and changing it in the event editor than in the bars view. That will depend on whether you're more comfortable with a textual or graphical representation.

Continuous-range controllers, like the pitch and mod wheels, are almost impossible to modify with the event editor. Each minute movement of such controls is recorded as a separate event. Pushing the pitch bend wheel upward might create dozens of controller events, and there could well be other events interleaved that make the beginning and end of the action difficult to locate. Some sequencers, including both Master Trax Pro and Bars & Pipes Professional, will let you draw a graph that represents the change of a particular control over time. Volume, pitch bend and mod wheel changes are most easily altered this way, and it's certainly the most sensible way to add controller events where they don't exist.

Transports, Tempo and Time

Dealing with a sequencer revolves around its transport controls. These are typically fashioned after tape recorder or VCR controls, giving you a comfortable way to move around in your MIDI sequence as well as play from and record to it.

By default, pressing the Play button in a transport control window will start all tracks of the sequence playing from the current location in the song. How you change that location varies from one sequencer to another, but you can generally move around via the transport controls (fast forward and rewind), clicking the mouse button inside some view of the sequence, or popping up a window that lets you directly enter the time value to which you wish to jump. Some portion of the transport controls are always active, so while you're playing you can at least count on being able to press the Stop button to halt playback.

You have control over what happens when you press Play. In the track view, you can choose to listen to certain tracks and ignore others by toggling the play/mute/solo control. This control is normally set to "play" for all tracks that have data in them so you'll hear the entire song with all its instruments. To cause a certain track *not* to play, you can set its control to "mute." The data doesn't get erased, but the sequencer doesn't send that track's data to your MIDI device when you play your song. If you want to listen to just one track, some sequencers save you the trouble of muting all but one track by providing you a "solo" option that serves the same purpose. As soon as you turn off the solo option for that track, the other tracks are unmuted.

Tempo and time signature adjustments also affect playback. These settings, which are either part of your transport controls or in a window of their own, determine the playback tempo of your song. Changing the tempo doesn't change your MIDI note data. You can alter the tempo with impunity, usually while your sequence is playing. The tempo setting is saved with the file and used to regulate the sequence's playback in other applications.

The transport control window also includes a Record button. You'll use this to bring new MIDI data into your song. While recording, a sequencer simulates the action of a multitrack recorder, playing already-recorded tracks (provided you set them to play mode) while recording the new MIDI data you create. Some sequencers offer an audible countoff prior to the start of recording, and you may also find a metronome option that clicks on the beat (as determined by the tempo and time signature settings).

Recording with a sequencer is very much like working with a multitrack tape recorder. Everything you play is captured in real time. Sequencers will let you filter unwanted data out. If, for example, you were playing on a velocity-sensitive keyboard but wanted all the notes in a particular song to play at the same volume, you could ask your sequencer to filter out velocity data. Filters are also handy when you're transferring a MIDI sequence from one sequencer (such as the one built into your synthesizer) to another (your computer). You might have a piece of music that goes overboard with pitch bends. Setting the record filter can remove pitch bend events from the captured data.

Filters can often be applied after the fact as well. Bars & Pipes Professional, which I've referred to many times as the best MIDI sequencer on earth, distinguishes itself by its unusual interface. The "pipes" in its name comes from its use of a plumbing metaphor, very appropriately applied to MIDI. The data flows from the source, which is your MIDI keyboard during recording, to the sink, which is your MIDI playback instrument. Bars & Pipes offers filter modules called tools that you can plug into the pipeline between the source and the sink. Each track has its own pipeline. Filters placed at the source side alter incoming MIDI data on the fly, saving the modified data in the track during recording. Bars & Pipes' filters range from the event exclusion filter I described earlier to unusual and exciting filters that add harmony, create counterpoint melodies, add grace notes, convert one type of controller event to another, and perform a host of other functions. More interestingly, tools placed on the sink end of the pipe work on MIDI data without modifying it. You can stack tools up to combine their function. The result is that Bars & Pipes will let you audition complex changes to your music without forcing you to save and load intermediate versions of your sequence.

Wrapping Up

After you've finished fooling around with your MIDI sequence, whether it's one you created yourself or loaded from some collection, you'll probably save the result as what's called a "type 1 MIDI file." This is a universal data representation standard that stores not only the MIDI event data, but also remembers the names you assigned to your tracks so you can run the file through a different sequencer without getting lost.

Of the systems discussed here, only Windows has a built-in ability to play MIDI sequences without additional software. MIDI sequence players exist in the public domain for the Amiga, and there's probably shareware for the Mac as well. Most often, though, you'll use whatever media integration package you've chosen to play your MIDI music. If you're doing interactive multimedia, you can't always assume that multimedia authoring tools support MIDI playback. Even under Windows where developers have no excuse not to include MIDI, there are still so-called multimedia tools that don't incorporate support for MIDI. That's the exception on all three platforms, though. It's no secret that MIDI is the most efficient and pliable way to record, store, and play electronic music. Smart vendors capitalize on that fact by including MIDI among their support audio types.

5

3-D Graphics and Animation

3-D graphics software can create convincing visual simulations, breathtaking business graphics, gorgeous titles and logos for video, and wild shapes that exist only in your imagination. With animation, you can move, reshape, change colors and textures, and otherwise make the worlds you create come to life.

I know the paragraph above lays it on a bit thick. It's hard not to get all starry-eyed over 3-D, and I'll confess to being as enamored of this technology as anyone. But I'll try to set my obvious lust for 3-D aside long enough to get at some of its practical uses. I mentioned some of the things you can do with 3-D in the opening paragraph. As this chapter progresses, you'll learn about some others.

If you watch any television at all, you're being subjected to computer-generated 3-D graphics in spades. Not long ago, 3-D was a lot more recognizable. Instead of being a realistic simulation of reality, the sharp, cubic shapes in most 3-D animation had a style of its own. Now, with faster computers and smarter software, it's a cinch that you've been hoodwinked several times into mistaking computer-generated reality for the genuine article. I've been working with 3-D a long time now, and the quality has gotten so good that even I can't tell with certainty whether some of the things I see on television are real or not.

Why 3-D?

The way 3-D is used in television and motion pictures helps us learn about how to apply it in our own work. Like most technology, 3-D isn't used because there are no alternatives. When some science fiction show wants to create a three-dimensional spaceship, its special effects people can still build models (and they often do). Commercial video producers used clay and styrofoam shapes and elaborate motion rigs to create the now-familiar "flying logo" prior to the advent of 3-D. And animators are still using paint and plastic sheets to draw tumbling and spinning graphics by hand. So if you can do everything that 3-D graphics software can do some other way, what's the attraction?

That's a trick question. The fact is, there are some things 3-D can do that can't be done, or done as well, using real objects. Setting that aside for a moment, even when you use 3-D graphics to create an image that could have been created through some other means, 3-D offers some attractive advantages.

Take the simplest and, for me, a very common use of 3-D: creating three-dimensional text. The alternative to using computer software is to cut shapes from some material, stick them to a background, light them and shoot them with a camera. An effect that could take days and multiple people to create with real materials can be done "virtually" by a computer and a single operator in minutes. 3-D becomes a labor-saving device in cases like this.

Future Vision

Another reason for 3-D's appeal is that it can create convincing simulations of things that will exist as objects someday, but which are impractical to build today. Architects are die-hard fans of 3-D, using it to show clients how buildings will look when they're completed. Miniatures used to be employed for this purpose, but only 3-D can place the client at the very same perspective he or she would have were they standing in front of the real building. Elements of the surrounding area can be added to make the scene more realistic, and even landscaping can be reproduced by the computer. Since the 3-D simulation comes from the architect's original CAD (computer-assisted design) drawings of the building plans, when those plans change, the changes can be reflected in the 3-D scene in minutes. Building a new model to incorporate radical changes could take much longer. Animation can be used to take the client on a tour of parts of the building, showing not only the structure, but offering a glimpse of how interiors might be designed.

The soda can, detergent bottle, food storage container and other household items you take for granted all had to be designed by someone. The same is true of your telephone, your computer, your television set, and so on. What these objects have in common is that they use packaging to contain something inside them. 3-D gives packaging designers the ability to test different designs before expensive and time-consuming models are made. The computer-generated models are often set into motion with animation so designers can see the package from all angles.

The artists who create the logos and other artwork that adorns packages of all kinds also use 3-D to see how that art will look on the package. One piece of sample art can be scanned into the computer and applied over and over again to different package shapes. The artist can use what he or she learns from the simulation to figure out where to place graphical elements that have to align with parts of the package. Computer-simulated lighting can give artists and designers a preview of how their package will look under department store lighting.

We're probably best acquainted with the fanciful 3-D graphics used in television commercials and motion pictures. These illustrate another key reason for 3-D's existence: to create visions of things that can't be created using real materials. In films, 3-D has been used to transform people into molten metal, destroy entire cities with nuclear explosions, portray deadly wars in space, and build mechanical creatures that come straight from our nightmares. Television ads use 3-D to make product packaging do things that no real package can do. Mouthwash bottles swing on vines and compete in boxing matches. A matchstick heaves a bag of inferior charcoal briquets into the distance. Then there's the bathroom, where toilets speak, bathtubs lean into a good scrubbing, and toothbrushes laugh. Doing these things with real materials would require clay models (which aren't as realistic), hand-drawn animation (expensive and time-consuming) or the dressing of actors in toilet costumes (no comment). While real materials always pose some limitation, computer graphics have the advantage of being completely changeable. The only real limits are imposed by the relative skill of the operator and the capabilities of the software.

Getting Ready for 3-D

The realistic and surrealistic worlds created by professional animators are accessible to us as well. All three platforms used for this book have several excellent 3-D software packages available for them. Using this software carries with it some burdens, many of which were described in Chapter 2. I'll recap some of that information briefly here and add a few details that weren't covered earlier.

The most significant burden imposed by 3-D graphics is the burden on your computer hardware. Equipping your computer to do 3-D means beefing it up as much as you can. Faster CPUs and floating-point coprocessor chips, bigger hard drives, more memory and faster graphics cards all figure into the speed with which your computer can generate 3-D images. The graphics card plays a central role in the quality of the generated graphics as well. If you're viewing images on your system's monitor, then you need only concern yourself with purchasing a graphics card with the best color depth you can afford (24 or 32 bits is vastly preferable). If you plan to record your 3-D graphics or animations to videotape or recordable laserdisc, then you must also worry about whether the graphics card you're using produces recordable video output at all, and if it does, whether that output is of sufficient quality for the work you plan to do.

With the Mac and Amiga, your excursions into 3-D will be best served by the fastest processor you can get. At this writing, the fastest main CPU for both of these systems is the Motorola 68040. If you're shopping for new hardware, keep in mind that the clock speed of the CPU affects performance; not all 68040-based systems perform equally. If you've purchased a system with an older, slower CPU, both Macs and Amigas can be upgraded with the addition of accelerator boards. These cost less than completely new systems and let you continue to use the box and peripherals you've grown accustomed to. You'll also want to stock up on memory. Expandable Amigas and Macs both allow users to upgrade their on-board memory; Amigas can be expanded with plug-in memory boards as well. Even experimentation in 3-D calls for a minimum of eight MB of memory.

The fastest processor available for PCs as of this writing is the Intel 80486. Depending on the system, the processor may be running at a clock speed of anywhere from 25 to 66 MHz. 3-D work wants the fastest clock speed it can get, and like the Mac and Amiga, a minimally capable PC 3-D system will have eight MB of memory. CPU accelerator boards are less common for PCs, but some manufacturers (including ALR, one of the vendors supplying systems for this book) mount their CPUs on replaceable modules. I upgraded my ALR's CPU from a 25-MHz 486 to a 66-MHz 486/DX2. The "DX2" designation means that the chip plugs into the socket of a 33-MHz CPU, but calculations are carried out at twice the clock speed by special double-clocking circuits inside the chip. It's a good compromise; double-clocked DX2 systems perform so closely to their single-clocked counterparts that it's seldom worth the extra money to get the "real thing."

Macintosh systems have a wide variety of available graphics cards, and all of them take advantage of the Mac's unique ability to manage multiple display cards and to run all Mac software on all cards regardless of their origin. That's a boon, since you can pick any software you like without worrying about whether it will support the display you've selected. That's not so with either the Amiga or the PC. Some of the Amiga's popular graphics software works only with the standard graphics modes of the Amiga which, while better than your average PC VGA, aren't quite a match for 3-D work. Bringing yourself a step up from there requires investing in a 24-bit graphics card. There are plenty of choices, but the Digital Creations' DCTV and Impulse's Firecracker 24 have fairly broad support among 3-D software vendors. I use the Video Toaster and its component 3-D software, Lightwave, for the 3-D work I do on the Amiga. The Video Toaster is not a general-purpose video display card (no other 3-D software deals with it directly), but the Toaster is so worth having, and Lightwave is such a good package, that I had no trouble sticking with that combination.

On the PC, there are an unbelievable number of graphics cards available. Most conform to one of two standards: VGA or Targa. Some vendors have extended the capabilities of VGA cards to include the ability to display 24-bit color images. Others have built VGA adapters that include recordable video output, with varying degrees of output quality. The Targa standard isn't really a standard at all but is more a reflection of that card's manufacturer's (Truevision) domination of the high-quality video card market. The Truevision Targa, in its many variations and third-party knock-offs, is probably the most widely used professional video card. Because of this, software aimed at professional users (as is the case with 3-D packages) usually includes the Targa among its list of supported graphics cards. A somewhat less popular card, the ATVista, also enjoys fairly wide support. A fast-rising alternative to the Targa and ATVista is the Illuminator Pro from Matrox. A version of this board is included with Matrox's Studio video production system, discussed in detail in an upcoming chapter. The Illuminator Pro is quickly picking up support from vendors of graphics software.

For this chapter, I configured my systems as follows: I loaded my UNIQ 486/50 EISA system with both Matrox's Illuminator Pro and Truevision's ATVista. The Mac used both the Apple 8•24 GC 24-bit graphics card and the Truevision NuVista+ card for its recordable video output. Again, I used the Video Toaster in the Amiga. All systems had eight MB of memory and plenty of hard disk space.

If you plan to record your animations to videotape, you'll need a VCR or recordable laserdisc player and a compatible VCR controller. These items, and the process of spooling animation out to tape, will be covered in the chapter on desktop video production.

The next step is to choose your 3-D software. I've worked with lots of different 3-D packages on the three system types used for this book. From that assortment, I've settled on a small group that represents a cross-section of the 3-D market. I've left out the very top end, occupied by the workstation-based software from companies like Alias and Wavefront, focusing instead on packages that perform well but don't command such high price tags. I also left out the low end and the public domain. From what remained, I chose those packages that generally represented good value for the money and were easy enough for those just getting started to use comfortably.

On the Mac, I chose Specular International's Infini-D. I used the Lightwave 3-D component (included with the Video Toaster) on the Amiga. On the PC, I worked with Crystal Graphics' Crystal Topas Professional.

Because of technical issues and time constraints, I was unable to grab screen shots from the PC software. That's a pity, because of all the software I use, Topas is the package I most often recommend because of its combined ease of use and functionality. The function of this chapter is to get you started in 3-D, though, and Mac and Amiga screen shots will accomplish that just fine. Topas gets plenty of representation; I just can't show you its interface.

If you go shopping for 3-D software, you'll find there are two categories of products, which are, unfortunately, not always clearly discriminated: *modelers* and *renderers*. As I described in Chapter 2, 3-D objects start life as *wireframes*, an appropriate name for the collection of lines that make up the skeleton of all 3-D objects. Modelers provide the tools to build these wireframes from scratch, from collections of objects you or someone else has already created, or from simple 3-D shapes (like cubes and spheres). The wireframe version of the 3-D object is then passed to a renderer. There, you place the object in a scene with other objects, assign visual properties to it, arrange lights and start your system computing (rendering) the 3-D image. The renderer saves the finished image to a file on disk and also frequently handles animation.

Different vendors handle the modeler/renderer split in different ways. On the Mac, most 3-D software is either one or the other—the functions of both are rarely combined in a single box. Infini-D is mostly a renderer, but it does include a primitive modeler. Combined full-function modeler/renderers are rare on the Mac. Dedicated renderers expect to import finished 3-D models from other programs. Macromedia's Swivel 3D is probably the most-used Mac modeler.

One facility that offers an intriguing modeling option is *publish/subscribe*. With this, you can create a 2-D shape in an illustration program like Adobe Illustrator and pass that shape to Infini-D where its internal modeler can turn the 2-D shape into a 3-D object. The combination of Publish/Subscribe, Adobe Illustrator and Infini-D make for an extremely powerful 3-D workshop. Just how this works will be described later.

The Amiga's Lightwave 3-D has grown to be one of the most revered personal computer 3-D rendering packages, and deservedly so. It combines an easy-to-use interface with a wealth of rendering options. Its pairing with the Video Toaster is a natural one. A Video Toaster system, likely put together to do video production, will already include a video recorder, and the quality of the output from the Toaster is excellent. Lightwave has a modeler component built in, but it can be difficult to learn and use. Fortunately, the renderer can import models from other 3-D programs.

My affection for Topas (PC) is well-earned. This software eliminates the distinction between modeler and renderer. You can draw and modify your 3-D objects, place them relative to one another in the scene, set them up for rendering and arrange animation, all from one unified interface. This unique approach is tremendous help to first-timers, for whom jumping back and forth between modeler and renderer can be frustrating. That's not to say that Topas, once learned, is any less powerful than the other tools. In fact, it includes capabilities that none of the other software described here can manage. Topas, by the way, does not run under Windows. It runs under DOS, but uses special "DOS extender" software to make use of all of your system's memory. If you're running Windows, you must exit it before launching Topas.

Coming to Terms

Before you can get started with 3-D, you need to acquaint yourself with some of the terminology you'll encounter in any 3-D package you use. If some of these terms or their descriptions seem a little confusing, just file them away until you get to a later section that offers a little more detail. You may have to jump around a bit; I wasn't able to put the definitions in an order than ensures you won't encounter an unfamiliar word in the definition of another.

> ***Z axis:*** This is the third dimension and represents the relative depth of the objects in the scene. If you were standing in a road, the painted line down the middle could be a *Z* axis. *X* and *Y* axes, representing horizontal and vertical position, behave in 3-D as they do in 2-D graphics (see Figure 5-1).

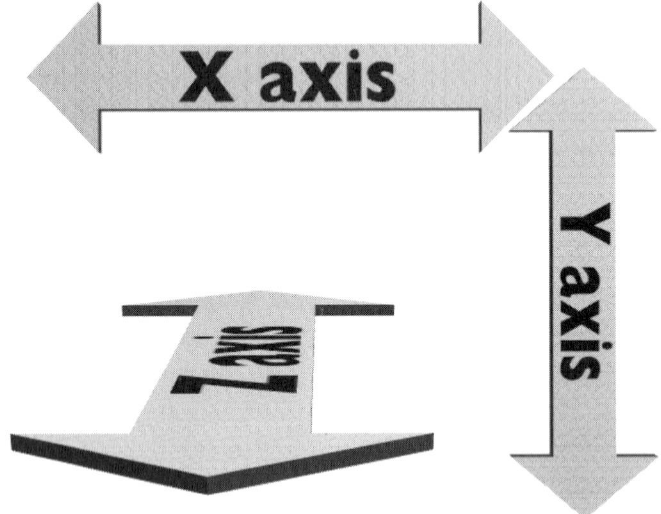

Figure 5-1: Three-dimensional axes

The combination of *X*, *Y*, and *Z* axis coordinates identify a single point in 3-D space. 3-D software uses a fixed *origin* for all three axes, a location in the scene where each axis' coordinate value is zero. Your software decides where zero is, and the location of zero may vary from one package to another. A common approach is to place zero for all axes at the center of the "stage," the invisible tabletop on which objects are placed. With a center origin, object coordinates can become negative numbers as objects are placed to the left (negative *X*), below (negative *Y*) or in front of (negative

Z) the center origin. Most software places no arbitrary limit on the range of coordinates, and you don't need to deal with numeric coordinate values very often. You can generally place objects wherever you like, but using the origin as a point of reference and organizing your scene around it can help you get your bearings when you get lost.

World: Sometimes called the *stage*, the world is the manageable universe of a 3-D package. As I mentioned above, the world has much in common with the real universe. While it could extend infinitely in all directions, the world of a 3-D package suffers the same limitations as our perception of the real universe. It's best to think of a 3-D world in terms of a stage with finite boundaries rather than as a limitless expanse. The latter is mathematically impossible—computers have limits on the size and precision of numbers they can handle. But tighter than the restrictions placed on you by your computer's numeric limitations is a practical limit: you shouldn't create a larger universe than you can reasonably manage and move around in. "Getting lost" in a world created by a computer program sounds like an odd concept, but it's far too easy to do.

The issue of the size of a 3-D universe most often arises when you're dealing with scenes that include lots of objects spread out over a large area. A common mistake made by those new to 3-D is the creation of too-complex scenes in the interest of impressing the audience or enhancing a scene's realism. Instead of constructing a scene based on a broad vision (an entire city), focus on building only what you can see from the camera's point of view (the face of a single building). Distant objects, like the buildings in a skyline, can be effectively simulated by background graphics or by making the background buildings smaller to simulate distance. You should always focus on keeping your 3-D world as small and simple as possible.

Scene: The collected objects, lights, cameras and properties you use to make up a graphic scene. 3-D renderers save scenes as single files for ease of loading and copying, but the objects (models) that make up the scene usually remain in the individual files saved by the modeler.

Views: Since a computer display cannot show three dimensions, and because 2-D pointing devices (mice, graphics tablets) are most often used to manipulate 3-D objects, 3-D software lets you see your scene from different points of view. A *front view* is useful for adjusting the vertical (*Y*) or horizontal (*X*) position of an object. A *side view* lets you adjust an object's *Z* and *Y* axis positions without affecting the *X*. A *top view* lets you adjust an object's *Z* and *X* position. Each view has its advantages. The top view is best for moving objects closer to or farther away from the *Z* axis origin. The front view is the one most often used for drawing new objects in modelers.

Traditionally, 3-D software shows multiple views at once, with each view in a different window (see Figure 5-2). You can travel among the

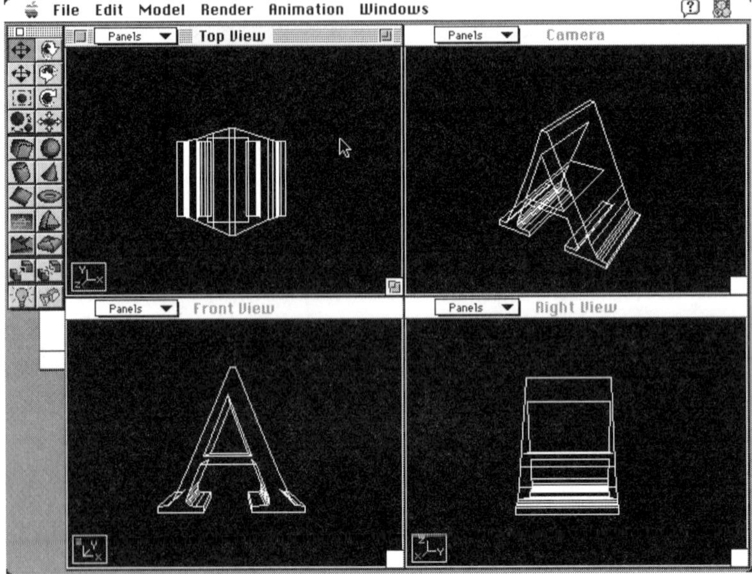

Figure 5-2: Multiple views (Infini-D)

views at will; moving an object in any given view moves the object relative to that view's prescribed coordinates (described above). Changes made in one view are automatically reflected in the other views. The default in Topas is to show you the scene only from the camera's point of view (see below). You can select the more common multiple-view interface if you prefer it. Lightwave's modeler uses multiple views, but the renderer uses a novel approach to positioning in 3-D space. You are presented with a single view on the entire scene, but you can alter your point of view or move an object in any direction (along any axis or across multiple axes) using only the mouse. The renderer's layout editor, which controls the point of view and the placement of objects in the scene, manages this feat by making use of the Amiga mouse's two buttons. *X*, *Y* and *Z* axis movements are possible through combinations of mouse buttons and left-right and to-fro rolling motions. It takes a little getting used to—it's something like learning to drive (or, perhaps more appropriately, fly)—but the movements become quite natural with practice.

Camera: In addition to the fixed views, described above, 3-D software supports an adjustable view. This view is managed by a virtual camera, which may be placed anywhere in the 3-D world. Like a real camera, this camera "sees" what it is pointed at, and it can often be zoomed in or out to bring objects closer or push them away without moving the camera. Good 3-D software (like Topas) places the camera on a virtual tripod. You can pan, tilt, and rotate it, and "dolly" it along a straight track. The tripod can be placed anywhere, but once you place it, Topas lets you work with the camera in a manner very similar to the real thing. More common, however, is the approach of making the camera a point in 3-D space that faces in a particular direction. You move the camera around in the scene as you would any object (Topas allows this as well if it is the method you prefer).

Wireframe: The skeleton of a 3-D object as seen without surfaces or shading. In the wireframe view, all lines and curves that define an object can be seen, even if they are normally obscured when the object is shaded. All 3-D objects are constructed of lines and curves that connect to form polygons. A wireframe is a mesh of these polygons (see Figure 5-3). A sphere, for example, is not a single round frame, but a frame made up of dozens of little flat polygons, fitted together to approximate the shape of a sphere.

Some software offers the option of viewing the wireframe with *hidden surface removal*, which takes away the lines that will be obscured by shading. You may also have the option of viewing the wireframe using *depth*

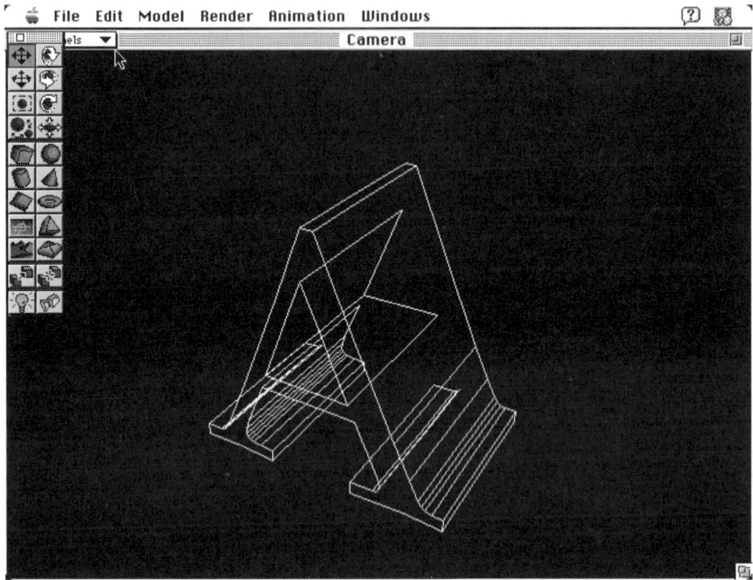

Figure 5-3: A 3-D object as a wireframe (Infini-D)

cueing, which shows distance by drawing points in a dimmer color as they recede into the distance.

Surface: The "skin" of an object is its surface. The wireframe representation of an object is usually covered by some kind of surface. You can select a different surface type for every object in your scene and sometimes for individual polygons that make up an object. Like surfaces in real life, surfaces in this context have properties that affect how they reflect light, how they interact with the skeleton (wireframe) that holds them up, and how they interact with other objects in the scene. The properties available to you depend on your software. Surface properties of most 3-D software include:

Color, the foundation color of the surface. Depending on other attributes, the surface may not be rendered entirely in its assigned color.

Transparency, the degree to which the objects behind a surface can be seen. Usually expressed as a percentage (100% being completely see-through, and 0% being completely opaque), transparency lets you create glass, water, and other transparent and semitransparent surfaces.

Diffuse shading, the degree to which a surface will spread the light reflected from it over a wide area. A matte surface, like a sheet of paper, will have a high degree of diffuse shading, while a metallic object has relatively low diffuse shading.

Specular highlight, the relative brightness of the bright spot made by the reflection of a nearby light source.

Shininess, the size of the specular highlight. The shinier the surface, the smaller the highlight.

Metallicity, the degree to which the specular highlight matches the surface's color instead of the light's color. Figures 5-4 and 5-5 show some of these properties in action.

Figure 5-4: Spheres rendered with specular highlight (left) and diffuse shading (right)

Color and texture maps: In addition to the color you assign to the surface, you may also be able to augment the surface's appearance with the application of additional color. A color map is usually computed inside the pro-

Figure 5-5: Transparency

gram, sometimes through a process called *procedural mapping*. A procedural map is a mathematical approximation of a natural pattern. If your 3-D software does procedural maps, then you'll probably be able to create wood, clouds, marble, granite, and other natural surfaces and patterns without having to draw or find a picture of the natural pattern. Procedural maps can also be used to produce color variations that are not seen in nature. These are obviously synthetic, but the 3-D program's application of realistic shading and perspective to objects covered by these synthetic surfaces creates a mesmerizing cross between the real and surreal.

Most 3-D software offers at least one other type of map: the *texture map*. This is a graphic that is drawn onto the surface of the object when it is rendered. If you created a wireframe model of a soda can and then covered that can with a colored surface, you'd still be missing the logo and text seen on all real soda cans. To make it real, you would create the label for the can as an ordinary rectangular (flat) 2-D graphic in some other package, saving the label as a graphic file compatible with your 3-D software. You would then load the graphic as a texture map and apply it to the soda can object.

This sounds pretty easy, but the proper sizing, positioning, and application of texture maps is one of the toughest tasks to master. If you don't care about realism, then you can just let the 3-D program run with its defaults. The results won't look much like a soda can label (unless it came from another planet). This chapter has a more detailed discussion of texture maps later on. If you study nothing else in this chapter, at least skim that section, because the proper use of texture maps is key to creating professional-looking 3-D graphics.

Lights: Without light, nothing can be seen. Our eyes see by absorbing the focused reflections coming from the objects around us. 3-D software uses light the way we do: it makes objects visible. Lighting in the simulated world of 3-D starts with *ambient light*, a light that shines equally bright in all directions. This is a 3-D pioneer's safety net, ensuring that objects you haven't illuminated with other lights can be seen. Ambient light, like all lights, can have an intensity and color. One frequent pitfall is to lazily use the ambient light as the only light in your scene. When you do this, the highlights and shadows normally brought out by individual lights vanish, making the scene appear flat and washed out. It's better to set the ambient light to a dimmer gray so that when you do your test renderings, you can see all the objects in the scene, but you can still see the dramatic effects that individual lights create. You can't usually remove the ambient light from a scene, but setting its color to black (or its intensity, if it can be set separately, to zero) will have the same effect. With no ambient light, objects out of the reach of other lights cannot be seen.

In most 3-D software, all other lights are objects that you can place and move around as you can any object. The most versatile individual light is the *point light* (sometimes called an *omni light*), which casts light in a manner similar to an uncovered lightbulb. The light originates from the point chosen for the light object and shines in all directions. As the distance from the light increases, the light's intensity decreases. Point lights can create specular highlights and cast shadows on objects that are close enough to them. More dramatic lighting is achieved by the use of the *spot light*. As does its theatrical namesake, a 3-D spot light throws its light in a cone. A spot is placed like any other light object, but unlike the point light, a spot must be aimed at whatever you wish to illuminate. The cone of light that comes out of a spotlight is not visible (even in fog, see below). As with a real spot, a 3-D spot illuminates whatever it's pointed at with a circle of brightness. If you point it at a flat object (like a floor or wall), that circle will be clearly visible. You can adjust the sharpness of the edge of that circle of light, as well as the degree to which (if at all) the circle is brighter in its center than at its edge. Like the point light, a spot gets dimmer as the distance from it increases. Spots can also create shadows, and they are frequently employed expressly to create the long, dramatic shadows that are their trademark.

Topas offers another type of light: *distant*. A distant light is like a point light whose intensity does not diminish with distance. It behaves somewhat like the sun, casting shadows and illuminating everything equally (if there are no clouds). Distant lights don't need to be pointed, but their position relative to the scene determines the direction and length of the shadows. A fun twist on the distant light is Topas' simulated sun. You can place your scene at a specific latitude and longitude on the earth, tell Topas what the time of day is and what the weather conditions are, and it will cast a distant light on the scene that has the color, intensity and direction of the sun for that place on earth at that time. In animations, the sun can be made to move over time just like the real thing, even rising and setting.

Each scene can contain multiple lights, and most scenes need several. You can change the intensity and color of any light to suit you, and most software also lets you decide whether a given light casts shadows or not. See the discussion on shadows below for more detail, but each shadow-casting light adds time to the rendering process.

Shading: Lights and surfaces don't translate into a visible scene until shading is applied. The software calculates the effect of light on objects in the scene and paints the scene based on mathematical models of the reflection of light. There are several such models, and each takes its place in the relative domains of speed and quality.

The bottom-rung shading model is *flat shading*. Each polygon that makes up an object is painted with a single, solid color based on its distance from your lights (see the left sphere in Figure 5-6). Most 3-D packages offer flat shading as a super-fast preview. Most packages won't apply texture maps, and you can't see the effects of spot and distant lights. Flat shading shows no shadows, either; it's really a very small step up from hidden surface removal. Flat shading's speed makes it handy for checking things not easily seen in wireframe. You might not be able to tell easily from the wireframe which side of an object is facing you, or whether two objects overlap. Flat shading will let you see a 3-D preview without making you wait too long for it.

More realism is offered by *Gouraud shading*. Here, the intensity of the light hitting the corners of every polygon is measured, and then the polygon is shaded with smooth color transitions between the values found at the corners. Depending on the object, Gouraud shading can give you all the realism you need, with the advantage that it computes very quickly. Because its precision is low, Gouraud-shaded objects can't show shadows, and specular highlights become angular instead of round (see the right sphere in Figure 5-6).

Figure 5-6: Flat and Gouraud shading

The second-best shading method, and one which is often the best a package has to offer, is *Phong shading*. Here, every point of every polygon is colored individually based on the amount of light striking it. Phong shaded objects can receive shadows and show round specular highlights as well as the circle of brightness cast by spot lights. In Figure 5-7, the two flat surfaces and the letters "Phong" are Phong-shaded. You can see the outline from the spotlight placed in front of the scene, and the shadows cast on the horizontal plane were created by a point light above and to the right of the letters. Shadow, spotlight and specular highlight effects are only pos-

Figure 5-7: Phong shading with spot and point lights

sible when the light hitting every point is measured separately. That process takes time; Phong shading even some simple scenes, if those scenes contain shadows, multiple light sources and texture maps, can take hours. Complex scenes can take *days* to render with Phong shading. The results are often worth it. Fortunately, most 3-D software lets you choose the shading model for each object in your scene. You can save rendering time by

Phong shading only those objects that require it.

The absolute best the packages described in this chapter can offer is *ray tracing*. This isn't a shading method, since it doesn't measure the light falling on polygons. Instead, ray tracing follows a ray of light from its source to its end and applies colors to the objects struck by the ray. The number of rays used affects the quality of the image; the more rays, the smaller each ray is, and the more precisely the effects of the light can be simulated.

Smoothing is a property of Gouraud- and Phong-shaded and ray-traced objects that makes the approximated curved surfaces created by polygon meshes appear to be smoothly curved. Without smoothing, a sphere that's viewed closely enough won't look like a ball. It will, instead, have a coarse appearance because each of the flat polygons that make up the sphere's surface will be shown flat. Smoothing, a property that can be turned on or off for an object (Topas refers to it as "rounded" as opposed to "faceted" shading), makes those flat polygons appear curved.

For most objects, Phong shading creates an acceptable degree of realism. Ray tracing takes things a step further by simulating two things that Phong shading can't: *reflection* and *refraction*. Normally, objects in a 3-D scene reflect only the light shining on them. Reflections of other objects in the scene don't appear, so if you placed a shiny sphere in the middle of a group of other objects, the sphere would not reflect the images of those other objects as it would in real life. Ray tracing changes the way light behaves by following rays of light not only until they strike objects, but until each ray has bounced off other objects in the scene and gone out into space (or its intensity has fallen to zero from distance). Each bounce is a potential reflection. The percentage of reflectivity of an object is something you can tune from within 3-D renderers that support ray tracing. As reflectivity is increased, the object's normal color is compromised in favor of the reflection. A perfect mirror would be 100% reflective. A matte surface, like paper or a painted wall, reflects nothing.

Refraction is the bending of light as it passes through a transparent or semi-transparent object. You remember, no doubt, the early science classes where refraction was demonstrated with a pencil in a glass of water. Viewed from the side, the pencil seems to split in two where the water's surface begins. Ray tracing effectively simulates refraction by using a refractive index you supply to deflect each ray passing through a refractive object. You could use refraction to simulate liquid or to make it appear that some object is encased in clear plastic.

If Phong shading takes a long time to generate, ray tracing takes an *excruciatingly* long time. In those days when minicomputers ruled the earth, they were set to work on ray-traced scenes that took days or weeks to render. Faster computers and more efficient algorithms have cut that time down considerably, but ray tracing should still be viewed as an expensive last resort for those times when Phong shading just isn't realistic enough, or when you seek a surreal effect that only ray tracing can provide. Ray-traced reflection and refraction effects are depicted in Figure 5-8.

Figure 5-8: Two ray-traced effects

One of the Mac 3-D packages in my lab, Presenter Professional from Visual Information Development (VIDI), is a combination modeler/renderer that does ray tracing, but with a twist. You can install a high-speed coprocessor board in your Mac along with a special version of Presenter Professional's renderer module that, combined, cut the time it takes to render ray-traced scenes considerably. The coprocessor board, from YARC, puts a fast RISC coprocessor at the command of your Mac's CPU. Other Mac software runs normally, but when you kick off a render in Presenter Professional, it sends commands to the YARC board that cause it to do the calculations. I received Presenter Professional after most of this chapter was already written. I've gone back to weave in mention of it (like this paragraph) because even without the YARC hardware, it's quite a good 3-D modeling and rendering system. I've left some room for it on the tape if you'd like a better look.

Some software, including Infini-D and Topas, can approximate one of the most important functions of ray tracing—reflections—through a process called ***environment mapping***. This is a "cheat" that gets you very nearly the same effect as ray tracing's reflections but in less time.

Creating and Manipulating 3-D Objects

Before we can progress to the important section on surface mapping, we need to build some 3-D objects on which to experiment. This needn't be a strenuous exercise. In fact, when you're just getting started with 3-D, it's best to work with simple objects. It's not at all uncommon for newcomers to spend fortunes in time painstakingly shaping a model to look just so, only to discover that some basic error was made that prevents it from rendering properly. So we'll start small. Even so, building simple objects requires knowing at least the basics of 3-D modeling. So here's enough modeling terminology and technique to get you started. It won't take you far; the manual for Topas is almost 600 pages long, so I can't hope to offer more than an introduction in the few pages I have to spare here.

When you first sit down with a new 3-D package, it's a good idea to figure out what the shortest path to a workable model is given the software you're using. If your program doesn't have a modeler at all, you'll either have to fire up an external modeling program to create a new object or grab an existing object from some collection. Newtek (creator of the Video Toaster) includes a marvelous assortment of pre-drawn 3-D objects with its Lightwave software. Specular International, the company that publishes the Infini-D 3-D modeler/renderer for the Mac, offers a series of what it calls "3-D clip art" under the product name Replicas. Specular provided me with two volumes of its Replicas series, and just browsing through the objects on those disks is ample evidence that, with patience, practice, and imagination, 3-D can do *anything*. Autodesk includes a CD-ROM of 3-D objects with its popular 3D Studio software for the PC, and Electric Image has a CD-ROM of samples for its Mac-based 3-D package.

What you'll find in these collections are objects that have already been drawn and had surfaces assigned to them. In many cases, you can grab an object from a collection, drop it into your renderer, and just click the "render" button. You may want to do that with a complex, detailed object or two to give yourself an idea of where the high ground lies. For our purposes, simple objects will serve us best. The soda can included with Lightwave, for example, is an excellent subject for experimentation. But perhaps the best object of all is text. Not all modelers can handle text (Lightwave is one that cannot), but very often, all you need to do to create a great-looking 3-D object is select a font and type in a character or two. Keep it small for now. You might be tempted to want to see whole words and phrases put up in the splendor of 3-D, but while you're learning, small, simple models take less time to render. That means less waiting and more active experimentation.

Text as an Object

Those modelers (and some renderers, like Electric Image) that can use text as objects rely on outline fonts. These are so named because instead of being digital snapshots of characters in a certain style and size, they are outlines of characters formed by lines and curves. That's perfect for 3-D work because shapes made of lines and curves are the starting point for all 3-D objects.

Topas handles text objects better than any 3-D software I've seen. The package includes an assortment of outline fonts, but if you want more, you can buy any Adobe Type 1 PostScript font and use it in Topas (see Chapter 3 for more discussion about PostScript fonts).

The advantage of an outline font is its scaleability. You can resize it to be as large as you like without any loss of quality. What's more, under the control of a program like Topas, objects created from outline fonts can be scaled nonproportionally: you can change the size on one axis and leave the others alone. This is called *stretching and squashing*, and it's a key component of animation. For our purposes, stretching and squashing lets us tailor the appearance of a particular font to suit our requirements.

To place text objects in your Topas scene, you use the Text option under Topas' Build menu. *(Note: the videotape includes a segment on the operation of Topas.)* This brings up a rectangular box matching the basic shape of the font and size you've selected. The box is mounted on crosshairs that move with the mouse or tablet cursor (for simplicity's sake, when I use the word "mouse" in this chapter, assume that I also refer to graphics tablets and other 2-D pointing devices). You line up the box with the spot where you'd like the first letter to appear and press the mouse button. Then type. Every character you type appears on the screen as a perfectly formed letter.

Drawing 3-D text in Infini-D is a little less direct. There, you type your characters into a dialog box rather than directly onto the screen. That same dialog asks you to specify the depth of the extrusion. Extrusion is covered very shortly, but for now we'll say that the Infini-D uses this depth figure to determine how far to extend the *Z* axis depth of your letters. In effect, it determines how "thick" they'll be.

When a letter hits the screen in Topas, it's a two-dimensional shape. Actually, it's got three dimensions, but the object's *Z* axis depth is one point. This is a good place to start—you can turn your text into all kind of 3-D shapes.

Working with a Modeler

Whether you choose a couple of characters of text or a simple predrawn object that comes with your software, your first stop on the way to the third dimension is the modeler. It's here that individual objects are given their shape. Part of a modeler's job is to act as a sort of database. You can name objects to make it easier to manage them, group several objects together under a single name, and some software (like Lightwave on the Amiga) even lets you assign names to individual surfaces to make it easier to attach properties to those named surfaces later.

Most modelers behave less like CAD software than like good 2-D illustration software, but with the added dimension of depth. You'll do all of your modeling work in wireframe because even flat shading would slow you down enough to frustrate you. Topas' single interface approach (one menu bar and one screen that are used for both modeling and rendering operations) is atypical. More often, the modeler is a distinctly separate part of the program (sometimes it is another program). You'll probably be presented with either a single or multi-view interface with a grid of lines or dots (Figure 5-9).

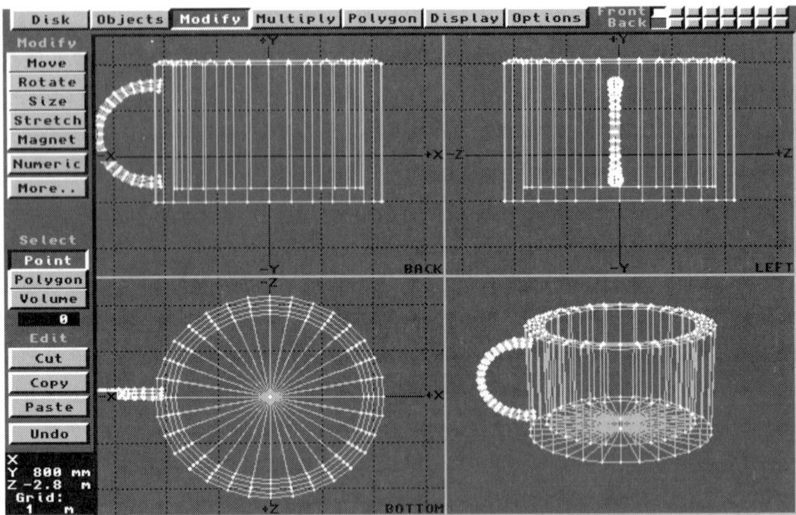

Figure 5-9: A 3-D modeler (Lightwave)

If you're working with a prebuilt object, you can load that object into the modeler to get a close look at it. That's not a necessary step, since an existing object can be carried straight to the renderer, or, if your 3-D software has a separate one, the layout editor. Loading a pre-existing object into the modeler lets you see it in the same setting in which you'll view your own work.

3-D Transforms

The real worth of the modeler is in the creation and modification of 3-D objects. Anything, even a single point, can be made three-dimensional by a modeler. 2-D shapes become 3-D objects through the use of *transforms*. The appearance of existing 3-D objects can be changed by transforms as well.

This discussion of transforms may seem a bit premature as I haven't yet given any time to using modelers to create the 2-D shapes that become 3-D objects, but to build good shapes, you should understand how the transforms work. The selection of available transforms varies from one package to another, but there are two that can be found virtually everywhere: *extrude* and *lathe*.

An extrusion is the simplest and most useful transform of all. It simply adds depth to an object. In Chapter 2, I used the analogy of the Play-Doh toy that pushes clay through a shaped outline cut in plastic. Extrusion works much the same way. The cut-out is the 2-D shape you've chosen to extrude. The modeler constructs a 3-D object by placing two copies of the shape to be extruded a specified distance apart (you specify the distance), aligning them perfectly with each other, and drawing lines between their corresponding points (see Figure 5-10). If you extrude a

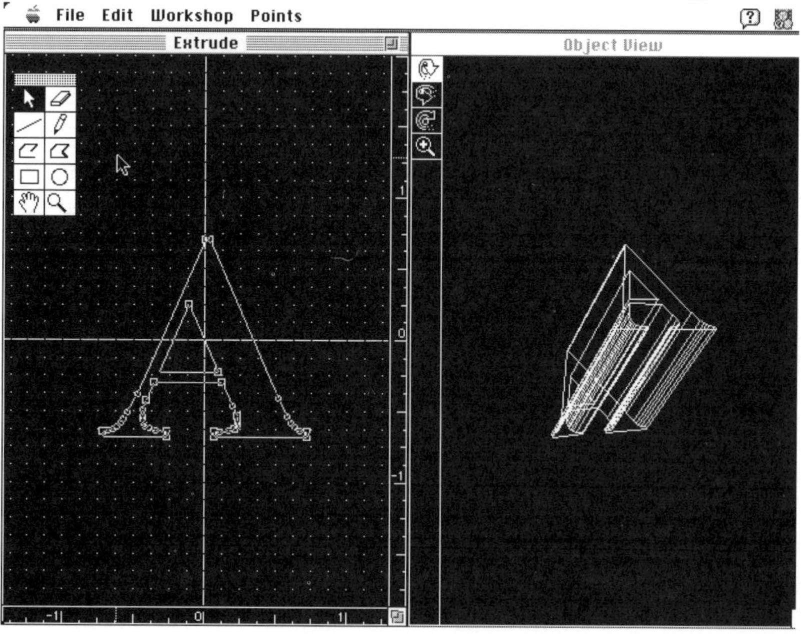

Figure 5-10: Extrusion (Infini-D)

square, a 3-D shape is built by running connecting lines between the four corresponding corners of two squares—upper-left to upper-left, upper-right to upper-right, and so on. The two copies of the object become *caps* that close off the top and bottom of the new 3-D shape. When you render an extruded object, it appears to be solid because the caps keep you from seeing inside the extrusion. The caps are single polygons that you can delete. If you remove a cap, the extrusion appears hollow.

Most software extrudes along straight lines only, but Topas lets you create an extrusion that is angled to the left or right instead of straight back. Presenter Professional and Lightwave can extrude along an arbitrary path.

An advanced flavor of extrusion is offered by some 3-D software. Topas calls its version of this transform *cross-sectional modeling*; Presenter Professional calls it *loafing*. Here, complex objects can be constructed by drawing a series of 2-D shapes. Those shapes will later be placed along a spine, rather like your own ribs, and then the ribs will be connected with lines to form a continuous surface. So an extrusion is really a cross-sectional model with only two ribs: one at either end. The shapes you use for the ribs don't have to be similar, but it helps. The 3-D software will find ways to connect two wildly dissimilar shapes, and it usually does an impressive job (it can, for example, do a fine job of running connecting lines between a circle and a square). But if you give it strangely complex shapes to connect, it might connect them in a way that isn't what you expected. Cross-sectional modeling takes practice to get right, but it's the best way to construct complex objects.

The other basic transform is one that, while practical, is also a lot of fun to work with. 3-D images have always been filled with soda cans and bottles, vases, building columns, lamps, bowling pins, cups and glasses, and other cylindrical objects because these are constructed by a 3-D transform called *lathing*. In a wood shop, a lathe is a tool with which you can shape wood by cutting into it as it turns. Lower the cutting tool at a spot one inch from the bottom of the stock, and you'll have an indent that cuts equally into the wood all the way around. Cut anywhere you like, and when you're done, you'll end up with a perfectly symmetrical, cylindrical sculpture. Slice it down the vertical center line, and the two halves will be precisely the same shape.

3-D lathing works on a rough adaptation of that principal. There is no stock. Instead, lathing starts with a 2-D shape that is the left or right half of the finished object's silhouette. That shape is spun around an axis (usually the *Y* axis; sometimes you can choose another or even define your own for creating asymmetrical shapes) and copies of it are made as it goes around. When it travels full-circle, connecting lines are drawn between the shapes to form a cylindrical model based on your half-silhouette (see Figure 5-11). In the figure, the silhouette is drawn for rotation around the thick *Y* axis line shown in the window on the left. You can adjust the smoothness of the lathed object by setting the number of *medians*, or more simply, the number of copies of the silhouette. The copies will always be evenly spaced, so specifying a greater number of medians will make the space between the silhouettes smaller, and the connecting lines between them will be shorter. That makes for a less faceted appearance when the object is rendered with

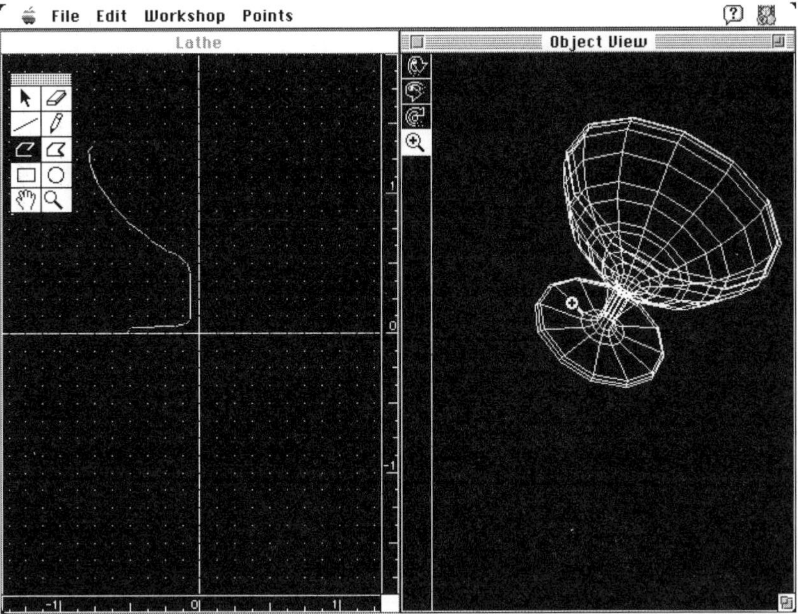

Figure 5-11: Lathing (Infini-D)

smooth shading. A high median count will cause your scene to take longer to display, even in wireframe, so test your software to see how few medians you can use while still getting a smooth surface. The fewer, the better.

Creating New Shapes

At the heart of any modeler is a 2-D drawing tool. This is what you'll use to create the outlines for extrusion objects, the silhouettes for lathe objects, and the ribs for cross-sectional models. The quality of the objects you can create will be determined, in large part, by the quality of the modeler's drawing features and your ability to master them. You may also have the option of using some other software to create your shapes. I've found that most 3-D software now supports the importation of shapes in EPS (encapsulated PostScript) form, the form used by 2-D illustration software like Adobe Illustrator. No matter how good your modeler is, it can't hold a candle to the likes of Illustrator. You should know whether the 3-D software you intend to use offers you the option of using an external 2-D illustration package. As I mentioned earlier, Infini-D uses the Mac's publish/subscribe facility to create a link with a program like Illustrator, making the two work in perfect concert. To use the link, you first create a shape in Illustrator that you'd like to lathe or extrude. You then select the shape and ask to publish it using an option in the Edit menu. You can give the shape a name if you like. When the shape is published, a rectangular outline will appear that encloses the shape. Then, with Illustrator still running, you launch Infini-D and enter its workshop interface (that's what Infini-D calls its modeler). Select the Subscribe option from Infini-D's Edit menu, and a dialog box will pop up with the names of all the currently published objects. You can have several items published at once from several programs, or several shapes published from one session of Illustrator. Select the object to which you want to subscribe, and it appears in the modeler window.

Publish/subscribe creates what's known as a *hot link.* Whatever changes you make to the published shape in Illustrator will immediately be reflected in Infini-D. Because of the flexibility of the link, you can legitimately use the powerful Illustrator as Infini-D's modeler.

It's more likely, though, that you'll use your 3-D software's own modeler, if for no other reason than that you can get where you're going a little faster. Modelers offer one or two ways to construct shapes: *polygons* and *splines.* Topas and Presenter Professional offer both; Infini-D and Lightwave are exclusively polygon-based.

A polygon in this context is no different from any other: it's a shape made of connected lines. Infini-D and Lightwave build polygons with straight lines only, while Topas and Presenter Professional let you use arcs as well. A polygon can be a closed or open shape. With a closed polygon, the first and last points are in the same place, creating a solid outline. In software that allows it, an open polygon is simply one in which the first and last points aren't connected. Open polygons are frequently used for lathing and cross-sectional modeling, but they can also be used to create hollow extruded objects.

Splines are curved lines, with the shape of the curve being adjustable. Those who work in Adobe Illustrator are well acquainted with splines—the way Illustrator manages them has earned it the respect of artists everywhere. Presenter Professional uses Illustrator-style spline controls, which are much more difficult to describe than to use. Each line segment in a spline object has points on either end. Each point has attributes that control the curve of the line associated with it. A line's curve can be set and modified by activating a set of control handles for one of its end points. Swinging those handles around change the curve's shape, and when you're done adjusting, the handles disappear until you activate them again. For building smoothly curved shapes, Illustrator-style spline controls are nothing short of magical.

Topas chose a different approach to represent and control its spline objects. A 2-D or 3-D spline object is made up of curved shapes, but it has an angular control lattice, a sort of scaffolding that determines the shape of the object. The control points around a 2-D spline make a straight-line polygon. The angle and length of each control lattice line determine the direction and angle of the curve controlled by that line. A 3-D lattice controls a mesh of spline shapes, perhaps created with cross-sectional modeling, that assemble to form a smoothly curved shape.

I realize the descriptions are a little confusing, so I'll cut to the chase: splines are able to create "organic" shapes that straight-line polygons can only approximate. Your finger, a drop of water, and a balloon are all examples of shapes that can be done more realistically by spline-based modelers.

Does that mean a modeler that can only do polygons is no good? Certainly not, and even when your modeler can do splines, you'll find yourself using polygons to build curved shapes sometimes just because it's easier. Remember that curved surfaces can be simulated by the renderer, so some rounded shapes will still be available to you. Every 3-D package on the market can do a lovely sphere without resorting to splines. The difference is that splines give you very precise control over the shape of the curve. When you use smooth or rounded shading, the software will take a guess at how the surface should be rounded and give you that. It'll get it right most of the time, but when it doesn't, that's when you'll wish you had splines handy.

Modelers employ labor-saving devices that help take some of the tedium out of building shapes. A good example is the *mirror* function, which takes something you've drawn and makes a mirror image of it. You can use this to build any symmetrical shape. Building an arrow shape, for example, is nasty work: you've got to get the points on both the top and bottom halves of the arrow to line up exactly, and all the angles must be identical. With mirror, you can draw half of the arrow and have a matching half created for you. Mirroring can be done along any axis.

Another helper is the *constrained line draw*. In most modelers, holding down the shift key while you stretch out a polygon's line segment will constrain the line to angles of 90 degrees (some modelers use 45-degree increments). No matter how hard you try to draw a crooked line, as long as you hold the shift key down, all your lines will be perfect parallels, perpendiculars, and diagonals. The top packages like Illustrator also allow you to set the constraint angle for more intricate constructions.

Modifying and Combining Shapes

Polygons and splines build 2-D shapes that you can turn into 3-D objects, but you won't always be fortunate enough to construct your scenes entirely with two-step objects: draw the shape, apply the transform. Instead, you'll probably have to combine the objects you create into super-objects. The ever-popular mug is one example. You can't lathe or extrude a mug complete with its handle (you could build it from a cross-sectional model, but don't bother me with details). To build one, you'll have to lathe the cup, construct the handle (you might use a cross-sectional model or a path extrude) and stick the two together somehow. A mug is only the simplest example. Modelers can be used to build models of cars, buildings, and even people through the combination of multiple objects.

Before you can combine objects, you need to size and position them appropriately. Modelers are equipped with tools for these operations. You can grab an object and resize it along one or more dimensions (or all of them equally), rotate it in any direction, and move it to any position in the mini-world of your modeler. You should build your objects with the knowledge that you can apply these operations later. You don't need to construct a complex shape using tiny line segments; build a huge version of the shape and resize it to its working size. Similarly, you don't have to build an object in the modeler in the position and attitude (rotational angle) in which it will be used. Instead, build it wherever and in whatever rotational angle is easiest for you, knowing you can place the object later.

Joining 3-D objects is usually not difficult, but it does require that you be adept at moving around in 3-D space. After you've sized your mug handle and rotated it to the proper attitude, you have to move it over to the mug and align it so that it lines up with the mug's horizontal center. That's no easy feat for a first-timer, and the biggest roadblock is wireframe. Without shading, it's impossible to tell how close or far away an object is. Depth cueing helps if you have it available, but it's still very easy to get tripped up. You can painstakingly line up the handle in the front view, only to discover that the handle is several inches *behind* the mug. With wireframe, you often can't tell. That's why multiple views are so important. The top view would show you the handle was in the wrong place.

There are two right ways to align objects in 3-D. The first is, as I said, to use your software's multiple view facility (Topas offers this as a user-selectable option). For our example, you would use the front view to line the handle up on the *X* and *Y* axes, and the top view to line it up on the *Z* axis. The other method is to use explicit coordinates. You ask the software to tell you where a specific point on the mug, near where you want to place the handle, lies in 3-D space. The program will report three coordinates which you can adjust and use as a position for the top of your mug handle. Most 3-D software will let you enter coordinates for all of its operations. Some let you bring an object into alignment with a selected point on another object, serving the same purpose as using coordinates but saving you the trouble of writing them down.

Once you've got the handle in the neighborhood, you'll probably have to adjust it to make it look like part of the mug. Objects are usually fitted together by purposely causing them to overlap. In our case, we want the ends of the mug handle to penetrate the outer surface of the mug. The handle only has to go in far enough that we can't see the caps at the handle ends; we don't want the ends poking through to the inside of the mug. You can do simple alignments like these by eye. By the time you get down to minute adjustments, you'll want to avoid any unintended movement of the handle. Most 3-D packages will let you do a *constrained move*, so that the object slides in a straight line along only one axis. Topas manages this in a typical way: holding the shift key down as you drag an object will constrain its movement to a single axis.

Overlapping shapes are rendered as angular joints. Modelers apply no filler to smooth the join. If you want the ends of the handle to flare out where they attach to the mug, you can either build flared ends into the model for the handle, or create a pair of short cone-shaped pieces that you then attach to the ends of your handle. The latter, it might seem to make the business of attaching the handle more difficult. After all, you'll have three objects to move and align instead of one. Once again, the modeler has a solution: *groups*. Every object you create in a modeler has a distinct identity and can be manipulated independently of the others. But for those times when you wish to create a super-object that is made up of two or more component objects, you can use your modeler's grouping facility to cause the super-object to be treated in some operations as a single 3-D shape. Most modelers do their grouping hierarchically, so the handle with the flared ends can be one group, and that group plus the mug can be another. You can name groups to keep track of them more easily, and some modelers will let you view the hierarchy for all the objects in your scene in an outline-style report.

Topas handles groups particularly well. Any time you request that an operation be performed on some object that is a member of a group, you'll be asked whether the operation should be applied to that object alone, or to its group (and to the super-groups above it). Some modelers require that you ungroup objects, that is, dissolve the group that links them together, before you can apply some operation to any of the group's individual objects.

Surfaces

A surface is the skin stretched over an object's wireframe skeleton. A surface is also the collection of properties that determine how that skin will look when it's rendered. The way surfaces are dealt with is, in large part, what sets 3-D packages apart from one another. Most 3-D software has enough in common in this regard, however, to make a discussion about working with surfaces worthwhile. For this section, assume that a surface is that collection of properties rather than an object's skin.

The set of surface properties available to you will vary depending on the software you choose; several surface properties were discussed earlier in this chapter. That discussion was mostly limited to solid-colored surfaces, the default surface applied by most modelers. Infini-D applies a surface called "white plastic" to all new objects, and that's pretty typical. Modelers default to shiny surface types because they show the effects of light more clearly. Topas assigns a different color to each new object so you can tell them apart in the wireframe view more easily.

While solid-colored, shiny surfaces are the default, the world isn't made of such things, and neither should 3-D scenes be. If you stick with solid colors, you can adjust surface properties like diffuse shading, specular highlight and shininess to wipe the gloss off of those objects in your scene that look better without it. But why stop there? Tinkering with surfaces is one of the most enjoyable exercises in 3-D work.

How you do that tinkering depends on your software. In Lightwave, you use the modeler to assign surface names to objects, then create sets of properties tagged with matching names in the renderer using a dialog screen (see Figure

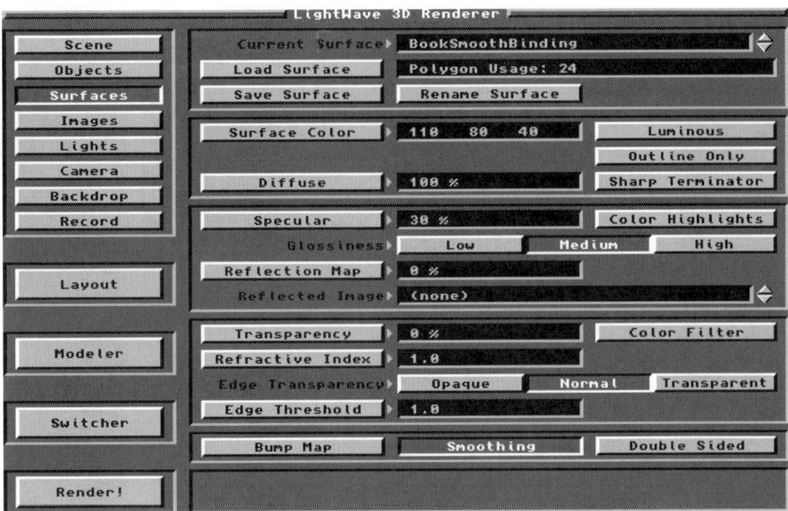

Figure 5-12: Lightwave's surface editor

5-12). Infini-D uses a pop-up surface editor (see Figure 5-13) that includes a shaded preview of the surface, mapped to a sphere. Presenter Professional's approach is similar, and Topas is unique among the software discussed here in that it lacks the ability to bring together all surface property settings under an assigned name. Named surfaces in Topas include only solid color and shading style (Gouraud, Phong, flat, rounded, and so on) settings. There is also no master surface editor; you need to visit several options under the Materials menu to construct a surface with more than the basic properties. That makes it more of a challenge to pull the surface assignments for large projects together.

Shading previews, like the one shown in the upper-right corner of the Infini-D surface editor window in the figure above, are becoming more common. Lightwave has none, so to see the effects of changes to surface properties, you have to render the scene. Topas has a preview window in its procedural map editor but nowhere else. Most Mac-based 3-D tools include the preview, and it's a tremendous time-saver. When you're without a surface preview facility, you can create your own by building and saving a scene containing only a sphere with a point light above it and off to one side. If your software handles transparency and reflections, put a rectangle underneath the sphere and texture map it with some repetitive

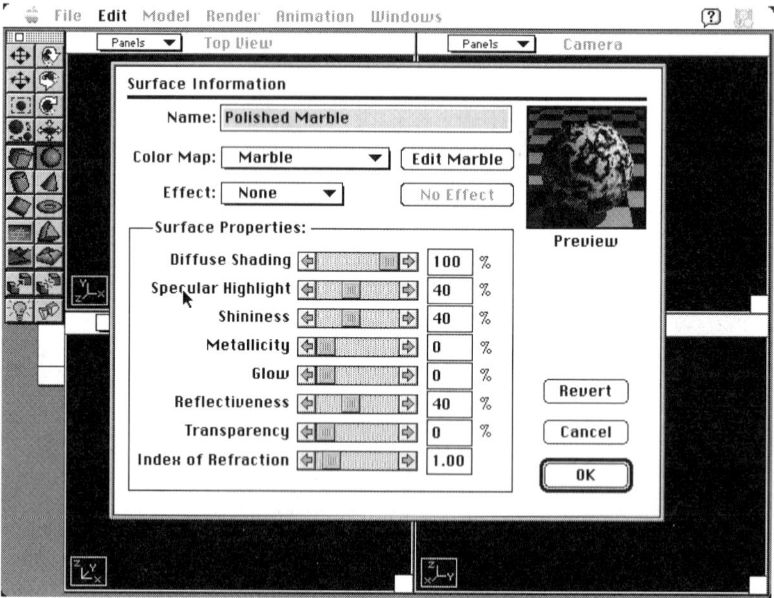

Figure 5-13: Infini-D's surface editor

pattern (see the section on texture mapping, below). That way, you can create your surfaces and test them on a preview scene that will probably render much more quickly than the real scene you're working on.

Texture and Procedural Maps

Taking the surface appearance of your objects beyond the ordinary can be a job for two alternatives to the glossy, solid-colored surface: texture and procedural maps. All good 3-D software supports texture maps, and most of the packages I've encountered now support at least a small number of procedural maps as well.

A texture map is, broadly speaking, a 2-D graphic that is painted onto an object. The graphic takes the place of, or is combined with, the solid color that would normally make up the object's surface. Text map graphics can come from anywhere, and they may be any size. The only limitation is that the graphics file must be in a format that your 3-D software can read directly. Your 3-D software may require that you preload the graphic into a buffer before you can apply it to an object as a texture map.

Once a texture map file is loaded, you have to choose how it will be applied to the object of interest. Each 3-D package has its own assortment of application methods. A texture map is either treated like a flat, flexible rectangular sheet that has the graphic printed on one side or as a slide in a projector that is pointed at the object. The former is sometimes referred to as a *wrap*, because the method of application produces a result that's something like wrapping your object in that printed sheet. A wrap always covers the entire object, no matter how large the graphic is in proportion to the object, but in doing so it can create distortions as it goes over uneven object topology. The *projection* map projects an undistorted graphic on the front and back face of an object, and the image "bleeds" around the sides in streaks.

Much of my use of texture maps comes from using 3-D packages as a way to attractively place a group of images (scanned photographs, for example) into a presentation slide or video title slide. I stretch out rectangles that roughly match the shape of the photographs I want to use, load the graphic files for those photos, and texture map the files onto the rectangles. The rectangles can be rotated and tumbled to add perspective, and you can set them above another Phong-shaded surface so you can cast shadows under the prints. You can even use two rectangular shapes or your software's texture map positioning tools to create photographic print-style borders or Polaroid print looks. By extruding the rectangle a little bit, the photo can appear to be mounted on a cardboard matte.

A rectangle with a texture map applied to it also makes a good backdrop for a scene. All 3-D programs let you load graphics files as backgrounds, but these sit motionless no matter how you change your viewing angle, zoom in or fall back. If you want a background that has as much perspective and depth as other objects in your scene, a texture-mapped rectangle is the best way to get it.

The best path to understanding how texture maps work is to apply a few of them yourself. You can start with a set of simple shapes (like the plane, sphere, cube and cylinder in Figure 5-14) and apply the same graphic to all of them as texture maps. Then you can see how your 3-D software handles texture maps. Infini-D's default mapping styles for primitive shapes work well, as you can see. Once you see how texture maps behave on simple shapes, you can use what you learn to apply texture maps to the more complex shapes you import and create.

Topas has a good assortment of texture map application styles, as shown in Figures 5-15, 5-16 and 5-17. These images show the *project*, *wrap,* and *apply*

Figure 5-14: Texture maps (Infini-D) (photograph by Howard Eglowstein)

styles individually. Particularly noteworthy in these illustrations are the traits that suit each texture map style to certain kinds of objects. You can see, for example, that of the three map styles, the projection map seems to distort the map graphic (parallel diagonal black lines on a gray background) of the lathed object on the left the least. The wrap covers the exterior of the extruded questionmark while leaving the front face the solid color assigned to it. And in both the wrapped and applied texture maps, seams are visible where the program joined the top and bottom of the map.

Seams are a frequent headache of 3-D artists. You can conceal them by positioning the map so that the seam falls on a part of the object that can't be seen. But if you're shooting the object from several different angles, or you're doing an animation that causes the entire object to be revealed, you will have to worry about seams. These were a particularly nasty problem for texture maps of natural surfaces like wood and stone. These were frequently called into service to add realism

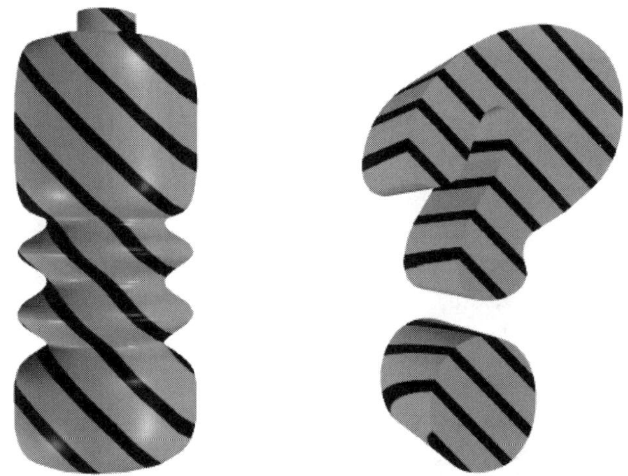

Figure 5-15: Projected texture maps (Topas)

to 3-D scenes, but hiding or minimizing the seams was sometimes more work than building the scene itself.

You're more fortunate than the early 3-D pioneers—you've got procedural maps (see Figure 5-18). These eliminate the searching for the perfect texture map graphic for a natural surface. Procedural maps simulate the random patterns of nature, as seen in woods, stones, clouds, sometimes even lightening. The simulations are done mathematically and created anew from scratch every time you render. You can tune the algorithms used to produce a pattern to create precisely the effect you want. If you load a procedural for wood and then decide you want the wood lighter and the grain darker and closer together, you can manage these things with just a few mouse-button clicks. A preview window will show you the new pattern you've created with your changed parameters. Figure 5-19 shows the interface Infini-D uses to give you control of a procedural map's settings.

The name of a procedural map—say, "marble"—shouldn't limit your imagination. The range of controls offered by 3-D software can turn any procedural into something nature never intended. You can take the gray-on-gray marble procedural

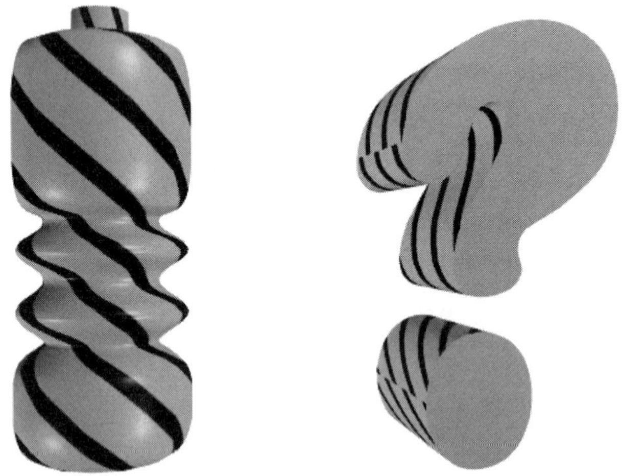

Figure 5-16: Wrapped texture maps (Topas)

and give it a twist to make it fit a surrealistic scene. But there are more practical reasons to use procedural maps beyond their named purposes: clouds can become realistic-looking mud splatterings or rust holes, the venous patterns of the marble procedural map can be made to look like sparks or streaks of flowing lava. Sometimes all it takes to put a new spin on an existing map is to change its colors. But don't stop there. Fiddle with all the settings to acquaint yourself with the range of patterns each procedural type can produce. The preview window is perfect for this kind of experimentation; you don't have to map and render the surface to see its effect.

In programs that support it, any texture or procedural map can be used to change the apparent shape of the object it covers. If you needed a golf ball for a scene, you could spend all night carving dimples in its outer skin. For a spinning planet earth, you could invest huge amounts of time designing a topologically correct 3-D surface. You needn't do either of these things, thanks to a special mapping technique called *bump mapping*. Any texture or procedural map can become a bump map. Brightness levels determine how far above or below the object's natu-

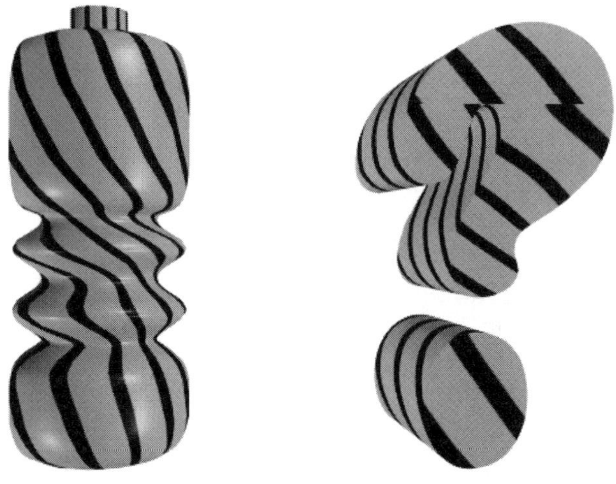

Figure 5-17: Applied texture maps (Topas)

ral surface height each pixel will appear to be. The golf ball's dimples could be reproduced by drawing a graphic of rows of dots and then using that graphic as a bump map with a negative displacement. Each dot would then appear to sink into the ball's exterior. Bump maps don't affect the shape of your objects. Instead, they trick the shader (Phong shading is usually required) into thinking that a pixel is riding higher or lower than its coordinates in 3-D space suggest. Some programs, like Topas, will also let you use alpha channel data for bump mapping. You can create an alpha channel bump map that draws no graphics on the object's exterior but which otherwise works like any other bump map. You may even place graphics that have nothing to do with the bump map in the other channels (red, green, and blue) of the graphics file holding the alpha channel data. Adobe Photoshop (version 2.5 or later, Mac or Windows) will create custom alpha channel graphics and store them as files that you can use for bump mapping. One of the most common uses for bump maps, by the way, is to place an embossed (etched into the surface) logo or other artwork on an object.

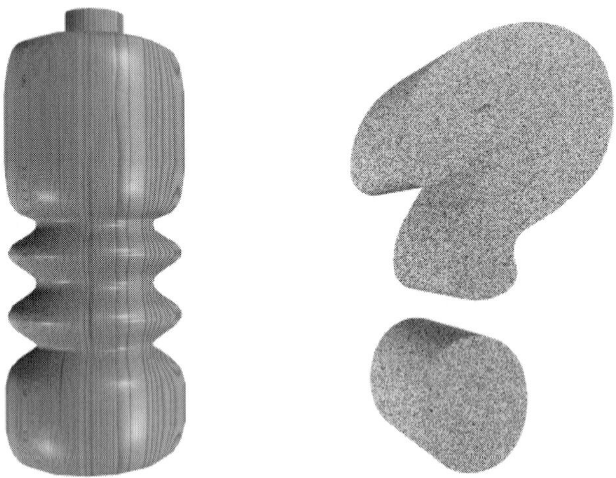

Figure 5-18: Wood and cork procedural maps (Topas)

In addition to bump mapping, you can sometimes switch on special attributes that change the way a texture or procedural map behaves. You may several options in the software you choose, including *transparency*, *shininess*, and *luminance mapping*. These increase the namesake properties of a surface based on the brightness level or alpha channel values embedded in graphics files. Transparency mapping makes it possible to "paint transparency" onto an object so that portions of it can be seen through. You might render a jet cockpit's window with a transparency map that combines the clear window pane sections with the metal frame that holds it together. A shininess map can give parts of an object a glossy appearance, while leaving others with the object's assigned surface properties. And luminance mapping can create objects that appear to be lit from inside. Luminance-mapped objects don't cast light on other objects in the scene, but those areas that have are mapped to the maximum luminance value appear brightly lit even when there are no nearby lights.

Transparency, shininess, luminance and other special mapping types can help you avoid assigning surfaces to individual polygons or groups of polygons to get

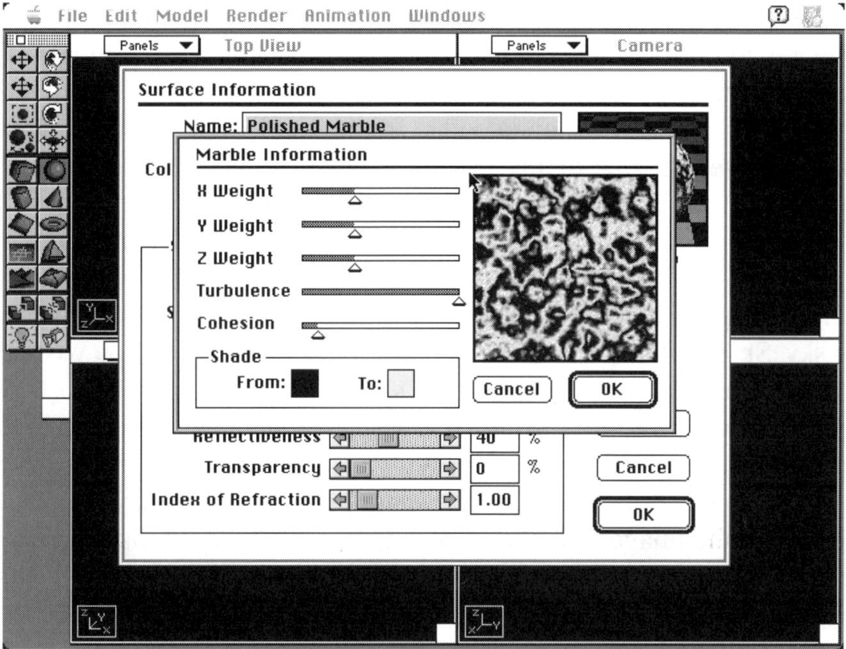

Figure 5-19: Editing a marble procedural map (Infini-D)

achieve the same effects. Without transparency mapping, you'd have to create a much more complex model for your jet cockpit. With a transparency map, that model can simply be a single curved surface.

Reflection and Environment Maps

There are two special classes of maps that create the appearance of reflections in shiny objects without incurring the overhead of ray tracing. The reflection map doesn't create reflections per se, but it simulates them by applying a special class of texture map. The graphic you select is seen as a semitransparent reflection in the object you reflection map. You could scan a photograph of a beach and reflection map it to a pair of sunglasses. A car windshield might reflect sky and clouds, and you might use reflection mapping on a chrome or other metallic surface to have it reflect the surrounding room. The reflection map offers you the advantage of adding visual elements to your scene which, while not directly visible, add to the depth and realism of the scene. A tendency some 3-D artists have when they first start out is to design scenes that are incredibly complex just so objects' ray-traced reflections can show something interesting. Its often just as effective, sometimes more effective, to use a scanned, video frame-grabbed or painted image as a reflection. You save the time of ray tracing. Equally important, you save yourself the aggravation of trying to line up the objects in your scene just right so they reflect the way you want them to. You might find, for example, that your car model's windshield doesn't point at the sky as you expected it to, or it points at a boring patch of your imitation sky, forcing you to either tilt the windshield or redesign your sky. Skip that; paint a reflection of your sky exactly as you wish it to be seen, and apply it to the windshield. You'll save a lot of time, and you'll get a perfect render even when you park your car in a scene that doesn't have a sky.

Your software will probably provide some sort of adjustment that determines the degree to which the reflection is magnified, and you may also be able to add distortion to the image to make it look more realistic on nonplanar objects. You'll also be able to choose the degree of visibility of the reflection. This is usually expressed as a percentage that is an inverse of the transparency of the reflection map. A 100% reflection obliterates the object's original surface in favor of the reflection. Lower numbers make the reflection increasingly transparent.

Environment maps serve nearly the same purpose as ray-traced reflections. An object can carry as a component of its surface the mirror image of the objects around it. Glass, chrome, and other metals and liquids can be environment-mapped to create reflections. I know that last sentence is a little confusing, but you can keep environment and reflection maps separate in your mind by remembering that only one of those two terms refers to the world surrounding the object. The environment map reflects the surrounding environment—all of it.

Your software (Infini-D and Topas both do environment maps) creates a map by placing a camera inside the object to be mapped and spinning it around to cover the object's visible area. This builds a graphic with a properly distorted panoramic view of the scene, which is then turned into a reflection map and mapped to the environment-mapped object. This all happens automatically, but it does take time. Parts of your scene may have to be rendered twice, and the environment map will probably show reflections of the backs of objects (which can't normally be seen). Because of this, you'll have to disable your software's "backface elimination" option (see the section on rendering speed, below).

Composite Surface Maps

Even with all these different flavors of texture and procedural maps, just one map on the skin of an object may not give you the effect you desire. Whether you're designing the exterior of a race car, rocket, or even something as seemingly unchallenging as a bottle of soap, you'll run into many situations that call for not just one surface, but a whole stack of surfaces, each of which adds its properties to the object. A rocket might call for one surface that is painted white, a bump map on top that gives it a slightly dirty, slightly dented appearance for added realism, and a third that contains the space agency logo and other markings. You'd spend a long time in a paint program creating a single texture map that served all of these purposes. Instead, most 3-D software lets you attach several surface maps to a single object (or, with packages like Topas, a single polygon if you need that kind of detail). These are often referred to as composite maps, meaning that the final surface is a composite (combination) of the component maps.

You obviously can't have several maps occupying the same space. You use composite maps when you want different maps to be visible on different parts of an object. Fixing the various maps to show up in different places is something of an art, and there's little sense in my describing it in detail here; the possible combinations are endless, and each package handles composite surface layering differently. In Topas, you can use the alpha channel of a texture map graphic to create a transparency mask. Transparent parts (portions where the alpha channel value, seen as shades of gray in most programs, is bright rather than dark) show through to underlying composite surface layers. Infini-D can automatically drop the blank space of a texture map graphic, making it transparent. This creates a useful decal effect without imposing the bother of creating an alpha channel mask.

Topas will, as I mentioned, apply surfaces to individual polygons if that's your wish. Autodesk's 3-D studio will do this, too, but not all packages include this feature. The combination of composite surfaces and individual polygon surfaces make just about any surface effect you can dream up possible.

Rendering

Rendering is the final step for most 3-D work. It is the most compute-intensive, and sometimes the most time-consuming part of 3-D. The product of a rendering session is a graphics file that depicts your scene with all the lights and shading properties you define, viewed from the vantage point you select. An animation is simply multiple consecutive renders, with each render being stored in a separate file, stored as a component frame in a specially formatted animation file, or sent out to a video or film recorder.

Once you've mastered object creation and placement, and you have spent some time working with surfaces, there needn't be anything difficult about rendering your finished scene. In most cases, it can be reduced to selecting a single option from a menu. But in other cases, the rendering component of your 3-D software may offer you some helpful options.

The amount of time it takes to render a scene depends not only on the content of the scene, but also on the settings you feed into the renderer. Once again, the way these settings are brought out to you differ from package to package. You may see the speed/quality trade-off expressed as a simple "low, medium, high" row of pushbuttons. Or, as is the case with Topas, rendering quality may be derived from a large collection of settings, each of which has some bearing on how long your render will take and how good the result will look.

Rendering Time

With everything else you have to think about when you do 3-D, you might prefer the idea of doing all the design and surface work, and then pressing one button and letting the computer do its thing unaided. But you should be concerned about the time it takes to render a 3-D scene. This is particularly true of animations, where the time to render any particular frame may determine whether the animation can be done at all in the time you have. Even a single scene can take an inordinately long time to render. Most often, the computer is tied up and pretty well useless for the duration of the render. Even if you are running a multitasking operating system and you *can* do something else with it, you shouldn't. It is a basic principle of 3-D rendering that it will use all the memory and CPU power available to it. Borrow from either by running another application at the same time, and you'll only make yourself wait even longer for your results.

Reducing rendering time is something you should plan for before you start building your first object. I'll list some shortcuts below; others will come to you as you work with your software. I encourage you to fiddle with all the surface and rendering-related parameters in your 3-D package. Most software will give you a measure of total rendering time after a render is completed, so you can perform your own benchmark tests.

Use reflection and environment maps instead of ray tracing for object reflections. Ray tracing produces cool results, but for most jobs, environment mapping will serve just as well for those times when you really must have objects showing reflections of other objects. But even this is expensive, so consider the worthwhile alternative of using the extremely fast reflection map. Some surface types, like chrome, show such distorted reflections anyway that you can often get away with using a paint program to draw a few streaks of the colors used in the rest of your scene. If you texture map that onto with a high level of distortion, it will look great and carry much lower overhead. The bottom line is: use reflection maps for the majority of your glossy and metallic surfaces that need to carry reflections; resort to environment maps only when the surface shows so little distortion that the hand-drawn reflection map shortcut will be too obvious; and use ray tracing for reflections sparingly, if at all.

Use backface elimination. No matter what point of view you choose, some portion of every object in your scene will be obscured. Odd as it may seem, your 3-D software still calculates those invisible surfaces, and that adds to rendering time. You can reduce the time spent drawing surfaces you can't see by activating your software's backface elimination option. This simply bypasses the calculations for obscured surfaces. Most objects will still look the same from the camera's angle. Backface elimination won't work if you have any semi transparent objects more than a point or two deep or if you generate reflections that show the obscured portion of any object in your scene. All it takes is one object to blow it for you; backface elimination is usually a global item, done for all objects at once or none at all.

Shrink your texture maps. Try to match the resolution of your texture map as closely as possible to its rendered size in the scene. Larger texture map images take longer to process, and tools (like Photoshop) make resizing images quick and easy.

While you're there, you might also check out whether your texture map can survive being represented in 16-bit or even 8-bit color. If your scene is going to be published in black-and-white, you can usually get away with knocking the texture map file down to 8-bit grayscale with no perceptible loss in quality. Not all software supports depth-reduced texture map files.

How much you can afford to trim in size or color depth depends on the image quality and content, and how the finished scene will be reproduced. If your destination is a 4000-line film recorder, you'll want your texture maps to be as big as possible to match the output medium's resolution. If the scene is going out to videotape or will be displayed on a computer monitor, then you can probably economize quite a bit.

Don't use maximum anti-aliasing unless you really need it. Anti-aliasing, which reduces the stair-stepped "jaggies" effect in graphics, is sometimes worth the time to apply, but often it isn't. Generally speaking, the higher the resolution, the less the need for anti-aliasing. At higher resolutions, there are more total pixels to represent curved and angled edges (the edges that tend to show up jaggies best), and at a high enough resolution, jagged edges won't be noticeable at all. All of the serious 3-D software I've used does its own anti-aliasing, and the better packages will let you choose how much to apply. The more anti-aliasing you use, the more time it will add to the render. The "low" setting is generally good enough for all but print work, and I recommend it for images rendered at the standard 640 × 480 or less. If you go *much* less than that, then I strongly suggest you live with the overhead of higher anti-aliasing. It has the effect of increasing the apparent resolution of an image by smoothing the sharp edges of objects. Your software may have a separate option to anti-alias texture maps, and I think this should always be used. If you use a texture map on a nonplanar object that isn't exactly perpendicular to the camera, the perspective and distortion applied to the image can show up as visual noise. Anti-aliasing will reduce or eliminate that. If your software can't turn texture map anti-aliasing on and off separately, then always use at least the "low" overall anti-aliasing setting to improve the quality of your texture maps.

Lightwave has a novel approach: it will render a high-res version of a scene, and then anti-alias and scale the result down to a more manageable resolution. This has the effect of very convincingly simulating the higher resolution while invoking the benefits of reduced file and display size.

Pick your shading methods carefully. If your software allows you to apply shading methods to individual objects (as Topas will), remember to save the most expensive methods for those objects that can't be represented any other way. In the case of Topas, the so-called materials palette will let you select a shading method for each object, or even for each polygon. In Topas, the top shading method is Phong, and there are specific conditions that call for Phong shading. These include receiving shadows cast by other objects, receiving the outline made by a spotlight being pointed directly at the surface, and showing round specular highlights. It's perfectly acceptable, even advisable, to have a mix of shading methods in a scene. You'll save yourself mountains of rendering time by Phong shading only those objects that require it, and Gouraud shading all the rest. I haven't found that flat shading, obviously the fastest method going, applies in many situations unless I'm looking for a completely solid color or an angular look.

Use shadows sparingly. Decide up front whether you need shadows in your scene. Shadows are always costly, whether done through shading or ray tracing. While they produce impressive effects, shadows can often be left out of a scene without doing much damage. If you use shadows, you can still trim rendering time by using them only where their effects will be most useful. Most software lets you determine whether a particular light casts a shadow, and you can sometimes choose which objects cast shadows as well. And remember that to receive a shadow, a surface must be Phong-shaded or ray-traced. So keep the number of shadow-casting lights and objects to a minimum, and use shadow-receptive surfaces only in those places where the shadow effects will be most noticeable and beneficial.

Ditto for reflections and refraction. If you're ray-tracing a scene, things will move a lot faster if you make sure that reflection and refraction are disabled for objects that don't need them. This usually means setting the reflection value to zero and the refraction index to 1.0 (no refraction). Changing either setting even one notch turns on ray tracing for that object, and you've added significantly to your rendering time. Even if you're running Presenter Professional with the YARC coprocessor board, you still can't afford to spread ray tracing around indiscriminately, although you can use it on objects that you'd never want to ray trace on an unassisted Mac.

Use 2-D wherever you can. If you created a beautifully detailed 3-D saddle, you could display it very nicely in a scene that depicted a corral. You might think about building the corral entirely in 3-D, but there's a far more sensible way: draw or take a picture of a real corral, scan it in, and use it as a background. Remember that the 3-D offered by 3-D software isn't *really* three-dimensional. It shows three dimensions on a two-dimensional medium the same way photographs do: by reproducing the effects of light and perspective. In this example, you'd use your picture of the corral as a background. You would take note of the direction of the sun in the photograph, using shadows and highlights as clues, and place an omni light over your saddle so it casts light at a similar angle. To add a little realism, you might drape the saddle over a piece of weathered fence wood (that might be easier than designing a 3-D horse) you could create with a wooden procedural map and a bump map to simulate distress. The finished scene, if done right, will enhance the realism of the saddle because of the obvious realism of the photograph.

One aid to using 2-D images in this fashion is *fog*. This often doesn't behave in the traditional sense. It is, rather a haze that blurs objects that are more than a specified distance from the camera. The haze increases in density at greater distances, so that if an object is far enough away, it is completely obscured by the fog. Fog's usefulness in this context is as a simulation of depth of field. In a 3-D scene, *everything's* in focus, just as though you shot the scene through a pinhole camera. Depth of field is the in-focus distance range of a camera given various lens settings. Everything outside that range, the starting distance of which you adjust with the lens's focus ring, is out of focus. The farther outside that range you are, the more blurry objects at that distance become. A mild fog can partially imitate depth of field by causing distant objects to appear blurry. Now if you have Photoshop or its like, and all you're after is to make the corral backdrop look out of focus, you can apply a blur filter to the texture map file and save it. That will be quicker than having your 3-D software generate fog, but fog is useful if you also have 3-D objects that you wish to share the blur.

Another way to use 2-D to save 3-D rendering time is to use previously rendered scenes as components of others. This is particularly helpful in animation, where each frame is rendered from scratch, even if only one object in the scene is actually moving. If that's the case, then render the nonmoving objects in the scene, save that as a graphic file, and bring it in again as a background, replacing the 3-D objects that were used to create it. Add the one moving object, and now, instead of rendering an entire complex scene, your software only needs to paint one texture map and a single object moving across it. That's a simplistic description, but there are plenty of times when you can get away with a prerendered background instead of using real 3-D.

Reduce the detail of distant objects. If you build a model of a car that contains dozens of highly detailed sub-objects, you'll have a model that looks wonderful close-up. But if you show that same car at a distance, most of that detail will be lost, but the software still ties up your computer drawing it. The farther away, the lower the potential for detail. Unless you're doing an animation that follows an object from close-up to far away, when the object is small and distant, substitute a *stand-in*, or approximated object. If it's really small, a blob in the same color as your car will suffice. If it's a little closer, you can still save time by removing some of the detail objects and replacing them with solid panels. You can build some of your stand-ins with groups of the primitive objects standard for your software. Try to stick with angular objects—rounded objects have more polygons and take longer to draw—and remember that there's no need to Phong-shade or ray-trace an object that's too far away to show the effect.

Do reduced-resolution test renders. There are few things more frustrating that waiting for a high-resolution render to finish, only to discover that the lights didn't work the way you expected. That's only one of many surprises that await you, but you can protect yourself easily. A favorite route I've found is in the "render window" facility found in both Topas and Infini-D. Here, you can drag a rectangle out on the screen, and the software will do a full render only inside that rectangular area. Topas will also render a single object. Window and object renders will let you see if the effects of lights and other scene settings are as you expect. But these options are rare.

More common is the reduced-resolution render. If you generate a postage stamp-sized image of your scene, it will render very quickly compared to a full-sized image. You can then view the result (Lightwave will show a reduced-resolution render at full screen size for scrutiny) to check for lighting and positioning errors. It takes some getting used to—like judging the quality of a photograph from a negative—but these test runs are invaluable for getting your scene straight before taking the time for a complete render.

When doing a test render, turn off all the fancy options you can live without. Certainly shut off anti-aliasing, and you can usually do away with shadows. Disable anything you don't need to see. Most test renders are done to check the placement of lights, and these go much faster without the frills.

Hide or delete obscured objects, cut partially obscured objects. Try to minimize the time you spend rendering what you can't see. If you're rendering a scene from several viewing angles, you can delete all the objects that aren't visible from a particular angle. Some software (Topas included) will make it easier for you by letting you hide objects. Hidden objects don't render, but you can pop them up again precisely where they were before in an instant.

Topas also supports the notion of cutting objects. If you wanted to show a sphere peeking out from behind a cube, you could do a cut operation on the sphere to hack off the portion of it that's not visible. A cut deletes the polygons in the cut portion and either spackles over the opening with a solid cap or leaves it open. The latter leaves you with fewer polygons to draw and less surface area to compute. Of course, if your software doesn't support cut (most won't), you can always design your objects "precut," that is, don't bother building anything that can't be seen. A scene of a car's rear end sticking out of a garage might inspire you to build the world's best car model, but settle for building the best half-a-car-model instead.

Check the performance of your software's procedural maps. Procedural maps are compute-intensive, but some software is quicker about it than others. You may find that your software is particularly slow. It's not usually slow enough to get in your way for a single-frame render, but an animation can be significantly slowed by procedural maps. You might speed things up by rendering a rectangle's worth of the texture, saving it as a file, and using that as a straight texture map.

Use as few medians as possible for lathed objects, and as few cross sections as possible in cross-sectional objects. Higher numbers of medians, the copies of the silhouettes used to build the frame for lathed objects, generally result in smoother, more contoured objects. More medians create more polygons, and therefore add to rendering time. Test your software to see how few medians you can get away with while still creating a smoothly contoured shape.

Similarly, the more cross (rib) sections you place in a cross-sectional model, the more polygons you'll get, and the longer the render will take. You shouldn't need more than two in a row of any identically shaped cross sections that are placed at the same relative position (except for an offset along a single axis).

Use polygons instead of splines wherever possible. Splines create beautifully rounded shapes, but they can take much longer to render than polygon-based objects. Topas, for one, offers you the tools you need to build most objects with either polygons or splines, and it will even let you use spline-line drawing tools to build polygon objects.

Use your software's batch render mode, or render on multiple machines. This is both a suggestion for saving rendering time as well as your own time. Most good 3-D software will let you pull together a list of scenes you want to render, and then render them all at once, unattended. This saves you having to load and render each scene, and it's an effective way to make use of equipment that sits idle on nights and weekends. Batch renders are probably the only way (without a YARC board) to make ray tracing an acceptable means of rendering complex scenes. It also helps break you of the habit of trying to do renders "while you wait," because every waking minute you spend waiting for the computer to finish rendering is a minute you could put to better use working on your next scene (or goofing off, for that matter).

Crystal Graphics, the company that makes Topas, has what I consider to be a positively winning idea. Their software, like virtually all 3-D software I've run, is copy-protected by a block that plugs into your PC's parallel (printer) port. But uniquely, Topas comes with a special version of itself, Topas Off-Line, that lets you run a reduced-functionality Topas on as many machines as you like. You need to plug the security block into the machine to start the software, but then you can unplug the block and move it to another system, and another, and so on. The block need only be used continuously when running the full-blown Topas. Topas Off-Line contains the renderer only, which you can use to put multiple machines to work rendering multiple scenes, or split a single animation up into sections and feed each section to a different system. Putting multiple machines to work can help offset some of the penalties invoked by higher-quality renders.

On the Mac, several companies selling 3-D software offer *distributed rendering*. With this, two or more Macs intelligently split the workload of a render, communicating with each other over a network. The finished render is pieced together from the output of both machines. There's no difference in quality, but the work is done faster than one machine could do it. Infini-D's distributed rendering solution is called Backburner. It installs on networked Mac systems and behaves like an ordinary screen saver, blanking the screen after a period of inactivity to avoid burn-in. But while the screen is blank, Backburner "advertises" itself to the rest of the network as being able to take on a piece of an Infini-D rendering job. If one is in progress on another machine on the network, the idle Mac is given a slice of the rendering job. If another Backburner-equipped Mac becomes idle during that render, the job is divided again, and so on. If a user sits back down in front of his machine and wants to use it again, all he or she has to do is press a key or move the mouse. Backburner will save its status and step out of the way. The user isn't inconvenienced at all. In a shop with a lot of Macs, it's a cinch that some number of them are idle at any given time. Running Backburner on every Mac in the place can make the time after working hours extremely productive, rendering-wise.

Animation

I'll close this chapter with a brief discussion of 3-D animation. This subject alone could fill several books this size, so I'll limit my own discussion to those aspects that are common to most 3-D animation software. I'll also delve into some of the hardware issues of recording 3-D animation to videotape.

On the face of it, there's nothing mysterious about animation. I described it earlier as "multiple consecutive renders," and that's true. Now, I'd add that those multiple renders are done to simulate some kind of motion or transition. Motion can be a tumbling object, a moving light, or a shifting camera angle. A transition can be a change of the surface properties of an object, the colors of lights in the scene, or a change to the shape of an object itself.

To animate, you must decide upon the movement and transitions you want your animation to depict, at which point in time each action should occur, and how long each action will take to complete. The software takes this information and builds an animation by *interpolating* movement and transitions over the periods of time specified for them. If you asked to move a square from the upper-left to the lower-right of your screen and specified a duration of three frames (more on frames in a moment), your software would produce three rendered images: one with the square in its original position (upper-left), one with the square in the center of the screen, and one with the screen in its final position (lower-right). Even though you never specifically requested that the square be placed in the screen's center, the interpolation made that happen. Generally speaking, the interpolation will create the smoothest movement or transition possible in the time allotted it.

A single frame of an animation is usually the same as a single render. Using the NTSC video standard (the standard in the U.S.), it takes 30 frames to make a second's worth of videotaped animation. So that means, for every second of animation, you'll need 30 separate renders. You can reduce the number of rendered frames per second by using each frame more than once. Recording each frame twice will save you half of your renders (you'll only need 15 frames per second instead of thirty), but the difference in the smoothness of the motion will be readily visible.

There are two basic classes of animation: *keyframe* and *path*. Most personal computer-based 3-D software uses keyframes, described below. Path animation involves the drawing of lines, usually built with splines, through 3-D space. These paths serve as tracks for object movement. Many high-end animation systems use spline-path as opposed to keyframe methods for defining motion, but keyframe is much easier to work with.

Creating and Previewing Keyframe Animation

The example I gave above of the diagonally moving rectangle illustrates keyframe animation at its simplest. Keyframe animation is so-named for the snapshots, called keyframes, of your scene that are used as place markers. To produce the three-frame animation I described, you would create two keyframes: one at either end of the rectangle's motion path. When you generate the animation, the interpolated frame will be created automatically.

A keyframe animation of any length is usually made up of several keyframe snapshots. The content of a single keyframe is a recording of all of the *animatable properties* of your scene. In Topas, object movement and object surface colors, light positions and colors, and some object shape changes are among the animatable properties. Infini-D has the ability to shape-shift (*morph*) any object into any other object over time. Each keyframe captures the status of those elements in the scene that can change between keyframes. Some items, like the background image in a Topas animation, can't be animated. The list of animatable properties should be one of the items on your list of details to look into if you venture out to buy some 3-D software. Even good packages can leave important things out, and some software offers unique animation features, like Infini-D's universal morphing, that, if you need them, makes that package an obvious choice.

A keyframe has a vital property associated with it: time. You set a keyframe's time using whatever interface your software provides. It usually involves telling the software what the "current" time is, that is, how far into the animation the next keyframe should appear. Creating an animation starts with setting an initial keyframe to record the starting positions of objects and other animatable properties. Then you move objects around and change other properties to reflect the way you'd like the scene to look at the end of this phase of the animation, and take another keyframe. You will assign a time value to the second keyframe that determines how long (usually in frames) it should take to transition from the scene status at the first keyframe to that at the last. If you wanted a duration of two seconds, you'd set the second keyframe at 60 frames. Keyframe values are relative to the start of the animation (time zero), not the previous keyframe.

Most software will allow you to create multiple streams of keyframes, one for each object if it suits you, plus one master keyframe stream for the entire scene that covers objects and properties that don't have their own keyframes. With object keyframes, objects can move independently of one another. If your software doesn't support this, it can be a serious challenge to organize the independent motion of objects. Object keyframes let you set up a keyframe spacing that's right for that object alone, but if you don't have it, all of your objects must be taught to work within a master keyframe rhythm.

If you place a keyframe accidentally, or if you decide later that it was in the wrong place, you can move or delete it. Moving a keyframe moves it closer to or farther away from the keyframes around it, changing the duration of the animated transitions and movements. Deleting a keyframe removes it completely. If have three keyframes and delete the one in the middle, the interpolation will take place between the two remaining keyframes.

An animation, then, starts as a series of keyframes, with the gaps between keyframes filled by the software to create smooth motion and shape and color changes. As a simple example, take a look at the graphics in Figures 5-20 and 5-21. Figure 5-20 shows a string of extruded text at its starting position in the animation. This example was done in Topas, and the starting object position (and other animatable properties) is recorded when you start the animation by creating the first keyframe. The first keyframe is always frame 1. Figure 5-21 shows the second keyframe, with the logo rotated 180 degrees around its *Y* axis and moved to the diagonally opposite corner of the screen. Moving and rotating the logo required

Figure 5-20: The first keyframe of an animation

Figure 5-21: The last keyframe of an animation

several actions, but keyframe animation doesn't track the way you make the changes to the scene. Instead, it is only concerned with the scene's state as of the time you grab the keyframe. It doesn't matter what convoluted means you use to get from one scene's keyframe to the next. The software will compare the two scenes and find the most efficient, and generally most aesthetically pleasing, way to interpolate the changes. In this case, there were two changes to the object between keyframes: its position and its rotational angle. In interpolating the intermediate frames, the software will make all the changes at once, in parallel rather than serially. Again, it doesn't matter which order you use to arrange a scene for a new keyframe. Do a move, then a rotate; or a rotate, then a move. Either way, the animation will show the object rotating as it moves. If you want the object to move first, then rotate, you'll have to keyframe it that way: take the first keyframe with the object in its starting position, snap the second after you've moved the object to the opposite corner, and snap a third after you've rotated it around 180 degrees. The object will move and then rotate in two separate actions. The object won't start rotating until it has come to a complete stop from the move. Interpolation is strictly limited to the changes made between a single pair of keyframes. Changes never bleed over from one keyframe pair to another.

Many animators who are just getting started frequently make the mistake of placing too many keyframes. In this example, it might seem as though, in order to ensure that the logo passes through the center of the screen as it makes its move from the upper-left to the lower-right, an intermediate keyframe should be placed that shows the logo smack in the middle, and with the angle of rotation that exactly matches the mid-point of the rotational action as well. It's always better to let the software's interpolation smooth things out for you. You can generally trust it to do the right thing, and when you decide you're better at interpolating than the program is, the result is usually a jerky animation.

Whether you use object or whole-scene keyframes depends on how many objects you think will be moving at once. Often, when you place several objects in motion, you want them all to move at the same time and to take the same amount of time to land at their final positions. In these cases, there's no reason to burden yourself recording object keyframes for all the objects in the scene individually. Use the whole-scene keyframe, and move all of the objects between keyframes. The only reason to use object keyframes is to separate changes to one or more objects from the rest. Whenever you have some change in mind that must happen at a rhythm that doesn't match that of the whole-scene keyframes, use an object keyframe rather than forcing the program to split the job of interpolation over three keyframes or more. When interpolation is split like that, it often doesn't come off as smoothly.

Object keyframes are particularly handy for keyframing changes to lights and cameras. These often move independently of the objects in the scene, and keeping object keyframes on lights and cameras makes it easier for you to try something different if you don't get the effect you seek. It can be difficult to isolate and modify the changes to any one object in an animation built with whole-scene keyframes, so keep light and camera changes separate.

The keyframes shown in Figures 5-20 and 5-21 produced a 30 frame (one second) animation. Even an inanely simple animation like this can still take several minutes to record (the process for that will be described shortly)—a long wait just to find out things didn't work as you expected. Your software will certainly offer some means of previewing the animation without waiting for the whole thing to record. The least you'll be able to do is take a look at the way the scene looks at any frame you request. If you ask for a frame number that isn't associated with a keyframe, the software will do the interpolation on the spot and put the scene on the screen (in wireframe) exactly as it will appear at that frame in the finished animation. If you wanted to see what the middle frame of our sample animation looked like, you'd ask Topas to call up frame 15. You could then render that frame to check on lights, colors, and other scene properties.

Topas offers more means of previewing animations than any of the other software described here, and these various preview modes are among its most appealing qualities. I already mentioned the ability to pull up any specific frame, keyframe or interpolated, and view and render it. Topas also offers a *real-time preview*, a rough wireframe preview of the motion and shape changes. The real-time preview is generated quickly and is displayed on your PC's main monitor (probably a VGA) in white wireframe lines on a black background. The wireframes are generated one at a time and stored in memory, then played back in real time to show object and camera motion. You can select any range of frames you like for previewing. The number of frames you can see is limited by your system's memory, but you can also skip frames (showing, for instance, every third frame instead of every frame) to preview a larger range. These wireframe previews, which are also available in nearly all 3-D software, are key to debugging the motion in your animation. They are generated so quickly that you can reasonably, on a fast machine, preview, make needed changes, and preview again in a cycle.

Topas also offers a preview mode called the *storyboard*. If you've ever seen a documentary on filmmaking (animated or otherwise), you know that a storyboard is a script for the visual treatment of a story, expressed in pictures. Topas' can produce an after-the-fact storyboard that will show you the status of your scene at regular intervals throughout the animation (or some portion of it that you select). Figure 5-22 shows a nine-frame Topas storyboard for our sample animation. The

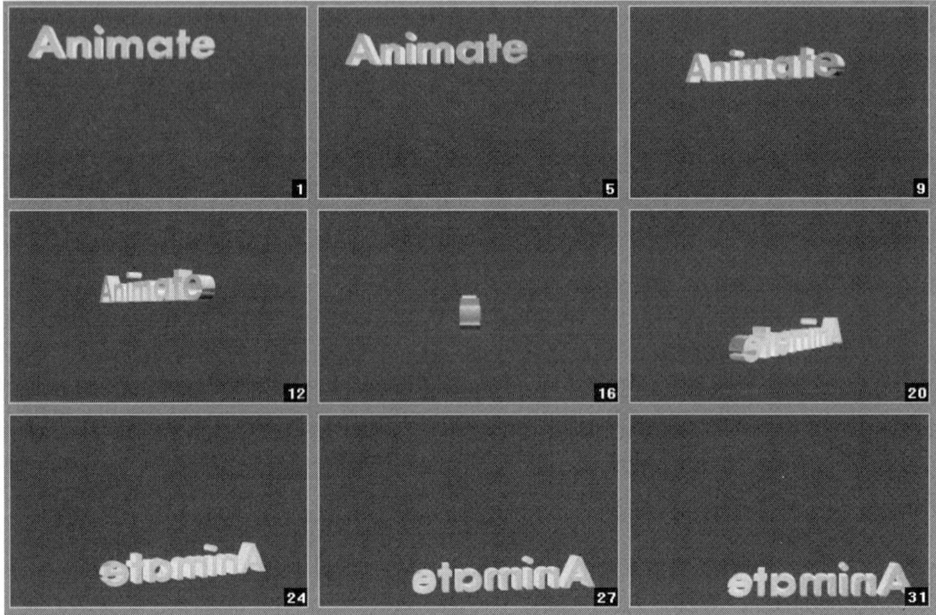

Figure 5-22: A Topas storyboard preview

animation frame number represented in each storyboard frame is shown in the corner. Topas will ask you how many frames you want to see on the screen at once, and automatically adjust the interval so that the first and last frames can be seen, and the frames in-between show the changes at even intervals. You can choose how much shading will be applied to a storyboard. This one was done with full shading applied, but you can still learn a lot from a wireframe or flat-shaded storyboard.

Yet another Topas preview method is the *flip book*. This is a cross between the real-time preview and the storyboard. To create a flip book, Topas generates a series of small color images (you determine how many), and then plays those images back at high speed to give you a moving preview of a selected portion of an animation. You can save flip books to disk and play them back later. The quality isn't good enough, and there isn't enough capacity to rely on flip books for even your least-demanding animated output, but its usefulness as a means of previewing an animation is unrivaled.

If, during the preview, you find something you need to change, you don't have to delete the keyframes and start over. You can load a keyframe (as described in the previous paragraph), change the scene content, and grab a new keyframe that overwrites the old one. Even if you've asked to look at a few interpolated frames, the software doesn't remember the interpolations, only the keyframes. Changes you make to any keyframe will force a new interpolation.

If you're looking at an interpolated frame (as you would be if you called up frame 15 of our sample animation) and you change it, your software may automatically create a keyframe at that position.

Topas has a special keyframe editing mode that applies changes you make to all of the following keyframes in the animation. Normally, if you edit a keyframe by loading it and changing it, changes are made to that keyframe alone. Let's say you created an animation with a blue sphere that moves across the screen over 30 frames. If you decided that you wanted that sphere to be green after all, and green through the entire animation, you'd load frame 1 and change the sphere's color to green. But if you didn't use the "apply changes to subsequent keyframes" option, the sphere would start green and then gradually change to blue as it moved. If you don't move the sphere while you're editing the keyframe, Topas will keep the object movement as it originally was, changing only the color.

Recording Animation

An animation is just keyframe data and scene data in your computer until, somehow, all of its frames are rendered and stored on a medium that makes it possible to play them back in rapid succession. I use the term "recording" broadly in this context; only one of the two methods available to you involves traditional recording.

The quickest route to a playable animation is to record the individual frames to disk in some standard animation file format. It's fortunate that animation has been around long enough on all three platforms in this book that a widespread animation file standard has emerged for each. On the Mac, a format called PICS reigned supreme until Apple's own QuickTime took over. Vendors of 3-D software quickly adapted their animation output modules to generate QuickTime movies. On the PC, the leading format is probably Autodesk's .FLI (and its variants), and the Amiga has its own "anim" format.

Having well-accepted animation file formats means that playback is easier to manage. On all three systems, you can get free software that plays QuickTime, .FLI and anim animation files. You'll also find that these formats are supported by the majority of multimedia applications.

Generating an animation file is easy, but it's not necessarily quick. Recording animation to disk saves time indirectly compared to taped animation, because disk-based animation is hardly ever done at videotape quality. .FLI animations are done in 8-bit color at a resolution of 320×200, and the other formats are similarly restricted in size and color depth. Reduced resolution means faster rendering; reduced color depth doesn't always mean that. Some programs always render frames to an internal 24-bit buffer, then reduce that buffer down to 8-bit color before storing each frame on disk. It generally takes just as long to generate an 8-bit image.

The advantage of disk-based animation is the ease with which it can be integrated into presentations and applications. Because playback requires no special equipment or expensive software, disk-based animations are supremely portable. But though they may be portable and easy to use, they are not small. An animation file is a collection of graphical images, and even when compressed using the advanced methods available today, these files are routinely multiple megabytes in size for a few seconds of animation.

There's another catch to using disk-based animation: playback rate. This issue is visited in greater detail in the next chapter, but I'll summarize here. While animations don't require any special hardware on the playback system, the less capable your hardware is, the slower the animation will play back. You might spool your animation out to disk at 30 frames per second, but even a blindingly fast machine will have a hard time keeping up with that rate. The Amiga, with its advanced video hardware (optimized for animation) on the motherboard of every machine, is probably the only system that can be counted on to routinely carry the burden of smooth animation playback. Macs and PCs vary so widely in their capabilities and configurations that unless you have complete control over the way the playback systems are built, you can't know what to expect when your animation is played.

Some animation files, including the .FLI, use delta encoding to reduce the file's size. You may recall that this stores only the changed pixels in an image. This scheme works extraordinarily well for files that have only a small object moving in an otherwise stationary field. Because the changes from frame to frame are isolated, the format can also make playback quicker by sending only the changed data to the display rather than updating the entire screen for every frame. But delta encoding and its playback advantages fall apart when large areas of the screen are changed at once. With most .FLI playback software, you'll notice a marked reduction in playback speed and smoothness for those frames containing greater numbers of altered pixels.

Clearly, if you can't count on your playback system being able to do 30 frames per second, there's no sense in wasting the time and disk space to create animation files that expect this playback rate. 3-D software that supports disk-based output will likely give you the option of selecting the frame rate for the file. You should choose a rate that will look good but that won't overburden the least capable systems you intend to target for playback. I've found that most systems can sustain playback rates of ten frames per second regardless of hardware, with the exception of .FLI files that depict massive frame-to-frame changes. Ten frames per second sits on the lower threshold of the mind's ability to merge consecutive still images into apparent motion, so you should try to avoid slower rates. At five frames per second, an animation looks more like a rapid-fire slide show.

Software that supports animation playback will either fill the screen with the animation or place it in a window on the screen. Amiga animations are usually displayed full-screen. .FLI files played under Windows, and QuickTime files played on either the Mac or under Windows, will, by default, play in a small window. The next chapter's section on digital video will discuss playback software, and the chapter on media integration will shed a little more light on the process of building animation into presentations and programs.

The "big time" for 3-D animators is recording to some analog media. Now before I take heat from video professionals, I will point out that there are devices that record video as digital data. But as that exciting technology is reserved only for those who can afford it, I'll focus my discussion on more accessible analog videotape equipment.

The best quality videotaped animation is recorded to tape one frame at a time. It is possible to send your 3-D output to an animation file first, then play that file while you're recording it to tape, but the quality isn't as nice as you can get from single-frame video animation. The issue of playback frame rate disappears, and as portable as an animation file is, a VHS videotape is practically universal (within its own video format (NTSC or PAL). What's more, video is an analog medium—you can output your animations at your video display hardware's best color depth.

There's a whole chapter coming up on desktop video production, and you'll find there quite a bit of material on single-frame editing video recorders and VCR controllers. I won't waste time or pages repeating that material here, but I'll give you a distant view of what it takes to record animation to tape.

You can't use your home VCR for single-frame animation. There are several innovative solutions that make consumer video equipment more suitable than it normally is for this purpose, but without professional quality gear, the results will always be flawed. An animation-capable VCR has three key properties: timecode, frame-accurate positioning, and single-frame editing. Timecode is a digital code that's recorded onto a videotape which stamps every frame with a user-settable hours, minutes, seconds and frame number. A frame-accurate deck can locate any single frame, using timecode, and position its heads precisely over that one frame. And finally, single-frame editing means that the deck can snap into and out of record mode on a particular timecoded frame fast enough to write the contents of *one frame* onto the tape without disturbing the frames around it. That one feature is what makes animation decks so expensive. It's not easy to make equipment that consistently precise.

Be wary as you look around for equipment, for while these features are often seen together, they are just as often seen separately. Plenty of hopeful animators have been duped, usually by salespeople who simply don't know better, into buying decks that lack the all-important single-frame editing capability. Timecode isn't enough, and timecode with frame-accurate positioning isn't enough. With these two features alone, you can sometimes get rough animations, but most often, you'll be disappointed with the results.

At the time of this writing, the least-expensive animation decks still cost around $7000. There's reason to hope, because that price is a steal compared to what animators were forced to pay just a couple of years ago. As animation and video editing become more popular, it's likely that prices on these decks will continue to fall.

To get animation to a videotape, your system needs two components: a display card with recordable video output and a VCR controller. The display card is half or more of the quality formula. Even if you've got a 24-bit display card, if the quality of its video output is questionable, you'll get bad-looking animation. It is worth the extra money for the better quality of professional display hardware. The Truevision (NuVista+, ATVista), Matrox (Illuminator Pro), and Newtek (Video Toaster) video equipment in my lab produces very clean recorded animation. The VCR controller sits between your computer and the video deck and waits for commands from your animation software. Your 3-D package will render a frame to the display card, and then send a command to the VCR controller that says "record one frame." The VCR controller then commands the VCR to position itself over that timecoded frame on the tape and lay down one frame's worth of fresh material, that material being the signal coming out of your system's display card.

That's the simplistic description of video animation. I implore you to refer to the chapter on desktop video production to learn more about video before you venture into becoming a video animator.

6

Digital and Overlay Video

Video is a truly universal medium; most of us deal with it daily. Now that video can be stored on your computer's hard disk, and video from a VCR can be played in a window on your system's display, you can put the power of video to work in your presentations and programs.

For better or worse, television has changed the world. After years of constant exposure, we've come to take for granted what was originally hailed as a magical device: pictures and sounds played together inside a glass tube. Now, far from viewing video as a magical medium, we see it as one of our primary means for receiving information from others. It's fitting, then, that multimedia technology, the sole purpose of which is to make our communication more effective, should include video as a pivotal media type.

This chapter may seem premature considering that the chapter on desktop video production, the chapter you'd consult to *create* the video this chapter shows you how to use, is still a few pages off. I chose to organize this book with discussions of media first, with closing chapters on their integration.

Compared with some of the other chapters in this book, this one is a quick and easy read. That's mostly because, while video is a compelling medium, there isn't a lot to tell about it now for various reasons. For starters, digital video hasn't been around all that long yet. It is most established on the Mac, where Apple's QuickTime software showed the rest of the world that digital video was possible and worth doing. Microsoft's equivalent (Video for Windows) came along much later, and as I write this, hasn't yet picked up the kind of nearly universal support that QuickTime enjoys on the Mac. I'm not suggesting that it won't gain such support; with Microsoft behind it, Video for Windows should do just fine.

Another reason for this chapter's quick handling of its subject matter is the disparity of implementation across platforms. The Mac is the undisputed digital video king thanks to QuickTime (and to Adobe Premiere, to which you'll be introduced shortly). The PC runs a distant second by the measure of the number of hardware and software products specifically aimed at producing and using digital video. The Amiga brings up the rear, for while there are some imaginatively crafted tools that can turn video into animation files, the Amiga stands alone as the only system here that has no native digital video support. Commodore is said to be working on it, and may well have a solution in hand by your reading of this.

Where overlay video (a definition is on its way) is concerned, the PC has the upper hand, thanks to Windows' clever design that makes it easy for software and hardware producers to plug new multimedia functionality into Windows. There are a small number of video overlay products for the Mac, but only Windows can boast hardware independence, a feature I consider invaluable. The Amiga can't manage the same flavor of video overlay as the many PC and few Mac products, but it can do something close to it far more cheaply than either of the other two systems.

This chapter, then, will necessarily present an uneven pattern of discussion. The Mac will dominate my coverage of digital video, the PC will get much of the attention with regard to video overlay, and the Amiga will be mentioned throughout but not with the frequency of the other two. I'm sensitive to those who feel loyalty to a particular platform and keep their eyes peeled for those who might slight it. But rest assured that the tilted coverage in this chapter is due to the state of the technologies being discussed and not my preference for some type of system over the others.

Selecting an Analog Video Source

One element common to both digital and overlay video is the original source: analog video. Some use a TV tuner or satellite receiver as a video source, and others rely on laserdisc players, but videotape is the most commonly used analog video source.

Strictly speaking, any VCR can serve as an analog video source. You can trot over to your favorite department store and pick up a bargain-basement VHS machine. It will certainly hook up to your video capture or video overlay board, and for some types of material, it may even be good enough. But the professionals that build multimedia playback systems that incorporate video will tell you that most consumer equipment lacks three fundamental requirements for serious use: video quality, computer controllability, and durability.

The video quality debate will rage forever, but the debate over digital and overlay video quality is framed a bit differently from the discussion of issues related to video production. In this case, nobody questions that it's insane to use the absolute best quality video gear for digital and overlay video. The limitations of these technologies, as they're currently implemented in all but the highest-end hardware, make investing in fancy, expensive video gear an outright waste of money. So quality, in this context, has more to do with flexibility and durability than with whether the VCR being used could be plugged into a broadcast console and sent out over the air.

Video capture is hardly demanding at all, and it's possible that, for low-volume work, you could get away with a cheap VCR. After all, no current mainstream solutions can capture the equivalent resolution and frame rate of even the lowest-quality VHS (6-hour mode) recording. There are high-end systems that will capture full-motion video at impressive resolutions, but those tools are still out of reach for most of us. Even if you can afford such a setup, you'll probably still have to knock the video quality down so it can be played on a more average system.

Overlay video expects more from a VCR, however, and you won't find suitable gear in most stores. The best deck is one that's packaged more as a computer peripheral than a piece of video equipment. One such deck is the Sony CVD-1000, nicknamed the "Vdeck." This is a computer-controllable VCR that uses the diminutive Hi8 (high-band 8mm) tape format to give the deck a delightfully manageable compact size. In many ways, it operates just like an ordinary VCR. A hinged front panel swings down to reveal a full set of familiar controls, and these controls are duplicated on the infrared remote as well. But the Vdeck has a few secrets hidden inside its case.

Among the first differences you'll see are the multiple video inputs. There are two composite video inputs (with accompanying stereo audio input), two video and audio outputs, and S-video input and output jacks. You can use these multiple connections to build systems that handle input from multiple sources and drive multiple monitors.

There's a computer system inside the Vdeck, and you can communicate with it through a serial I/O connector on the deck's back panel. You hook the Vdeck into your computer just like a modem. The deck listens to its serial port for commands that switch video inputs, get the tape transport moving (play, record, fast-forward, and so on), fade video and audio in and out, and even switch the power on and off. The Vdeck enjoys a rich command set that's shared by a number of video devices that employ Sony's VISCA serial control protocol. If you're a programmer, you can get documentation from Sony that describes VISCA in detail; there's enough in the Vdeck's manual to get you started as long as you understand a little about hexadecimal arithmetic, bit fields, and serial I/O. If you're not comfortable rolling your own, applications that speak VISCA's language are coming up fast, like Macromedia's MediaMaker (Mac), Mathematica's Tempra Show (PC), and Gold Disk's VideoDirector (PC/Amiga).

Like MIDI, VISCA supports daisy-chaining multiple devices together. You can place several Vdecks under the control of one computer. The decks automatically assign unit numbers to themselves when your computer sends a "reset" command down the line. From that point on, your software can issue commands to up to seven decks. Those commands will be acknowledged when they're received, and because each deck has its own controlling computer inside, the commands can be carried out asynchronously, that is, while your computer is busy doing other things.

One of the attractive aspects of VISCA is that it can be adapted to all kinds of equipment. The Hi8 video camera I use, the Canon A-1 Digital, has a tiny phono jack on one side that's labeled "Remote." This can be connected to a wired remote control, but it is also a highly functional serial control interface. Sony offers an inexpensive device called the Vbox that can turn the A-1 Digital, or any other LANC-compatible (also classified as "control-L," and a variation called "control-S") video device, into a VISCA-compatible device. The VISCA protocol leaves a lot of room for future device types; audio mixers and video switchers are examples of devices that might be controlled by VISCA in the future.

The Vdeck has another feature not found in consumer video equipment that's often important to overlay video applications (and sometimes digital video work as well): timecode. The previous chapter defined timecode as the unique digital identification of every frame on a videotape. The Vdeck supports timecode both by reading timecode written to tape by other Hi8 devices (Sony sells some professional camcorders that write timecode) and by adding its own timecode to both prerecorded tapes and those recorded in the Vdeck itself. Tapes don't automatically get timecode—blank tapes don't come from the factory with timecode already written to them, and even video devices that support timecode must be asked to produce it. The code is written to the tape either along with the material being recorded or before or after material is placed on the tape. Placing timecode on a tape prior to or following the recording of video on that tape is called *striping*.

A tape with timecode on it, combined with the Vdeck, creates a powerful capability that no consumer VCR can match: frame accuracy. You can, through software, send a command to the Vdeck that tells it to advance (or rewind) to a specific timecode location. The deck will then use the timecode on the tape to find that location for you. Timecode is expressed as four numbers: hours, minutes, seconds, and frames. There are 30 frames per second in NTSC video, and a frame-accurate deck can position itself over any one of them you choose. As I said, commands are handled asynchronously. Your software doesn't have to do anything but listen for the Vdeck's response—it will notify the software when it has located the timecode you requested. From there, you can do whatever you like. The Vdeck can record or play from that spot, perform audio dubs (recording new audio over already-recorded video), and even lay down as few as four frames of new video for time-lapsed recording.

The Vdeck's timecode capability is applicable not only to video overlay work, where the output from the deck is routed directly to the computer's screen during a presentation, but also to digital video work. Some digital video capture/editing applications, like Adobe Premiere (Mac), use VISCA and timecode to digitize precisely located and timed clips from a videotape. The software lets you hunt around on the tape and mark the segments you wish to record. Premiere will then locate those segments automatically and record them, without forcing you to mash buttons on the remote control.

There are plenty of other Vdeck features that make it perfect for video overlay in particular. The ability to fade audio and video in and out makes for smooth transitions from other media to video and back. The PCM stereo digital audio supported by the Vdeck in both recording and playback lets you use the Vdeck as a source of high-quality audio as well. And the video switching capability lets you use live video (such as a camera pointed at the podium) along with the videotape.

Digital Video

The premise is simple: you can record video onto your hard disk and play it back later. But for a few surprises along the way, this is one of those rare simple premises that turns out to be nearly as simple to implement.

Digital video isn't a new idea. We've had the roots of the technology for years in the form of video capture boards. These digitize a single frame of video and store it on disk as a graphics file. In fact, the hardware used to capture full-motion digital video today is either very similar or identical to the video capture boards of long ago.

The software took a long time to appear, and much of the delay was thanks to two stumbling blocks. First, there was no sense in doing digital video at all if it couldn't be done right. That meant being able to capture sound along with the video and being able to play the digital video on all kinds of systems without requiring special hardware. The other delay was imposed by performance. Either capturing or displaying digital video takes a lot of juice from all corners of your system. Your CPU will be working full-time directing the data traffic and deciphering the compressed data. Your disk controller and drive will be pumping that data at a heavy sustained clip. And your display hardware will be straining to get several frames of video onto the screen each second. Getting the most out of digital video means having a system that's configured to handle it.

The perfect system for digital video varies depending on whether you intend to do mostly playback, or a lot of your own capturing as well. You also need to consider how important video quality is to you; the higher the quality, the higher the cost.

Two factors figure equally to both Mac and PC-based digital video systems for which capture will be a part: disk and memory. The disk should be as fast and as expansive as you can afford, and you should load your system up with plenty of memory. The disk is most important, because of all the media discussed in this book, digital video is far and away the most disk-hungry of the lot.

The Mac is almost irresistibly easy to equip for digital video, and the fact that it has the best selection of applications doesn't hurt, either. The QuickTime capture board to beat on the Mac is Supermac's VideoSpigot. This is as close to plug-and-play as it gets. The board installs in a couple of minutes and has one connector on its back panel: an RCA jack for a composite video input. As far as optimizing your system for playback goes, there are a number of vendors hawking video cards that claim to accelerate the performance of QuickTime movie playback. Try to see the card in action before you buy into the claims, but in general, any card with hardware display acceleration (if it's any good) will improve QuickTime playback performance over the standard Mac display hardware.

PCs are catching up fast, thanks in part to Supermac's own VideoSpigot (being sold for PCs by Creative Labs). Here, too, the card installs quickly and has only video connections on the back. There is a huge market for accelerated PC graphics cards, with the buying public showing a marked interest for those that make Windows display faster. As with the Mac, any display card that speeds up Windows will speed up Video for Windows. You may find a few vendors that boast specific acceleration of digital video playback. Once again, check the claims in person before you spend your money.

Unique to the PC is the variety of video capture boards available for it and the multiple roles those boards can play. Truevision's Targa can be used for full-motion video capture as well as for creating high-quality video output of a rendered 3-D scene. Other cards do double duty as Video for Windows capture boards and video overlay boards, letting you do both with a single card, saving both money and precious slot space. Matrox's Marvel, for example, is a Video for Windows capture board, video overlay board, *and* integrated VGA controller all on one card.

If you want to capture audio with your video, the Mac is already equipped. On the PC, you'll need an MPC-compatible sound board. That shouldn't be a problem, since Video for Windows requires the Windows multimedia extensions to begin with (which, in turn, requires a sound card).

The playing of a digital video clip is no cakewalk for your computer. To make it possible to play the video with synchronized audio, video and audio data are interleaved into a single stream. To play a video file, that data must be split up. The audio frames are reassembled and sent to your system's audio hardware. The video frames take considerably more work. If the video is compressed, it has to be run through the appropriate decompression software or hardware. Then, if the video's color depth is higher than the display's, as when you play a video file with 16-bit color on an 8-bit display, the colors must be dithered to fit within the display's color restrictions. If you've selected a playback window size that differs from the resolution at which the video was originally captured, each frame has to be scaled. Only then can the frame be painted onto the screen. During all this, the software must keep audio and video in sync, and still leave some time for other critical tasks to run; the Mac OS or Windows can't just shut down completely when a video is playing.

When your system is, in some way or ways, not up to the challenge, both QuickTime and Video for Windows do their best to adapt. By default, the continuity of the audio is maintained at all costs; a halting audio track is at least distracting, so the basis for audio priority (even though this is ostensibly a video system) is understandable. When the burden of the video must be reduced, QuickTime and Video for Windows skip frames during playback. They adjust continuously; they must, because under Windows and the Mac OS, resource usage patterns can change from moment to moment.

Because the best performance is seen with video captured (or processed to) a window at or about 160 × 120 pixels in size, the best viewing is done when your system is running at the 640 × 480 resolution. At higher screen resolutions, the video window can look like a postage stamp floating in an immense space. You can demand that the video play in a larger window by scaling the video, but as you expand the window size, your video's frame rate declines.

QuickTime

This Mac-based software technology involves more than digital video, but I'll discuss it here strictly in the context of its digital video capabilities. Since its creation, Apple has been giving QuickTime away for free, and now all releases of the Mac operating system include a disk with QuickTime on it. Without applications software, QuickTime won't do a thing for you; it's just a driver that installs into your Extensions folder. It's completely invisible until some application kicks it into action.

From a user's perspective, QuickTime is a file format standard. A QuickTime digital video file (called a "movie") contains a combination of digital video and audio data. The audio is optional, but if you use it, you can capture it at any rate and resolution supported by your audio hardware. Similarly, the video can be captured at any resolution, frame rate and bit depth allowed by your video capture board.

QuickTime's rapid rise to acceptance can be seen on the software shelves of any Mac dealer. Apple wisely made QuickTime movie playback capability ridiculously easy to add to applications, and aggressively encouraged software vendors to do so. Now it's hard to find a Mac application that doesn't have a sticker on the front boasting QuickTime compatibility. Even spreadsheets and word processors have taken on QuickTime playback.

As I said, the QuickTime extension can't play back movies on its own. Capturing and editing movies require third-party software. Most QuickTime capture boards include at least a limited capture application. The Video Spigot includes Adobe Premiere, the leading QuickTime editing tool. Recently, Apple standardized the movie capture interface as well, so now QuickTime applications have a device-independent means of capturing new movie files.

Shortly before this book went to press, Apple also released QuickTime for Windows, a playback-only module that lets developers on that platform build movie support into their applications. The movie files are portable between systems without modification. It's a bit too early to tell yet whether QuickTime for Windows will eat into Microsoft's own Video for Windows territory. It's likely that the two will co-exist, with software vendors hedging their bets by supporting both. One early indicator of this can be seen in Macromedia's Action, a Windows presentation program that plays both QuickTime and Video for Windows movie files, and even includes runtime versions of both sets of software.

QuickTime Digital Video: VideoSpigot and Premiere

Under both QuickTime and Video for Windows, you need at least two components to capture digital video: a capture board and capture software. My Mac system is equipped with a VideoSpigot card. That device includes its own capture program, called Screenplay, shown in Figure 6-1.

Note: all of the still video images shown in this and future chapters are taken from two sources, both produced by Firstlight, Inc., a company specializing in analog and digital stock video footage. Firstlight provided a videotape with several clips on it for use with this book, and coincidentally, also produced the sample video clip library CD-ROM included with Microsoft's Video for Windows software. Firstlight's clips are all of the highest quality, but you can't see that from the screen captures used in this chapter. The videotape will give you a closer look at Firstlight's work in a more appropriate medium.

Screenplay, like nearly all video capture programs, lets you see a live view of the external video source so you can position the tape, change the channel or focus the camera. This isn't really a live view in the manner that video overlay provides.

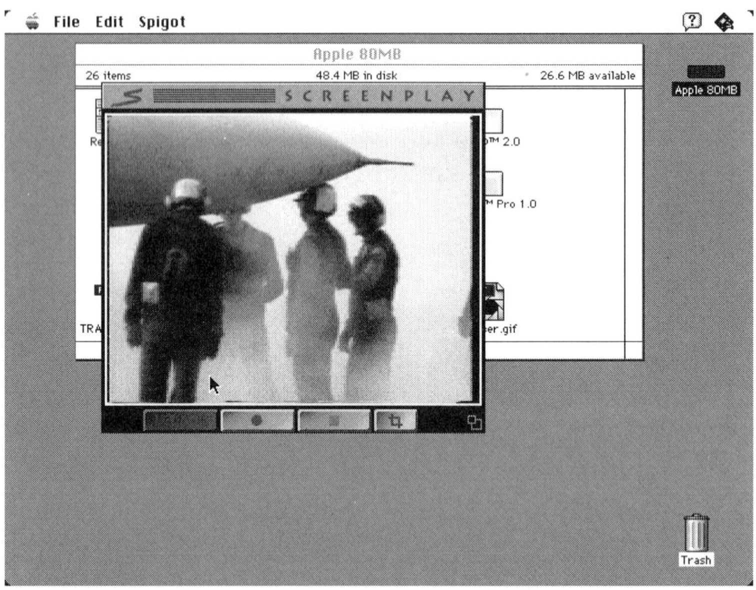

Figure 6-1: The VideoSpigot capture program

It is, in fact, video capture, with the board and software rapidly grabbing frames and shooting them directly to the screen. They're just not being recorded to disk.

QuickTime capture programs offer you control over the resolution and bit rate of captured files. You usually control the resolution by grabbing a corner of the capture window with the mouse pointer and resizing it manually. It doesn't resize continuously. Instead, there are only a few specific resolutions supported by the combination of hardware and software you're using. As you resize the window, you'll see a ghosted rectangle that shows you what the movie file's resolution would be if you released the mouse in its current position. You can also pop up a window with a pair of sliders in it that control hue and saturation. Hue applies a sort of master color correction to a video signal that, for one reason or another, comes into your capture board with bad color. If people's faces are looking too purple or too green, you might be able to tweak the hue slider to get things back in line. The saturation slider controls the intensity of the color. Not the brightness, but rather how far from a grayscale representation the image is. A yellow road sign at low saturation will look either gray or pale yellow. At high saturation, the yellow will be very intense; you could even say it glows. If the saturation is set too high, the colors will start to bleed "outside the lines." Color controls usually appear with the sliders set at their mid-points, settings that reflect the factory-set defaults that work for the majority of uses. If your video source is good, you shouldn't have to mess with the hue and saturation settings.

All you have to do to start a capture from Screenplay is click on the record button. A running clock will appear that shows you how many seconds (and tenths) of video you've captured so far. You'll also see a display of the average frame rate. You can't choose that rate directly, but you can set a maximum that reflects the best performance you expect from the least-capable target playback system. Screenplay starts up with a default limit of 10 frames per second, a reasonable setting that both conserves disk space and matches the likely maximum playback rate for slower Macs.

QuickTime captures are written to disk in a raw format, meaning that no data compression is applied during the capture. This won't be universally true once QuickTime capture boards with hardware compression become more common. But you do need compression, because raw files are much too large to store efficiently and play at reasonable frame rates. QuickTime capture software applies compression after the video is captured raw. The raw capture data is run, one frame at a time, through the compression module and saved in a new file.

Most video compression methods will deliver a minimum reduction in file size of about 50%. You'll have a choice of several compression schemes, some standard with QuickTime, and possibly some that are unique to the capture hardware and software you're using. The relative efficiency of the compression is adjustable through a slider labeled "quality." This is a more apt label than "compression efficiency" because it keeps you mindful of the effect of increased levels of compression: as compression is increased, quality decreases. With most compression methods, there's a point of diminishing returns, a compression level above which no further significant savings in disk space can be achieved, but which will degrade the quality to unacceptable levels. You can usually get a preview of how a certain level of compression will affect your video. You'll be shown a compressed version of the currently displayed frame. The preview isn't saved, and you can move the quality slider around, change compression methods, and click the "preview" button as many times as you like. This is helpful, because once the compression starts, it can take as long as several seconds per frame. You shouldn't wait until the compression is finished before you decide the compression settings you selected won't do.

Just where to draw the balance between your need to conserve disk space and your need to maintain quality is up to you. The choices are sometimes made a little clearer by looking at the extremes, and finding something in-between them that meets your requirements. Figures 6-2, 6-3 and 6-4 all show a similar frame from a Firstlight video clip, captured fresh and enlarged a bit to show the detail here. Again, keep in mind that video looks horrible in print. The point of these figures is to show you the effects of compression. Before I explain how to classify the quality of each figure's image, flip ahead and look at the figures on your own; see which one you like best.

Figure 6-2: Video capture, no compression (VideoSpigot)

For my money, the image done with the mid-line compression looks pretty good. It's grainier than the original, but that actually makes some of the edges sharper. Compare the tread on the front tire between Figures 6-2 and 6-3. Look, too, at the beams supporting the operator's cage. You should notice both an increase in sharpness and a loss of detail. Figure 6-4 shows an image that is

Figure 6-3: Video capture, mid-point compression

entirely unacceptable. The details, like the tire tread and the letters on the side, are completely lost. Maximum compression has turned the subtle variances in shade to blobs of solid color.

Screenplay isn't meant to be anything more than a convenience. It certainly doesn't show off all the power QuickTime has. The one missing piece is editing. For that, most QuickTime video producers turn to Adobe Premiere. I'll ramble about this product for a while because I can't show you a screen shot of Premiere for a couple more pages. That works out just fine, because Premiere deserves some discussion. Just as digital video wouldn't have made it into the mainstream without QuickTime, Apple owes Adobe, makers of Premiere, a huge debt. There aren't many "killer apps" (the one piece of software that no one can live without) in multimedia; Premiere is one.

The concept behind Premiere is to provide you with the kind of tools professional video producers have at their disposal, but done entirely in software. Pre-

Figure 6-4: Video capture, maximum compression

miere can produce effects than even top-of-the-line systems would have trouble with, and it does it all inside the computer on your desk without any special equipment.

Let's forget about Premiere's nifty effects for a moment and concentrate on the basics. Premiere is a digital video editor. You can take a batch of digital video clips, raw or compressed, and edit them just as you would if they were on videotape. In the simplest case, you can trim unwanted material from a clip and resave it as a compressed file. In the extreme case, you can use Premiere to build complex and impressive digital videos that employ multiple video and audio layers and transitional effects. Either way, Premiere saves the finished edit to disk as a QuickTime movie, applying compression as you request.

An editing session in Premiere starts with a collection of clips. You can browse around your disk (or CD-ROM) from within Premiere, previewing the clips you find and selectively adding the clips you're most interested in to the Premiere session you're running (called a *project*). Only clips you load into the project can be used in edits.

Premiere is dominated by a construction window, in which tracks of video and audio are assembled. A preview window lets you see a single assembled frame from any point in your sequence.

Premiere also has its own movie capture facility. For this feature to work, Premiere requires a module called a VDIG (video digitizer) that matches the capture board you're using. This provides a device-independent layer that Premiere and other QuickTime applications can use to build in recording with minimal hassle. No VDIGs are included with Premiere; they all come from capture board vendors.

Premiere's capture interface calls out to the VDIG not only to capture video, but also to adjust the capture board's settings, select the frame rate and compression method, and otherwise tune the capture system. Video can be also be brought into Premiere not only in real time, but also one frame at a time. If you connect your Mac to a VCR through VISCA, Diaquest, V-LAN, or another supported VCR control interface, Premiere can automatically step through a video and capture it one frame at a time. You can then edit that video digitally in Premiere, and finally record it back to the VCR (also one frame at a time). It's a time-consuming operation, but the resulting video can be of much higher quality than is possible with real-time capture and playback, and it becomes the very rough equivalent of an editing suite for those long on patience but short on cash.

As video capture boards with hardware compression and decompression engines become more accessible, Premiere already has most of what you'd want from a high-quality digital editing system. The hardware compression would allow Premiere to deal with digital video in closer to real time, and at a resolution that's suitable for direct recording to videotape.

You perform your editing tasks through Premiere's construction window (the largest window in the figure). You place a clip by dragging it into one of the construction window's tracks. There are three tracks of video (titles and graphics count as video) plus three tracks of audio. The audio tracks can be mixed however you like—you can alter the playback volume of each audio track over time by moving points on a graph, making for cross-fades and other dynamic effects. If a video clip was captured with audio, the audio and video are locked in sync and placed in the construction window together. Stand-alone audio clips containing music, narration, or sound effects can be dragged in and aligned with a particular location in your video.

There are two main video tracks (A and B), and one "Super" or superimposition track. The A and B tracks are mixed according to their overlap, and icons dragged into the FX (transitional effects) track. A *cut edit*, in which one video source is immediately replaced by another, is arranged simply by butting the end of one clip against the beginning of another (either in the same or in different tracks). If video tracks A and B overlap, an FX icon can be placed between them to arrange a transition. The transitions are varied, running the gamut from simple wipes and dissolves to page turns and cube spins. You can gain a more professional look by adding colored borders and anti-aliased edges to transitions that use moving shapes. When appropriate, transitions can be adjusted to create unique effects. A zoom transition can be stopped in the middle, for example, to create a picture-in-picture effect.

The Super track can hold anything the other two video tracks can hold, but its primary duty is to handle titles and overlaid graphics. Premiere has a versatile software keyer that simulates many of the functions provided by broadcast video keyers, including *chroma* (color) and *luminance* (brightness) *keying*, and image mattes (video is played through a text or graphical shape). Keying is explained in more detail in the chapter on desktop video, but here's a quickie: the basic job of a keyer is to analyze a video source and turn some part of the image "transparent" so that a background graphic or another video source can show through. The television weather reporter uses chroma keying to create the illusion of standing in front of a full-size weathermap. Premiere can do chromakeying, so if you want to play weatherperson, you can shoot some video of yourself in front of a solid-colored background (some color that doesn't appear in you or your clothing). You can then digitize that video and use Premiere to place yourself in front of a stationary or moving weathermap (or whatever suits you better). One particularly unusual key mode that's hard to find even in high-end gear is the *difference keyer*: it compares each frame of video to the one before it and makes everything that doesn't move transparent. So if you shoot a basketball game with a stationary video camera, you can extract just the parts that move (the players and the ball) and lay them in front of another video source.

Most edits done in Premiere will place one video source on the screen at a time. You can open up a "picture-in-picture" effect, but Premiere takes it even further than that. Motion effects let you animate the movement of a video or graphics clip through another (or across a colored background). The animation follows a path you create, and at each point in the path you can apply rotation, scaling and distortion to create wonderful pseudo-3D effects.

Transitional and motion effects take time to compute. Whoever said "there is no free lunch" could have been talking about Premiere, because for all its incredible power, the effects it places at your disposal can take a long time to generate. They are created one frame at a time, using graphical scaling and warping algorithms that exact a heavy toll on your system's CPU. When you design your Premiere video, you should try to keep the heaviest effects to a minimum. They'll slow down the generation of the finished video. Fortunately, Premiere is loaded with ways to preview virtually everything it does before you commit to saving the edit back to disk.

In addition to transitions and key effects, you can apply filters to video clips to change their appearance. If you've used Adobe's equally impressive still image processing software, Photoshop, then you're already familiar with the way filters behave. There are 41 Premiere filters in all, and most of them are special-effects oriented. You can create an undulating dream sequence effect, make your video ripple like waves in a pond, or spin your video into its center like water down a drain. More practical filters handle gamma (brightness) and color correction, tinting and colorization, and color filtering. Filters change the clip's contents directly, that is, when you apply a filter, you change the contents of the original video clip. That's not true of other editing tasks inside Premiere. You can generally hack and slash away at your material in the construction window without touching the original clips.

The last major piece of Premiere is its integrated titler. Premiere creates very nice-looking anti-aliased text that you can place in the Super track to superimpose over other video or graphics. Premiere's titler is only a time-saver; Adobe's own Illustrator or even presentation package like Aldus Persuasion will do a better job of creating professional-looking title graphics. Titles and other material placed in the Super track can be faded in and out on cue just like the titles on the television news.

Using Premiere can get to be an addiction. Most video producers will tell you that the editing is their favorite part of the job, and with tools like Premiere to unleash your own creativity, it's easy to see where their enthusiasm comes from.

Video for Windows and VideoSpigot

The venerable VideoSpigot that helped make QuickTime the champion it is today is also available to PC users running Windows. The software side of Windows digital video, simply called Video for Windows by its creator, Microsoft, is difficult to compare to QuickTime, and there's really no reason to. QuickTime is clearly established on the Mac through Apple's complete control over its own operating system. Microsoft can exert similar pressure on Windows developers to fall in line behind Video for Windows.

Not that Windows developers shouldn't be delighted to build Video for Windows support into their software. Video for Windows adds digital video to Windows' current mix of digital audio, MIDI, animation, graphics and external video device control as provided by the multimedia extensions. Existing software may not even have to be adjusted to make room for digital video support.

From a user's perspective, Video for Windows offers the first hardware-independent means of capturing, editing, and playing digital video on a PC. It's been done before, but solutions always required you to pair certain capture boards with certain applications that dealt with those boards. Video for Windows offers you the freedom to choose your hardware and software without worrying about whether they'll work together. As long as everything's compatible with the multimedia extensions and Video for Windows, you can be fairly confident that any combination you put together will work.

At this writing, Video for Windows is packaged as a separate product. There have been rumors that Microsoft may bundle some or all of Video for Windows in a future edition of the Windows operating environment itself. You may find that your capture board or editing software includes the Video for Windows software. That's all speculation for the time being, since as I write this, there is only one dedicated Video for Windows capture board (the VideoSpigot) and *no* editing software save what's included with the Video for Windows package. That's bound to change, probably during the delay while this book is prepared and printed. I hope to show you at least one Video for Windows editing application on the videotape.

Picking up the box that says "Video for Windows" doesn't quite give you everything you'll need to work with digital video on your PC, but it will take you most of the way there. If you've already got Windows 3.1 installed, and you have an MPC-compatible audio board, Video for Windows will give you the ability to play clips encoded in Video for Windows' AVI (audio video interleaved) format.

You will be able to convert Quicktime movies and Autodesk Animator (.FLI) animations to AVI format using the included software. You can also edit and combine prerecorded clips (like those on the included CD-ROM from Firstlight) using the bundled editor, VidEdit (see Figure 6-5). An audio editor, WaveEdit, is also part of

Figure 6-5: VidEdit (Video for Windows)

the bundle, along with a graphics editor (BitEdit) and a color palette tool (PalEdit). Also included is a copy of Media Browser, which helps you keep track of your video clips and other multimedia material.

Video for Windows plugs itself into Windows' multimedia extensions architecture with Windows-level drivers. By default, the capture drivers aren't loaded, meaning that you can do everything but grab your own video from an outside source. Once Video for Windows' installation program runs to completion, you can immediately start playing and editing video clips from within the standard Windows Media Player and Video for Windows' VidEdit.

If you add a capture board and driver, another application in the Video for Windows kit becomes useful: VidCap. This is similar to SuperMac's Screenplay on the Mac in that it's a quick, easy way to capture fresh video clips.

Like QuickTime, Video for Windows includes an assortment of software data compression modules. Again, these aren't normally applied to the data as it comes in from the capture board; that would incur too much overhead and slow down the frame rate. Compression is applied after the video is captured, while the captured or edited video file is being saved to disk.

Video for Windows or, more appropriately, the multimedia extensions allow even programs that have no specific support to take on the ability to play digital video files. Any application that has OLE (object linking and embedding) client support will let you embed a Media Player object. All you have to do is load the Media Player, use it to load the video file you want to embed, select Copy Object from Media Player's Edit Menu, and then use the appropriate Paste option in the client application. This will create an icon in your document which, when you double-click it, will load Media Player and play the video file that was loaded when you did the copy and paste.

Media Player includes a set of options that make OLE video objects appear a little less foreign. Selecting the "Play in client document" box plays the video in place, at the location and size of the object's icon. The Media Player controls don't appear, so it looks like the video is playing from inside the client application. The client's Edit menu is extended to allow you to pop up Media Player to "edit" the video clip. Actually, the only editing you can do from within Media Player is to mark a start and end point for the embedded clip. This doesn't change the clip file itself; the selected range is simply made part of the embedding data.

Of course, once you embed a clip in a document, you may want to make the document and clip available to someone else. Microsoft allows free distribution of the run-time components (not the edit or capture applications) of Video for Windows so those who haven't bought it for themselves can play your clips.

If you want to do something closer to real editing, you have to run VidEdit. Even if you're working with prerecorded clips that you have no interest in editing, you might want to run them through VidEdit. The video you load into VidEdit can be saved to another video file in an altered form, changing any combination of resolution, color depth, compression method, audio format, playback frame rate, and color palette. You can also use VidEdit to change the way the audio track is synchronized to your video. A trip through VidEdit is a common procedure for a clip moving from CD-ROM to hard disk, for example, so the clip's size can be trimmed through compression or color depth reduction. VidEdit will resample your audio, too: resampling from 22 KHz, 16-bit stereo to 11 KHz, 8-bit mono will quarter the size of the audio portion of your AVI file, with a corresponding reduction in sound quality that might be acceptable depending on the clip.

VidEdit is not a full-fledged digital video editor—Microsoft can't close the market to likely future players like Adobe Premiere. In fact, all VidEdit will do is let you select portions of clips and do cut-and-paste editing. There are no transitional effects, no superimposed titles or graphics, nothing fancy. The most useful part of VidEdit is its interface to the compression modules (see Figure 6-6). This

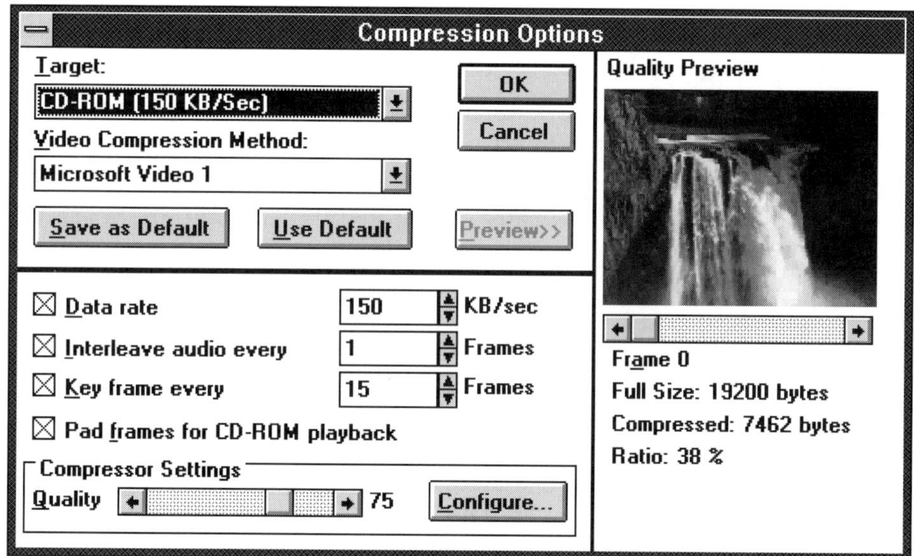

Figure 6-6: Adjusting video compression (Video for Windows)

dialog box gives you an instant preview of the effect any selected compressor would have on a video file's size and appearance. Some compressors are tunable, letting you select a quality/size ratio that suits you. As with QuickTime, the preview helps you see when the quality of the video falls below an acceptable level due to the application of too much compression. Video for Windows also lists the statistics for the current video frame, showing you the size reduction your compression settings will achieve, and both the preview picture and the statistics change as you move the quality slider back and forth. You can see for yourself where that point of diminishing returns, where video quality is damaged without a worthwhile reduction in file size, is located and avoid it.

With the included VidCap video capture program and some video capture hardware, you can create your own AVI video clips. The capture process itself isn't difficult, but setting up your system to capture video can be a challenge.

Two of the systems in my lab used to have 16 MB of memory. I had to trim them back to 8 MB to accommodate the video capture boards I work with, since all but one (the VideoSpigot) are memory-mapped into the space between the 8 and 16 MB marks. A memory-mapped PC board looks like memory to your computer, but it's not general-purpose memory like that installed in your system now. Instead, the memory in a memory-mapped video capture board creates a faster path to your system's hard disk; data can be copied directly from the capture board's memory to your disk. That's a nice feature, but your PC won't allow two blocks of memory to occupy the same location. So if you have a memory-mapped peripheral card that wants to be placed in your system's memory space between the 8 and 16 MB mark, that means you probably can't run the board if you have more than 14 or 15 MB of memory in your system. That's ironic, since Video for Windows runs best when you have lots of memory to throw at it. The whole experience of getting memory-mapped capture boards to work in my systems gave me a strong preference for the Video Spigot, which is still memory-mapped, but it only takes up a tiny space between 640K and 1MB, an area reserved for peripherals; you can have as much system memory as you want.

A video capture board, if it was made since Video for Windows' release, probably comes with a capture driver. The Video for Windows package includes capture drivers for some older boards. With the board and driver installed, you can proceed straight to VidCap. This capture utility gives you good control over the parameters that affect quality. Audio, which is brought in through your system's MPC-compatible digital audio board, can be captured in any of the board's supported rates and resolutions, and a level meter pops up to let you see how "hot" your audio source is.

Freshly captured video is generally written directly to disk in a raw format (8, 16, or 24 bits, depending on your capture board's capabilities and your preference). It takes up a lot of space on disk but requires the least processing time during capture. That's a key consideration, since good video captures depend on proper system configuration. If your Windows isn't running at peak performance, VidCap will drop frames. The more real memory, faster CPU, more contiguous disk space, and better disk I/O performance you have, the smoother your video captures will be. If your disk cache, buffer count or Windows virtual memory settings aren't right on, your maximum capture bandwidth can be halved or worse. VidEdit lets you tune your video file's compression for a particular data rate, but when you do the capture, the only choices you have cover bit depth and frame rate. And while QuickTime will knock the frame rate down to adapt to slower hardware during capture, -Video for Windows will struggle to maintain the rate by dropping video frames. So if you specify a capture rate of 30 frames per second, VidCap will do its best to achieve that, and it won't change that rate on you (although you'll probably wish it would). If hardware or software isn't up to the frame rate you've asked for, Video for Windows will drop frames, sometimes huge blocks of them, and then try to catch up. These dropped frames leave noticeable gaps in the video playback (audio is usually maintained) during which a frame freezes on screen for some period of time and then the video starts moving again. Doing an effective Video for Windows capture means playing high-low with the frame rate, jockeying to find the maximum frame rate that results in no dropped frames. It's not much fun, but you should only have to play that game once when you start working with your capture setup. You should be able to use the frame rate you pick up from your experimentation for all the captures you do until you make some major change to hardware or software.

Video for Windows can represent video clips in 8-, 16- or 24-bit color or gray-scale. A special mode called "8-bit palettized" is notable because *you* select the size and content of the color palette. You can load a palette built with PalEdit, or you can ask VidCap to derive one from your video source. Colors in the video that aren't in your palette will be approximated, and you can redo the palette in VidEdit if you're not happy with it. Choosing your own palette can result in fine-looking 8-bit AVI videos, better than any 8-bit QuickTime video I've seen. Sixteen- and 24-bit color modes are useful for boards that feature accelerated display of high-color graphics. Any 16- or 24-bit file can be resampled down to 8-bit palettized for space savings and to allow the file to be played on a wider range of system types.

Digital Video Futures

Since I've been tracking the progress of multimedia technologies for years now, I've got good reason to be hopeful about where digital video will wind up in the future. I've already seen the arrival of professional-quality video editing systems, with Adobe Premiere-like interfaces, which run in otherwise ordinary PCs (see the discussion of Matrox Studio in the chapter on desktop video). Those in the video business already know that the old reliable analog videotape is a dying medium. The low-end digital video solutions described in this chapter are a precursor to the appearance of full-blown professional editing systems that don't use videotape at all. You'll be able to go from camera, through editing, and back out to a storage and playback medium without the video signal ever crossing over to analog. That means no loss of quality, no matter how many times the video has been transferred and manipulated. Future systems will also be able to apply Premiere-like transitional and other effects in much less time with the aid of hardware, and such effects may even take place in real time.

Video professionals are already using expensive *nonlinear editing systems* as replacements for traditional videotape editing suites. Having the video in digital format on the hard disk means being able to edit material of any length without having to wait for the tape decks to spin around locating a particular spot on the tape. Similar time savings are found throughout, with another example being the ability to preview an edit or effect exactly as it would appear in the finished program. If that preview works, it can be committed to the digital final edit. If it doesn't, it can be thrown away and another approach attempted with no hassle. But rarely are these systems used for direct editing. Instead, video producers use nonlinear systems to create an *edit decision list*, a script that lists where the edits will take place and specifies the effects to apply. That list is then carried over (on diskette, perhaps) to a videotape editing suite. That might seem like an added step instead of a convenience—why wouldn't a producer just sit in the videotape suite to begin with? The advantage offered by nonlinear editing is its speed. Besides, once the edit decision list is carried over to the videotape suite, all the producer has to do is pop the tapes into the decks and order the editing computer to run the list. The process can often proceed from there unattended while the producer attends to other things.

The life of a video producer may seem far removed from your own, but it's a snapshot of how your life may be changed by future digital video technologies. Just as people who have been doing video all their lives can use digital technology to grant themselves a huge leap in productivity, so can you use digital video to make video, a medium that was previously unavailable to you, part of the work you do. As things get easier for video producers, that technology will find its way into your hands in the form of multimedia tools. The things being done by the likes of Adobe Premiere aren't new. What's so new, and so exciting, is that digital video lets anyone with enough time and creativity tap into video's power.

Digital video has other potential applications, too. We're just beginning to see more affordable video teleconferencing systems. These take video from a camera mounted on top of your computer or in your conference room, digitize it in real time, and shoot it across a network connection to a machine that plays it back on the other side of the building, or the other side of the world. You may have seen videophones, real and imagined. You know that the ability to *see* the person you're talking to brings conversations to a much higher level than you can obtain over a blind phone connection. Video teleconferencing has existed for years, but it's been expensive, requiring satellite links or costly dedicated high-speed data telephone lines. But digital video capture, storage, and compression technologies are making it possible to send that data over ISDN digital lines at a fraction of the cost of other types of dedicated data lines. Video teleconferencing is advancing so rapidly that just in the year I spent writing this book, doing teleconferencing from your own desk went from fantasy to reality thanks to the technologies seen in products like QuickTime and Video for Windows.

Where will it all lead? Once technology paves the way with larger, faster hard drives, more efficient data compression and decompression through hardware, and faster display cards, video will become as easy to manage as text. We're already seeing this playing out to some extent with audio, although it is not as universally useful as visual media. If video becomes easy to manage, it will certainly advance to the level of text and graphics as a widely-accepted means of presenting information. How quickly video advances to this status will depend on the rapidity of the advance of related technologies. It shouldn't take long. Major players in the computer system, peripheral hardware, telecommunications, video equipment, and software industries have all made developing digital video-related technologies a top priority. Within a couple of years, you can expect most computer systems to include digital video playback hardware. Systems that don't include it will be upgradable, at very low cost, with expansion cards that add hardware-assisted digital video decompression and playback. I'm hopeful, too, that video capture hardware will be nearly as universal. You may well see RCA composite video and S-video input jacks on the back of systems in the not-too-distant future. That's a vision I applaud, because I believe the information delivery potential of computers won't be fully realized until video graduates to a standard data type.

Video Overlay

While analog video may be heaving its final breaths, it's not dead yet. And until it is, there are still distinct advantages to analog video for some applications. Compared to digital video, analog video always plays in full color, at its full frame rate, takes up no space on disk, and it can be copied to a tape that anyone with a VCR can play.

Using analog video with a computer usually involves setting up some kind of video overlay system. This takes the video signal from a VCR, laserdisc player or TV tuner (for the rest of this section, let's assume we're using a VCR), combines it with the video coming from your system's main or auxiliary display, and shows that combined signal on a shared monitor (usually your system's main monitor). There are two primary classes of video overlay devices. The first class is the video overlay device, which presents the external video source on your computer's display as a full-screen image. Your computer can create text and graphics that will be displayed on top of the video (hence the term "overlay"). You can create graphics that include video-transparent pixels, showing through to the video source wherever they appear, but nontransparent colors obscure the video in favor of the graphics. True overlay devices are the most common type on the Mac, where cards like Truevision's NuVista+ do double-duty as Mac display cards and video overlay devices. The NuVista+ has recordable video output as well, so you can send both the external video source and the overlaid computer graphics to a VCR, allowing for some very creative presentations and simple video productions.

The Amiga has something like video overlay, but it's done differently because of the Amiga's design. The Amiga was built from its first day to be adaptable for use with video, so it costs less to get the Amiga's video signal combined with an external source. It's usually done through an external device called a *genlock*. Commodore sells one of its own that's good enough for casual use, and other vendors offer units that fairly match output quality and price. An Amiga with genlock provides the same kind of functionality as a video overlay card. The video source always fills the screen, and the Amiga lets you create graphics that contain transparent pixels. The advantage offered by the Amiga is that genlock has been available for that system so long, most Amiga presentation and other multimedia applications are all set to work with it. This isn't as true of the Mac, where there is no standardized approach to video overlay. You're dependent on the software and hardware vendors whose products you select to provide you with video overlay drivers.

On the PC running Windows, you'll find an approach to video overlay that's as sensible as the rest of the multimedia extensions. Video overlay is a standardized component of the multimedia extensions. Any card that includes a Windows-compatible MCI driver will work instantly with any application that expects an overlay card. Most such cards that are built for the PC can display the external video not only full-screen, but in resizable windows as well. The latter integrates nicely with Windows, where *everything* is presented in resizable windows with attractive shaded borders. Sometimes referred to as video-in-a-window cards (I'll keep calling them "video overlay," a mild misnomer that keeps the callouses off my fingertips), these boards provide a remarkable level of functionality. Staying within the boundaries of the standard set of video overlay commands provided in MCI, you can make the video window appear and disappear, resize and move it, freeze-frame the video, and even save and load still video images. What's more, if your video overlay card comes with Video for Windows drivers, you can use the card for both video overlay and digital video capture.

Matrox Marvel

At this writing, there is no video overlay board on any system that's as capable as the Matrox Marvel for the PC. The Marvel is a one-slot card that combines video overlay, Video for Windows capture, passed-through audio, two channels of video input and, on the best models, an on-board VGA controller capable of displaying 16-bit color.

The Marvel connects to your external video and audio source (or sources) through a bundle of long cables. If you use the version that has an on-board VGA, all you have to do is plug your system's main monitor into the 15-pin connector on the back of the card. Then, from the moment you boot your system, the Marvel acts as your system's primary display adapter.

The video overlay capabilities of the Marvel kick in when you use software that either supports video overlay directly or has support for Windows' MCI. If you can issue MCI string commands from within your application, you can immediately take advantage of the Marvel's immense features set. To give you an idea of its capabilities, Table 6-1 lists some of the functions the Marvel places at your disposal and the MCI commands associated with them. If you don't understand what MCI is all about, you'll find more information in the next chapter. For now, at least read over some of the descriptions. This is far from a complete list, but it will give you some idea of what this board can do.

Using the Marvel is a pretty straightforward business. Plug your video and audio sources in, get Windows and your multimedia application running, and instruct your software to open a video overlay window. Some software, including some Windows-based video editors I've seen, don't need to be told to open the video window—they sense the existence of the overlay board and open the window automatically. In other cases, you'll have to tell the software when you want the overlay window opened, and specify a size and position for it. If you have a Vdeck or other computer-controllable video player (including laserdisc players), you can use that in combination with the Marvel to build program-directed video playback into your presentations and applications. With good multimedia software, you can synchronize the appearance of the video window with the start of the playback of a video clip from tape or disc. To give the user something to look at while you're locating the clip, you can use the Marvel's load command to place a stationary graphic in the video window. If you were creating a real estate database, for example, you might put up a still image of the property while the Vdeck searched for the clip of the walk-through tour. By the time the salesperson gets done filling the customer in on the property, he or she can click on a button to start the walk-through playing instantly. At the end of the clip, you could reload the still image and stop the Vdeck.

The Marvel has one facility that makes it unique among video overlay cards. It has a specialized DVE (digital video effects) circuit on board that makes it possible to perform a limited (but impressive) set of Adobe Premiere-like special effects on the incoming video. You can use Matrox's Keyframe Editor application (see Figure 6-7) to program the DVE with a script of actions. The Marvel's effects include scaling, inverting (horizontal or vertical flip), moving, posterization (an art effect), tint, mosaic (turning the image into blocks of large pixels), strobe and fade. Any number of these may be combined into a single DVE event and programmed with the Keyframe Editor to start at a specified time. As with 3-D keyframe animation, the Keyframe Editor interpolates the changes you make between two events. With that, you can create simulated 3-D tumble effects, have the video window fly onto and off of the screen, fade the video in and out, and perform countless other combinations of effects through the DVE. The script you create with the Keyframe Editor is saved there, and later loaded with the "load" command. All you have to

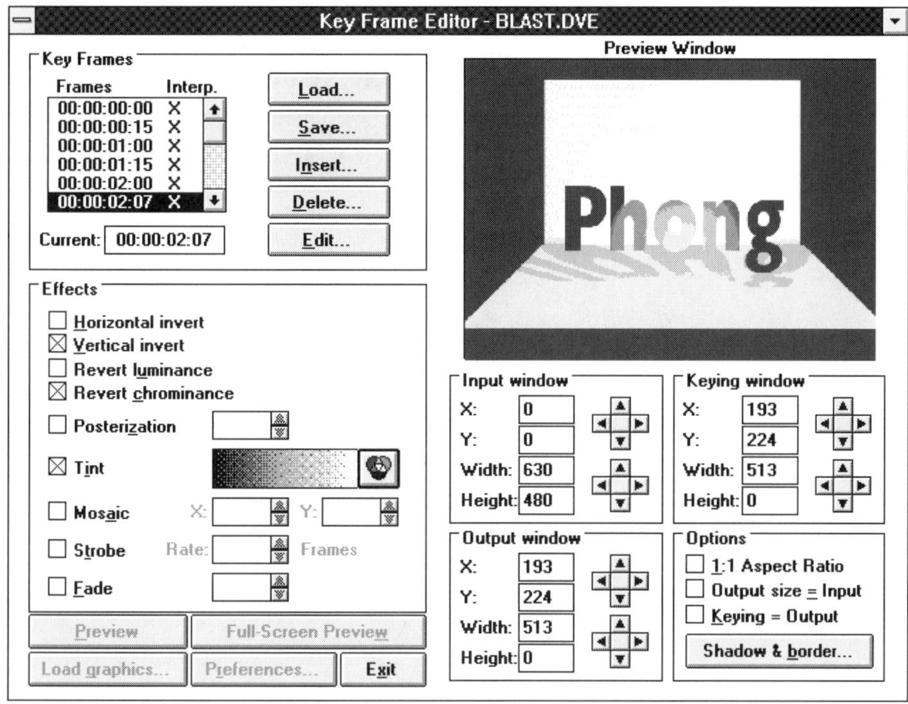

Figure 6-7: Marvel's Keyframe Editor

do is send the "play" command from any MCI-capable application, and the DVE script you created will run, with the events you selected occurring at precisely the time offset you requested for each. DVE adds a dimension to video overlay applications created with the Marvel that can't be reasonably achieved through any other means.

Table 6-1: Matrox Marvel MCI commands

Command	Description
capability	Gets information about the capabilities of the Marvel overlay driver. Inquiries include: **can save** (returns true if device can save still image to disk), **can stretch input** (true if device can resize video window), and **can freeze** (true if device can freeze a video image. All three inquiries are answered "true" for the Marvel.
close	Closes the video window.
copy	Copies current contents of video window to Windows clipboard. A video still frame be pasted as a graphic into other Windows programs.
freeze	Captures (but does not save) a single frame of video, displaying it instead of the incoming video in the window until an **unfreeze** command is issued.
load	Loads a graphics file into the Marvel's buffer and displays it in the video window. Also used to load a DVE (digital video effects) program, described below.
open	Initializes the Marvel, opens a window, and displays the currently selected video source in it.
paste	Pastes the contents of the Windows clipboard into the video window.
play	Plays a DVE program loaded with the **load** command. Marvel can move, resize, invert, tint, and apply other effects to the incoming video based on a program you create with the Keyframe Editor. See chapter text for more details.

Table 6-1: Matrox Marvel MCI commands

Command	Description
save	Saves the contents of the video window to disk.
setaudio	Controls the Marvel's passed-through audio. Commands include: **bass to *value*** (sets bass level), **treble to *value*** (sets treble level), **volume to *value***, **source to input *value*** (1 or 2), and **mute *on/off***.
setvideo	Controls the appearance of the video in the Marvel's window. Commands include: **brightness to *value***, **contrast to *value***, **source to input *value*** (1 or 2), and **source to svideo** (to enable S-video input).
status	Returns status of Marvel. Commands include: **audio source** (returns 1 or 2) and **video source** (1 or 2).
unfreeze	Releases a frozen video frame and starts displaying live video in the window again.

7

Desktop Video Production

While there are many ways to bring media together, there are none so compelling as video. This medium is uniquely able to incorporate virtually all other types of media, as well as being part of a multimedia presentation itself. This chapter is a fitting close to this book because it uses video production as an example of media integration, bringing together all of the elements discussed in this book.

While multimedia technology makes it possible to package information in all kinds of intriguing ways, it carries with it an unavoidable burden: how do you share what you've created with others? Until the day comes that the hardware and software required to play back multimedia presentations are cheap and widely available, we often need to consider what form our final work will take. It's true of most media types that the more technology you must have to create them, the more technology is required to play them back.

There is one exception: video. When properly used, video has the power to sell, convince, and inspire thought in a more efficient way than any other medium. From a technological standpoint, a television is an amazing device that incorporates the elements of color, movement, and sound in a way that so closely simulates life that we're helplessly drawn to it. It's no wonder that advertisers spend billions producing and placing ads on television: if you've got a point to make, we presently have no more efficient path into other people's minds than through television.

A VHS videotape is as close to a universally playable multimedia format as you can find today. About $4 U.S. buys a good-quality tape capable of holding up to two hours of material at a higher resolution and frame rate than all but the most expensive digital video solutions. Modern consumer VCRs offer high-fidelity stereo audio, so your presentation gets good treatment on both the visual and aural fronts. Videotape is cheap, lightweight, easy to duplicate, and can be viewed anywhere. It makes an extremely attractive final destination for any multimedia work.

That's not to say the video is without drawbacks. The best image quality VHS tape can offer is still not good enough for highly detailed charts and graphics, so there will still be plenty of situations in which you'll want to use your computer to display the graphics live. It's also not very interactive. You can build video into a presentation, as I described in the previous chapter, by using computer-controllable VCRs and video overlay boards. But on its own, a consumer VCR and a wireless remote control make a poor companion for a live presentation.

This chapter is all about producing your own videos. Doing it well means understanding video's strengths and limitations, and those elements are framed by your budget and time. It also requires that you possess some sense of aesthetics and style; not everyone who can learn to produce video can be assured of someday producing *good* video. You need only watch TV to understand that there are plenty of people doing video for a living who should consider an alternate occupation.

While video is a wonderful way to bring other media together, it is also the most complex and expensive medium to employ properly. You can truck over to your local TV shop and buy what looks like video editing equipment for relatively little money. But for reasons explained in this chapter, cheap gear produces cheap results. The focus here will be on producing professional-quality results, but not so professional that it'll put you in permanent hock.

Most of the discussion on the desktop video front revolves around the last step in the process: editing. True, that's the place where the computer plays the largest role, but you've got to have something to edit first. So this chapter opens with some video basics, moves on from there to discuss equipment choices, and then it's hands-on the rest of the way with discussions that cover everything from the video shoot to the final edit.

This is the most involved chapter in this book because video is a dense topic. It's also one of the least-illustrated chapters in this book because video moves and speaks and uses color. I'll try to paint as clear a verbal picture as I can, but there are some concepts that may not make it through to you until you see them. You might follow this chapter with a course on video production, or you might use the form in the back to inquire about this book's videotape. Whatever route you take, don't expect what you learn here to give you a professional's knowledge. Only experience can do that.

Why Video?

If you're going into a conference room or boardroom to sell something, chances are you've got a lot invested in whatever it is you're about to hawk. I've gotten all kinds of enthusiasm about the value of various media types, but consider how video can change the way you present information to others, compared with more traditional media like flip charts and 35mm projected slides.

On video, facts and figures become computer graphics, *animated* graphics if you like, that go beyond mere columns of numbers. The graphics can be interspersed with video that pops up in a window, voice-over narration, and music that advance your audience's respect for your company and ensure that the facts are building the case you want them to build. Building and product plans become virtual prototypes, 3-D models viewed in motion, from several angles and even from the inside. Video also lets you transport your audience to other places. Take them to your offices where your designers can be seen working closely with the manufacturing staff. Let the audience sit in briefly on a planning meeting where your staff is discussing a project similar to the one in question. Let your audience see the people behind the statistics and the models. On video, everyday objects become art, as the camera takes the viewer on a carefully guided tour, ensuring that important details aren't missed. And all the while, music and voice-overs help support an image of professionalism, of stability.

Of the traditional presentation methods, none offer the combination of sound, color, and motion. These things attract and hold an audience's attention, and video combines them all. Video is also unique in its ability to condense information. A five-minute video can hold the equivalent information of innumerable transparencies because you have the freedom to combine graphics, video, voice, music, animation, and other elements to tell your story.

Video Roots

"Desktop video" is a misnomer; there are very few worthwhile video production systems that can fit on a desk (unless it's a desk about the size of a king-sized bed). I prefer the phrase, "computer-assisted video production," but the shorter version is both much easier to say and much more widely used.

Computers have a long history of involvement with video, dating back to the first days when videotape recorders were cabled to specialized computers—*edit controllers*—so raw video could be edited into a finished product without the tedium of manual editing. Early editing systems were expensive, slow, bulky, and noisy. The television station in my hometown took years to give up its old 16mm film editing and processing suite because, for a long time, film was quicker and easier to work with than video. Early "portable" video cameras were beastly things, too, two-piece units that separated a very heavy shoulder-slung deck from a very heavy on-the-shoulder camera. Weightlifting was a popular spare-time sport among field camerapeople.

It was determined early on that computers could be trained to do things that expensive analog circuits couldn't do very well. Specialized computers were used as *video switchers,* devices that switch smoothly from one video signal to another, as when a newscast goes from the anchor, to a tape, back to the anchor and then to the weatherman. More expensive video switchers could do more than just cut or fade between two video sources—they could apply *transitional effects*. The least of them did wipes (the new video replaces the old in a sweep across the screen), but the best of the early digital video switchers managed advanced effects like mapping video sources to sides of a cube and spinning it through space.

Computers also replaced the old art card, the bit of stiff paper on which credits, weather forecasts and other text and graphics were drawn for on-air use. Computers proved able to outgun the art card with multiple type styles, instant changing between pages of text, and even credits that rolled up the screen electronically. These *character generators* were later expanded and given the ability to draw custom graphics for weathermaps, advertisements, and such. Banks of slide projectors were replaced with *frame stores*, dedicated systems that stored and displayed video graphics at a producer's command.

Today's television station, video production center, or better-equipped cable outlet is packed to the rafters with digital gear that produces results of uncompromising quality. Now even videotape has gone digital, and bigger stations are gathering and editing their news and other house-produced material entirely in digital formats. That's the kind of equipment you can get on a huge budget, and when you have video engineers at your disposal to run and fix these massively complex systems. This chapter aims a bit lower.

Much of the computer-controlled equipment in use in video today—editing, switching, effects, character generation, and graphics—is packaged into specialized components capable of doing their assigned tasks and nothing else. The old-fashioned edit controller still exists, as do stand-alone character generators and specialized graphics systems. To be fair, some component technologies have advantages (sometimes small) over their desktop video equivalents. But some professional users are climbing into desktop video because as quality improves and prices come down, they realize there's not much reason to spend the extra money on components.

Among the advantages of the expensive, component-based gear is quality: everyone who spends large sums on specialized equipment expects *broadcast quality.* That's a phrase you'll hear a lot associated with video, and it has different meanings depending on who's saying it. For our purposes, let's simply place broadcast quality as the topmost mark on a quality scale. It's the best you can get, and to get it you need to invest in the kind of gear you'd find at CNN or CBS. At the bottom of the scale, place a tick at consumer or hobby-level video. This is where standard VHS VCRs and most camcorders fall. You can also find very inexpensive titlers, editors, enhancers and other modules at this level, but what works well for video snapshots falls apart on a 20" monitor in a boardroom or on a projection television in an auditorium. And it's an inescapable property of video that if you start with mediocre-quality material, editing and duplicating will turn it to absolute mush.

Between consumer and broadcast-quality lies a somewhat newly defined market area known by several names, and that's where this chapter will spend its time. Some call it *pro-sumer,* while others call it *industrial* or *commercial*-quality. The equipment often looks and acts like broadcast-quality gear, but is at least slightly less capable and produces results you couldn't quite put on the air. Compared to VHS, this middle-of-the-road gear produces significantly better results by all measures: resolution, clarity of color, generational stability (an increase in the number of times a video can be passed down a generation during editing), and often audio quality as well.

You can buy equipment that comes very close to industrial gear at most department stores now, but true industrial video equipment has qualities that no store-bought gear possesses. The most important of these is that the equipment can be controlled by computers. That's what makes desktop video production possible. The computer takes control of the VCR, telling it when to play, record, pause, and search for a particular scene on tape. If you install a graphics card that has good-quality recordable video output, the computer becomes a character generator and frame store, too. The combination of computer-controllable video decks and a computer graphics card with video input and output create a minimal desktop video editing system. Add switching and transitional effects, and you get even closer to what the pros use. As you add audio production equipment, more video decks, professional video monitors and other good gear to your setup, you can start cranking out video that could rival what you can buy from people who do video full-time.

The Video Crash Course

I won't pretend that teaching yourself video production is easy. In fact, I can tell you that while there are few things as rewarding as seeing a finished video that you know you've created, I can't remember any set of skills I've acquired that took more time and focused effort.

The best way I can think of to get you into the water quickly is to organize my video tutorial around video terminology. All the video tools you're likely to use expect you to understand these terms, but I'll give you more than a working definition. Under each term, you'll find a discussion that places the term in its context and raises issues that you should be thinking about as you get started in video. I've framed the coming discussions with the equipment and software in my lab, but the information is applicable to all kinds of situations and products.

Once again, I find myself explaining the relative absence of a certain system type from the pages in this chapter. Of the three systems discussed here, the Amiga and PC have the best assortment of desktop video production tools. The Mac does have some good solutions, but none which I could get my hands on in time for this book. The bulk of the Mac's desktop video solutions are built around products that are very similar in feel and function to Matrox Studio, which is covered in detail here. I'm sure my discussion of that product will give you a headstart on most Mac-based solutions you might go after.

With that out of the way, here are some terms to absorb. I didn't arrange them alphabetically. Instead, I've attempted to arrange them so that the most basic terms are presented first, followed by the more complex definitions that depend on the earlier ones.

Video format: A standard defined by the width of the tape, the shape of the cassette used to carry it, and the method used to record the video data onto the tape. VHS is the most popular video format, with players available for as little as $100 U.S. VHS tape is 1/2-inch wide and is carried in a cassette that's roughly 7.5 inches wide and 4 inches deep. The front of the cassette is spring-loaded, covering the exposed tape at the front when the cassette is not in use. A modified version of VHS, dubbed ***Super VHS***, is currently gaining favor as an industrial format. Super VHS (or S-VHS) uses the same 1/2-inch tape and the same cassette, and S-VHS tape can still record and play ordinary VHS programs. When used with S-VHS video equipment, however, the tape carries a much higher-quality video signal, significantly enhanced in resolution and clarity. Better S-VHS decks offer "hi-fi" stereo audio to go along with the video. It's not digital, but the quality is excellent, and decks often include built-in noise reduction on the hi-fi soundtrack. Hi-fi audio can only be heard on S-VHS decks with hi-fi sound (which is virtually all of them). Lower-quality stereo audio tracks, playable on any deck, are included. S-VHS decks can record ordinary VHS videotapes as well, in either hi-fi stereo or lower-quality stereo or mono sound. Most decks can record both the high- and low-fidelity audio tracks simultaneously to ensure that all decks can play the recorded material. S-VHS tapes cannot be played in ordinary VHS decks, but you can play VHS tapes with S-VHS equipment. Some industrial decks will only play VHS tapes recorded in SP ("two-hour") mode.

Industrial S-VHS decks are increasing in number and can now be had from several manufacturers. I do all of my editing on two Panasonic models that hit the market fairly early and, in effect, defined the industrial S-VHS equipment market: the AG-7750 and the AG-7650. These are computer-controllable, frame-accurate editing decks. The only difference between them is that the AG-7750 is a recorder/player; the AG-7650 is a player only.

Another popular industrial format is ***Hi8***, which is short for high-band 8mm. This is an enhanced version of the 8mm tape format popularized by consumer camcorders. At roughly 3 3/4-inches by 2 1/2-inches, both 8mm and Hi8 cassettes are very lightweight and fit easily in a shirt pocket. Even at its reduced size, the cassette can hold up to two hours of tape (recorded at the best available resolution). The advantages of Hi8 over standard 8mm are the same as for S-VHS over VHS: better resolution and greater clarity. One feature found in some Hi8 and 8mm equipment is *PCM audio*, stereo digital audio of superb quality. PCM audio can only be played on certain equipment. Hi8 decks also offer hi-fi stereo audio, which can be played on any Hi8 machine. Hi8 tapes cannot be played on regular 8mm decks, but 8mm tapes can be played in Hi8 decks. You can use 8mm tapes in a Hi8 deck, but the tapes will be recorded with the reduced quality of the 8mm format.

Many in-house video facilities use some combination of S-VHS and Hi8 equipment because each of these formats has its advantages. S-VHS is well-suited to video editing. The tape is wide enough to resist stretching and *drop-outs*, losses of video information (seen as streaks and sparkles on playback), which occur when the tape's magnetic coating flakes off. Professional-quality S-VHS cassettes are sturdy enough to survive the knocking around they get in the average production session. Hi8, on the other hand, excels in the field. The cassette's light weight and diminutive profile translate to small, lightweight camcorders that transport easily. There are now several professional video cameras that record in Hi8. Sony is the primary champion of this format and has the widest selection of Hi8 camcorders. I selected a Canon model, the A-1 Digital, because I found it had a combination of features that was hard to find elsewhere in the same price range, and because the unit can be found at most upper-rung video stores. I also liked the Sony EVO-9100, which is a little harder to find, but which adds the benefit of timecode.

Within certain boundaries, a video format guarantees that someone with matching equipment can play the videotape you send them. The exception occurs when you cross certain national boundaries. Regions of the world are carved up into sections that adhere to one video encoding standard or another. If you sent a VHS tape recorded in the U.S. to a buddy in Great Britain, for example, he or she wouldn't be able to play it. The U.S. uses an encoding standard called NTSC that governs the way video data is encoded on the tape. Great Britain shares a format called PAL with other nations, and still others adhere to an encoding standard known as SECAM. These formats are not cross-compatible, but you can buy equipment that converts video from one format to another. There are also service bureaus that specialize in video standards conversions.

Composite and ***component signals:*** Between devices, video data is carried through cables. When you use S-VHS and Hi8 equipment, you have two types of cables you can use: composite and component. A composite cable has two conductors, or wires. The entire video signal is assembled and sent over one of those wires. The term "composite" comes from the fact that several components of the video signal must be assembled into a single stream before it can be sent through a two-wire cable. At the other end, the signal is broken down again into its components and recorded or otherwise manipulated. Consumer equipment often connects together using inexpensive RCA plugs and jacks. Industrial and high-end consumer equipment is more likely to employ BNC connectors. A BNC jack is a cylindrical shape with two short posts sticking out of the sides. BNC cables have twist-locks on their connectors that grab those posts and ensure a firm connection. This also keeps the cable from being inadvertently pulled out.

A component cable, often referred to as "S-video," uses a small, round connector with four conductors plus the metal shield around them. Equipment that supports cables of this kind are able to handle component video signals. Specifically, the luminance (brightness) and chrominance (color) data are separated. That leaves both signals more pure and makes edits and copies clearer. S-VHS and Hi8 decks usually have S-video connectors, and they also record video onto tape in component format. Because of this, when you're using equipment that supports both composite and component signals, you should always use the S-video connectors. If you use composite connections anywhere in your stream of connections amongst video devices, you lose the benefits of the separation of luminance and chrominance.

Video cables can have a dramatic impact on the quality of your work. When you're just learning, it's okay to cheat by using less-expensive RCA cables and, where necessary, RCA-to-BNC adapters. But before you record your first serious tape, you should invest in professional-quality cables. BNC-to-BNC cables should be shielded and rated for 75 ohms. Don't worry if you don't understand what that means just yet, but that will help you know what to ask for. If you're using a Video Toaster-based setup, which uses BNC cables, you'll want to make sure that all of the cables running from the Toaster to your video equipment are exactly the same length. You can buy premade video cables of specific lengths from most professional video supply houses and catalogues.

As I said, if your equipment can be connected with S-video cables, use them exclusively to avoid dropping your video signal down from composite to component. Matrox Studio deals with S-video signals, but it comes with all of its own high-quality cables.

Sync: When you're editing video, bad sync is the most common disease behind bad edits. Sync is the invisible clock that runs inside a video signal. It tells the equipment where the top of the picture is, what the picture's resolution should be, and generally keeps the video signal steady rather than jumping all over the screen.

To do professional-quality edits, you need all of the devices putting out video to be locked to the same sync. In effect, all of your equipment must draw the upper-left-most pixel on the screen at precisely the same moment, and that lock-step must be established continuously. With good sync, you can use video switchers and effects units to superimpose one video signal over another and take advantage of a host of other visually appealing effects. These all depend on using a computer to decide, on a pixel-by-pixel basis, which of the available video sources to display, or if a combination is used, what proportion of each video source is displayed at that pixel.

A video production studio needs a *sync network*. Here, a master sync signal is distributed to all of your video sources, and you need to arrange to lock each device's video output to that master sync. If you use a computer with a graphics card as part of your studio, the adjustment should be easy. Truevision and Matrox professional video cards will automatically lock themselves to whatever video is fed into them. Some cards also have separate "Sync In" or "Ref In" connectors in case your master sync source doesn't produce a video signal you're interested in using. When a graphics card locks to an external sync source, it's called ***genlock***. Some video cameras, particularly studio models that don't have attached video decks, also have genlock capabilities.

Sync is a little more difficult to manage with devices that can't do genlock. Videotape can't be genlocked. A graphics card can adjust its own internal circuitry to delay the drawing of the video data until the external sync signal says "go." But video recorded on tape has an indelible sync of its own. To lock a VCR or other nongenlockable device to an external sync source, you need to use a ***time-base corrector*** (TBC). Simplified, this device makes an electronic recording of the video signal coming off the tape and delays the transmission of each video frame until the master sync source says it's okay. Because a TBC holds an electronic version of each video frame, these units often have controls that let you alter the appearance of the video as it passes through. Typical adjustments include the following: *video level* adjusts the relative strength of the outgoing signal. This can help adjust for a bad recording. Higher video levels appear brighter. *Set-up* raises or lowers the brightness of the color black. Dropping it can give you very deep, dense blacks, but it can also make the picture appear muddy. Raising it turns blacks to gray, but it may help salvage tapes recorded at insufficient brightness levels. *Chroma level* (also called *saturation*) determines how much of the chrominance component of the signal will be displayed. With the chroma level set at zero, the picture is black-and-white (only luminance can be seen). With the chroma level boosted, colors get brighter. Boost it too high, and colors will go neon, glowing around the borders of the objects they represent and bleeding into other colors. *Hue* adjusts colors. If your video shows green or purple people, you may be able to fix it by turning the hue control. Hue adjusts all of the colors in the video at once. If you have bad color on some objects in your video because of poor lighting, hue won't fix that. And finally, you may find a *Y/C delay* adjustment. This corrects for timing problems between the luminance and chrominance signals. You need to adjust Y/C delay if the black-and-white outline of an object is offset from the color that should be associated with it. Turning the Y/C delay knob will move the color until it's "inside the lines."

TBCs come in lots of shapes and sizes. Most common are external TBCs, self-contained units that accept a video input and a sync input, and they output a sync-locked video signal. Their front panels may have some of the adjustments I described (plus some others), and many of them will also let you do a digital freeze of the incoming video signal. This isn't of much use in modern studios, nearly all of which include computer graphics cards that can digitize video instantly. It is sometimes useful when you're trying to adjust the TBC's settings. You can freeze a frame that is a good test for the adjustment you're trying to make and work with that instead of waiting for material to come around on the tape.

There are also a number of companies selling TBCs on expansion cards that plug into your PC or Amiga. Some don't interface with the computer hosting them except to draw power, but others let you make front panel-type adjustments through software. Card-based TBCs are less expensive than external units because you don't have to pay for the package or the power supply. The video and sync sources plug directly into the back of the card, and the output is taken from there as well.

The best place to find TBC is built into your equipment. The Panasonic AG-7750 and AG-7650 topped my list of choices when I set out to build my lab partly because they have their own TBCs. Without relying on any other gear, all three of my decks will lock to a master sync source. Their front panels provide a full set of TBC controls.

Whether you must use time-based correctors on your video equipment depends on what you're using to do your edits. If you have a Video Toaster-based studio, everything going into your Toaster *must* be locked to a master sync source. Matrox Studio solves the problem by placing three time-base correctors on the

Studio boards themselves. The version of Studio I have supports up to six video inputs. The three TBCs attach themselves to whatever inputs you're using for a particular edit; they "float," so if you use Studio, you don't have to buy any time-base correctors. If you have some equipment, like the Panasonic AG7750 and AG-7650 decks, that are already time-base corrected, you can tell Studio not to waste a TBC on that video source.

Even when you don't have to lock to an external sync, a TBC is a helpful thing to have around. It's the only way to get all the adjustments I described above, and TBCs generally clean up video signals; most anything looks better run through a TBC, even if you don't need one for the work you're doing.

So what's a master sync source? The requirements are simple: it has to put out a clean, constant video signal. Video supply houses sell boxes that put out clean, constant *black burst*, effectively a blank video signal. Many professional graphics cards also have black burst outputs so you can use them for master sync. Don't use a VCR as a sync source. With a TBC, a VCR can put out a signal stable enough for sync, but often, when you switch in and out of play mode, the sync will glitch long enough to confuse all of the video devices that are reading sync from it. In the case of the Video Toaster, you probably wouldn't want to plug a VCR into the Toaster's input #1 (from which sync is drawn). You would instead plug the output of a black burst generator or the video signal coming from a professional graphics card. In a pinch, you can draw sync from a video camera (one that's showing live video, not a camcorder playing a tape), or even from a video game. A black burst generator or a graphics card's video or black burst output is still the best place to draw sync.

Timecode: In the previous chapter, I introduced the concept of timecode, a digital code that brands each video frame with a unique marker. Timecode is an essential element of editing. Without it, you could set up an edit to cut to a woman just as she begins to speak, but when the edit executes, it might miss the cut, lopping off her first word or showing the odd face she made just before the cut point you selected. Timecode, once laid down on tape, is locked to the video. A particular timecode value, expressed with colon-separated numeric values (*hours, minutes, seconds, frames*), will always represent the exact same frame on the video every time. Editing software uses timecode to ensure precise edits every time. You can create a list of timecode-based edits, save them on disk, and lock that disk away with the associated tapes for years. If you drag those tapes out later, insert them in decks (even if they're not the same ones you originally used) and execute that list of edits again, you'll create precisely the same result as your first edit.

There are two methods of recording timecode to tape are *VITC* and *LTC*. VITC (vertical interval timecode) uses the space between the bottom of one frame of video and the top of the next, space you can see if you purposely throw your TV's vertical hold out of whack—the vertical interval is the black bar between pictures, to hold the digital code. If you look at the vertical interval on some prerecorded tapes, you may see the timecode there as flashing patterns of dots and lines. VITC records the digital code to the vertical interval as graphics. Since the vertical interval is tall enough to have several lines of graphics, equipment that supports VITC allows you to set which line in that space will be used to hold the timecode. You should set all of your equipment to write and read VITC to and from the same line.

LTC, linear timecode, is recorded as audio onto one of your deck's audio tracks. The AG-7750 has four tracks of audio: two hi-fi and two called "normal." The normal audio tracks are of such low quality that they're not of much use (except that they're the only tracks the cheapest VHS decks can play), but one of them can be used to hold LTC. If you use LTC, your deck will probably have a switch that turns off the audio output for the audio channel you're using for timecode. It's not very pleasant to listen to. LTC, because it's audio, has the advantage of being recordable onto audio tape as well. Professional multi-track audio tape decks often have some facility for recording, and sometimes even interpreting, LTC. The Tascam MIDIstudio 688, for example, is an eight-track cassette recorder. You can flip a switch to reserve one of those eight tracks for LTC, which runs through an audio cable from the back of your record deck to a special jack on the MIDIstudio. The value of this will be explained later.

Timecode can be managed through two means: internally and externally. The Panasonic decks I use have option boards installed in them so that they generate and read their own timecode (VITC and/or LTC). If your VCR doesn't support timecode directly, you can purchase an external device called a *timecode generator* that sends out a timecode signal you can record onto your tape, usually on one of your audio tracks. If you use externally generated timecode, you must also use an external timecode reader so that your editing software can know what the tape's position is. Some VCR controllers (definition coming) have timecode inputs built into them for this purpose; some can generate timecode, as well.

It's best to build timecode directly into your video decks. For one, the front-panel displays will show the timecode value rather than the far less useful "tape counter." And most decks with built-in timecode will pass that timecode through the serial control ports at the back to the VCR controller, eliminating the need to string another set of cables to pass timecode around.

Timecode can be placed on a tape anytime you record it, but to be useful, it should be recorded in one pass. Producers usually record timecode onto an entire tape (or at least enough of it to cover the length of the material) using a process called ***preblacking*** or ***striping***. This records a video signal, usually black, along with timecode that starts counting at a time you specify. Some decks will let you stripe new timecode onto an existing tape without disturbing the material on it. Timecode can count up to 23 hours, 59 minutes, 59 seconds, and 29 frames, far more than a single tape can hold. A common practice is to stripe tapes with an hour value that helps identify the tape. The first stock tape you stripe might start counting at 00:00:00:00. Since that tape will run to two hours or so, you might start your next tape with a timecode of 03:00:00:00. You might also stripe all the tapes you use for a certain job with matching timecode hours. Inserting a timecode-striped tape and pressing Play will bring the timecode up on the display after a delay of a couple of seconds. Using the hour encoding can help you tell your tapes apart if, like me, you're a little lazy about labeling your videotapes.

Continuous striping is important because if the timecode sequence is broken, your editing software can lose track of where the tape is and abort or botch the edit. It helps to think of it in the same light as formatting floppy disks before using them. Just pop any fresh tape you buy into your record deck and stripe it while you're having lunch or conferring with associates. Some software will stripe a tape for you automatically. Striping takes as long as the real playing time; a two-hour tape takes two hours to stripe.

VCR controller: This device sits between your computer and an industrial or broadcast VCR and translates between them. Your editing software sends commands to your VCRs through the controller, and the controller passes data back to the software.

When you choose a video deck, you should make sure it's supported by the VCR controller you plan to use. Support isn't universal; each vendor has its own pet control protocol that VCR controller vendors must adhere to. Brand-new decks, those on the market less than a year or so, may not have controller software written for them yet. A quick call to the controller's vendor will get you a compatibility list. One other item you need to notice, primarily in shopping for used decks (which is a good way to save money), is whether the deck has a serial or parallel control port. Serial ports are almost always better, and nearly all of the newer decks have them. VCR controllers that communicate with parallel ports are usually more expensive.

To work properly, a VCR controller needs to be plugged into your sync network. Professional edits are done frame-accurately. To make an edit come off precisely when the video frame associated with a particular timecode begins, the controller must rely on the master sync to tell it when the frame starts. Most VCR controllers have sync inputs. Be wary of those that don't. An off-sync edit can show on tape as anything from a barely noticeable split-second tear in a part of the picture to a full-blown screaming glitch. Either way, off-sync edits are ugly, and there's no reason to spend good money on good video equipment only to drive it with cheap VCR controllers that don't watch your sync.

Like everything else in this business, VCR controllers come in different shapes. They can be cards that plug into your computer's bus, sit in an external box, or install inside the VCR you're using. An external unit, be it in its own box or installed inside your VCR, connects to your computer through one of its serial ports. The main advantage of card-based controllers is that they don't tie up any serial ports, and they're usually a bit less expensive for the lack of a case and power supply.

My facility uses both kinds of controllers, but for different kinds of jobs. The three-deck video editing system goes through a unique VCR controller network called a ***V-LAN***, made by Videomedia. The hub of a V-LAN network is a transmitter module. It connects to your computer's serial port and also has an input for a master sync source. The transmitter then attaches to one or more receiver modules through BNC network cables. This allows you to place the receivers wherever they're most convenient. Each receiver has a serial or parallel control port that connects, through a cable, to the port on the back of your VCR. Each V-LAN module is encoded with a unique node number, so that when you turn the network's power on and start your editing software, the V-LAN transmitter reports the node number of each receiver module connected and the status of the deck attached to it. In AmiLink VT, the Video Toaster-based editing software I use, there's one button, labeled Config, that automatically configures the editing software for the V-LAN configuration.

Each V-LAN module is actually a self-contained computer system. Newer V-LAN modules, like the VLX system I use, let you change their operating software by downloading new code from a disk. That way, you can keep the V-LAN software matched to the decks you're using.

V-LAN uses a proprietary code between the transmitter and the computer; only registered developers have access to it. That doesn't pose much of a problem for most applications, since the V-LAN system is one of the most widely supported VCR control systems on the market.

There are times when I want to write my own software that talks to my video decks, and times, too, when I prefer the convenience of an in-system VCR controller card. Diaquest makes internal VCR controller boards for the Mac (***DQ-Animaq***), PC (***DQ-422***), and Amiga (***DQ-Taco***). I use Diaquest cards primarily for the custom applications I create and for single-frame animation recording. Unlike the V-LAN, which uses proprietary commands between your system and the transmitter, the Diaquest manuals include all the information you need to command the board from within your own software. In my lab, I use a PC with a Diaquest board in it for my Mac and Amiga single-frame animation control. The Amiga is connected to the PC through a serial cable, and a short Basic program passes incoming commands from the Amiga to the PC's DQ-422 board. My record deck's serial control port plugs directly into a cable attached to the DQ-422, and it also has a handy black-burst output that works as a clean master sync source whenever the PC housing it is turned on.

Which of these two solutions you choose will depend on what your software supports and what kind of work you do. There are no absolutes, but in my studio, I've found the Diaquest boards to work best for animation and custom video processing applications, and I use the V-LAN for my video editing. I should note that both Videomedia and Diaquest have both internal and external units.

At this writing, Matrox Studio doesn't yet support any standard VCR controller. Support for the V-LAN is planned. For now, Studio comes with a four-port serial card and cables for direct control of up to four decks. This remote doesn't have sync input, but because the Studio software has its fingers in the video signal through Studio's video boards, it will sync the edits up for you.

Assemble and ***insert edits:*** An edit is the laying down of a segment of video, the location and duration of which are identified by ***in*** and ***out points*** (expressed in timecode), onto your record tape. An editing system includes one or more source (playback) decks and usually one record deck. During the editing process, you'll collect segments from the tapes in the source decks and move them to the record deck, laying the end of one edit against the beginning of the next. The result will be a recorded tape that is either your finished program or an intermediate edit master that will become a source for another edit.

When you record new material onto a tape in a professional editing deck, you can choose between two methods. An assemble edit records everything simultaneously—video plus all audio channels and timecode if you have it—completely erasing whatever was on the tape before. You can record an assemble edit onto a completely blank piece of tape, that is, one that hasn't been preblacked, but it's not advisable. If you should try to play a blank portion of the tape, your editing software (and possibly your deck) could get hopelessly confused. Assemble edits are good for creating edit masters because they copy everything from one tape to another.

The insert edit is more common because of its flexibility. It must be done on tape that has already been recorded, but it lets you choose what you want to record. In the case of my Panasonic decks, I can record the video, hi-fi audio, and the left and right channels of my normal audio tracks independently. Whatever I choose *not* to record during an insert edit is left alone. I can use insert edits to do ***audio*** and ***video dubs***. An example of an audio dub would be the after-the-fact recording of production music to an animated logo. The production music could go in as an audio-only insert edit, leaving my animation untouched. You could also use the audio dub to lay down a foreign-language audio track on one of the normal audio channels. A video dub would let you cut to a view of a graphic while the voice of the person you were taping continues underneath.

When an insert edit ends, that is, when the out point timecode of the source material is reached, the VCR stops recording instantly. The next frame of the video and all the audio tracks will reflect whatever was there before your edit. You can't count on being able to do that with an assemble edit; those are meant to proceed in a beginning-to-end fashion. Use an insert edit whenever you're going back over already-recorded material.

Cuts-only and ***A/B roll***: A cuts-only video editing system, as its name implies, can only perform cut edits, in which every video clip you record hits the tape instantly (one frame it's not there at all, and the next frame it's all there) and goes away just as abruptly. An A/B roll system uses two source decks and a video switcher to create gentler, more visually appealing transitions (like fades) between clips. The sections on the Video Toaster and Matrox Studio describe transitions in more detail.

A/B roll editing is more complicated than cuts-only because you have to organize your material. You must arrange your clips so that every pair of scenes you wish to transition between is split: one clip on the A deck and one on the B deck. If you have two edits in a row that take clips from the A deck, you must do a cut edit between them. That's because in order to do a transition, the video switcher (under the control of your editing software) must have two running video sources. It can't pick up material that's already been laid down on your record deck and use that for a transition. You may only transition from deck A to deck B, and from deck B to deck A.

All that arranging can make A/B roll a bother. Fortunately, too many fancy transitions in a video are annoying. In any given production, probably 90% of your edits should be cuts. In my own work, the A/B roll tends to manage itself, since I use one master tape to hold my opening logo, closing credits, and any intermediate animations. I tend to limit transitional effects to edits that go from one type of video shot (a person talking, for example) to one that's completely different (like a 3-D animation). Here, it can be reasonably argued that the transitional effect lessens the jolt of the abrupt change in scenery.

Having a cuts-only system doesn't mean you're on bread and water. The Video Toaster, with the cuts-only edition of the AmiLink VT editing software, can use the toaster's dual frame buffers (which hold 24-bit color graphics) as if they were video sources. So even in a cuts-only environment, you can make a smooth transition between video and graphics, or between video and character generator pages, even ones that move.

One advantage of an A/B roll system, or of an A/B/C roll (and so on) system, is that you can use picture-in-picture and other layering effects. Matrox Studio has an impressive set of layering capabilities (see "keying," below) that will be of no use to you if you don't have multiple video sources. The Video Toaster, too, can set multiple video sources up to share the screen simultaneously, but Studio has far more advanced keying and layering support (that's one of its greatest strengths). These facilities will be of no use to you if you lack multiple video sources. To have the day's animated stock quote graphic float over a news reader's shoulder, for example, you'd need the news reader on one tape and the stock quote on another. If you had a third source deck, Studio could float still another graphic or somehow use that video source in the edit.

Both Studio and the Video Toaster will allow you to use video sources that aren't directly controlled by the editing software. You can use a live camera, the output from a graphics board in another computer, a laserdisc player, or a feed from your cable TV hookup. The only requirement, in the case of the Toaster, is that the source be genlocked or time-base corrected to alignment with your master sync. I don't recommend trying to save money by hooking up a manually controlled VCR to turn a cuts-only system into A/B roll. You'll never be quick enough on the remote to keep up with the editing software.

Preroll: Videotape is very thin and flexible. It bends and twists when your deck's transport changes directions, as when it goes from Stop to Play. From the time you push Play, it can take several seconds for the tape to align itself with the deck's heads to the point where the video is clean and the audio tracks can be heard. The same kind of alignment delay occurs when you record. To allow for this, VCR controllers and editing software use preroll. When you execute an edit, all of the involved source and record decks are rewound to a fixed period (usually five or six seconds) before the in point. Then all the decks are started simultaneously, at precisely the same time. The preroll also gives the VCR controller a chance to catch-up any of the decks that might have started a fraction of a second behind or ahead of the others by applying minute speed adjustments. The record deck is prerolled, but it doesn't click into Record mode until its in point is reached.

If your edits look bad, and you're confident that your sync network is in order, you can try raising your preroll time to a higher number. VCR controllers, editing software, and sometimes the decks themselves can be programmed for whatever preroll period you like. Don't put the precision of your edits at risk just to save a couple of seconds off the front of each edit; it's not worth it.

Jog and ***shuttle:*** In addition to the expected Play, Stop, Rewind, Fast Forward, and other transport controls on your VCR, most professional decks often feature a jog/shuttle control. Jog rolls the video forward or back very slowly, one frame at a time or less, so you can zero in on a particular timecode frame or find the timecode associated with a certain on-screen event. Shuttle moves the video back and forth at variable speeds, ranging from a fraction of normal playback speed to several times faster. Both jog and shuttle are for visual location of material, so they do their work visibly; you can see their effects on the screen. The Panasonic S-VHS decks I use have what has come to be a typical control, a large wheel that handles both jog and shuttle. Editing software usually offers at least a shuttle control that you can operate through the software's user interface.

Standby mode: Tape follows a complex path through a VCR's innards, during which it's wrapped around various read/write head assemblies and capstans. When you first insert a cassette, a loop of tape is pulled out of the cassette and into the deck. Once the tape is threaded in this way, the deck can change modes (such as from Play to Stop) very quickly; all it has to do is set the tape in motion. While the tape is threaded, it is at greater risk of damage due to stretching or kinking, both of which can cause the tape's magnetic coating to flake off. Professional decks often allow you to leave the tape threaded for extended periods of time so that editing commands can be carried out without waiting for the tape to thread. When the deck is stopped but the tape remains threaded through the system, the deck is said to be in standby mode. To protect your tape, most decks will take themselves out of standby mode after a certain period of inactivity. You can usually program the deck to change the duration of this standby period. A VCR controller can send a "standby off" command to a deck that has a standby mode, and many editing packages and 3-D animation software let you specify that at the end of each operation, the deck will be taken out of standby mode to protect the tape.

It's probably not necessary to remove standby mode after every operation. The only situation that calls for concern is when commands to the deck will be separated by long inactive periods. This is particularly true when recording single-frame animation, which can invoke delays of up to several hours per frame. In that case, and in any case where you're likely to leave the deck idle for more than a few minutes, protect your tape by taking your deck out of standby mode.

The best protection for a tape, of course, is to remove it from the deck completely. It's a good idea to fully rewind the tape first. This helps maintain the tape's tight winding around its reels and also reduces the chance that the elements or some other force will get at an important piece of tape. Rewinding usually pulls all of the recordable tape into the cassette, exposing only a plastic leader. Even without a plastic leader, you should consider the first several seconds of a tape unusable. It's not at all uncommon for that portion of the tape to get chewed up pretty badly after several uses. Start recording at least 10 or 15 seconds into the tape. Preblacking for timecode, however, should start from the very beginning of the tape so that your software can get its bearings when you insert a fully rewound tape.

Keying: This is the electronic compositing of two or more video sources into a single output signal. Most keying modes depend on making some part of a video image transparent. Keying creates layers of video images. Whatever is on the top layer is most visible. If the top layer has no transparent pixels, you won't see any of the underlying layers. Wherever a layer has a transparent pixel, the layer directly underneath it will show through.

Keying depends on real-time analysis of the video image. The video switching hardware decides, based on the content of each frame of video, which pixels to turn transparent. There are two popular keying modes: ***luminance*** and ***chroma keying***. A luminance key uses the relative brightness of each pixel to decide whether to turn it transparent. To use a luminance key, you configure the switcher for a specific luminance threshold. In the case of the Video Toaster, this threshold is represented as a number between zero and 257. A luminance key effect will turn every pixel that is either darker than (black keying) or lighter than (white keying) the threshold transparent; you choose which to use based on the content of the video.

Luminance keying works very well for titles and graphics. All you need to do is design your graphic with an all-white or all-black background, and avoid using white and black in the graphic itself (unless you want something in the interior of the graphic to turn transparent). It works less well for people and live video. Dark keying can turn shadows, dark shirt buttons, and the pupils of your subject's eyes transparent. White keying can make teeth, the whites of eyes, and reflections from the lights transparent. It's possible, with careful lighting and wardrobe preparation, to make luminance keying work for weathermap-type keying. But for most live work, chroma key is the better choice.

Chroma key turns a selected range of colors transparent. If you've ever been in a television studio, you've probably seen the trademark blue paper or paint behind the news desk. Chroma key allows you to select a range of colors that is very unlikely to appear in a person or an article of clothing and turn it transparent. Chroma key works even better for titles than luminance keying (better, because it leaves black and white alone), but it requires a bit more preparation. You may have to take some care that the color you're using for transparency in the graphic matches your settings in the luminance keyer.

The Video Toaster does luminance keying only, and can mix a maximum of two video sources together with it. Matrox Studio offers both luminance and chroma keying and can combine up to three video sources.

Equipment Choices

You won't always be fortunate enough to be able to pull together complete productions using material handed to you by someone else. Stock footage from companies like Firstlight can add spice and depth to the videos you produce, but most of what you roll into any video you produce yourself will come from video you shoot yourself.

Deciding to shoot video yourself involves making several choices, the most important of which is your choice of video camera. The most common packaging for video cameras is the camcorder, a combination camera and VCR. There was once a distinct advantage to having the video deck separate from the camera. Generally, this meant better quality in both the camera and the deck. Now, even the most expensive digital tape formats have been packaged into camcorders. While huge and heavy compared to consumer-style camcorders, these top-end all-in-one units serve pretty much the same purpose as their more petite and less costly counterparts.

I'm inclined toward Hi8 as a convenient camcorder acquisition format that delivers good results. There is also a miniature version of the S-VHS format, called S-VHS-C, that uses cartridges roughly the same size as Hi8 (but a little thicker). S-VHS-C camcorders are usually about the same size and shape as Hi8 units. Camcorders are not, however, all created equal. Depending on the kind of shooting you plan to do, certain types of cameras work better than others.

These days, it seems the primary goal of camcorder manufacturers is to make the smallest, lightest device. While the notion of a shirt-pocket video camera is technologically appealing, the super-small, super-light camera is often not the best choice for serious work. For starters, the smaller cameras often sacrifice a number of things to get down to size: features, optical and video quality, and accessibility of controls often suffer. Starting with the Hi8 format excludes most of the bargain-basement consumer camcorders that only use ordinary 8mm or VHS-C. And while a super-light camera may be a joy to carry with you everywhere you go, it can be impossible to hold steady.

I've worked with a great many Hi8 camcorders, and I've reached some conclusions about what to look for when you shop for one. I hesitate to offer specific recommendations because the video business moves so fast, it's easily possible that the camcorders I like as I write this will be obsolete by the time you read this.

I will describe the units that most impressed me to illustrate some of the points you may wish to consider before you buy.

The first good camcorder I encountered was a Sony EVO-9100, an extremely solid Hi8 camcorder. Among its winning attributes was its built-in 8mm timecode, a huge help if you're planning to use Hi8 gear in the editing process; you can often pull the tape out of the camcorder and edit it directly. The Sony camcorder also had the fastest, most accurate autofocus I've ever used, and it turned out absolute gorgeous video.

I now use a Canon A1 Digital for most of my field work. This is a popular high-end consumer camcorder that includes an infrared remote and a handful of digital special effects. It doesn't do timecode, but it sports an excellent set of optics (one model up the line, the L-1, offers interchangeable lenses) and it also has a Control-L remote control port.

I described Control-L in the previous chapter during the discussion on VISCA. The A1 Digital's Control-L port looks like an ordinary pause control jack. It's actually a serial interface that allows an edit controller, computer or other device to control the camcorder's functions. For tape editing operations, Control-L's positioning of the tape is not very precise. Accuracy is only about a second or so, meaning that if you try to use the A1 Digital in an edit, it can miss an in or out point by as much as a second. That's unacceptable, so don't plan on building a non-timecode-equipped camcorder into an editing suite. The A1 Digital's Control-L port can save you the hassle of using the camera-mounted controls or the wireless remote to transfer the good material from a camcorder tape to an edit master. You can find editing and cataloguing software that uses the remote port to do quick and dirty edits or to create a list of scenes on the tape. Even if you don't plan to invest in Control-L editing devices or software now, it's wise to look for camcorders that have this capability since you may want it later.

When you shop for a 35mm camera, it's nice to get one that's loaded with automatic features. Automatic exposure and autofocus are great time-savers, but you'll always encounter situations that fool the camera's automatic circuits. With camcorders, you should look for a unit that lets you take control over the exposure and the focus. Backlighting, over- or under-lighting, and other adverse conditions are ones you'll want to be able to compensate for. Most camcorders include at least a manual iris control that brightens or darkens the picture, and some, like the A1 Digital, let you zoom in, take an exposure reading from your subject, and lock that exposure setting so that brighter objects in the scene don't confuse the meter. Likewise, most cameras have a switch that disengages the autofocus. When disengaged, you can usually get the camera to do a one-shot automatic focus by pressing a button on the camera.

The A1 Digital sports an array of digital special effects, and you may find similar bells and whistles on the camcorders you see when you shop around. The frills are mostly a come-on and a means of driving up the price of the camera. Be smart about looking at camcorders; don't be snookered by glitzy features you don't need. Some of the A1 Digital's neat-o features are just plain silly, like the strobe and posterization effects, but there were a couple of worthwhile gadgets thrown in. The A1 Digital can instantly digitize a frozen frame of video with excellent clarity. The camcorder also offers a 2X digital zoom (effectively doubling the camera's zoom range), and record in extraordinarily dim lighting with a 1/8-second shutter speed (the normal speed is 1/60). I have used this camera to shoot in moonlight, and while the resulting video is nothing to brag about, it is viewable.

In choosing a camcorder, you also want to consider how to get the video out of it. In my own facility, I have a separate Hi8 VCR (the Sony CVD-1000 Vdeck), but most people who shoot in Hi8 have only the camera to use for playback. If you create that situation for yourself, check to make sure the camera you choose has good video and audio output options. If you use Hi8 or S-VHS-C, make sure the camera has an S-video output. If you plan to record any stereo audio, check the camera for stereo line output jacks. Don't plan on using the camcorder's headphone jack for audio output; you'll only add the noise from the camcorder's headphone amplifier to your edits. Also, RCA jacks are more durable and create better connections than the 1/8-inch stereo phone jacks that are sometimes used to save space. These tiny jacks are notorious for going bad after lots of plugging and unplugging.

Professionals will tell you, and with some basis, that the camcorders the average Joe (or Janet) can buy in a retail store is not suitable for professional use. Depending on the outlets available near to where you live, that can be true. It's important that you not settle for what you can buy locally, because you may not find professional-quality gear in any area store. You will probably fare better if you at least check with your closest dealer of professional video equipment. While they'd probably rather sell you a high-end device, if you walk in looking for a Hi8 camcorder, chances are you'll find units there that don't appear on local store shelves. There is such a thing as a professional Hi8 camcorder, and that's where you should set your sights. My A1 Digital is considered to be at the bottom end of that class. I sprung for it because it was affordable, and I don't regret the choice. I have, however, often rented better cameras for more serious work, but I always choose Hi8.

If you want to step up from Hi8, you'll definitely want to pay a visit to a professional dealer. There are innumerable formats that outgun Hi8 in resolution and overall image quality, and I haven't the space to discuss them here. The leap in price for that improved quality is considerable, but it may be cushioned somewhat if you're willing to settle for used or reconditioned gear. My counsel to first-time buyers is to spend wisely and to trust your own eyes. When you shop, don't just look through camcorders and fiddle with the controls. Put in a tape, record some footage that forces the camera to deal with different lighting situations, and play that tape directly out of the camcorder onto a good-quality monitor at the dealership. That's something you can't do mail-order, and that's the reason I am willing to pay the extra money to shop in a real store. If, after you've looked at the best Hi8 has to offer, you're disappointed with the quality, forget my experiences and move up to the next level (if your budget will allow). I decided that Hi8 is good enough for the corporate-style work I do. Your eyes may tell you different, and if they do, believe them.

Hold Still

I think the most valuable advice I ever heard regarding shooting video with a camcorder is, "never hold the camera in your hands." Hands shake, the body sways, and if you're zoomed in far enough, you can see the picture move up and down in the frame as the camera operator *breathes*. I favor two fixes for this predicament: the tripod and a device called the Steadicam JR.

Now that everyone is buying camcorders, good video tripods are easy to find, and acceptable ones are even cheap. I've found tripods of acceptable quality for less than $150 U.S. What makes a video tripod suited for video is mostly the way the head—the part of the tripod to which the camcorder attaches—is designed. A good video tripod uses a *fluid-filled head*. The fluid hydraulically dampens side-to-side (pans) and up-and-down (tilts) movements. With a fluid-filled head, you can do exquisitely smooth pans because the fluid regulates the speed of the pan, compensating for varying pressure on the tripod's lever.

More expensive tripods are usually either made better or just carry some famous tripod company's name. The only reason to spend more for a tripod is to get a better-quality device that's more likely to survive if you do a lot of traveling. If you're setting up a studio, you may want to get a tripod that has or accepts casters. Video supply shops also offer casters that you can place under any ordinary tripod. Rolling the camera around isn't necessarily something you'd do with the tape running, but it is more convenient (and easier on the gear) than picking the whole contraption up and moving it to a new spot.

My favorite choice for field work is the Steadicam JR. This device, manufactured by Cinema Products, helps you hold your camcorder still for handheld shots, but it does so much more than that.

The device itself sounds simple enough by its description: it is a perfectly balanced platform resting atop a handgrip. A gimble mechanism maintains a single point of balance while allowing a remarkable range of motion. A monochrome LCD monitor displays the video coming from your camera, and frees the operator from being glued to the camera's viewfinder.

Fully extended, the Stedicam JR reduces camera shake by adding weight and isolating the camera from the minute body motions we make when we breathe, move about or just try to stand still. The handle and LCD monitor let you shoot from just about anywhere your hand will go—from your hip, over your head, near the ground, whatever the shot calls for. The gimble mechanism also allows you to make perfectly smooth pans by just giving the JR's platform a small push and letting it pan on its own.

Uniquely, a Steadicam JR will let you walk while you're recording. You can shoot from a person's point of view and navigate around corners, up and down stairs, through doorways, and all without the bounce and shake that normally accompany hand- or shoulder-held moving shots. If you're doing a walking tour of a piece of real estate, there's no better way to shoot it than with the Steadicam. With some practice, you can spice up an interview or a plant tour video by following the speaker around. The Steadicam JR adapts so well that you can walk in front of someone, pointing the camera back at them, without having to walk backward. A good demo of the Steadicam JR can be seen on this book's tape.

The Steadicam JR, with a mounted camcorder, feels like a mighty weight because it's all balanced on one hand. You get a feel for just how heavy six or seven pounds really is when you've held it with one hand for a few minutes. Because of this, and because the gimble setup isn't something you need for every shot, the Steadicam JR's platform folds into a more-or-less flat package that you can park on your shoulder (there's a fold-out "whale tail" that adds length for more stability), or hold any way you like; the LCD screen remains viewable in this mode. As an example, I once shot a sports competition by holding a folded JR at full arms' length over my head. By doing this, I was able to shoot over the crowd, and gain enough height to get a view of the entire game from over the players' shoulders; this shot would have been impossible without the JR. The LCD panel pivots vertically so you can view it from any angle, and a bubble level shows you whether the camera is flat or not.

The Steadicam JR has become, for me, an essential component for any video shoot. I leave my camera mounted to it (Cinema Products offers a bag specially designed to carry the Steadicam JR, its accessories, and a mounted camera) and use it as though it were part of the camera. You'll need lots of practice before you get the hang of using the device, but once you compare the results with hand-held, you'll never think of going without the JR.

Sound and Lights

No matter how good your camera is, and no matter how still you hold it, you're guaranteed bad video if you don't spend at least a little time thinking about sound and lighting. While modern camcorders are able to shoot good video snapshots using their built-in microphones and available light, these are generally not acceptable for professional work.

The microphone is probably the cheapest way to greatly improve the quality of your video. Many first-time producers make the mistake of taking the audio for granted, but believe me, there's nothing that can drag an otherwise good video down like bad audio.

On-camera microphones frequently pick up zoom and autofocus motor noises, and every time you touch the camera it records booms and snaps onto your audio. If you're shooting one person, have him or her wear a small microphone on the tie or lapel, fastened with a grip or pin, and plug it directly into the microphone jack on your camcorder. If you're shooting multiple people, you can either lapel-mike them individually and use a mixer to combine the signals, or use one or more table or floor-standing microphones. But no matter how carefully you prepare, sound has a way of fooling you: what you hear with your own ears never comes close to what gets recorded on tape. For this reason, you must use headphones, plugged directly into your camcorder, to listen to the sound while you're recording. That way, you can catch serious problems and fix them before everybody disperses. You can correct minor variances in recording volume later, but you can't really fix distortion, background noise, or room reverberation inexpensively after the fact. If you hear any of these problems and can't figure out how to fix them, you'll probably have to find a new location. Also, if you're shooting a speech or some function that has its own sound system, tap directly into it rather than recording the sound in the room. It may sound fine to your ears, but sound from loudspeakers doesn't record well.

The arsenal of products available to assist in the recording of audio is vast. A couple of lapel microphones with long cords (acceptable battery-driven electret models cost about $30 U.S.), an assortment of patch cables of various lengths, an audio mixer, and a set of audio adapter plugs are a good start. Some camcorders, including the one I use, can record audio in stereo, but it's rarely worth the fuss to mike a room in stereo, and the editing process is a little simpler when you're using one channel of audio. Again, it's a matter of taste.

You may also elect to use a wireless transmitter/receiver pair. These either include their own microphone or have a jack that accepts a mike of your choice. The transmitter is worn by the speaker, usually clipped to back of the pants or stuck in a pocket. The receiver usually winds up taped to the side of the camcorder (making it almost impossible to use the Steadicam JR because of the added weight). A good wireless microphone (there are plenty of toy ones—avoid them) puts out clean sound and frees you from tripping over cords.

Lighting can be a hard problem to solve. In a studio, you can set up fixed lights and backgrounds, plant people in chairs, and move the lights around until the shadows disappear. But when you're shooting in the field, getting the lighting right can be a full-time job. If you're going to be doing a lot of indoor field work, I suggest you pick up a book on video lighting. My own preference is to use two or three relatively low-wattage, inexpensive reflector lamps. These have matte white interior surfaces that spread the light evenly. If you're shooting a person, onc light on either side of the face, either at face level or slightly above or below, can light the face acceptably. The goal is to minimize shadows without blinding your subject. For that reason, I generally hang the lights low or high so the subject can look straight ahead (into the camera) without having the lights permanently engraved on his or her retina.

Professional video dealers offer packaged sets of field and studio lights which, if you can afford them, are the best way to go. It's not that cheap lights don't work. They do; I use them all the time. What the package deal offers you is a complete set of not only lights, but the equipment that holds and shapes the lights. In a good kit, you'll get light stands, several kinds of video lights, and sometimes the clamps and arm assemblies that let you turn office furniture and its like into light fixtures.

Planning a Shoot

Those of us who grew up on television have come to take it for granted. The expertise of the people who create the images we watch makes it all look easy. When you're shooting "video snapshots" on vacation, it can be as simple as point and shoot. A good camcorder can keep the image in focus and properly exposed. What video technology won't take care of for you, however, is planning, and that's the element that often makes the difference between a professional-looking production and one that looks like an ad for a tractor pull.

Planning a video, like any large project, is best handled by breaking the task into pieces. Where video is concerned, those pieces can be grouped the way you would material for a book. The opening, for example, should set the viewers' expectations, and put them in a frame of mind appropriate for the message being delivered. It should also grab their interest and make them want to keep watching. But before you begin, you must think of the central message, the "big idea" that the video must get across. Most videos sell something, be it a point of view, a product, a service or a corporate image. So you might ask yourself, "what am I selling?" If you can boil that down a brief narrative or series of video clips, that becomes your opening segment, and something similar also finds its way into the summary at the end. The front of the video should answer the audience question, "what will I learn from watching this?" The tail of the video should answer the question, "what *did* I learn?"

The main body of your video can be split into segments, each of which revolves around a major premise. To support that, segments employ multiple sequences, groups of video scenes that illustrate a contributing minor premise. Within those sequences, your case, as it were, is made by individual scenes. For simplicity, think of a scene as all the video that is shot at a single time. A scene may include changes of camera angle and subject, but it's generally shot in one place with the same group of people or products (or whatever you're shooting). A change in subject, that is, when the video starts making a new point, usually makes for a new scene. When you set about finishing the tape, scenes are combined into sequences, sequences combined into segments, and segments are pulled together to make the video.

When you group things this way—segments, sequences, and scenes—a hierarchy begins to appear that suggests a natural way to organize it: an outline. Use whatever tools you like, but I will counsel you to use a computer. You will want the freedom to rearrange parts of your outline without having to recreate it. After you build your outline, you can print it out, stick it on a clipboard, and use it as a guide during the shoot. Later, when you're editing, a marked-up version of the outline can help you keep your material organized and guide you through the edit.

I employ several tools for my outlines, with my choices depending on what kind of equipment I have available. FrameMaker, the document publishing software I used to produce this book, does killer outlines, and I frequently use it when I can produce the outline in my office. You may find that the presentation graphics software you use includes a good outliner. Failing that, any spreadsheet or word processor will at least do the job. Whatever you choose, don't make learning the outlining tool a major part of your project.

In creating my outline, I find it helpful to work from the top of the organizational hierarchy down, adding detail as I go. I name and describe all the segments first, creating a sort of table of contents. Then I go back to add the sequences as outline sub-items under those segments, and I finally break up the sequences into scenes. Don't forsake the outline, for you'll almost certainly find sequences that don't flow well, or small ideas that need to be promoted to larger ones. This in itself is enough to recommend outlining as a first step—once you start shooting, it's often too late to figure out your plan won't work. Using an outline as a shooting plan also helps avoid wasting your time, and perhaps more important, the time of others involved (which you or your client may be paying for).

The scene-level detail section of your outline offers you an opportunity to think things through. Think about where each scene will be shot, how the room needs to be prepared, who will speak, what they'll say . . . try to leave no detail to chance. A good outlining tool will let you include all that minute detail in the outline, but also allows you to collapse the outline to a less detailed view so you can see the "big picture." As far as the scene-level detail is concerned, forget about technical issues like lighting and sound for now, but try to imagine the scene playing out in your mind, and get as many of those thoughts down on paper as you can before the day of the shoot.

Doing a bit of composition in advance can also save you considerable time later. Go to the room where you plan to shoot the scene; bring your camcorder if you can. Imagine where your subject will be placed, and where you'll stand with the camera. Try to find a couple of workable angles in case you need to switch on the day of the shoot, or if you want to spice things up by shooting parts of the scene from different points of view. Pay particular attention to what's behind your subject. Avoid background clutter (unless it reinforces your message, as when you're doing a documentary on mismanaged landfills). If clutter is both unavoidable and undesirable, try to put as much distance between the subject and the background as possible. Greater distance allows the camera to focus on the subject, casting the background in an out-of-focus haze. You may also free yourself from concern about the natural surroundings by using background paper. This is thick, colored or patterned paper that comes in long, seamless rolls. It's commonly used in portrait photography, but it works just as well for video. It works particularly well if you're shooting a subject that will later be keyed onto a new background. The disadvantage of some background paper is that it can make the scene look sterile, as though it were shot in a studio. The natural environment disappears. On the other hand, a scene shot against background paper is sometimes much easier to light. If you don't use background paper, and your video camera doesn't do backlight compensation (or if you don't feel comfortable with the camera's features), avoid shooting a subject in front of a lamp, window or other brightly lit object. You must remember that the tiny black-and-white monitor inside your camcorder's eyepiece does a poor job of showing flaws in exposure. It's wise to bring a small color monitor with you to a field shoot so you can see either the live feed coming out of the camera or the playback immediately after some test scenes are shot (you should do both). A number of companies now sell tiny, lightweight, battery-operated color LCD monitors that can give you a better idea of the scene's lighting and color, but even a small, real color monitor (nine diagonal inches or less) will show you more detail. It's hard to tell using an LCD panel, for example, whether the scene is tightly focused. A color television monitor will show you that.

A lot of video is shot of people talking to the camera. If this is to work, it needs to be planned. The best approach is to have the subject prepare a script or read from a script prepared for him or her, because ad-libbing, while it has its folksy appeal, can both do tremendous harm to the message and waste a lot of time in retakes. Find out whether the speaker can take the time to memorize his or her script. Sometimes you can carve the script up into manageable sections that an alert speaker can memorize just before shooting the scene. If so, you'll gain the freedom to shoot from any angle, in any surroundings, without making room for papers and a flat surface. If you're stuck, you can go all-out and use a teleprompter (a computer that rolls large text up a television monitor), or trek to the art store, buy some matte board, and create cue cards with a marker. If at all possible, avoid having the speaker read from a piece of paper in hand or on a desk or podium. This creates a shifty-eyed look on tape as the speaker looks at the camera, then down to the script, then up again. If you must shoot someone reading from a paper script, make sure the script can be seen in the shot (or at least one of the shots in the scene) so that the audience knows why the subject's eyes are dancing up and down.

If you decide to split the scene into multiple shots, remember to change camera angles when you stop and start again; leaving the camera in place produces an unnatural (and sometimes comical) jerking motion as the speaker's head and body move instantly from the position at the end of one shot to the beginning of the next. This can be corrected in editing by inserting some intervening material, such as a shot of the interviewer if the speaker is being questioned.

The Day of the Shoot

Print your outline, your speaker's script, and all your notes onto paper and bind them together. I tend to run them through a three-hole punch and place them in a looseleaf binder; you might prefer to use a clipboard. Make sure each scene has some unique identifier associated with it. The outline may take care of this for you. Segment II, sequence 4, scene A might become scene II-4-A. You can also assign scene names or arbitrary scene numbers. *How* you identify a scene isn't important; *that* you identify it is crucial, and it's important to use the same identifcation scheme every time you refer to your material. You should also identify each *take*, or each attempt to capture a particular scene, by number. You usually use multiple takes to go back over mistakes. They're also handy, however, to give yourself the option of editing in different points of view for the same material. You can shoot a speaker saying precisely the same lines both head-on and from a pulled-back angle that shows his or her surroudings. When you edit the tape, you can break up the monotony of a stationary camera shot by occasionally (once is enough) editing in the long view.

Your script, your shooting notes, and the cassettes themselves should be labeled with this segment-sequence-scene code. Even the video itself should be marked: pick up a cheap erasable memo tablet and pen at a department store and write the scene ID on it. Point the camera at that tablet and record 20–30 seconds of this marker prior to each new scene so you can identify it on the tape, even when viewing it in fast-forward or rewind. A camcorder that uses timecode is immensely helpful in organizing the video you generate during a shoot. You can write down the timecode associated with the beginning of each take. The tape counter value, provided you remember to reset the counter to zero when you insert a new tape, is of lesser use, but still worth writing down. Anything you can do to limit the amount of time you spend visually searching for material during the editing session will cut your effort considerably.

If you have a specific amount of time to fill, you may need to determine a target duration for each scene. If you have advance access to the script, read through scripted portions aloud and time them. You can also budget time for shots that don't include dialogue; just time the shot as you shoot. The danger in not planning for time is that you may end up with a finished product that's much longer or shorter than you expected.

Then there are the last-minute preparations. If you're going portable, make sure you have enough consumables—batteries, spare lightbulbs, some kind of fastening tape, and, of course, videotape—for the entire shoot. Pack more blank videotape than you think you'll need. If you're shooting for anything but the heck of it, always use new tape; there's no reason to let frugality force you to shoot something again.

Once you've set up the lights for your scene, you should white-balance your camera. This is usually simple: aim the camera at any white surface (you should carry a white matte board or something like it with you for this purpose) and push your camcorder's "white balance" button. This will adjust the camera for the color of the lights you're using. All lights may seem white to you, but failing to white balance for your shooting environment can result in nasty surprises when you sit down to do the edit. To be most effective, you should place the white board where your subject will be, especially if you have a mix of different kinds of light in the scene. Since it only takes a few seconds, grab a new white balance every time you change the lights or move closer to or farther away from a natural light source (like a window).

There are some basic laws of composition that apply to video, but they leave plenty of room for creativity. No scene should last less than five seconds unless you're shooting for a rapid-fire effect. Shoot with later editing in mind; don't try too hard to do in-camera edits. That is, don't worry about making the scenes start and end so cleanly that you could take the tape right out of the camcorder and use it directly. Your camcorder doesn't always respond instantly to start and stop commands, so it's best to leave some slop on both ends to make editing a little easier. Besides, it ruffles the subject less if you start the camera and let him or her begin speaking when they feel comfortable. Go easy on all camera motion—when in doubt, stick it on a tripod and leave it alone. Zooms and pans are hard on the eyes. Use them sparingly, and when you do, you should never do pan or zoom quickly. It's often better to pause the camera, zoom or pan, and then start recording again; you'll get a clean cut that won't tax your audience. The exception is panning for panoramic shots (to get a wider view of a landscape or interior than you can get from one place) and to follow a walking speaker.

If you're shooting a speaker, it's not necessary to keep them constantly in the center of the frame. This is one area where you can learn a lot from watching television and movies. See how professional camera operators frame their shots. You'll see very few straight-on shots because they look stiff and overly posed. Instead, you'll often see seated speakers framed against the left or right side of the screen. It's okay to be creative in your composition as long as that creativity doesn't create a distraction.

Your camcorder's auto-focus is there for convenience. It is not able to adjust to every subject or every composition. If you get creative, for example, and place your main subject anywhere but the center of the frame, you'll confuse most auto-focus systems; they'll focus on whatever's in the center. There are other odd situations, like shooting through glass, shooting low-contrast subjects or patterns of horizontal lines that can also make auto-focusing uselessly slow or completely ineffective. If your subject moves, or you do, while the camcorder is running, remember that whenever the distance between the subject and the lens changes, your camcorder must refocus. The A1 Digital's auto-focus can track a moving subject, even if it moves out of the center of the frame, but that's not a common feature, and some camcorders' auto-focus systems are just plain inadequate. You might consider practicing manual focus, particularly if you intend to shoot a lot of moving subjects. It's a good idea to practice manual focus if you intend to do your own shooting. With practice, you can learn to focus more quickly and precisely than most camcorders' auto-focus systems.

There are also some cheap tricks that can help make the video you shoot look more professional. Grab detail shots when you're done shooting the main scene. I sometimes need to shoot a person being interviewed, and detail shots can help break things up. First, I grab an interview-like straight or side shot of the person delivering his or her answer a question. I then shoot a separate scene of something that illustrates what the speaker is describing in his or her answer. When I edit this scene, I'll cut the detail footage in as a video-only insert edit, so the speaker's voice can still be heard until the supporting video. Also, you can simulate a "two-camera shoot" by using a similar method. If you want to show the interviewer asking the question, for example, shoot him or her *after* the interview is finished, over the shoulder of the person being interviewed. You can shoot the interviewer as he or she speaks, or just looking intensely interested in what the subject is saying. Once again, the "my, that's interesting" looks can be edited in as video inserts. If you want to catch the questioner speaking, you'll need to insert the audio as well. Both look perfectly natural after editing provided you take care to avoid showing the interviewee speaking or gesturing in a manner that obviously differs from what the soundtrack represents. This technique also takes a seasoned interviewer who doesn't feel silly nodding or looking interested when nothing's being said.

Don't stop, rewind, and record over gaffs; just leave the tape running, scribble "take 2," "take 3" or whatever on the bottom of your scene marker, record a few seconds of it and keep going. Tape usually costs less than the time of the people involved in your shoot, and if all else fails, you may get what you need from editing together the usable portions of the bad material. The last bit of advice I'll offer about setting up for a video shoot is to keep graphics in mind. If, for example, you're shooting a speaker and you plan to overlay his or her name during the editing process, be sure to leave room for that. Consider other opportunities to mix computer-generated graphics with your scene. Any video scene can be overlaid with graphics. While it's possible to size and position the video within the graphic during editing, it's easier to shoot the video to place the subject at a size and position appropriate for the graphics overlay.

Video Editing: The Video Toaster and AmiLink VT

The rest of the material in this chapter will be devoted to bringing together the video you shoot, the audio you digitize and edit, the stationary 2-D and 3-D graphics you create, and 3-D animation into a finished video presentation. The term "editing" may bring to your mind images of streams and reels of film and a jig with a razor blade. But with video, editing isn't only about piecing together bits of video footage. Once computers get involved, everything from MIDI music to animated graphics can enter the mix. Editing becomes more than just mixing together material you've already created. It is at the heart of the creative process that is video production.

This chapter builds its hands-on discussion around two editing systems: Newtek's Video Toaster and Matrox Studio. Both of these are, in their own way, revolutionary technology. The Video Toaster started the whole desktop video business. Matrox Studio took many of the concepts proven by the Toaster, added some capabilities that users were asking for, and turned out a product that takes a completely different approach to video production.

I don't believe I can teach editing technique in a book. Like most things, studying how others do it will help show you the way. And in this task, I believe it's important not to encumber you with a lot of rules and recommendations. This is one area where your own creativity, your own sense of what works and what doesn't, will determine whether you have what it takes to produce your own videos. Even if I could, I wouldn't will you my technique. I'd rather see what you can do on your own given the knowledge you gain from this chapter and the books and courses that I advise you to follow this up with if you're serious about this subject. To that end, I'll focus here on giving you an overview of the features and operating procedures associated with two popular desktop video production systems. Even if you don't plan on buying either of these specific products, you should find this section valuable because the Video Toaster and Studio provide good illustrations of the two basic classes of desktop video editing setups.

I chose to start the Video Toaster-based system because, of the two systems, the Toaster takes the most to set up. If you want what the Toaster's got to offer, however, you'll find it worth the effort.

My lab has the Toaster installed in an Amiga 3000T/040, a very fast, very expandable tower system that makes an excellent host for the Toaster. The Video

Toaster was originally built to fit in the Amiga 2000, a short desktop case, and the Toaster boards itself won't fit into a 3000T or 4000 unless you take a metal-cutting tool to the case exterior. That's what I did (it took about an hour), but now there are external expansion chassis that make it possible to house a Toaster outside the Amiga's case, solving the problem of having to mangle the system case to make it fit. Check with an Amiga dealer or video dealer to find out more about these external boxes.

Understanding how to use the Toaster for video production means understanding what it is and what it *isn't*. The quick description of the Video Toaster hardware goes like this: it is a four-input, two-output video switcher, dual 24-bit frame buffer, and a digital video effects processor on an Amiga card. The card, by itself, does nothing. It's the software that makes the Toaster work.

Included in the Video Toaster software bundle are five tools. The switcher (see Figure 7-1) is the Toaster's primary interface. Much of it is fashioned after a tradi-

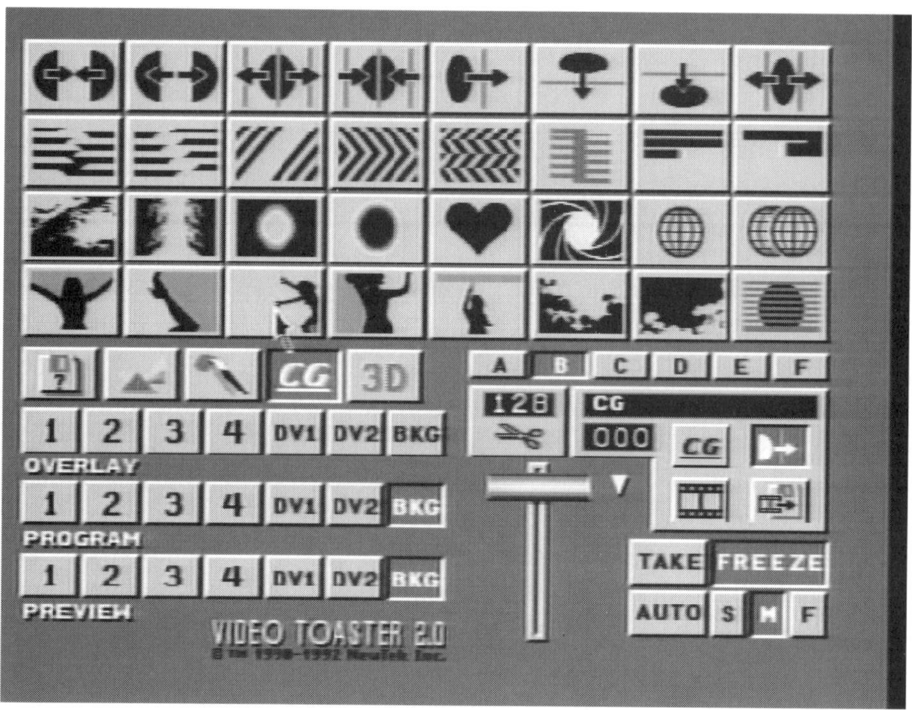

Figure 7-1: The Video Toaster switcher interface

tional video switching console. The large buttons (Newtek calls them *croutons*) with the designs on them select from among the Toaster's available transitional effects. You may recall that a transitional effect is a spiced-up way to transition from one video source to another. A few examples of the Toaster's effects will be shown here, and the videotape will highlight many more of them. The effects are represented graphically in the switcher interface by grids of croutons. There are six separate grids in all, labeled A–F, and each grid contains 32 effects for a total of 192. This may seem like an unbelievable number, but many of them are variations on other effects, and most video switchers with digital effects you offer more different effects than you could ever use. The idea is to present a wide range of effect types to suit the work you're doing. The Toaster's switcher can adapt itself to any kind of work from super-conservative to downright bawdy, with effects ranging from simple cross-fades to silhouettes of a shapely woman dancing through the frame.

Toaster Effects

What most people remember about the Toaster, after seeing a demonstration, is its effects. It is an impressive array, to be sure, and even though it's not even close to all there is to the system, no discussion of the Toaster would be complete without a discussion of its effects.

Most of the Toaster's transitional effects are split into classes. You have dissolves (or fades), wipes, DVE (digital video effects), and organic effects. With everything the Toaster can do, the effect I employ most often is the dissolve. This gradually superimposes one video source over another. The new source starts out filmy and transparent, then becomes more solid over time until it completely replaces the old video. A dissolve has two uses: to cross-fade between two video sources and to fade the video in or out. The Toaster has three internal video sources, one of which is a background generator. This is a video source that is either a solid color (you can pick from a fixed palette of commonly used colors) or a simulated video "snow," similar to what you find when you tune your television to a channel that has no nearby station. The snow background is one of those strange, wonderful twists the Toaster offers video producers who want to go their own way. At any rate, a dissolve becomes a fade-in or a fade-out when you dissolve from or to the background generator. A fade to black can be accomplished easily by setting the background color to black and fading to it.

A wipe uses motion and patterns to reveal the new video source. A simple wipe reveals the new source in a sweep across the screen, starting from one side or corner and sweeping in a straight line to the other. The Video Toaster offers a mind-boggling assortment of wipe effects, covering everything from the traditional diagonal and horizontal straight-line wipe to wipes that use irregular shapes to reveal the new video source (see Figure 7-2). The wipe in the figure uses an

Figure 7-2: A wipe effect (Video Toaster)

undulating thick line, made of the special "snow" color, to sweep across the screen. Other wipes fall like a stack of books, paint the new video source onto the screen with falling sheep (no kidding), and weave the new source in with an interlocking pattern.

The distinctive feature of the wipe is that it only reveals the new video source. It doesn't reshape or in any way modify either video source's picture. If you stop a wipe in the middle, half of the screen will show the old source, and half will show the new source, both unaltered except where the leading edge of the wipe passes through.

There is a special class of Toaster wipe that uses a moving silhouetted shape to bring the new video source onto the screen. A baseball player winds up and pitches a fastball right at the screen. The new video source *is* the ball, which grows to reveal the entire image with a rapidly growing circle. In another of the animated wipes, a shadow of a sexy woman walks into the frame, catches you watching her and pulls down the shade (which brings in the new video from the top of the screen). In the interest of equal time, there are also several male-dominated effects, like the weightlifter shown in Figure 7-3.

Figure 7-3: An animated wipe (Video Toaster)

If you want to alter your video, the Toaster offers an assortment of digital video effects. Actually, all of the Toaster's effects are digital, but the DVE classification is borrowed from component effects units that specialize in reshaping video in real time. Most often, the video source is resized into a smaller window on the screen, and that window's shape is caused to undergo an animated change over time. One of the more impressive Toaster DVE tricks is the sphere: the old video pulls away from the sides of the screen and wraps around a sphere that spins rapidly off into the distance. The new video source acts as a background for this. Another effect does a simulated real-time texture map onto a spinning cube. More laid-back effects in this class include fly-ins (the new source flies onto the screen as if from a distant corner) and tumbles (the old video flips, end over end, while receding into the distance). A tumble-in-progress is shown in Figure 7-4.

Figure 7-4: A tumble effect (Video Toaster)

The drawback with the Toaster's DVE effects is that the device can't compress video cleanly. In other words, the Toaster can't take a full-screen video image and shrink it down so that the same image fits in one-quarter of the screen. It will do it, and many DVEs use resized video, but it's only an approximation. The Toaster takes advantage of the fact that, if it's moving, your eyes will be tricked into thinking the shrunken image contains all the detail the full-screen image did. In fact, the Toaster resizes video by dropping image data. If you stop a DVE in progress, the image looks blocky as the Toaster expands image pixels to cover up the ones it removed. This shortcoming is sometimes pointed to by video professionals as a reason not to be impressed by the Toaster. What they're missing, of course, is that you don't have to use the DVEs. In fact, I find most of them so gaudy that I've never found a use for any of them except when I'm fooling around with material I know no one else will ever see. For me, the Toaster's DVEs are eye candy, impressive examples of what the Video Toaster hardware is capable of.

Perhaps the most unique and beautiful of the Toaster's effects are the organics. These animated wipes use moving, feathered edges to bring the new video onto the screen. They look like clouds, pouring liquid, smoke or fire (see Figure 7-5). These mesmerize the audience with their smoothly animated movement.

Figure 7-5: An organic effect (Video Toaster)

Using the Switcher

There's more to using the switcher than selecting from among the Toaster's immense collection of effects. Before you can get anywhere with the switcher, you have to hook up the Toaster's video inputs and outputs.

The Video Toaster has four composite video inputs and two composite outputs. You make connections to the board through a column of six BNC jacks on the back. The four inputs work with any device that puts out an NTSC video signal. Except for that case when you're connecting only one video device, all of the devices feeding into the Toaster must be locked to the same sync source through genlocking or time-base correction as appropriate. The Toaster itself takes its sync from whatever's connected to input #1.

As I mentioned earlier, the switcher has three internally generated video sources. These can be used just like external video; you can transition between any two video sources, internal or external, using any of the switcher's effects. The three internal sources are the background generator (described earlier) and the Toaster's two frame buffers. The latter provide two separate buffers, each of which can hold a single 24-bit graphical image. You can grab a frame of video from any external video source into one of the buffers and save it as a file. The frame buffers also load and display images created with ToasterPaint, the Video Toaster's 24-bit paint package, Lightwave, the 3-D graphics system, and the Toaster's character generator. The software compresses graphics so they take up less space on disk, and they load very quickly into the frame buffers (three seconds or so). Dual frame buffers make it possible to transition from one still-image graphic to another from within the switcher.

You store and recall still images using a special interface on the switcher's main screen. Images are numbered from 000 to 999, and you can maneuver among them quickly using the plus and minus keys on the Amiga's keyboard. A small window on the switcher screen displays the short name you associated with each graphic when you created it. When you press the Enter key, the switcher loads the graphic you requested into one of the Toaster's frame buffers.

The video sources (1-4), frame buffers (DV1 and DV2) and background generator (BKG) are assigned columns of pushbuttons, with each row of buttons making up a *bus*. The Video Toaster has three busses: overlay, program, and preview. To put a video source on the main monitor (or VCR, or whatever's connected to the Toaster's program output jack), you need only select the button assigned to that source on the program bus's row. Switching this way is instantaneous, effectively a cut (or *take*) to the new source. The preview bus also has an output jack of its own, so you can see another video source or load and view frame buffer graphics without disturbing the main (program) output. But the preview bus serves another, more important function. Whatever you punch up on that bus becomes the destination for the next transitional effect. If you want to wipe between external video source #1 and the graphic loaded into frame buffer DV1, you punch up input #1 on the program bus and DV1 on the preview bus. Then, when you apply a transition, the current program signal (input #1) will be replaced by the frame buffer graphic (DV1) using the transition you select. Once the transition is complete, the switcher swaps the program and preview busses, so that the program bus shows DV1, and the preview bus shows input #1. That way, you can select two sources and flip between them just by executing the transition over and over again; you don't need to re-select the source and destination of the transition unless you want to change them.

Transitions are speed-adjustable (slow, medium or fast—editing software can adjust it more precisely) and can be activated from either the keyboard or the mouse. If you tap the spacebar, the switcher will execute the currently selected effect at the speed you've requested. If you drag the mouse while holding down the right mouse button, you can vary the speed of the effect by moving the mouse vertically as fast or as slow as you like. With some effects, you can create split screen and picture-in-picture effects by using the mouse to start the wipe, stopping after you drag the effect halfway to completion.

The overlay bus works with the Toaster's luminance keyer. Whatever is on the overlay bus will be keyed over the program output, using either a white or a black key, with the luminance threshold set through the switcher interface. Any graphic or video source can be punched up on the overlay bus for keying.

ToasterPaint and the Character Generator

There are five buttons on the switcher's interface that shuttle you between the Video Toaster's software modules. Those you're most likely to access from the switcher are ToasterPaint and the character generator.

Because the Toaster can't scale graphics in real time, if you want to do an over-the-shoulder graphic, you'll have to load it, at full size, into ToasterPaint and scale it down to a smaller graphic that is at the size and position you require. The result will be a full-screen graphic of a huge, blank background and a little rectangular floating image. You can use the switcher's luminance keyer to drop the graphic in, or you can use a special class of effect called a positional effect. These are meant to be used with scaled graphics. One of them opens up a rectangular window to show a selected portion of whatever's on the preview bus as an over-the-shoulder-type graphic. You can move the rectangle around the screen and resize as you need to before you go "on the air," and the switcher will remember the size and placement of the rectangular window when you go back to execute the effect later. It takes a little preparation, but it works well enough.

Other uses for ToasterPaint are mostly related to retouching and modifying captured video frames. You can smear or blur a cluttered background to make a foreground image stand out, create a cut out in the shape of a face or object so you can luminance key it (without the background) onto your video, and you can add visual elements like gradated backgrounds to create professional-looking video graphics. ToasterPaint (see Figure 7-6) can also distort (or warp) images to create

Figure 7-6: ToasterPaint (Video Toaster)

pseudo-3-D effects. In general, ToasterPaint is a pretty respectable package. Like everything else on the Toaster, though, it does all its work on the Amiga's display, not your program or preview monitor. ToasterPaint, Lightwave 3-D, and the character generator all require you to work on the Amiga's display, then render your work to the Toaster's 24-bit frame buffer for display. While the Toaster has two 24-bit frame buffers, you must operate ToasterPaint on a screen that's only able to display 4,096 colors (quite a step down from 16.7 million). What you need to keep in mind is that the Toaster includes many of the tools you need to do video, but the tools are not, in every regard, as good as other software. ToasterPaint is no Photoshop, but then again, Photoshop doesn't come free with a video production system. It's easy to rag on the Toaster's software while sitting in a lab (as I am) with a vast selection of tools in every category. I can, however, easily imagine myself getting by with nothing but the Toaster and the tools that come with and connect to it.

Another vital software component of the Video Toaster is its character generator. This creates clean, professional-looking titles using an interface fashioned after stand-alone professional character generator systems (see Figure 7-7). This program uses bitmapped fonts (an assortment is included; others are available both in the public domain and through commercial sources). Characters and lines can be drawn in any solid color, and can cast either a dropped or extruded shadow at a position and in a color you choose. A drop shadow looks as though a wafer-thin letter was suspended above a background and lit from an angle. The shadow is the complete letter shape, but part of it is usually obscured by the letter itself. An extruded shadow roughly simulates the effect of a 3-D extrusion, with the side of the letter facing away from the light source shown completely in shadow.

The character generator creates numbered pages, and you select among them from within the switcher interface just as you would frame buffer graphics. The character generator stores most pages in a condensed format rather than taking up the space needed for a full-screen graphic. The condensed pages are reconstituted when you call them up from the switcher. This effectively repaints the page from scratch on demand, and the process can sometimes take several seconds. You can trim the delay by saving some types of pages as graphics files which you can then load as frame buffer graphics in three seconds.

The character generator creates different types of pages depending on their intended use. The *framestore page* is intended to be loaded and displayed on its own. The software lets you place solid-colored or gradated backgrounds behind your text. Working in concert with ToasterPaint, you can also put artwork or a still frame video image behind the page and save the whole thing as a frame buffer file.

You may also create *key pages*, pages of characters that have no background of their own because they're meant to be luminance keyed over some video source. When you load a key page, the switcher automatically punches up the page on the overlay bus so that when you do your next transition, the keyed text will fade in over the video. Transition again, and it fades out.

Variants of the key page, the *scroll* and *crawl* page types create moving titles. A scroll page rolls more than a screen's worth of text vertically at a speed you select from within the character generator. Similarly, the crawl page sends a single line of text moving, ticker tape style, across a selected portion of the screen, also at a speed you choose. The text and the speed setting are saved together; loading a scroll or crawl page from the switcher puts the page on the overlay bus. When you transition, the text will appear and start moving, and you regain control after the last text has scrolled or crawled completely off the screen.

What's most impressive about the Toaster's character generator is its level of

Figure 7-7: The character generator (Video Toaster)

integration with the switcher. The two work so well together that you can jump out of the switcher, type up a quick character generator page, and jump back to the switcher in plenty of time to get the new page on the air. There are a few things you can't do from the character generator. The interface is completely run from the keyboard (the mouse is inactive), and you don't have scalable fonts. You can generate bitmaps, usable in the character generator, from a scalable font if you want to use a font in a size you don't have. This isn't the same as being able to specify an arbitrary size for your type. Also, the character generator can only do one font, one size, and one color for every line. I bring up these points not to take pot-shots at Newtek or their incredible product. Rather, I point these things out because it's best not to be surprised. The expectation of some, after looking at the Toaster's specifications, might be that this package can do *everything*. It can't (what can?), but it's quite possible to use the tools the Video Toaster bundle provides you to create fine, professional-looking video.

The Toaster as Editor

Out of the box, the Video Toaster can't do video editing. The switcher's layout and behavior are built for live, in-studio video switching. The switcher interface offers no control over external video decks. There's also no provision for switching or mixing the audio that accompanies your video. Equipping a Video Toaster system to handle editing means adding the editing-related hardware and software the Toaster is missing.

The first step is to select a video editing program. The other equipment you buy will be governed by the equipment with which this software works. I use a package from RGB Computer and Video called AmiLink VT (see Figure 7-8). This software takes advantage of the Amiga's multitasking capabilities by running alongside the Video Toaster's switcher. AmiLink acts as the master controller, sending commands to your video decks (through a set of V-LAN controllers) to get them rolling in step with your requests, and it also pulls the strings of the Toaster's switcher so that video switching, transitional effects, character generator pages and frame buffer graphics are all placed at your disposal through AmiLink's interface.

AmiLink's interface is a useful mix of old and new. All editing in AmiLink is done using timecode. The current timecode locations of up to three decks are displayed simultaneously. You can set in and out points either manually, by typing in the timecode value, or visually, using AmiLink's controls to search around the tape

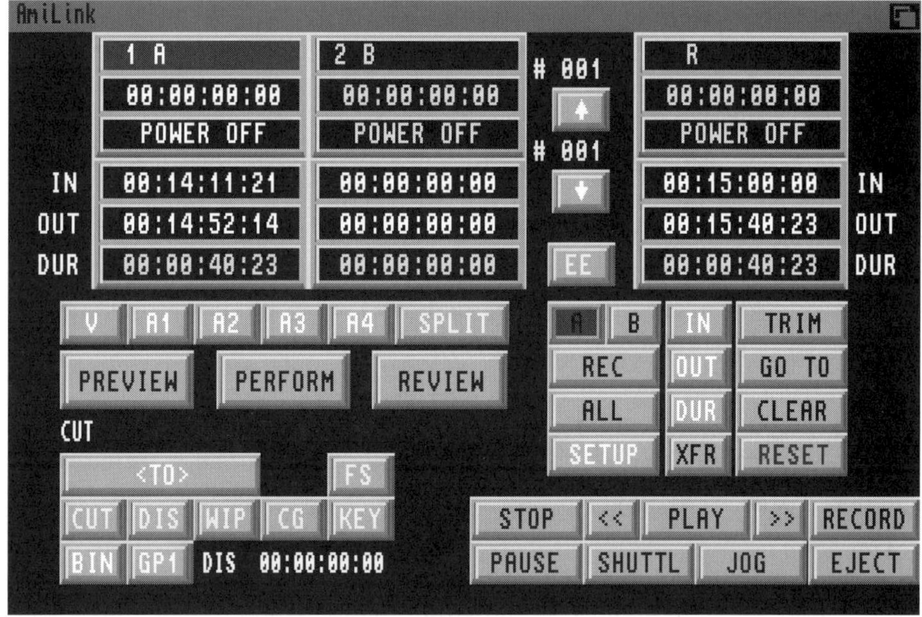

Figure 7-8: AmiLink VT

until the in or out point goes by. When you see what you want on the monitor, you can click the in or out button on the interface screen to make the selected deck's current timecode location the in or out point for that edit.

A single edit in Amilink has at least one player side and a recorder side. On the player side, you can select either the A or B deck and use AmiLink's transport controls to actively control that deck. Once you find the material you want, you create the player side of the edit by setting either in and out points, or an in point plus a duration. You can use a duration to make sure an edit lasts for exactly a specified period of time. The duration and out point fields fill in automatically; you fill in one, and AmiLink will fill in the other. In most cases, the duration is the difference between the in and out points.

AmiLink does insert edits, so you also need to select which tracks (audio and video) you wish to use for the current edit. You can also do a split edit which, over the duration of the edit, toggles video and audio tracks on and off. An example of a split edit is to show the face of a speaking subject, but not having the audio cut in until he or she starts saying something interesting. You might start with a video insert that replaces the video of the reporter but leaves his or her voice running as narration. Then the split would kick in, and the audio tracks would join the video just in time to hear the speaker.

On the recorder side of the edit, you also need in and out points. These are expressed relative to the timecode on the tape in your record deck. The in point determines where the edit will land on the recorded tape. Usually, you'll copy the duration field from the player side of the edit over to the record side.

That describes a single cut edit. There's only one source, and the video is cut into the record tape (at the record in point) without any effects. AmiLink VT comes in an A/B roll edition, which is the version shown in the figure. An A/B roll edit has *two* player in and out point sets. The edit may include switching between the two video sources with a Toaster switcher effect. The total duration of an A/B roll edit depends on how you organize it. You can create an edit that rolls video A, then does a transition, then rolls video B. In that case, the duration of the edit is the rough sum of the A and B clip playing times. I use the word "rough" because, in order to do a transitional effect, both videos must overlap for at least a second or so. You may also create an edit that rolls video A, then brings up video B as an overlay. You could key in a 3-D logo animation over a live shot this way.

Fact is, AmiLink lets you do pretty much whatever you want, even if it doesn't make sense. It takes some practice to get the hang of A/B roll. Much of the learning is in figuring out how to set ins, outs, and durations so that edits come off the way you want them to.

AmiLink can operate a Video Toaster that's either running on the same Amiga or a different one. You can take advantage of the availability of inexpensive Amigas (almost any of which, given a reasonable amount of memory and disk space, can run AmiLink) to set up an editing console that's nowhere near your Toaster and video decks. I've seen this done to keep the producer's working environment quiet and cool. If you're alert, you may gather from that that most video equipment is noisy and hot. The monitors and the Amiga running AmiLink can be in one quiet room, with cables run into a separate equipment room. You only need to visit the equipment room once to load the tapes into the machines. You can run either a parallel or a serial communications cable between your AmiLink Amiga and the system with your Toaster in it. You'll also need a serial cable running to your V-LAN transmitter, but the V-LAN gear can sit in the equipment room as well. AmiLink works the same way whether the Toaster is running locally or remotely.

AmiLink's control of the Toaster is primarily exerted through a simple interface that uses row and column designations to select the Toaster effect you want to use, and which also shows a mockup of the overlay, program, and preview bus buttons. The settings you create in the AmiLink mockup will be transmitted to the Toaster's switcher before the edit begins. As the edit progresses, when the time to kick off the transition occurs, AmiLink will run the switcher exactly as you'd run it if you were operating it manually. The difference is that AmiLink runs the switcher with frame-accurate precision. Everything happens exactly as you order, on the very timecodes that you specify for the various events of the edit.

As you create your edit, you can preview it without recording it to tape and interrupt the preview at any time to go back and tweak some settings. Because AmiLink is not terribly visual in its interface, you'll find yourself doing a lot of previewing, but you'll find yourself falling into a very natural rhythm before long. Once you're happy with a single edit, you can either run that one edit out to tape or move on to the next edit (they're identified numerically; the first edit is #001) without performing the one you've just finished. A new edit, by default, copies the record out point of the previous to the record in point for the new edit. Because of this, you typically only need to set a record in point once, at edit #001, and let AmiLink compute the rest for you.

AmiLink's control of the Toaster is not limited to transitional effects. It takes on the "everything is a video source" approach of the Toaster's switcher by letting you use the frame buffers and the character generator as though they were video decks. All you have to do is set durations for these alternate sources that determine how long they stay on the screen. You can create a pseudo A/B roll system by using one playback deck, one record deck, and one of the Toaster's built-in sources. AmiLink will apply transitional effects between a rolling tape and an internal source. You can also make a request for a specific numbered frame buffer or a certain character generator page a part of an edit. Before the edit is performed, AmiLink will command the Toaster to load the frame buffer or page for you. In the case of key pages, you can create an offset that fades the key page in and out during the course of the edit, as when you put a speaker's name at the bottom of the screen for a few seconds.

The combination of the Video Toaster, AmiLink VT and a set of V-LAN controllers creates a powerful editing environment. Both the Toaster and the AmiLink software is very well written, and I've found them to be tools that stand up to demanding professional use. One thing that's lacking is any handling of audio. AmiLink can send commands to an audio mixer, but I didn't have a chance to test that capability in time to write this chapter, although it clearly seems like the best way to go. Generally speaking, you'd arrange for the mix to take place at the same time as the transitional effect in an A/B roll. You don't have to worry about mixing for a cut edit, except to ensure that the output from the player you're using is somehow routed to the recorder. You can get by with a manual mixer and some patience. Place the mixer (make it a good one—remember that, at least for the gear I talk about in this book, the audio tracks are of very high quality) near your Amiga keyboard and mouse. You can mix your audio manually by watching the timecode displays on the AmiLink screen (they always update in real time, even during an edit) and anticipating the mix, or you can go more seat-of-the-pants and watch the monitor connected to the Toaster's program output.

Audio for Video

Another approach to audio is to do all the mixing in advance of the video edit. This takes a *lot* more planning than using an automated or manual mixer, but it also lets you do things that are impossible to manage any other way. Production of audio isn't something you need to do for an entire videotape program. You should only invest the additional effort in those edits that require it.

The fist step in producing audio for video often involves copying the audio tracks from your video clips onto either analog audio tape or into a digital recording system. I've used both analog and digital gear, and I have developed a strong preference for the SunRize AD516 Amiga digital audio board and its Studio 16 software. I'm so impressed by that combination that I use it even when I'm running my PC-based editing system. I'll describe working with the AD516, but the procedure is roughly the same for analog recording gear.

You bring your audio into Studio 16 one or two channels at a time. When you connect the audio outputs from your playback deck to the AD516's inputs, make sure you also connect that deck's timecode output to the timecode jack on the AD516. To be useful, the timecode must be taken from the same deck that's playing the audio. You'll generally create separate files on disk for each of the audio sources you wish to combine. You'll then use Studio 16 to modify the files as you like, perhaps adding fade ins and outs, bleeping expletives, adding sound effects, or otherwise changing the shape of the sound.

Once you've altered the audio files to sound the way you want them to, you can add them to Studio 16's cue list. This will cause the software to listen to the timecode coming into the AD516 (timecode that is now connected to the record deck, since that's the only constant timecode source during an edit) and kick off the playback of audio files at the timecodes you specify. It's very precise, starting on exactly the frame you request, so Studio 16 can maintain lip sync with a speaker or cause a sound effect to come off exactly on cue. By organizing the cue list to match record in points or other AmiLink timecode events (such as split events), you can create very complex audio maneuvers that would be impossible to do manually.

Matrox Studio

Studio's basic hardware and software design differs significantly from that of the Video Toaster. Studio is built to be entirely self-contained, providing all of the hardware and software you need to do video editing. It includes a character generator (Image North's Inscriber/CG) and a 24-bit paint package (Mathematica's Tempra Pro), but the emphasis on Studio is clearly on editing. Studio has other capabilities, but even setting those aside, what makes Studio unique is its incredible completeness. In one package comes all the hardware, software, cables, and connectors you need to edit your own professional-quality videos; all you have to add are VCRs. You can blend graphics and titles with your video, add broadcast-quality transitional and other effects, and use the automated, computer-controlled audio mixer to manage the audio portion of your production. All of this is presented through an unintimidating Windows user interface. Once the hardware's installed, you can have your first edit in hand in about ten minutes.

Studio's completeness can be seen in its hardware specifications. It includes an eight-input video switcher with digital effects; a six-channel computer-controlled stereo audio mixer with DSP digital audio; a 32-bit graphics frame buffer with alpha channel; three channels of built-in time-base correction; and VCR control for up to four decks. This combination leaves you having to go outside Studio for practically nothing; 3-D is about the only thing I do frequently that's not covered by Studio, but you can still use the Studio hardware, a component of which is Matrox's Illuminator Pro video board, to create your 3-D animation. You're spared the expense of additional components, and Studio doesn't require you to have the kind of expertise typically needed to purchase and set up a video production system from scratch. All you have to do is install the five-board Studio set in your PC, invest in some compatible VCRs and a monitor or two, and hook things together using the cables Matrox provides. After that, you're ready to roll.

In my lab, Studio has a dedicated home in a Uniq 486/50, a cube-shaped system that suits Studio well because it fits on a shelf alongside my video equipment, has lots of expansion slots and a hefty power supply. Studio itself is a set of five expansion boards and accompanying cables. The three video-related boards link together inside your system's case, so all video is processed internally, making it less susceptible to noise. That internal video bus also allows for the addition of future boards that plug into that high-speed video data stream. There is one EISA board—the Virtuoso audio processor—so you must shop for a PC with an EISA bus. If you don't need Studio's audio capabilities, you can save yourself the cost of the Virtuoso and run Studio in an ISA system. It's been my experience, however, that Virtuoso is worth the expense. Even without it, you'll probably want an EISA-based PC because Matrox has aggressive plans to upgrade Studio's capabilities. One or more of those upgrade may well be packaged in the form of EISA cards.

To run Studio, you'll need a system with 14 MB or less of total RAM. That's because some of Studio's hardware is memory-mapped, in a system with more than 14 MB of memory, there isn't enough room to map Studio's boards. Studio also requires Windows 3.1. Matrox wisely programmed all the hardware support into Windows drivers that allow you to make configuration changes on the fly, and Matrox supplies its own special applications (accessible both from Windows' Control Panel and from inside Studio) for managing Studio's hardware configuration. The configuration software built into Studio give you a very simple way to track changes to equipment and cabling.

Most of configuring Studio is telling it what it's connected to. You use the configuration interface to identify the types of the VCRs you're using (you may mix and match to your heart's content), and how they are connected to Studio. A complete Studio configuration makes four sets of direct connections to each video deck you'll use as a player: video input, audio input, and remote control I/O. A recorder is connected to Studio's video and audio outputs and also gets a remote control connection. The video cables have four S-video inputs. You may convert one or more of these, using supplied adapters, to transform a single S-Video connection into two composite video connections. In that way, Studio supports between four and eight inputs; you may mix S-video and composite inputs however you like, keeping in mind that running everything as S-video has its advantages. Studio's audio cables all have RCA connectors, except for a pair of monitor outputs which use 1/4-inch phone plugs, and four microphone inputs, which also use 1/4-inch phone jacks. Studio comes with adaptors that let you use the RCA audio input and output cables with three-pin XLR connectors. Sometimes called *balanced audio* inputs and outputs, these connectors are commonly found on professional video gear. Once again, the inclusion of enough adapters to connect to four video decks saves you a lot of time. All of the video and audio cables are *very* long and are clearly labeled near their connectors. The cables aren't bundled together until they reach the system, where they are gathered into two large pin connectors that attach to the backs of the Studio cards.

Studio's integrated VCR controller is a four-port serial I/O card. Matrox supplies four sturdy serial cables with nine-pin connectors. You can use any kind of video source with Studio, including video cameras and even consumer equipment, but Studio will only control professional, serially controlled video decks. There are plans to support some external VCR control interface (V-LAN is mentioned in company literature), and when that's done, you'll be able to use Studio to operate a wider range of video equipment. Even at this writing, the list of supported equipment is quite sufficient.

You'll run Studio through your PC's VGA-compatible monitor. Studio requires a VGA card with a feature connector, just as a video overlay card does, because Studio uses video overlay to place a window with your video in it on the screen in some of its interfaces. With Studio installed, Windows runs mostly as it normally does, but with two differences. First, you can use the Illuminator Pro video board that's part of Studio to run Windows applications in 32-bit color. Adobe PhotoShop, for example, runs remarkably well in this environment. Second, Studio requires that the display resolution be limited to 640 × 480 pixels. That doesn't cause any trouble for Studio, because all of its interfaces are designed to fit a screen that size. If you're used to having more room to maneuver in Windows, you may want to set up another machine for general-purpose work.

To understand Studio's software, it helps to know something about Studio's hardware. Studio gives you three independent channels of video that you may combine virtually any way you like. Any three of the eight video inputs can be switched into this three-channel virtual bus, and Studio's internal graphics frame buffer can also be used as a video source.

Obviously, you can't just throw three video sources onto a screen at once.

Each video channel has its own digital processing unit. Each unit operates independently of the others, contributing to your output in the way you define. Studio can resize a video image in real time. Resizing video smaller creates window or picture-in-picture effects, while making video larger than full-screen creates a zoom effect. A video source can be positioned anywhere you like, regardless of its size, even completely off the screen. Each channel can also have any combination of posterization, negative, monochrome, mosaic, inversion, or strobe effects applied to it, the same assortment of effects available in Matrox's Marvel video overlay board. You may also apply a solid-colored border or a drop shadow to the rectangle containing a video source.

To get to the screen, the video passes through Studio's switcher/effects unit. This decides which of the three channels actually show on the screen and how. Studio's assortment of transitional effects include wipes, dissolves, and slides. Wipes can have colored leading edges, done with either hard or soft lines. Slides bring video sources onto and off of the screen by sliding the entire image at once. All effects can be applied to both full-screen and resized images.

Studio's keyer lets you create a composite of up to three video sources. The keyer offers luminance, chroma and alpha key modes, plus a special mode called Ultimatte. This uses the blue component of a graphic to determine transparency—the more blue there is in a pixel, the more transparent it is. This is useful for creating semitransparent graphical effects in software that doesn't support the alpha channel. Most of Studio's key modes can be used on both video and still images.

Virtuoso is an MPC-compliant digital audio board, capable of digitizing and playing back audio at up to 44.1 KHz, in 16-bit stereo. It also has an on-board music synthesizer and supports external MIDI devices (MIDI in and out connectors are included in the standard cable set). Virtuoso's mixer controls up to six stereo audio sources, with volume, balance, bass, and treble for each channel. A master volume control determincs the loudness of the monitor output. Matrox used a powerful general-purpose DSP, which will later bring digital audio effects to Studio, and there are plans to update Virtuoso's software to provide multitrack digital audio recording and editing. Until it does, I find the combination of Studio and the Sunrize AD516 (the latter running in an Amiga, of course) very effective.

Studio Software

When you first launch Studio, a blank window pops up. Behind the scenes, Studio's drivers reach out through the VCR controller and commands each of your video decks to play for a few seconds. This tells Studio whether the decks are connected and working properly, and also causes the decks to read the timecode stripes off their tapes, updating both the deck's front-panel displays and Studio's notion of the current timecode for each deck.

All that raving about hardware leaves me precious little time to discuss Studio's software. For all Studio can do, Matrox's programmers have done a marvelous job wrapping Studio's complexity in a friendly, versatile application called Personal Producer. This software is available separately, and you can use it to build editing systems that cost less (and do less, of course) than Studio.

Personal Producer's main interface (see Figure 7-9) uses graphics to represent

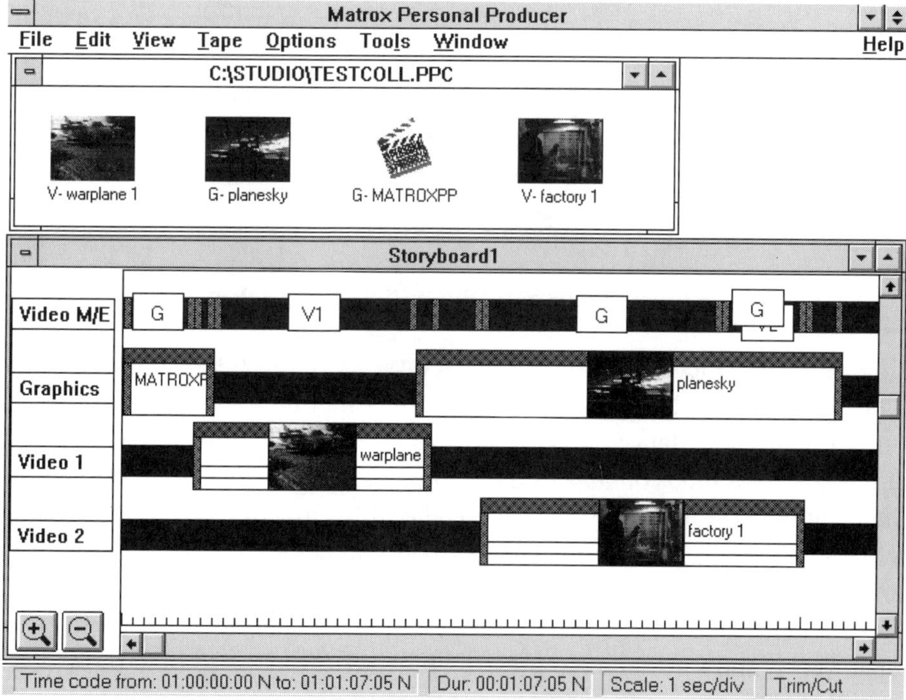

Figure 7-9: Studio's clip collection/storyboard interface

video clips and editing sequences. Instead of organizing a series of edits, when you use Studio, you start by collecting a series of video clips. These come together

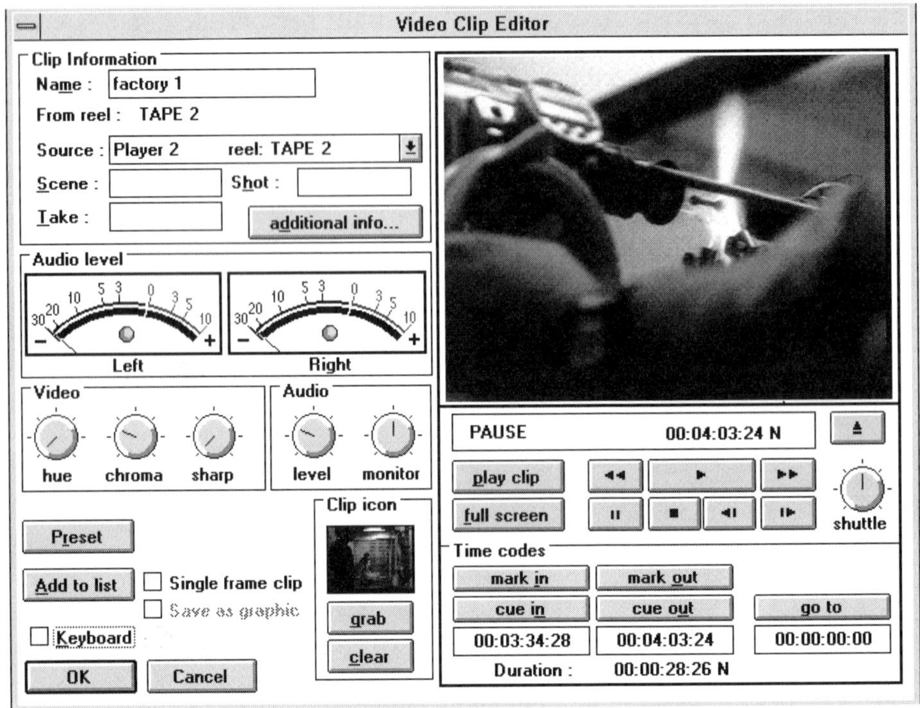

Figure 7-10: Studio's video clip editor

using Studio's video clip editor interface (see Figure 7-10). This screen combines video transport controls, video quality adjustments, audio controls, edit information, and arbitrary data you with associated with the clip. Each video clip gets a name and a graphic; you assign the name, and Studio automatically grabs a frozen video frame and turns it into a icon. The editing information associated with a clip includes that clips in and out points. You can set these using Studio's on-screen transport controls or by typing the timecode locations directly into the appropriate fields. "Cue in" and "cue out" buttons transport the video to the in or out point, respectively, and you can also press a "play clip" button to play the video from the in point to the out point.

A video clip can come from any connected video source, and you may switch sources from within the clip editor through a pull-down option menu. Studio lets you associate *reel names* with the tapes you use in an edit. That name is saved with the video clip, so later, when you carry out your edit, if the clip calls for a reel that you don't have loaded into a deck, Studio will pause and prompt you to insert it. Any time you eject a tape from a deck and insert a new one, Studio will ask you for that tape's reel name.

The large window in the figure is a video overlay window in which Studio provides a real-time view of the selected video source. This is mostly a convenience; you can also see the video on the monitor connected to your record deck. Having it in a window on the clip editor's screen lets you concentrate exclusively on your system's main monitor.

Once you mark in and out points and provide a name, you've created a clip. When you close the editor window, the clip becomes a graphical icon that appears in a clip collection (the top window in Figure 7-9). The name you assigned to the clip appears underneath the graphic as a caption. As I said, Studio automatically grabs a representative image from your video to place in the icon, but you may grab an icon from any part of the video you like.

Studio has other clip editors as well, most notably the graphics clip editor (see Figure 7-11). The figure happens to show a character generator page created in Inscriber/CG, but the clip editor can load any graphics file in Truevision TGA, Windows BMP, or an Inscriber format called VII. A graphics clip becomes an icon

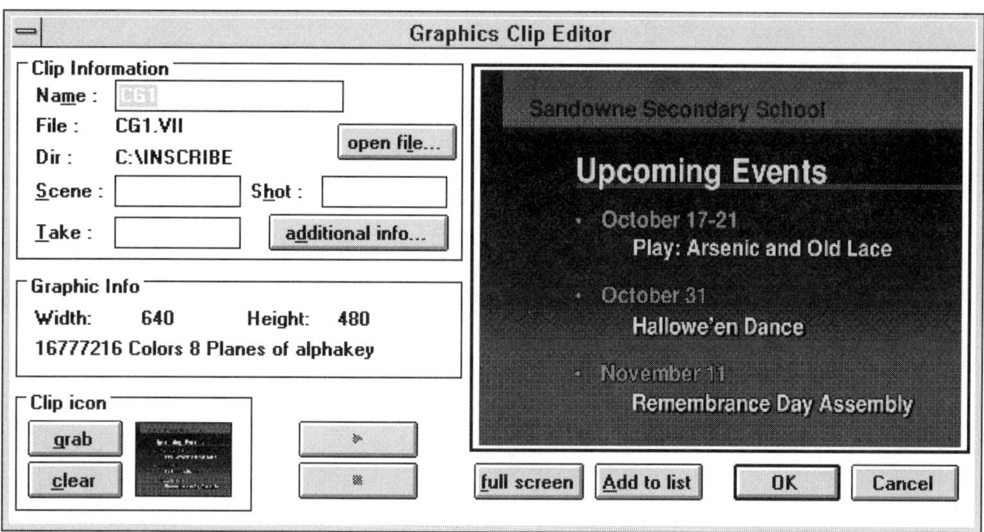

Figure 7-11: The graphics clip editor (Studio)

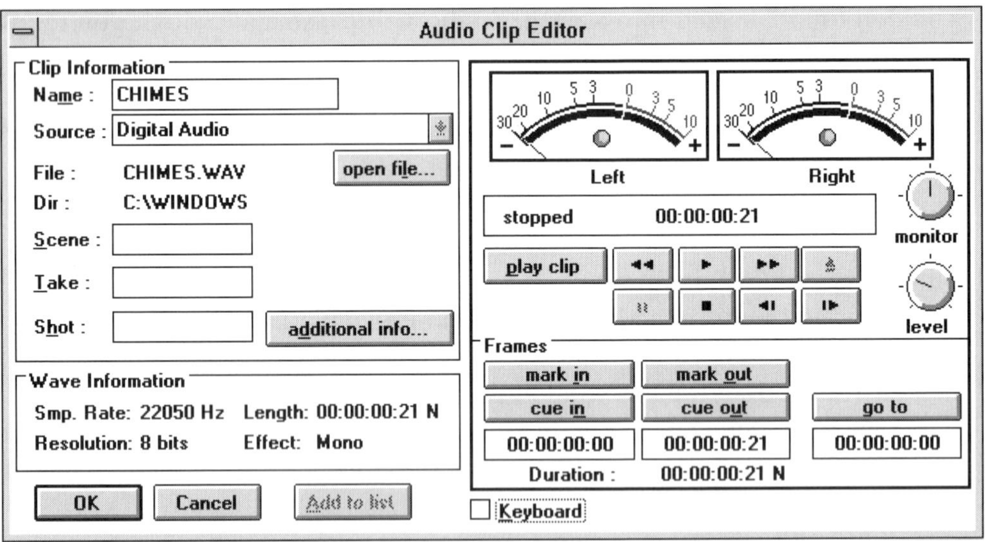

Figure 7-12: The audio clip editor (Studio)

in the clip collection, just like the video clips. One interesting way to create a video clip is to check off the "single frame clip" and "save as graphic" boxes on the video clip editor's interface. This will preroll and play the select video source and do a single-frame grab of the video at the in-point frame you specify. The graphic will then be saved as a graphics clip.

There is also an audio clip editor (see Figure 7-12) that lets you create a clip from any Windows digital audio file. An audio clip can have in and out points, just like video, so you can selectively play portions of audio clips under Studio's control.

You may invoke the editor associated with any clip by double-clicking on it. Studio allows you to change any property of a clip after you've added it to the clip collection.

Once you have a bunch of clips in your collection, you start building your edit by dragging and dropping the clip icons into the storyboard window. Studio's storyboard has separate tracks, each of which accepts clips of a certain type: graphic, video, or audio. When you drop a clip onto a storyboard track, a graphic appears there which depicts the start, end, and duration of that clip. There are three video tracks in keeping with Studio's ability to combine up to three simultaneous video sources.

Two special tracks—Audio M/E and Video M/E (M/E stands for mix/effects)—are automatically filled in as you drop clips onto the storyboard. You double-click the icons on the M/E tracks to change the default audio or video mixing. The Video M/E track controls the type and duration of transitional effects and determines how video channels are stacked by the keyer. By default, all video edits are done with cuts. If you want to add a transition, you can click on a bar in the clip's graphical representation and drag it out until the status line shows the effect duration you want. These transition bars are set up whenever you drop overlapping video or graphics clips into the storyboard. A cut transition is represented by two pairs of bars—one pair each at the clips beginning and end—which have no space between them. By stretching out the space between the transition bars, you make room for an effect.

Double-clicking between the transition bars on the video M/E track pops up the video mix/effects editor (Figure 7-13). Most of the interface is given over to arranging transitions, which transition from the "initial state" to a "final state" over the duration of the transition period you stretched out. A simple transition would take one full-screen video source and transition to another. You can also arrange transitions that fade to or from a selected background color (usually black). If you

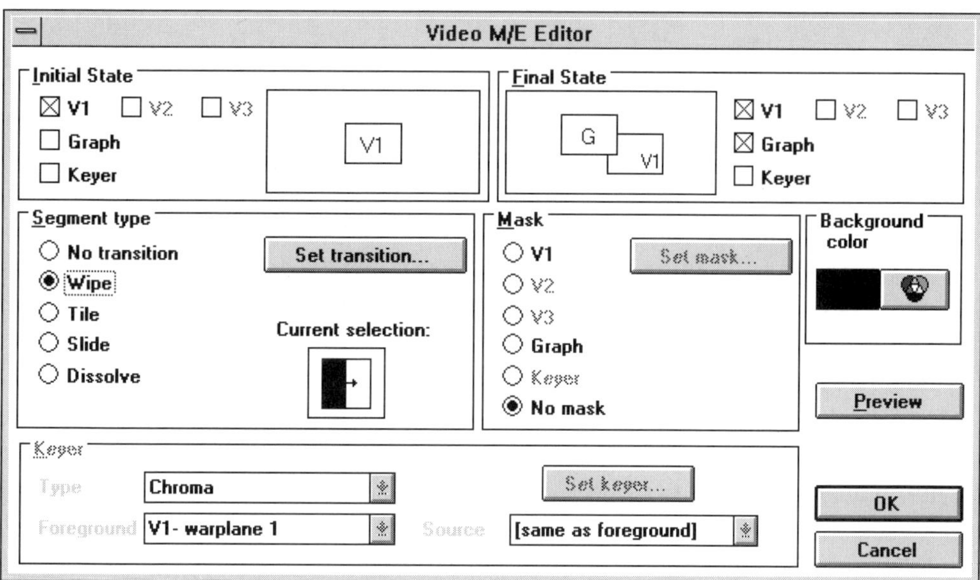

Figure 7-13: The video mix/effects editor (Studio)

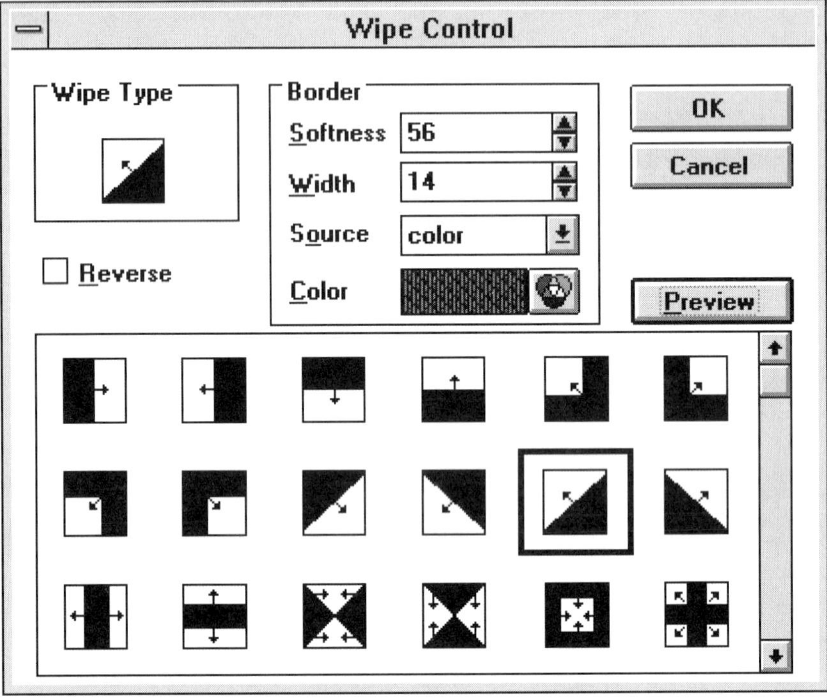

Figure 7-14: Studio's wipe effect control

select the wipe or slide effect, you can press the "set transition" button to bring up a window with the choices for the wipe or slide's path across the screen. Figure 7-14 shows the wipe effect control interface, with some of the wipe path selections available to you.

The video M/E editor also controls Studio's keyers. You may have up to three video sources stacked, in any order, with the means of displaying each partially under the control of the keyer. It's here that your titles get superimposed over your video, or the weathermap placed behind the person giving the report.

You can take more minute control over how each video source appears on the screen through Studio's keyframe effects. These allow you to assign starting and ending attributes to a clip in the storyboard and then have the software interpolate between them automatically (see Figure 7-15). Resizing, positioning, and certain nontransitional video effects are among Studio's keyframeable attributes. Through the keyframer, you can create fly and tumble effects like the Toaster, but with the

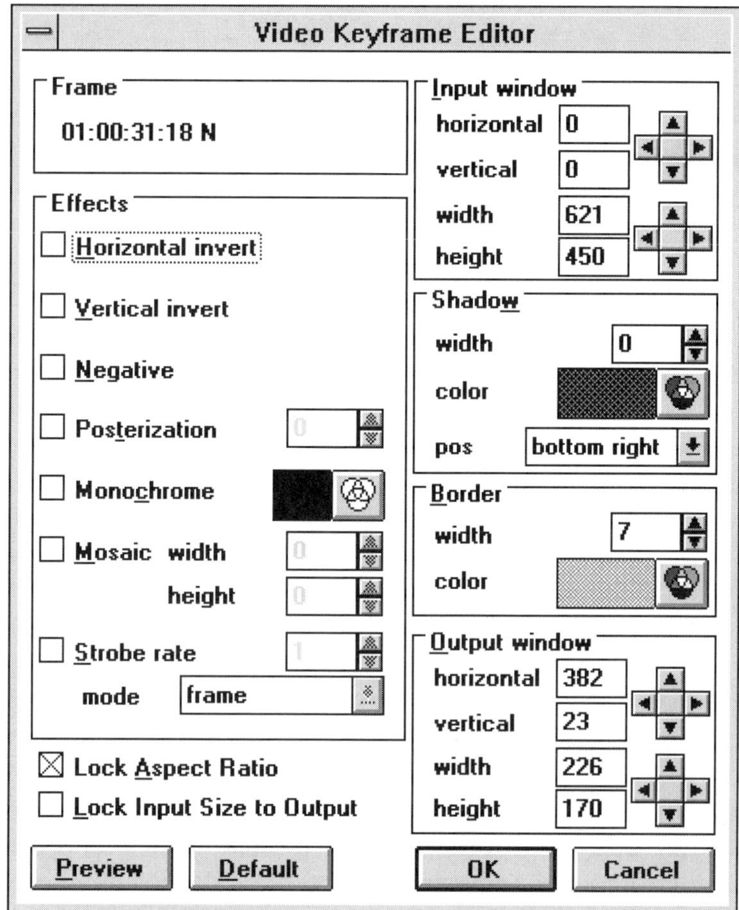

Figure 7-15: The keyframe editor (Studio)

advantage that when Studio resizes video, it does it cleanly. All you need to do to create a keyframe effect is enter size, position, and effect settings for the beginning keyframe, enter another set of information for the closing keyframe, and ask Studio to interpolate. Studio will then determine the intermediate size, position, and effects changes needed to make the video source's window. You may have more than two keyframes associated with a single clip, and each track in the storyboard can have its own independent keyframe activity. When you record the finished video, keyframed events are animated smoothly in real time. It's an impressive facility.

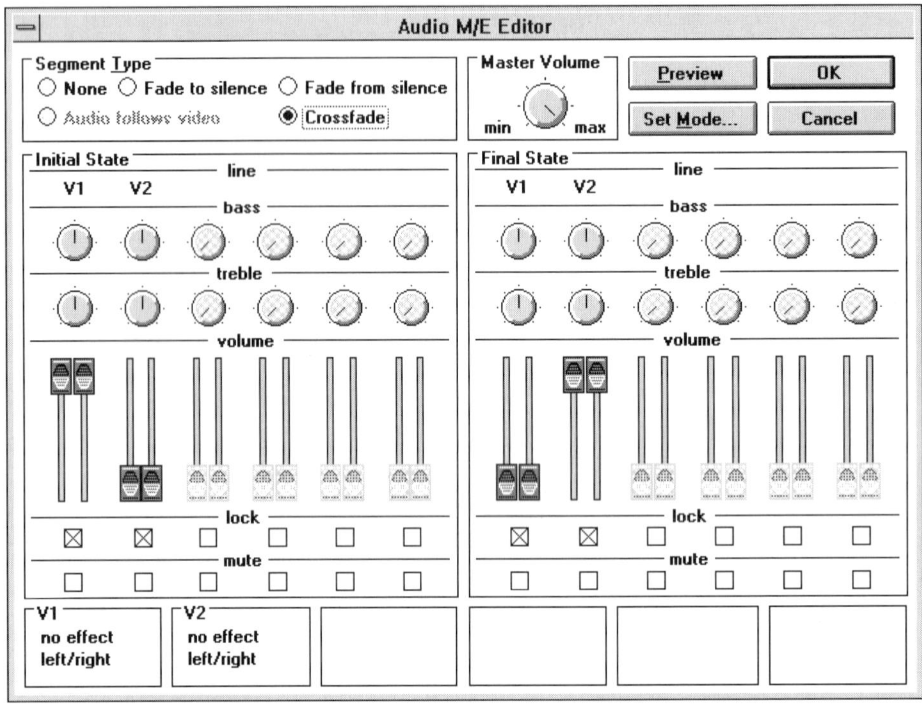

Figure 7-16: Studio's audio mix/effects editor

The audio M/E track manages automated audio mixing. The same transition bars interface that's used for the video M/E track appears in the audio M/E track, and you can create audio transitions of any duration you choose. Studio's internal audio mixer will do precise cross-fades, and quality of the Virtuoso's audio output is exceptional. The audio M/E editor interface (see Figure 7-16) has two sets of mixer sliders: one that depicts the mixer's status of the beginning of the transition, and one that shows its status at the end of the transition.

Once you have more than one item in your storyboard, you can ask Studio to preview a portion of it. In fact, Studio is loaded with "Preview" buttons throughout the various clip and effects editors so you can see what impact your choices will have on your finished video long before you commit them to tape.

Nearly all of working with Studio is setting up clips and arranging the storyboard. After that, all you have to do is select a menu option that sends the whole storyboard to videotape. You only have to baby-sit it if you have clips on reels that aren't currently loaded.

Storyboard or Edit List?

I selected AmiLink VT and Matrox Studio as the examples for this chapter because they represent the two most commonly implemented interfaces to video editing. Studio uses a storyboard and timeline approach, while AmiLink has what's called an edit list interface.

Each method has its advantages. The storyboard approach builds a thumbnail view of the editing sequence as you drag in your clips and arrange transitional and keyframe effects. Every action is represented in the storyboard somehow, and you can use that graphical view to create a preview of the edit in your mind long before you commit anything to tape. The storyboard itself is a graph, with the horizontal axis representing the progression of time. Every event on the storyboard has its starting and ending times precisely represented by its horizontal placement on the storyboard.

By their nature, clip collections and storyboards lend themselves to projects that change a lot. It's possible to make huge changes to a storyboard quickly, simply by dragging off old clips and dragging in new ones, extending or shortening the time any clip spends on screen, or adding and removing effects. The equivalents of these actions are harder to manage with an edit list program. The object-oriented approach of Studio, in which video clips, graphics, audio, effects, and other elements are individually manipulable objects, makes life much easier for producers who have a lot of material to pull together and who need the flexibility to make quick changes.

Another advantage of Studio is the clip collection. You may have several of these open at once, and you can drag clips back and forth between collections. This allows you to create libraries of commonly used material like animated logos and credits. Anything you plan to use more than once should be placed in a clip collection that makes the clip easy to find when you need it. For large collections, Studio can switch to a textual view that shows lists names and attributes of clips instead of icons.

AmiLink VT, and other edit list-style editors, have the advantage of being much quicker to use when you know what you want in advance. If, through careful planning, you have your edits all mapped out before you get underway, an edit list program like AmiLink will let you practically pour your edits into the interface. The list comes together quickly because there are so few frills, and some video producers prefer the AmiLink interface precisely because it isn't so cozy as Studio. They feel they can work faster if they can simply see their edits expressed as timecode. Also, AmiLink has the advantage of constantly accessible transport controls. With Studio, you must be in a clip or effects editor to have access to the remote controls for your video decks. That's the way object oriented software works: you don't get the controls associated with an object until you open it. There are no objects in AmiLink, so you might say that an edit list-based editor has more "road feel" because you always have direct access to all of your video decks.

That an edit list interface has no objects means that the elements of your edits have less potential for reuse. You can print out your edit list and even copy in and out points around, but for the most part, when you sit down to an editing session with AmiLink, you're starting from scratch unless you're making changes to an existing edit list. The only real reuse you have available to you is that you can load a prepared template that has the edit points and effects associated with a project's front matter (logos and such), and you can build the rest of the tape from there.

Pros who have been in video a long time sometimes express a preference for edit-list software because it feels like the specialized editing systems they've been using for years. They've tuned their minds so that they can envision their edits without getting much help from the software, and for them, timecode seems a much more natural representation of video than icons and storyboards. AmiLink suits these users because it doesn't force them to deal with unfamiliar interfaces.

That's not to say that professionals aren't turning on to Studio and its like. The clip collection reusability, the quick access to previews at every step in the process, and the do-everything approach offer more freedom to video producers. You can spend more time thinking creatively and less time worrying about the process of editing; Studio takes care of the detail work for you. While Studio's design makes video accessible to people who don't understand much about it, it clearly offers the most benefits to those who either have or acquire a deeper knowledge. Certain aspects of Studio, such as its multi-layer keying, are more likely to go unused by someone with very little video production experience. Perhaps what makes Studio special is that it adapts itself to users at all levels of expertise and, in effect, can help bring a novice up to proficiency as a producer. Every time an object's editor pops up, it's loaded with knobs and buttons that beginners are bound to play with. Studio makes it easy to experiment, and therefore, easy to learn.

Studio can't guarantee to turn you into a video producer; nothing can. You still have to have the seeds of creativity and aesthetic sense inside you. With Studio and the other tools described in this chapter, you no longer have to become an engineer to produce video. The software does most of the work for you, and in the case of Studio, even the hardware is designed to shield you from needing more than a high-level understanding of video technology. It is that level of understanding which I have attempted to impart to you in this chapter. If you've absorbed it, you should be able to move on to doing your own video work, either using the tools I've described or something like them. I hope I have an opportunity to see what you create.

Index

Resource Guide

AdLib Multimedia, Inc.
(sound boards)
350 Franquet St., Ste. 80
Ste. Foi, QB, CD G1P 4P3
(800) 463-2686
(418) 656-8742
fax: (418) 656-1646

Adobe Systems, Inc.
(Photoshop, Illustrator, Premiere, TypeAlign, Streamline)
1585 Charleston Rd.
P. O. Box 7900
Mountain View, CA 94039-7900
(800) 833-6687
(415) 961-4400
fax: (415) 961-3769

Advanced Logic Research, Inc. (ALR)
9401 Jeronimo Rd.
Irvine, CA 92718
(800) 444-4257
(714) 581-6770
fax: (714) 581-9240

Aldus Corp.
(Persuasion, PhotoStyler)
411 First Ave S, Ste. 200
Seattle, WA 98104-2871
(800) 333-2538
(206) 622-5500
fax: (206) 343-3360

Apple Computer, Inc.
(Macintosh computers, Hypercard, QuickTime player for Windows)
20525 Mariani Ave.
Cupertino, CA 95014
(408) 996-1010

ASDG, Inc.
(Art Department Professional)
925 Stewart St.
Madison, WI 53713
(608) 273-6585
fax: (608) 271-1988

AT&T Graphics Software Labs
(RIO, TOPAS, Panorama)
Note: At press time, this company was preparing to close down. TOPAS is now being sold by its developer, Crystal Graphics (see their entry in this guide for contact information). RIO and Panorama have been transferred to another AT&T division. At this time, only the division name and toll-free number are known. This book's videotape will include updated contact information.
AT&T Systems Development Organization
(800) 448-6727

Autodesk
(3D Studio, Animator, animation player for Windows)
2320 Marinship Way
Sausalito, CA 94965
(800) 445-5415
(415) 332-2344
fax: (415) 331-8093

Bitstream, Inc.
(fonts)
215 First St.
Cambridge, MA 02142-1270
(800) 522-3668
(617) 497-6222
fax: (617) 868-4732

Blue Ribbon Soundworks, Ltd.
(Bars & Pipes Professional, SuperJam)
1293 Briardale Lane NE
Atlanta, GA 30306
(404) 377-1514
fax: (404) 377-2277

Brown Wagh Publishing
(Curtain Call)
160 Knowles Dr.
Los Gatos, CA 95030
(800) 451-0900
(408) 378-3838
fax: (408) 378-3577

Canon USA
(camcorders & still video)
1 Canon Plaza
Lake Success, NY 11042
(516) 488-6700
fax: (516) 354-5805

Cinema Products Corp.
(Steadicam JR)
211 South La Cienega Blvd.
Los Angeles, CA 90016
(213) 836-7991
fax: (310) 836-9512

Commodore Business Machines
(Amiga computers, AmigaVision, CDTV multimedia players)
1200 Wilson Dr.
West Chester, PA 19380
(215) 431-9100

Computer Presentations, Inc.
(ImagePrep)
1117 Cypress St.
Cincinatti, OH 45206
(513) 281-3222

Corel Corp.
(Corel Draw)
1600 Carling Ave., The Corel Bldg
Ottawa, ON, CD K1Z 8R7
(800) 836-7274
(613) 728-8200
fax: (613) 728-9790

Creative Labs, Inc.
(Sound Blaster)
1901 McCarthy Blvd
Milpitas, CA 95035
(800) 998-5227
(408) 428-6600
fax: (408) 428-6611

Crystal Graphics
(Crystal Topas Professional)
3110 Patrick Henry Dr.
Santa Clara, CA 95054
(800) 394-0700
(408) 496-6175
fax: (408) 496-6988

Diaquest, Inc.
(DQ-Animaq, DQ-422, DQ-Taco)
1440 San Pablo Ave.
Berkeley, CA 94702
(510) 526-7167
fax: (510) 526-7073

DigiDesign
(Audiomedia II)
1360 Willow Rd., Ste 101
Menlo Park, CA 94025
(800) 333-2137
(415) 688-0600
fax: (415) 327-0777

Digital Creations
(DCTV)
P. O. Box 97
Folsom, CA 95630-0097
(916) 344-4825
fax: (916) 635-0475

Electric Image
(3D images)
117 E. Colorado Blvd, Ste. 300
Pasadena, CA 91105
(818) 577-1627
fax: (818) 577-2426

Electronic Arts
(Deluxe Paint)
1450 Fashion Island Blvd
San Mateo, CA 94404
(800) 245-4525
(415) 571-7171
fax: (415) 571-7995

Ensoniq
(EPS 16 Plus)
155 Great Valley Pkwy
Malvern, PA 19355
(215) 647-3930
fax: (215) 647-8908

Firstlight, Inc.
(Stock video footage)
15353 NE 90th Street
Redmond, WA 98052
(800) 368-1488
(206) 869-6600
fax: (206) 869-6605

Frame Technology Corp.
(FrameMaker)
1010 Rincon Circle
San Jose, CA 95131
(800) 843-7263
(408) 433-3311
fax: (408) 433-1928

Fresh Music
(production music on CD)
80 South Main Street
Hanover, NH 03755
(603) 643-1388

General Parametrics
(VideoShow HQ)
1250 Ninth St.
Berkeley, CA 94710
(800) 223-0999
(510) 524-3930
fax: (510) 524-9954

Gold Disk, Inc.
(Showmaker)
5155 Spectrum Way, Unit 5
Mississauga, ON, CD L4W 5A1
(800) 465-3375
(416) 602-4000
fax: (416) 602-4001

Handmade Software, Inc.
(Image Alchemy)
15951 Los Gatos Blvd, Ste 17
Los Gatos, CA 95032
(408) 358-1292
fax: (408) 358-2694

Image North Technologies
(Inscriber/CG)
180 King St. S, Ste. 360
Waterloo, ON, CD N2J 1P8
(800) 363-3400
(519) 570-9111
fax: (519) 570-9140

Impulse, Inc.
(Firecracker 24)
8416 Xerxes Avenue North
Brooklyn Park, MN 55444
(612) 425-0557
fax: (612) 425-0701

International Business Machines (IBM)
(Ultimedia PS/2, M-Audio Capture and Playback adapter)
Old Orchard Rd.
Armonk, NY 10504
(800) 426-3333
(914) 765-1900

Iomega Corp.
(Bernoulli & Floptical drives)
1821 West 4000 South
Roy, UT 84067
(800) 777-6179
(801) 778-1000
fax: (801) 778-3450

Killer Tracks
6534 Sunset Blvd.
Hollywood, CA 90028
(800) 877-0078
(213) 957-4455
fax: (213) 957-4470

Macromedia, Inc.
(MacRecorder, SoundEdit Pro, Action!, MediaMaker)
600 Townsend St.
San Francisco, CA 94103
(800) 288-4797
(415) 252-2000
fax: (415) 626-0554

Mathematica, Inc.
(Tempra, Tempra Pro, Tempra Show)
402 S. Kentucky Ave., Ste. 210
Lakeland, FL 33801
(800) 852-6284
(813) 682-1128
fax: (813) 686-5969

Matrox Electronic Systems, Ltd.
(Matrox Studio, Illuminator Pro, Marvel)
1055 St. Regis Blvd
Dorval, QB, CD H9P 2T4
(800) 361-4903
(514) 685-2630
fax: (514) 685-2853

Media Vision, Inc.
(Pro Audio Spectrum 16)
3185 Laurelview Court
Fremont, CA 94538
(800) 348-7116
(510) 770-8600
fax: (510) 770-8648

Microsoft
(Windows, Video for Windows, PowerPoint, Windows Sound System)
One Microsoft Way
Redmond, WA 98052-6399
(800) 426-9400
(206) 882-8080
fax: (206) 883-8101

NewTek, Inc.
(Video Toaster)
215 Southwest Eighth St.
Topeka, KS 66603
(800) 847-6111
(913) 354-1146
fax: (913) 231-0101

Oxxi, Inc.
(Aegis SoundMagic, Presentation Master)
P. O. Box 90309
Long Beach, CA 90809-0309
(310) 427-1227
fax: (310) 427-0971

Panasonic Broadcast and Television Systems
(AG-7650, AG-7750, VTR decks)
1 Panasonic Way
Secaucus, NJ 07094
(800) 524-0864

Passport Designs, Inc.
(Master Tracks Pro)
100 Stone Pine Rd.
Half Moon Bay, CA 94019
(415) 726-0280
fax: (415) 726-2254

PC Video Conversion Corp.
(Hyperconvertor)
1340 Tully Rd., Ste. 309
San Jose, CA 95122
(408) 279-2442
fax: (408) 279-6105

Prosonus
(production music and sound effects)
11126 Weddington St.
North Hollywood, CA 91601
(800) 999-6191
(818) 766-5221
fax: (818) 766-6098

RGB Computer and Video
(AmiLink VT)
4152 West Blue Heron Blvd., Suite 118
Riviera Beach, FL 33404
(800) 535-7876
(407) 844-3348
fax: (407) 844-3699

Roland Corp.
(SC-55 Sound Canvas)
7200 Dominion Cir.
Los Angeles, CA 90040-3647
(213) 685-5141
fax: (213) 722-0911

Scala, Inc.
12110 Sunset Hills Dr., Ste 100
Reston, VA 22090
(703) 709-8043

Sony Corp. of America, Business and Professional Group
(CVD-1000, EVO-9100, camcorders & still video)
3 Paragon Dr.
Montvale, NJ 07645
(800) 523-7669

Specular International, Ltd.
(Infini-D, Replicas, Backburner)
P. O. Box 888
233 N. Pleasant St.
Amherst, MA 01004-0888
(413) 549-7600
fax: (413) 549-1531

SunRize Industries
(AD1012, AD516, Perfect Sound, Studio 16)
2959 S. Winchester Blvd, Ste 204
Campbell, CA 95008
(408) 374-4962
fax: (408) 374-4963

SuperMac Technology, Inc.
(VideoSpigot)
485 Potrero Ave.
Sunnyvale, CA 94086
(800) 334-3005
(408) 735-7250
fax: (408) 735-7250

Symantec
(More, Norton Utilities)
10201 Torre Ave.
Cupertino, CA 95014-2132
(800) 441-7234
(408) 253-9600
fax: (408) 255-9341

SyQuest Technology
(removable cartridge drives)
47071 Bayside Pkwy
Fremont, CA 94538
(800) 245-2278
(510) 226-4000
fax: (510) 226-4100

Tamron
(Fotovix)
99 Seaview Blvd.
Port Washington, NY 11050
(516) 881-5400

Tascam Division of Teac America
(MIDIizer, MIDIStudio 688)
7733 Telegraph Rd.
Montebello, CA 90640
(213) 726-0303
fax: (213) 727-7656

Truevision, Inc.
(Targa+, ATVista, NuVista+)
7340 Shadeland Station
Indianapolis, IN 46256-3925
(800) 344-8783
(317) 841-0332
fax: (317) 576-7700

Turtle Beach Systems
(Multisound, Wave for Windows)
1600 Pennsylvania Ave., Cybercenter, Unit 33
York, PA 17404
(717) 843-6916
fax: (717) 854-8319

UNIQ
(PC-compatibles)
49090 Milmont Dr.
Fremont, CA 94538
(800) 866-3656
(510) 226-9988
fax: (510) 266-1188

Videomedia, Inc.
(V-LAN)
175 Lewis Rd.
San Jose, CA 95111
(408) 227-9977
fax: (408) 227-6707
info: (800) 937-8526

Visual Information Development, Inc.
(Presenter Professional)
16309 Doublegrove St.
La Puente, CA 91744
(818) 918-8834
fax: (818) 918-9935

Voyetra Technologies
333 Fifth Ave.
Pelham, NY 10803
(800) 233-9377
(914) 738-4500
fax: (914) 738-6946

YARC Systems Corp.
(coprocessor boards)
975 Business Center Circle
Newbury Park, CA 91320
(800) 798-9272
(805) 499-4048
fax: (805) 499-4048

The Multimedia Production Handbook: The Video

As this book was bring printed, production was already underway for the accompanying video tape described in these pages. It illustrates many of the products and procedures discussed here, and lets you experience them with the sound, motion, and color this book cannot convey.

If you'd like to know more about the video, please fill out the questionnaire below and send it, along with a self-addressed, stamped business-size envelope to:

Tom Yager
P. O. Box 48391
Fort Worth, TX 76148

You will receive an information package as soon as the tape becomes available.

- - - - - - - - cut here - - - - - - - - - - - - - - - - - - cut here - - - - - - - -

Company ____

Name ____

Address ____

____

City ________________ State ____ Country _________ Zip/Postal code ___________

Video standard: ☐ NTSC ☐ PAL

Format preferred: ☐ VHS ☐ Super VHS ☐ Other _____________ (specify)

Only VHS duplication is assured. Depending on interest, other formats may be made available.

Please answer the following questions: (feel free to use the back of this sheet)

What does your company do?

What is your involvement or projected involvement with multimedia?

Which multimedia technologies interest you most?

How will multimedia help you or your company meet objectives?

Of the subjects covered in this book, which would you like to learn more about?